A Regarded Self

A REGARDED SELF

Caribbean Womanhood and the Ethics of Disorderly Being

Kaiama L. Glover

Duke University Press   Durham and London   2021

© 2021 Duke University Press
All rights reserved

Designed by Drew Sisk
Typeset in Portrait Text and ITC Avant Garde Gothic by
Westchester Publishing Services

Library of Congress Cataloging-in-Publication Data
Names: Glover, Kaiama L., [date] author.
Title: A regarded self : Caribbean womanhood and the ethics of
disorderly being / Kaiama L. Glover.
Description: Durham : Duke University Press, 2021. | Includes
bibliographical references and index.
Identifiers: LCCN 2020044478 (print)
LCCN 2020044479 (ebook)
ISBN 9781478010173 (hardcover)
ISBN 9781478011248 (paperback)
ISBN 9781478012757 (ebook)
Subjects: LCSH: Caribbean literature—History and criticism. |
Women in literature. | Feminism in literature.
Classification: LCC PN849.C3 G568 2021 (print) | LCC PN849.C3
(ebook) | DDC 809/.88969729082—dc23
LC record available at https://lccn.loc.gov/2020044478
LC ebook record available at https://lccn.loc.gov/2020044479

Cover art credit: Mafalda Mondestin, untitled, 2019. Ink on
archival paper. Courtesy of the artist.

*For Salome and Ayizan,
my glorious girls.*

CONTENTS

Acknowledgments ix

Terms of Engagement xi

Introduction 1

1   **SELF-LOVE** | Tituba 39

2   **SELF-POSSESSION** | Hadriana 68

3   **SELF-DEFENSE** | Lotus 111

4   **SELF-PRESERVATION** | Xuela 146

5   **SELF-REGARD** | Lilith 188

Epilogue 219

Notes 225

Works Cited 249

Index 267

ACKNOWLEDGMENTS

The irony is not lost on me.

Over the nearly ten years I have spent thinking, researching, and writing into fruition this project that is so adamantly about the self, I have relied on a rhizomatic community of individuals that is a joy to mention here.

There are those who were there at the very beginning, when this book was no more than scattered bits of curiosity and intuition; and there were those who showed up along the way to point me down marvelous rabbit holes previously unconsidered. They are the colleagues, collaborators, administrators, and dear friends who have offered me their support, encouragement, and example, along with all manner of delightful libations. Thank you, Bashir Abu-Manneh, Alessandra Benedicty-Kokken, Elizabeth Boylan, Tina M. Campt, Soyica Diggs Colbert, Maryse Condé, Edwidge Danticat, Marlene L. Daut, Colin Dayan, Laurent Dubois, Brent Hayes Edwards, Christian Flaugh, Alex Gil, Farah Griffin, Kim F. Hall, Maja Horn, Régine Michelle Jean-Charles, Régine Joseph, Kelly Baker Josephs, Tami Navarro, Caryl Phillips, Rose Réjouis, Ronnie Scharfman, Carina del Valle Schorske, David Scott, Faith Smith, Maboula Soumahoro, Deborah A. Thomas, Omise'eke Natasha Tinsley, Mengia Hong Tschalaer, Gina Athena Ulysse, Gary Wilder, Nancy Worman, and those whose names have, regrettably, been buried within the folds of my memory.

I have had the privilege of sharing and receiving feedback on the ideas that make up this manuscript in the intellectually generous and intimate collegial spaces of the Caribbean Epistemologies Seminar (The Graduate Center, CUNY); the Engendering the Archive working group (Barnard College, Columbia University); the Practicing Refusal working group (Barnard College, Columbia University, and Brown University); the Columbia University Global Center in Paris; the Greater Caribbean Studies Network (University of Virginia); and the cohort of Fellows at the Schomburg Center for Research in Black Culture (New York Public Library). I have presented this research at convenings of the Caribbean Philosophical Association, the Haitian Studies

Association, the Caribbean Studies Association, the Council for the Development of Social Science Research in Africa, the Society for Francophone Postcolonial Studies, the Winthrop–King Institute for Contemporary French and Francophone Studies, and the CUNY Graduate Center. This book has been meaningfully enriched by exchanges with audiences in each of these settings. It has also benefited immensely from the generosity of my graduate student interlocutors at Columbia University and the University of Virginia, whose rigor and insight kept me well on my toes.

I am grateful for the opportunity to include in this volume portions of *A Regarded Self* that have been published previously in other venues. Sections of my first chapter appear in *French Forum* and *Contemporary French and Francophone Studies*, and fragments of chapter 3 figure in articles for *Small Axe* and *Legs et Littérature*.

I am also deeply thankful to Duke University Press for the patient and careful shepherding of this manuscript into the world. Lisa Lawley, Olivia Polk, Christopher Robinson, Chad Royal, Liz Smith, and Joshua Tranen are an editorial force I have been thrilled to have on my side. They understand the precious thing that is one's own book. Ken Wissoker's at once gentle and exacting engagement with my work in our very first conversations has been invaluable, and the comments of my two outside reviewers truly helped take this manuscript to the proverbial next level.

All along this journey I have had the constant support of my closest and dearest community: my mother, Marsha Bacon Glover; my partner, Stephan Valter; and my daughters Salome and Ayizan—all of whom see me clearly and love me thoroughly for who I am, beyond the work.

TERMS OF ENGAGEMENT

DISORDERLY, adj. Not acting in an orderly way; not complying with the restraints of order and law; tumultuous; unruly; offensive to good morals and public decency.

SELF-DEFENSE, n. The act of defending one's own person, property, or reputation.

SELF-LOVE, n. An appreciation of one's own worth or virtue; proper regard for and attention to one's own happiness or well-being.

SELF-POSSESSION, n. Control of one's emotions or reactions especially when under stress; presence of mind; composure.

SELF-PRESERVATION, n. Preservation of one's self from destruction or harm; a natural or instinctive tendency to act so as to preserve one's own existence.

SELF-REGARD, n. Regard for, or consideration of, one's own self or interests.

Definitions derived from *Merriam-Webster's Collegiate Dictionary*, Eleventh Edition, and other sources.

INTRODUCTION

The "I" is unseemly.
—Adriana Cavarero, *Relating Narratives* (2000)

There is power in looking.
—bell hooks, *Black Looks* (2015)

This is a book about practices of freedom. Its focus is women, for reasons that I hope will become apparent, but many of its arguments are not, in the end, rigidly gender-specific. This is also a book about community—about assemblages of individual beings bound more or less comfortably together by a shared set of attitudes and interests, aims and imaginaries. By narratives.

More precisely, this is a book about the challenges posed by certain practices of freedom to the ideal of Caribbean community. *A Regarded Self* proposes an inquiry, within the geocultural space of the French- and English-speaking Caribbean, into the ethics of self-regard. It offers a sustained reflection on refusal, shamelessness, and the possibility of human engagement with the world in ways unmediated and unrestricted by group affiliation. It asks how, given a regional context that privileges communal connectedness as an ethical ideal, individual women can enact practices of freedom in its wildest sense. What alternative modes of being do their noncommunal or even anticommunal choices suggest? How do such freedom practices disrupt North Atlantic theorizations of the individual in/and community? How capable are we, Global South scholars and beings-in-community ourselves, of maintaining commitments to read generously in the face of antisociality or moral ambiguity? What ordering codes do we inadvertently perpetuate through our own ways of reading? These questions animate my reflections in these pages.

Reading "professionally"—critically—very often encourages our investment in the act of analysis as political undertaking. As scholars, especially those among us who are raced and gendered both within the academy and in society more broadly, we are inclined to read for our own politics. We tend to dismiss, decry, or question the value of creative works that do not plainly generate or gesture toward programs or possibilities for political change. In the worst instance, we become ensnared, as Anne Anlin Cheng has written, by "identity politics and its irresolvable paradox: the fact that it offers a vital means of individual and communal affirmation as well as represents a persistent mode of limitation and re-inscription" (2009, 90). Our critical selves risk falling into the trap of empathetic identification, a phenomenon Adriana Cavarero describes as the articulation of the self through "the use of a history of suffering and tribulation told by another—most of all by someone who belongs to the ranks of the oppressed" (2000, 91). This is an understandable desire, but it is a consumptive form of engagement, a selfish form of relation. It tends to want moral or political clarity at the potential, if not likely, expense of the other's unique experiences.

For while it is true that we have arrived at a moment in postcolonial and Global South studies wherein assumptions about national sovereignty as the ideal political formation or about the continuing symbolic power of communal narratives of suffering and redemption have been widely disavowed, we remain very much bound to the political. If we have become wary, that is, of placing too much faith in collective forms of governance, we nonetheless persist in evaluating individual actions through the prism of communal politics. In this, we inevitably invest in "whole sets of assumptions that our academy and society continue to make about marginalized subjects and the politics that surround them and the social preconditions that constitute them" (Cheng 2009, 91). In our desire to confront and contest the spiritual, intellectual, and material deprivations that are the direct result of long-standing global injustice, and to identify allies in those efforts, we risk deeming only a very narrow set of acts recognizable as legitimate forms of agency.

This book means to hold up a mirror to a broader critical community of readers that, with all the best intentions, implicitly demands allegiance to its moral principles and politicized practices. Though my inquiry is sited in the Caribbean, the questions I pose here resonate in other contexts as well. Indeed, writers in geocultural spaces beyond the Caribbean and its diasporas have also asked to what extent our own uninterrogated expectations can amount to a differently repressive dimension of contemporary critical theory, especially where these expectations interpolate raced and otherwise vulnerable women. As Toni Morrison has queried urgently: "What choices are available to black women outside their own society's approval? What are the risks of individualism in a determinedly individualistic, yet racially uniform and socially static community?" (2004, xiii).

Morrison's questions are useful to pose as much with respect to the kinds of disorderly female characters I consider throughout this book as with respect to their various creators. The authors of the works in my corpus are themselves disordering. They present characters who remain morally ambivalent, politically nonaligned, and adamantly unrecoverable and so call attention to the inadequacy of any model that suggests a binary moral context. They remind us how often and how easily victim and perpetrator come to inhabit the very same being. Their narratives resist easy co-optation into any preexisting system. As such, they caution us not to get too comfortable in our righteousness. Perhaps most important, they encourage us to imagine refusal itself as a legitimate critique and to not burden the refuser with an obligation to fix things or to refashion the world for all of us.

I have wanted to honor refusal in my own readings here. Recognizing that it is our inclination to consume certain characters and the narratives that contain them in order to satisfy a latent desire for empathetic identification, the challenge both in reading these works and in writing this book has been to "remain in the gift of discomfort" (Cheng 2009, 90) these novels offer. I have sought not to systematize but to suggest useful commonalities among the works I engage here—this body of literature that has been so thoroughly read for its political intent, or lack thereof.

Admittedly, it may very well be that "without community there is no liberation, only the most vulnerable and temporary armistice between an individual and her oppression" (Lorde [1984] 2007, 112). And it is certainly true that communal affiliation of the right sort can provide an individual (woman) with both protection and deliverance. In the extended postplantation context of anticolonial nation-building and antiracist activism in the Americas, communities of contestation and resistance have transformed the hemisphere and defined freedom in unequivocal terms. But it is equally true that a certain communal imperative has emerged out of this context, an imperative that has posited normative social and political principles to which proper citizens are expected to conform. Adhering to these principles has meant a broad dismissal of individualism as an ethical subject position, wherein by *ethics* I mean the collectively determined frame within which moral legitimacy and consequent deservingness of social approbation are situated. Given the weight of this imperative, the significance of "simply" investing in the self must not be underestimated.

Writers in the postcolonial Americas, and in the Caribbean in particular, have long figured community as an objective to be achieved—to be actively crafted both in language and in law. Be it via masculinist discourses of nationalism, womanist conceptions of intergenerational cultural connections, or transnationalist and diaspora-based discursive frames, the Caribbean has been cast, from both within and without, as irrepressibly buoyed by a deep-seated ontological potential for the communal. The Caribbean literary tradition has been dominated to a large extent by those writers who affirm the existence of an organic, counterdiscursive collective ethos among the people they strive to represent in their work. Committed to articulating parameters for defensive solidarity and creative validity, male writer-intellectuals of the region have long pledged to give voice to silenced communal stories they insist need telling. Works by women novelists similarly insist on communal affiliation as the foundation for individual empowerment.

Such privileging of collective self-definition is a phenomenon that bears out in the critical context as well. As I have argued elsewhere, scholars of Caribbean literature tend to celebrate those writers whose texts focus most vocally on representing the valor of the unheard and disenfranchised insular community (see Glover 2010). The postcolonial Caribbean collective these authors and many of their theorists describe is placed in opposition to the exploitative capitalism and bleak inhumanity of Europe and North America—a strategic refusal of "the unmitigated market-centered, selfish individualism, and rampant materialism of contemporary globalization" (Meeks 2002, 166). The Caribbean presents a space of resilience, resistance, and fruitful heterogeneity—creolized but ultimately coherent, poor in resources but rich in "folk." Irrepressibly buoyed by a deep-seated ontological commitment to the communal, the Afro-Creole Americas declare themselves a Global South cultural corrective to a soullessly technologized, alienated First World order.

Taking as a point of departure this investment in communalist ideology in the Caribbean, *A Regarded Self* looks closely at the linked matters of freedom, community, and ethics—freedom as an ethical practice within and often in conflict with community. While the idea of community as an essentialist, romanticized, and forcibly affiliating social structure has been contested within multiple and diverse academic and political spheres, few have attended to the particular place of Caribbean letters in these debates.[1] Moving in that underexplored space, I consider the motivations and the methods, the stakes and the consequences, that inform representations of women's contestatory grapplings with community, taking as my point of departure five works of prose fiction: Maryse Condé's *I, Tituba, Black Witch of Salem* (*Moi, Tituba . . . sorcière noire*, 1986), René Depestre's *Hadriana in All My Dreams* (*Hadriana dans tous mes rêves*, 1988), Marie Chauvet's *Daughter of Haiti* (*Fille d'Haïti*, 1954), Jamaica Kincaid's *The Autobiography of My Mother* (1996), and Marlon James's *The Book of Night*

Women (2009). The woman at the center of each of these narratives exists in a state of conflict vis-à-vis her textual community that more and less explicitly queries the extratextual ordering practices of the postcolonial Caribbean literary community. Her privileging of the self emphatically resists co-optation, both by repressive narrative communities and by ostensibly liberal and liberating critical discourses.

It is the "radical indeterminacy" (Cheng 2009, 91) of their protagonists that positions these works outside of certain canons and has earned them greater and lesser degrees of disapproval, if not disparagement, from postcolonial scholarly and broader reading communities. In their representations of adamantly self-articulating, sexually self-defining female characters, these writers present self-love—physical and emotional—as both provocation and critique. Their respective creative positions in many ways unsettle the ideological imperatives outlined by the region's most prominent writers. As a consequence, most have seen their political loyalties and ties to a national or regional Caribbean identity called into question by their contemporaries, or their works insufficiently or reductively attended to by literary scholars. *A Regarded Self* thus takes into account both the extratextual and the textual. I look here not only at the ways in which these characters disorder their narrative communities but also at the ways in which their creators disturb and have been misapprehended by communities of theorists and readers, more broadly. I am interested in the critical context within which the writers of these disorderly texts have been implicated, and I ask what the cost of advocating self-regard can be within postcolonial Caribbean literary communities. In this respect, *A Regarded Self* proposes an interrogation of our reading practices—a consideration of the ways in which we as theorists engage in processes of gatekeeping, naturalizing, and otherwise ordering the subjects of our inquiries.

Emerging from a variety of national spaces and historical moments, the novels I consider are united in their crafting of stories that uncover and break apart inflexible constructions of regional collective identity. In representing women characters animated by preservationist self-regard, these works critique the phenomena of totality, unity, and closure that so often endanger those who, by virtue of their race, gender, sexuality, class, citizenship status, or otherwise personal identification, constitute the world's most marginal. Although not one of these works suggests a viable alternative politics (and this very deliberately, I argue), by revealing the insidious pathologies of the social, they create space for the articulation of an ethic.

The self-regarding women at the center of these novels are frustratingly equivocal beings. Every one of them is controversial. Some are downright unpalatable. Always removed from the explicitly political, and often manipulative or even dangerous, they elicit profound ambivalence from the reader. It is admittedly difficult, for example, not to be frustrated by Condé's Tituba, the free Black woman in the colonial Americas who resigns herself to servitude not once, but twice, in the name of love and lust. It requires an initially counterintuitive reading of Depestre's white Creole beauty Hadriana to understand fully her abandonment of an adoring Black community in the interest of her own (sexual) liberation. It calls for an unflattering reassessment of Black radicalism not to dismiss out of hand Chauvet's Lotus, a frivolous Haitian girl who plays at revolution like a game of seduction. It takes some work to see past the simmering rage that fuels Kincaid's Afro-Carib antiheroine Xuela, faced with her stubborn refusal to get on board with the Caliban-as-hero machine so fundamental to anticolonial subjectivity. And it is, yes, an especially great deal to ask the reader to accept the very fact of James's Lilith, an enslaved woman-child who, quite frankly, is not a very nice person. Tituba. Hadriana. Lotus. Xuela. Lilith. These provocative names announce the disruptive power of the women who bear them—women who defy rather than defer to communities that will not have them or will not love them as they are. Each of these women is an audaciously disordering force within, and on the margins of, her social world. Her defiance of gendered expectations subtends what is ultimately a wide-ranging discourse of dissent.

Whereas the self can be devoured by public scrutiny, it can be saved by private self-objectification.
 —Iké Udé, "The Regarded Self" (1995)

The criminal and the narcissistic woman are subject to, yet outside the law; both are attempting to evade its effects, if only momentarily.
 —Jo Anna Isaak, "In Praise of Primary Narcissism" (2005)

The practices of freedom and disorder—the practices of refusal[2]—enacted by the women in the works of my corpus demonstrate an unwavering devotion to what I have come to call the "regarded self," a formulation I borrow from a context entirely ex-centric to that of the writers and characters who concern me. Coined by Nigerian visual artist and photographer Iké Udé, the *regarded self* describes the ambivalent nature of social being, wherein it is at once crucial to love oneself, deeply and protectively, and to publicly perform modesty, selflessness, and love for one's community. For Udé, as for me in my analyses of these Caribbean texts, the regarded self proposes a strategy for navigating the individual's vulnerability to the gaze of more powerful others.

Being gazed upon is a matter of being beheld, which literally—etymologically—implicates both regard and possession.[3] Thus, the anxiety produced, as psychoanalytic theory would have it, by the fact of being seen and known as an object-being that exists for others—of being grasped or seized and "understood"—is arguably compounded in the postcolonial context. Postcolonial studies is deeply preoccupied with the question of the gaze and the hierarchies of power it determines. The field has been influenced definitively, for example, by Édouard Glissant's notion of opacity as a strategy of Global South resistance to the degrading transparency imposed by the North Atlantic imperial gaze. Frantz Fanon's memorable account of devastating interpolation—"*Look*! A Negro!" ([1952] 2008, 89; emphasis mine)—similarly demands we consider who, historically, has regarded whom and with what consequences. Jean-Paul Sartre's passionate opening salvo in his essay "Black Orpheus" offers yet another expression of this concern: "Here are black men standing, *looking* at us, and I hope that you—like me—will feel the shock of being seen" ([1948] 1964–65, 13; emphasis mine). As these canonized instances attest, the stakes of the (formerly) colonized individual's exposure to the regard of the metropolitan Other (and, later, vice versa) animate regional intellectual production. It is against this backdrop that I situate the women of these novels at varying points on a continuum of *self*-regard—that I highlight their indulgence of behaviors ranging from self-concern to selfishness, from self-care to something brazenly akin to narcissism.

Admittedly, *narcissism* is a big word. First conceived of by Sigmund Freud as a normal psychological condition constitutive of the fundamental human drive to defend the integrity of the self, narcissism so defined amounts to a "libidinal complement to the egoism of the instinct of self-preservation" (Freud [1914] 1957, 73–74). If the individual's childhood environment is emotionally stable, so Freud's logic goes, a balance is maintained in adulthood between love/desire for the self (ego-libido) and love/desire for others (object-libido). If, however, this balance is somehow upset (via improper parenting or trauma, for example), that healthy "primary" narcissism can become pathological, causing the individual to withdraw any love for or attachment to other objects in the world and to direct libidinal energy exclusively toward the self. Since Freud, narcissism has been in fact most readily associated with pathology: the gaudy frivolity of the reality television star, the humble-bragginess of social media, the vanity of the millennial. Narcissism triggers our innate suspiciousness regarding the individual and, especially, the autobiographical subject. It is perceived viscerally and adamantly as incompatible with ethics—and it is "a characteristic commonly and pejoratively attributed to women" (Isaak 2005, 50).

Over a decade before historian and social critic Christopher Lasch (1979) denounced narcissism as the scourge of post–World War II modernity, however, psychoanalyst Heinz Kohut called for consideration of a narcissistic continuum and of the pop-cultural propensity to obscure its complexity. As Kohut observed in his 1966 essay "Forms and Transformations of Narcissism," "although in theoretical discussions it will usually not be disputed that narcissism, the libidinal investment of the self, is per se neither pathological nor obnoxious, there exists an understandable tendency to look at it with a negatively toned evaluation as soon as the field of theory is left" (1966, 243).[4] In other words, while narcissism is, according to early psychoanalytic theoretical principles, a natural and neutral human behavior, it is anxiety producing in the practical context of human relation. This anxiety is particularly acute when it comes to the postcolonial Caribbean, wherein the very possibility or desirability of a lone, integrated self is itself a question, and narcissism is perceived as a distinctly North Atlantic pathology, the inevitable product of a coldly individualist culture.

Given that *narcissistic* is an epithet that has been used to describe (condemn) not only several of the fictional characters I consider but also their creators, my reflections throughout this book are overlaid or undergirded to varying degrees by this analytical conceit. Recognizing that narcissism is overburdened by pathological connotations, I pointedly lean into its pejorative and unsettling dimensions in my analyses here. Accusations of narcissism attach to several of the novels I discuss, making apparent the threat they issue to the communities they represent as well as to certain communities of readers. I mean to underline the discomfort and even outrage these characters and their texts produce—to home in on their disordering effect, in both the medical and the metaphorical sense. The popular understanding of narcissism as a "relational malady" (Schipke 2017, 5) accords with what the American Psychiatric Association names a "personality disorder"—"an enduring pattern of inner experience and behavior that deviates markedly from the expectations of the individual's culture" (American Psychiatric Association 2013, 645). I want to insist on the fact that the term *disorder* is meant to signal a fundamental maladaptivity of the self with respect to externally constructed models of acceptable or reasonable social (communal) behavior. In the works in question here, the maladaptivity of their protagonists produces a disordering effect that crosses the boundaries of the text.

Digging further into the literal-cum-metaphorical purpose of the concept, it is crucial to note that pathological narcissism—like every other personality disorder—arises foremost as a coping mechanism. It is an individual's means of contending with her or his perceived vulnerability to the psychosocial assaults of the outside world and, as such, can be a far more nuanced term than popular understandings would have us believe. It is important, then, to examine Kohut's rearticulation of narcissism as a necessary adaptive strategy, a survivalist impulse to provide resources for the self in moments or spaces wherein that self is denied sustenance—or denied altogether.

This nonpathologizing conception and deployment of narcissism in a Western, European context as a defensive response to one's community and its order is taken up explicitly, albeit ambivalently, by Frantz Fanon in *Black Skin, White Masks*. On the one hand, Fanon condemns narcissism as an essentialist obstacle to his ideal of race-blind human solidarity.[5] Yet, on the other, he hints at the possibility of a dynamically narcissistic practice of individual disalienation whereby it becomes possible to refuse the psychic violation of hostile external forces—"I grasp my narcissism with both hands and I turn my back on the degradation of those who would make man a mere mechanism" ([1952] 2008, 23). I am interested in this latter instance, the instance attended to by Sylvia Wynter, who reads Fanon's deployment of narcissism as a veritable "counter-manifesto with respect to human identity" (2001, 37)—the means by which to negotiate, if not resist, being "locked in thinghood" (Fanon [1952] 2008, 193), which is the result of one's being determined from without the self, being posited as lack, either sexual (in the Freudian context) or racial (in the postcolonial context). For Fanon, the concerted denial of the individual colonial subject's interiority reflected the primary malignancy of colonialism and racialization. The reduction of the colonized body's use value to the desires of racial capitalism was a violation that could be countered only by a retrieval of self-awareness in its most robust form. Decoloniality and the psychic survival of the colonial subject depended on this operation. Inasmuch as Fanon, a practicing psychoanalyst, understood the phenomenon of the nonwhite-raced individual's inferiority complex and alienation as socially conditioned—as something imposed on that individual's subconscious—narcissism as a praxis of extreme *self*-consciousness offered something of an escape valve.

Admitting the existence of a continuum from healthy to pathological narcissism makes it possible to understand narcissism as something other than the product of a "culture of competitive individualism" (Schipke 2017, 5). It allows us to tease out what Monica Miller elegantly names, in her analysis of Udé's and others' work, "a narcissism more compensatory" (2009, 245).[6]

Narcissism thus understood would signal the performance of self-love in a context wherein that self is improperly loved or unlovable on its own terms. Narcissism thus understood dovetails with Udé's call for defensive self-regard.

Self-regard exists in a wide and slippery ethical space. While it is defined as "regard for or consideration of oneself or one's own interest," it is also synonymous with "egocentricity, egocentrism, egomania, egotism, narcissism, navel-gazing, self-absorption, self-centeredness, self-concern, self-interest, self-involvement, selfishness, selfness, [and] self-preoccupation" and "related to" "complacence, complacency, conceit, conceitedness, ego, pomposity, pompousness, pride, pridefulness, self-admiration, self-conceit, self-esteem, self-importance, self-indulgence, self-love, self-partiality, self-respect, self-satisfaction, self-sufficiency, smugness, vaingloriousness, vainglory, vainness, vanity, self-assumption, self-consequence, self-content, self-contentment, [and] self-glorification."[7] This connotative concatenation reflects the ambivalence with which we tend to approach expressions of self-regard in general. And the stakes are particularly high in contexts wherein self-sacrifice and solidarity are the privileged modes of social identification and interaction. The stakes are arguably even higher when it comes to nonwhite women, perhaps because Black and brown women are presumed neither to have nor to aspire to such a relationship with the self.

Community presupposes the visibility, and concomitant policing, of its members. And some members are decidedly more policed than others. Women's bodies—be they placed in a colonial, nationalist, postcolonial, or even feminist context—are particularly vulnerable to the regulating impulse of the communal. To be in community is, above all, to be exposed, "to be posed in exteriority, having to do with an outside in the very intimacy of an inside" (Nancy 1991, xxvi). To be in community is to be vulnerable to the regard of others. It is to be always considered. Beheld. Rendered, ultimately, transparent to the gaze of others. Given this, self-regard constitutes an effort at individual liberation from, or at the very least resistance to, being beheld and judged from without. And to the extent to which this external regard can be intrusive, coercive, or otherwise violent, efforts to render oneself illegible or to see oneself otherwise certainly may be read as attempts at self-protection.

Every one of the narratives I examine in this study encourages a careful consideration of the extent to which a woman's self-regard might be recognized as an achievement—a justifiable response to the prejudices and other perils of the existing communal order. The female protagonists in all of these fictional works at some point become aware of the literal and symbolic threats posed by the often dangerously fragile community in which they are embedded. They attest to the fact that many supposedly safe spaces contain the possibility for great harm, depending on who inhabits them. They reveal the insecurity of home—the extent to which the domestic is under siege by or complicit in the maneuverings of politics. All of these women engage in some degree of narcissistic pushback with respect to persistent, structural social trauma—self-regard is the tactic they adopt in the face of impossible satisfaction from their community. What, they compel us to ask, should we make of an individual's "misbehavior" in social contexts that are themselves pathological? Do conditions of enslavement and its traumatizing aftermaths expressly call or allow for radical narcissism? Under conditions of constraint, might deviance better be understood as defense? Might self-regard be a legitimate recourse—the best and only recourse—for a self ever vulnerable to the violent, consuming force of the ordering social gaze?

I am certainly not the first to consider the challenges to individuated being in community in the Caribbean—what Alessandra Benedicty-Kokken pithily articulates as the question of "how personhood has been constructed under the weight of the notion and practice of 'nationhood'" (Benedicty[-Kokken] 2013, 7). Nor am I the first to do so in foregrounding matters of gender—to ask "how national belonging and the nation-state continue to play a fundamental role in circumscribing Caribbean people's lives" (Horn 2014, 3). Notions of (in)decency and (dis)order have long been understood as having everything to do with women's social—and especially sexual—(non)conformity to behavioral conventions governing the public sphere. Further, as Donette Francis reminds us, "conditions of belonging presuppose a raced, gendered, classed, and sexed body, and . . . for women and girls the struggles have often been against kin as much as colonizer" (2010, 2). It is no coincidence that the novels I consider feature disorderly women characters in contexts of nation-building, wherein the stakes of communal identity formation are particularly high and wherein incautious women too easily find themselves cast as necessary Others to a developing idea of Same.

The claims of both literary theorists and social scientists of the postcolonial Americas—put forward in works like Belinda Edmondson's *Making Men: Gender, Literary Authority, and Women's Writing in Caribbean Narrative* (1999), Omise'eke Natasha Tinsley's *Thiefing Sugar: Eroticism between Women in Caribbean Literature* (2010) and *Ezili's Mirrors: Imagining Black Queer Genders* (2018), Donette-Francis's *Fictions of Feminine Citizenship: Sexuality and the Nation in Contemporary Caribbean Literature* (2010), Mimi Sheller's *Citizenship from Below: Erotic Agency and Caribbean Freedom* (2012), M. Jacqui Alexander's *Pedagogies of Crossing: Meditations on Feminism, Sexual Politics, Memory, and the Sacred* (2005), and Deborah

Thomas's *Exceptional Violence: Embodied Citizenship in Transnational Jamaica* (2011)—advance compelling critiques of the heteronormative and misogynist continuities between colonialism, nationalism, and postcolonialism. Moreover, as these studies make apparent, the diverse societies of the Caribbean have long adhered to an entrenched Protestant ethic of respectability—with women in particular expected to conform to codes of "decency" as part of their commitment to shore up liberatory anticolonial projects as well as postcolonial nation-building efforts—to adhere to and "perform normative scripts of sexual citizenship such as the good mother, the respectable woman, the worthy Christian, or the father of the family ... which involved the harnessing and simultaneous disavowal of the erotic potential of the body" (Sheller 2012, 10). These masculinist ordering codes are well known and have been well studied. Also well known and well studied are the gendered expectations of and constraints on Caribbean womanhood intrinsic to colonialism, along with those resulting from the blind spots of white feminist politics.[8]

On the one hand, there is little surprising about the phenomenon wherein women in colonial and postcolonial spaces, literary as much as extraliterary, are called upon to do battle with misogynistic and patriarchal white supremacy, with misogynistic and patriarchal Black nationalisms, and with hegemonic North Atlantic feminisms. These are the "enemies" we know ("we" being postcolonial, Caribbeanist, womanist scholars). Of interest to me, however, are coercions slightly different from those to which we already have become attuned. I am interested in texts and authors that not only defy the usual suspects but also deeply unsettle *un*usual suspects—ostensibly progressive, antiestablishment communities of readers and critics—thus revealing the strictures to which that same "we" is perhaps insufficiently attentive.[9] Crucial here is my effort to enact the praxis David Scott outlines in *Refashioning Futures: Criticism after Postcoloniality*, notably, "to imagine an ethos, or perhaps even a *habitus*, of critical responsiveness to the tendency of ... identities to harden into patterns of exclusion that seek to repel or abnormalize emergent or subaltern difference" (1999, 217).

Throughout this book I propose possibilities for thinking more broadly about human efforts that are not overtly state-centric but make affective calls for transformation. In this respect, my project dovetails meaningfully with our current suspicion regarding existing modes of revolutionary upheaval and calls for greater attentiveness to risky individual expressions of defiance. Whereas, for the most part, the theorists with whom I engage seek in their work to identify or construct coherent counterdiscursive (literary) strategies via which sexed Caribbean subjects claim the status of citizen, *A Regarded Self* attends to literary configurations of individual refusal that not only transgress existing models of postcolonial Caribbean community but also caution against the codification of potentially constraining counterdiscourses. Insofar as a distinction is maintained between the notion of communal identity and that of bourgeois individualism, I am interested in the space between the presumed virtue of the one and the unseemliness of the other. What *do* we get when we don't get what we expect—ideologically or politically—from these women, these authors, these texts?

Order

One of the basic impulses in Caribbean thought is undeniably the need to reconceptualize power. The fascination with worlds of closure; the need to ground a new society on a visionary discourse; the exploration of a foundational poetics . . . [are] manifestations of the desire to establish a new authority, to repossess time and space . . . pursuit of an ordering and ordaining vision.
—J. Michael Dash, *The Other America* (1998)

Our cultural identities reflect the common historical experiences and shared cultural codes which provide us, as "one people," with stable, unchanging, and continuous frames of reference and meaning, beneath the shifting divisions and vicissitudes of our actual history. This "oneness," underlying all the other, more superficial differences, is the truth, the essence, of "Caribbeanness," of the black experience.
—Stuart Hall, "Cultural Identity and Diaspora" (1994)

The border between the political and the literary in the Caribbean has always been permeable. Over centuries of official colonial exploitation and in the interminable wake of North Atlantic empire, peoples of the Caribbean have struggled to delineate and to assert a geoculturally specific, resistant identity. Community has been a particularly significant concern for Caribbean writer-intellectuals in their efforts to determine empowering sociopolitical identities in the face of centuries-old practices of dispossession, historical erasure, and disenfranchisement—both by racist Euro–North American imperial structures and by rapacious neocolonial regimes. Confronted with the relentless twinned forces of psychosocial alienation and military repression, Caribbean social actors have understood that purposeful national and regional unification is critical to cultural and political survival. In the anticolonial context of the first half of the twentieth century, especially, community clearly amounted to a political imperative—"a militant and strategic response to a situation of oppression which [could] only be overturned by organized collective action . . . predicated on a strong sense of unity and solidarity" (Britton 2011, 5). To define community in opposition to clear and common enemies was a political necessity. And it was politically advantageous given the vulnerability of European empires in the wake of World War II.

The construction of Caribbean community as refusal had—and has—at once tactical, ethical, and creative dimensions. It has served as a political rallying cry, undergirding long-standing masculinist discourses of nation-building and Black radicalism as well as more recent narratives "of globality, transnationalism, diaspora and various other forms of international community" (Forbes 2008, 17) so critical to the sociopolitical survival of peoples of color. Integral to these interventions in the realm of policy and governance has been an investment in the communal on the part of the Caribbean cultural elite. The centrality of strategically constructed community in the domain of politics has manifested with equal clarity in Caribbean letters. As Celia Britton (2010) and Lucy Evans (2014) have outlined in their studies of literary representations of community in the putatively former colonies of the French and British Americas, respectively, Caribbean fiction is marked by a commitment to highlighting and promoting the collective specificity of the region.

Both Britton and Evans consider the diverse challenges prose fiction writers face in seeking to give voice to the people whose stories, they argue, have been globally silenced. They consider the "*models* of community" (Britton 2010, 4) these writers propose not merely as representations of communal solidarity but also as so many "self-conscious engage[ments] in the act of community-building" (Evans 2014, 16). Britton argues that the writers of her corpus—among whom are Jacques Roumain, Édouard Glissant, and Patrick Chamoiseau—understand the creation of community to be "their duty *as writers*" (2010, 3).[10] Evans identifies a parallel phenomenon among anglophone intellectuals: "Brathwaite concludes his study [*Contradictory Omens* (1974)] with the phrase 'The unity is submarine,' suggesting that beneath the region's plurality of cultures and ethnicities lies the unifying experience of migration. Derek Walcott's vision of Caribbean culture as a 'shipwreck of fragments' places a similar emphasis on the unification of disparate parts" (2014, 9). Evans goes on to cast a wider net, noting that "the cultural theory of [Wilson] Harris, Glissant and [Antonio] Benítez-Rojo engages with the concept of communal identity in relation to broader visions of a Caribbean regional consciousness" (28).

This assessment echoes Stuart Hall's reflections on "cultural or national identity" and "forms of cultural practice" (1989, 69) in the Caribbean. Hall points to two, largely chronological understandings of culture in the Americas. The first, the "oneness" model, undergirds Negritude, Rastafarianism, and other forms of Pan-Africanism up to and through the 1950s and 1960s and defines "a sort of collective 'one true self'" (69) in opposition to the imposed version of selfhood by which colonizing forces relegated African-descended peoples to positions of degradation and lack. The more recent, more modern approach to identity—"which qualifies, even if it does not replace, the first" (70)—Hall sees as a movement beyond Africa-sited "imagined community" and "imaginative geography and history" toward a recognition of difference and discontinuity among Caribbean subjects.[11] It marks the "play of 'difference' within identity" (73) and aligns with Glissant's *antillanité* (Caribbeanness), the doctrine of *créolité* (Creoleness), and the antiessentialist cultural multiplicity of the Caribbean Artists Movement.[12]

The postcolonial (as opposed to anticolonial) intellectual landscape Hall, Britton, and Evans describe proclaims the internal diversity of cultures and nations in the Caribbean as a decisive refusal of the homogenizing, ethnocentric, universalizing practices of the North Atlantic. This refusal remains bound, however, by a persistently communal intention. These later-century conceptions of the human are, at their most granular, invested in *collective* specificity. Be it in the context of Glissant's Relation, Benítez-Rojo's "repeating island," or "the collective human substance of the Village" celebrated by George Lamming (Lamming [1970] 1991, xxxvi), the smallest unit of engagement is the community. Moreover, such "corrective theories of creolization, métissage, and hybridity have often ended up reinforcing the empirical, geographical, and biological fact of boundaries and borders, recalling the imperatives they seek to undermine" (Cheng 2009, 89). These writers advocate for the significance of discrete cultures in relation and account for exchange and contradiction among diverse nationally or regionally identified collectives. Yet they never go so far as to consider the particular identifications of individuals unmediated by cultural or national identification.

It is well understood that "Caribbean literature deals more with the cultural and political problems of the region than with the inner conflicts of individual souls" (Torres-Saillant 2013, 275). There are consequences to this well-established phenomenon—notably, the codification of a prescriptive order that risks "increasing, not diminishing, the fragmentation in the individual subject" (Lee-Keller 2009, 1297)—the creation of a reified center with respect to which particular, individual souls are (made) marginal, their inner conflicts elided. Directly paralleling the sociopolitical arena, it is the case, as Curdella Forbes plainly asserts, that Caribbean literary culture, "whether diasporic or nationalist, has insisted on the ascendancy of the communal over the individual" (2012, 40–41).

Women in particular have found themselves inhibited and/or left on the margins by such calls to communal order—obliged to conform to and sacrifice for social and political objectives that in important ways fail to account for or even address the specificities of women's existence or that prescribe fixed gendered modes of adherence as a condition for belonging. Caribbeanist sociologist Mimi Sheller emphasizes the myriad ways in which contemporary constructions of citizenship (and its corollaries, inclusion and legitimation) reflect profound "entanglement in deeply seated colonial *and* postcolonial ideologies of gendered, ethnic, and heteronormative boundary drawing and exclusion" (2012, 7). Caribbeanist gender theorist M. Jacqui Alexander puts forward an even fiercer critique of these constraining continuities: "Black heteropatriarchy takes the bequeathal of white colonial masculinity very seriously," she writes. "Heteropatriarchal nationalist law has neither sufficiently dislodged the major epistemic fictions constructed during colonial rule, nor has it dismantled its underlying presuppositions" (2005, 62).

The absenting or narrow representation of the Caribbean woman in works by male authors of the region—the "consistent erasure of the figure of the black woman in both African American and Caribbean male-authored texts" (Edmondson 1999, 99)—is a much-discussed phenomenon. The very authors credited with providing lexical and philosophical tools for undoing the psychosocial binds of colonialism are guilty of more and less subtle sidelinings of women from the postcolonial canon. Scholars like Omise'eke Natasha Tinsley have criticized the rhetoric of Black male Creole radicalism for having done battle with white patriarchy only to "reinvent heteropatriarchy in black and brown, in Creole" (2010, 208). Caroline Rody has argued that "the male authors whose texts dominated the Caribbean canon until the 1970s, generally tended to objectify women and delimit their figural possibilities" (2001, 113).

Susheila Nasta identifies only two possible representations of "woman" in Caribbean fiction: "either as the rural folk matriarch figure, representing the doer, the repository for the oral tradition, the perpetuator of myths and stories, the communicator of fibres and feelings, or, alternatively, woman, as a sexy mulatto figure, a luscious fruit living on and off the edges of urban communities belonging to no settled culture or tradition" (1993, 214). Allocated the role of auxiliary or sister, advocate or mother, martyr or lover, Caribbean women have been configured in regional fiction as infinitely willing and expected to orient themselves in service to communities that are little attentive to their individual needs and desires. With few exceptions, canonical texts of the mid- to later twentieth century omit the presence of women altogether, relegate them to the status of romantic partners and muses to politically awakening or awakened men, turn them into metaphors for the violated and exploited homeland, or position them as noble mother-warriors who "battle to provide for their families" (B. Thomas 2006, 12) and, by extension, their communities.

Theorists have been, to a large extent, complicit in reinforcing this order, as Vèvè A. Clark has outlined compellingly in her foundational essay "Developing Diaspora Literacy and *Marasa* Consciousness":

> The New Negro, Indigenist, and Négritude movements of the 1920s and 1930s constitute the grounded base of contemporary Afro-American, Caribbean, and African literary scholarship. Critics return repeatedly to this textual field as if to embrace a heralded center, familiar and stable. . . . New letters works became communal property to be read and revised across national boundaries. . . . .
>
> Even as the predominantly male new letters voices were materializing in the Caribbean, their narrative and discursive strategies were being redefined in terms of gender by women novelists the likes of Suzanne Lacascade and Annie Desroy, whose texts inaugurated "la littérature féminine" in the Guadeloupe and Haiti of 1924 and 1934, respectively. Scholars consistently overlooked these early texts primarily because none of the authors participated in either Indigenism or Negritude. A separate tradition developed for over five decades and was not recognized as such until Maryse Condé published her study of Antillean novelists, *La parole des femmes*, in 1979. (1991, 9, 10)

Not only was Condé instrumental in recognizing the contributions of Caribbean women writers to global literature at a time when few readers were paying attention, but she also analyzed the specific ways in which women's literature had been dismissed within the region itself. No one has been more thorough and succinct than Condé in outlining the tendency of Caribbean literary canons to oblige allegiance to a masculinist status quo and, more broadly, to a representative "we." In her oft-cited 1993 essay "Order, Disorder, Freedom, and the West Indian Writer," Condé insists that literary history in the French-speaking Caribbean has been dominated by the consecration of limiting artistic models to which "acceptable" works of literature tacitly have been expected to adhere. Pointing to Jacques Roumain, Aimé Césaire, Édouard

Glissant, and the Creolists Patrick Chamoiseau and Raphaël Confiant, among others, she argues that an exclusive and excluding order has long diminished the significance of women's literature or kept it on the margins, in large part by its suggestion that female authors are insufficiently committed to what is assumed to be the common struggle of the Black postcolonial collective—what in the anglophone context Edmondson identifies as the presumption "in the black community that feminism is incompatible with the project of black liberation" (1999, 99).

According to Condé, holding to the criteria for authenticity posited by male authors has been tantamount to abolishing portrayals of individual struggle, personal tragedy, and female sexuality in regional literature. She famously argues that novels conforming to this literary order ultimately restrict themselves to depicting only messianic male heroes working to revolutionize their communities and to "rehabilitate the exploited Black Man" (1993, 125). Condé cites a number of points of "order" that make up the homogenizing masculinist template, which are (paraphrased): (1) individualism must be resisted, as only the collective should express itself (led by an individual male hero, if need be); (2) the masses should be considered the sole producers of Beauty and sole source of inspiration for the writer; (3) the principal, if not unique, purpose of writing should be to denounce one's political and social conditions and thereby join the liberationist struggle; (4) poetic and political ambition should be viewed as inextricable from one another; (5) the spatial framework should be the native land; (6) the hero should be male and of peasant or proletarian origin; (7) the brave and hardworking woman should be the auxiliary in the man's struggle for his community; and (8) although children are produced, no reference should be made to sex (and, if any, only to male sexuality).[13]

Disorder

Like any movement with integrity, [feminism] requires that a person live her/his life entirely by its principles, and not many are prepared to go that far at this stage, especially in the Caribbean where small societies exert tremendous pressure for conformity on the individual.
—Elaine Savory Fido, preface to *Out of the Kumbla* (1990)

As a counter to this pervasive sidelining and constrictive stereotyping, a discourse of (Afro-)feminist scholarship has become highly visible in critical approaches to Caribbean women's writing since the early 1990s, most often in critical studies devoted to discovering and promoting a female authorial voice. These studies emerged in response to the late 1960s and early 1970s "literary explosion" (Larrier 2000, 4) of postcolonial women's writing in Africa and the Caribbean. They point out that, before this period, few of the women who wrote were ever published, and certainly none were included in regional canons, which meant, of course, a silencing of women both as creators and, largely, as agentive characters.

Feminist scholars of the 1980s and 1990s made it a point to identify certain character types and forms of storytelling as subversively feminine, highlighting the degree to which women authors have sought to dismantle frames put in place by their male predecessors and contemporaries from what, it is generally maintained, is a decidedly feminist—or, at the very least, feminized—perspective. Groundbreaking Afro-Americanist and Caribbeanist women scholars in particular, among them Carolyn Cooper, Carole Boyce Davies, Belinda Edmondson, Elaine Savory Fido, Françoise Lionnet, Pamela Claire Mordecai, and Susheila Nasta, have taken up the task of establishing a place for women writers in the postcolonial canon, offering sophisticated articulations of the challenges women's prose fiction presents to the region's male-authored (national and nationalist) narratives. As Lionnet has affirmed, postcolonial women's narratives offer "an important site in which to study the personal, cultural, and political transformations that are the legacy both of the colonial encounter and of the postcolonial 'arts of resistance' it produces" (1995, 3).

The original project of building feminist community relied on a number of specific, cohering preoccupations and presumptions, all of which affirmed the legitimacy and political necessity of a gendered analysis of literary production—"a specifically female position" (Davies and Fido 1990a, 1)—on thematic as well as formal levels. The most prominent of these points of connection is unquestionably the matter of voice. There has been a decided consensus regarding the essential linkage between individual women and their local and global, historical and contemporary feminine communities through storytelling—an extolling of "the voices of black women who bind together, through memory, voice, and metaphor, the quotidian detail of community life, moral and spiritual insight, and the profoundly personal" (McKinney 1996, 22).[14] From Condé's *La parole des femmes: Essai sur des romancières des Antilles de la langue française* ([1979] 2000) (*The Voice of Women: An Essay on Novelists of the French-Speaking Antilles*) to Myriam J. A. Chancy's *Framing Silence: Revolutionary Novels by Haitian Women* (1997a) and Adele S. Newson and Linda Strong-Leek's edited volume *Winds of Change: The Transforming Voices of Caribbean Women Writers and Scholars* (1998) to Isabel Hoving's *In Praise of New Travelers: Reading Caribbean Migrant Women*

Writers (2001), whose introductory chapter is titled "Place, Voice, and Silence," scholars of Caribbean women's literature and of the representation of women in Caribbean literature have consistently touted strategies via which women, on behalf of their communities, challenge the "inability to express a position in the language of the 'master' as well as the textual construction of woman as silent" (Davies and Fido 1990, 1).

Crucial to these and other studies is an investment in telling "herstory" from a first-person perspective, with fictional "I" narrators presenting the single most important element of the subversive stance taken by their creators.[15] Emphasizing the relationship between communal focus and the agency accorded the self-telling individual featured in writings by women authors, Valérie K. Orlando, for example, notes that the authors in her corpus "do agree that when a woman steps outside the confinement of village and home to speak in her own words she becomes automatically politically engaged and compelled to become an active agent for herself and other women within her society" (2003, 6). Myriam Chancy maintains that the specific practice of first-person narration "reflects a political strategy used not only to create a sense of extra-textual intimacy, but also to create a space within the parameters of the genre that redefines national identity in terms of the personal" (1997a, 6). And Renée Larrier describes the practice wherein women writers encourage conflation with their first-person fictional narrators as one of "dual authorship," a formal approach in which the Afro-Caribbean and African women authors she discusses in her study "create first-person female narrators who relate their own story" and so "wrest the representation of their experiences from others." She argues that the technique "moves them—writers and characters—toward subjectivity, empowering them, thus conferring authority on women and their communities" (2000, 1–2).

The parallel discourses of genealogy and community consistently mark scholarly examinations of women writing and written. Critical works like Chancy's *Searching for Safe Spaces: Afro-Caribbean Women Writers in Exile* describe a foundational feminine (comm)unity anchored in female ancestral linkages that persists despite differing geographic, social, and national affiliations. Chancy writes, "Although these writers do not form a 'cohesive' community, in the sense that they are not all from the same island [and do not] reside in the same country of exile, they do speak from similar vantage points and express the same concerns for the necessity of preserving Black women's ancestral and contemporary voices, as they emerge from the Caribbean and other nations where descendants of the African diaspora remain" (1997b, xix). Davies and Fido, for their part, posit that "the new Caribbean woman's text becomes a locus for the reinscription of the woman's story in history.... Storytelling becomes a central cultural metaphor for the ability to communicate oral history through the generations" (1990a, 6). Ancestral connections and, implicitly, then, maternity and procreation are presented as the key to strategies of insubordination deployed within female-centered narratives as well as to processes of historical and cultural insertion that concern women writers themselves.

The essentialist subtext of these discursive feminist and womanist challenges to a masculine literary order has not gone unnoticed. As Edmondson remarked in 1999, "any articulation of feminist consciousness *necessarily* involves an essentialist construction of the subject" (89).[16] Moreover, the initial decades of the twenty-first century have seen ever-increasing political, social, and artistic awareness of gender identifications that undermine or escape classifications like "male" and "female." The work of Caribbeanist scholars like Omise'eke Natasha Tinsley, M. Jacqui Alexander, Vanessa Agard-Jones, Christian Flaugh, and others have provided compelling accounts and analyses of "gender complexity" (Flaugh 2013, 46) in Caribbean culture. Yet while the very category of "woman" has certainly been upended in many ways with respect to Caribbean social orders, it remains crucial to take seriously the persistent heteronormative demands on and conscriptions of the (Afro-)postcolonial feminine. Even as theory turns toward the fluid and the unbound, notions of womanhood remain tethered to standards set for the roles of mother, wife, daughter, muse, and so on. And the privileging of a feminine creative community as a framework for the critical study of women's fiction has created a valuable and productive space for the consideration of transnational and transcolonial phenomena—sociopolitical and aesthetic. Discursive feminist and womanist challenges to the masculine literary order have brought much-needed attention to the role and particular struggles of women in the Caribbean and the wider context of the Global South.

The purpose of my investigation here is not to oppose this perspective, nor is it to enter (directly) into the rich and important conversations currently being held among scholars, activists, artists, and others regarding the (il)legitimacy or (un)usefulness of the categories of woman and man in the Americas. I do want to draw attention, however, to the presumption that women's politicized self-conception is inherently and, ultimately, freeingly based in either maternal or sororal community—the presumption that a woman's recognition of herself as responsible for protecting and preserving a transgenerational feminine community is essential to her coming to full subjectivity. It is crucial to examine the ways in which such discursive challenges to a masculine order are marked by the constraining presence of gendered expectations and thus risk flattening, albeit differently, the experience of individual women. I want to dig into the irony of Fido asserting "[feminism] requires" in the same breath with which she laments "the pressure for conformity on the individual" in the Caribbean (Davies and Fido 1990c, xi).

I want to look closely, that is, at texts in which the female protagonists do not behave in ways that fit asserted parameters of feminine solidarity—characters who do not successfully exist in, who are not necessarily nourished or empowered by relationships with other women, who are not generatively linked to mothers or daughters, who do not come to voice within their narrative space, and whose author-creators subsequently find themselves in tension with extratextual communities of readers and scholars. The disorderly women who are the subject of this inquiry fall short of promoting "the reconstructive powers of female community" (B. Thomas 2006, 13) articulated by Caribbean feminist discourse. If the centrality of the relationship between grandmothers, mothers, and daughters to history-making is a veritable touchstone of regional "women's literature," the works I consider here unsettle customarily positive readings of intergenerational knowledge transmission between women and decouple resistance from the maternal-cum-communal. In these novels, sisterhood proves unreliable, and mothers betray. Girls have to fend for themselves.

Not only do these works not propose "the counter-order of a matriarchy" (Dash 1998, 109), but some also explicitly contest it. They do so primarily via a persistent questioning of the value—or, conversely, an exposing of the negative consequences—of certain matrilineal connections, focusing on difficult, even dangerous relationships between mothers and daughters rather than on—or without the counterpoint of—the more readily idealized connections between grandmothers and granddaughters. Rather than affirm "the dominance of the French Caribbean matrifocal family where the all-powerful mother reigns supreme and the father is noteworthy for his frequent absence and unreliability" (B. Thomas 2006, 8), several of these texts privilege complicated relationships between fathers and daughters, inevitably setting up a Freudian schema. Their protagonists tend to question, if not outright reject, a maternal heritage that conflicts with their own understanding of the world and their place in it—or they simply have no access to such a heritage. They cannot trust the advice or the emotions of mothers they do not really know, may not respect, and by whom they may even have been betrayed. The tenuousness or nonexistence of these mother–daughter relationships thus has the effect of interrupting the correlation between postcolonial womanhood and memory-as-history.

Absent a sustained relationship with a maternal ancestor or personal experience of maternity, the women of these narratives are for the most part focused on the present; none of them engages significantly with long history. Preserving, reclaiming, and reinscribing community are not their concern. Neither, then, does any sort of communal feminist project emerge from the stories they tell. As such, they challenge claims regarding the presumed politicization of "voiced" women. They question the presumption that self-telling equals empowerment or that it is a de facto feminist gesture. The truths these women speak, moreover, are often unsettling. Although they in many ways subvert well-known enemies of the marginalized—heteropatriarchy, classism, and other forms of bigotry—they nevertheless fail to identify or interpolate their readers as allies. They demand, that is, by the very fact of their "I"-narrating selves, a measure of intimacy with a reading "you" whose sympathy they ultimately seem to discourage. In their insistent refusal or inability to embrace sisterhood, they undermine the potentially "ethical relationships between writing selves and reading others," the "bonds of mutuality or coalitions of resistance" (Campbell 2010, 34) we have come to expect women's narratives to generate.[17] They push against assessments of the singular importance of first-person female narration as inherently indicative of a communalist, politicized intention; their narratives amount to so many individual stammerings.

If these women stammer, it is perhaps at least in part because they are angry. None of them is a madwoman, but they are all mad women.[18] Their behavior is, in fact, reasonable. This is a crucial point. Each of them has experienced the childhood trauma of not being seen or of being subject to abuse; each is or becomes keenly aware that her situation is unsafe and unfair—and that she is far less at fault for her unhappiness than the world would have her believe. Each comes to realize that her safest course of action is to take care of herself.

Freedom?

How does one call into question the exhaustive hold that such rules of ordering have upon certainty without risking uncertainty, without inhabiting that place of wavering which exposes one to the charge of immorality, evil, aestheticism. The critical attitude is not moral according to the rules whose limits that very critical relation seeks to interrogate. But how else can critique do its job without risking the denunciations of those who naturalize and render hegemonic the very moral terms put into question by critique itself?
—Judith Butler, "What Is Critique?" (2001)

For what is ethics, if not the practice of freedom?
—Michel Foucault, "The Ethics of the Concern for the Self as a Practice of Freedom" (1997)

In a 1984 interview, Michel Foucault makes a case for the paramount importance of self-care as a practice of individual freedom. "One must not have the care for others precede the care for self," he comments. "The care for self takes moral precedence in the measure that the relationship to self takes ontological precedence" ([1984] 1987, 118). Over the course of the conversation, he affirms the primacy of self-care over manifest political alliance. He pointedly distinguishes between ethics as an individual "practice of freedom" and processes of liberation that have to do with institutional possibility. For Foucault, practices of freedom are contingent on but distinct from a politics of liberation. Referencing anticolonial independence struggles in particular, Foucault acknowledges the legitimacy of emancipation discourse but argues that "the act of liberation is insufficient to establish the practices of liberty that later on will be necessary for this people, this society, and these *individuals* to decide upon receivable and acceptable forms of their existence or political society" ([1984] 1987, 114).

Foucault's context is explicitly Greco-Roman and proto-European, despite his brief, punctual references to the (post)colonial. Yet a turn to Foucault in thinking about the right- or wrongheadedness of the disordering Caribbean women at the center of the narratives I discuss here is warranted not only by his insistence on the inherent ethical value of the individual's "voluntary insubordination" (Foucault 1997b, 47) but also by the nature of the consequent criticism of his work by materialist scholars.[19] Multiple theorists have taken Foucault to task for the perceived moral and political insufficiencies of his ethical paradigm—his espousing, as Karen Vintges notes, of what are perceived as "unrealistic notions of radical freedom and moral nihilism" (2001, 166). Foucault has been accused of a "lack of ethics," his work marked by "an attitude of narcissistic self-absorption" and thus devoid of any "discernible trace of human solidarity, mutuality or fellow-feeling" (Wolin 1986, 85). Such critiques point to the absence of a definitive, explicit, normative political stance in Foucault's work—to the absence of a categorical right and wrong and an indifference to the project of achieving social justice. Such formulations unambiguously posit "bad," "narcissistic" self-focus against "good" communal entanglement, making plain the intuitive hurdle to reconciling a privileged self with a humanist notion of morality.

Those who would defend Foucault argue, however, that not only is Foucault's philosophical position ethical, but it is also deeply political. They note that Foucault advocates for caring for oneself "*correctly*," with the objective being "to *behave correctly* in relationship to others and for others" ([1984] 1987, 119, 118). Foucault is clear: "Care for self is ethical in itself, but it implies complex relations with others.... Care for self renders one competent to occupy a place in the city, in the community or in interindividual relationships which are *proper*" ([1984] 1987, 118; emphases mine). Theorists like Campbell, Vintges, and Richard Wolin, among others, argue that Foucault's concept of self-care is foundational to an ethics of empathy wherein understanding the self allows for an appreciation of others' equally legitimate projects of self-knowledge, "a respect for the (self-understanding of) others" (Vintges 2001, 173).[20] Thus do Foucault's defenders deem his work, which he himself characterized as "a few fragments of an autobiography" (1988, 156), fundamentally ethical in its solipsism. Foucault "made philosophy out of his life and 'lived' his philosophy," writes Vintges, thereby transforming "an individual attitude into a challenge to society, charging his experience with an ethical significance" (2001, 166–67).

Judith Butler similarly recovers Foucault's self-focus and the broader matter of self-telling as central to ethics and a precursor to politics. She offers acute insight into Foucault's "What Is Critique?" in her own essay of the same title (2001), as well as in her more expansive philosophical treatise *Giving an Account of Oneself* (2005). Butler affirms Foucault's perspective on the inherent morality of self-construction, evoking in particular the subject's opacity to itself and its inextricable, engaged positioning within the community by which that self is conditioned, what J. Aaron Simmons identifies as Butler's "recognition of sociality at the heart of subjectivity" (2006, 86). Thinking through Foucault's propositions in the specific context of self-narration and ethical responsibility, Butler argues that there exists no "outside" of the (constrictive, coercive, possibly violent) communal space from which the individual might somehow look objectively upon and give an account of a coherent self.[21] Self-narration necessarily occurs within and participates in the "domain of unfreedom" (J. Butler 2005, 42) that is the social order. "When the 'I' seeks to give an account of itself," Butler explains, "it can start with itself, but it will find that this self is already implicated in a social temporality that exceeds its own capacities for narration; when the 'I' seeks to give an account of itself, an account that must include the conditions of its own emergence, it must, as a matter of necessity, become a social theorist" (7–8). Following Butler's logic, to "indulge" in "I" narration must not be understood as the expression of a "nomadic self that escapes" without "taking responsibility and making basic moral commitments" (Vintges 2001, 177), as Foucault's critics would have it, but rather as a form of active engagement with a "beyond-oneself," an enacting of the simultaneous or doubled gesture of critiquing at once the self and the community that is constitutive of that self.

Butler takes the survival stakes of self-construction and critique into consideration. Thinking with Foucault, she makes explicit the extent to which performing self-scrutiny against the backdrop of an alienating normative social order represents profound risk. "To question the norms of recognition that govern what I might be, to ask what they leave out, what they might be compelled to accommodate, is, in relation to the present regime, to risk unrecognizability as a subject," she posits (2005, 23). Moreover, such questioning amounts to virtuous performance. That is, "if that self-forming is done in disobedience to the principles by which one is formed, then virtue becomes the practice by which the self forms itself in desubjugation, which is to say it risks its deformation as a subject" (201).

In an earlier text, referencing in particular the question of gender and also channeling Foucault, Butler insists that for the marginalized subject "survival depends upon escaping the clutch of those norms by which recognition is conferred" (1999, 3). The very possibility of achieving "a livable life"—of facilitating one's "persistence as an 'I'" (1, 3)—demands the foundational capacity to pose an "interrogation of the terms by which life is constrained in order to open up the possibility of different modes of living" (4). Through interrogation, critique stages a "confrontation with authority" (Foucault 1997b, 46) that, while it does not necessarily propose a moral or political alternative, does reveal the "mechanisms of coercion" (59) on which community relies to suppress threats to its coherence. The retreat into the intimacy of the self amounts, then, to a "critical attitude" (42) with respect to the group in and to which that self presumably belongs. And herein lies the potential for the discernment of an ethic.

But what kind of ethic, precisely? On the one hand, Foucault's reluctance to supplant a critiqued normative order with another, presumably "better" normative order proceeds from the distinction he establishes between morals (externally determined rules of social conduct, requiring/demanding obedience) and ethics (internal reflections on the praxis of self-making, requiring/demanding virtue), a distinction I read in parallel to that which separates the gaze and self-regard. Nonetheless, those seeking to "rehabilitate" Foucault foreclose the very zone of liberty such a distinction allows. The ethical purchase of the twinned practices of critique and self-construction Foucault outlines is, in the end, community focused:

> For Foucault [and those who would defend him] the ethical subject is always already a political subject. "Being occupied with oneself and political activities are linked" [1998, 26]; and "freedom is thus inherently political" [1997a, 286]. Foucault's concept of ethics is political through and through. A concern for who you want to be in life and how you want to act is a political concern. It is a concern about acting in the polis—making politics. (Vintges 2004, 286)

By the same token, while Butler raises the stakes in *Gender Trouble: Feminism and the Subversion of Identity*, positing individual survival as the principal objective of critique and self-creation, her contextual frame is nevertheless alliance politics and communal solidarity (intersex advocacy, a critique of same-sex marriage, queer theory and activism, etc.). As with Foucault, for Butler, "individual agency is bound up with social critique and *social transformation*" (J. Butler 1999, 7; emphasis mine). In positing the legitimacy of individual self-care but then making it into a polis-facing practice, both Foucault and Butler ultimately conjure an ethical possibility they do not pursue. They do not go so far, that is, as to imagine the potential value of refusal that does not explicitly yield a political program for engagement.

This neglected (rejected?) ethical opening is, however, precisely the path chosen in the works of my corpus. The women they present neither build nor transform their worlds: they escape or they survive them. Yes, these Caribbean women characters' refusal to cede the primacy of their self approaches what may be understood as a Foucauldian ethics of self-care, insofar as it puts them in critical relation to the normative social codes governing not only their textual but also their extratextual existence. Yet, if "there is something in critique which is akin to virtue" (Foucault 1997b, 43), it is also true that we do not demand the same virtue from all subjects. There are those we would much prefer keep their critique to themselves. Moreover, if there is anything virtuous about the critique these characters stage, it is not contingent on a constructive or productive political contribution, or even on the promise thereof. They do not posit the communal good as the ultimate aim of self-regard. They are not interested in mastering their appetites or in being on their best behavior.[22] And this is only logical. For what sense would it make, really, for these women to base any project of self-*cons*truction on fealty to a polis that relies on the *des*truction of (some part of) their true self? In their largely self-imposed personal solitude and political isolation, however, these women are not recoverable within the project outlined by Foucault, Butler, and others. Rather, their self-regard supports an ethics of sustained dissent.

In a myriad of ways, we have been instructed that to enter the fold of collectivity, be it familial or revolutionary, we must first be liberated of our sexual deviance, our politically incorrect desires.
—Juana María Rodriguéz, "Queer Sociality and Other Sexual Fantasies" (2011)

Dissent. Disobedience. Practices of refusal. Not riot, not revolution, barely resistance. The women of my corpus are solitary creatures whose affirmative nonbelonging is, in and of itself, a form of persistent critique. In this respect, these novels would seem to fit within a fascinating genre outlined by Curdella Forbes to describe prose fiction works that present "the ultimate ascendancy of personal desire as narrative strategy and aesthetic value" (2008, 20).[23] Such works, which Forbes names "individualist texts," are adamantly incompatible with communal discourses. They embrace a practice of "sly disobedience" that "seeks to remain true to itself first and foremost" (2012, 24). Although often reclaimed by "discourses such as postcoloniality, Caribbean identity, diaspora and . . . feminist resistance" (2008, 21), they "are not easily identified with the mores of collectivist terms such as nation, the folk, diaspora, women's community, collective cultural resistance," or other platforms for solidarity, "whether of the nation or globe or academy" (2008, 17). They are not narratives of alternative community and are not identifiable with progressive communal discourse.

The works I discuss here accord in many ways with these principles. However, they stop short of "negat[ing] the concept of community and privileg[ing] the individual as a form of alternative unbounded universe within and of her or his self" (Forbes 2008, 20), a crucial element of Forbes's individualist texts. The heroines of these narratives, though unquestionably preoccupied with themselves and their own self-realization, nevertheless are obliged to navigate and negotiate the explicitly gendered expectations and limitations of their social world. They at no point deny their intersubjectivity and are by no means free from their communities. Nor do they truly desire to be untethered. Rather, they have been compelled to withdraw by the fact of their incongruity. Each believes in and desires integration into a group but finds herself singularized, and most often scapegoated, with respect thereto. In their self-focused humanism, they do not (cannot) belong but want to—if only the world were better. They are not welcome in their communities but would like to be. They practice refusal in the absence of acceptable conditions for belonging.

The question is not that of Foucauldian self-mastery or of Butlerian activism. Nor is it that of a Forbesian indifference to the communal. It is a matter of defensive self-regard. These women struggle against the "constitutive dispossession" (J. Simmons 2006, 86) that would render them opaque to themselves while leaving them to be determined by others. Their solipsistic qualities thus work to safeguard their individual psychological self as it is contained within, and to an extent constrained by, a body that is de facto at risk—a physical self all too vulnerable to humiliation, sexual violence, and other forms of predation. These women's affirmation of a desiring, desirable, and desired self is a critical component of a broader, innate self-valuation. In other words, these self-regarding female characters (come to) believe that they matter and, as such, that to love and be loved is their right. But, like the Haitian goddess Ezili so exquisitely theorized by Colin Dayan, they "demand that the word [*love*] be reinvented" (Dayan 1995, 63).

This question of love—of romance and the erotic—is central to the praxes of self-regard I point to in these novels.[24] Given that "systems of sex and gender operate at the juncture of the disciplining of the body and the control of the population" (Alexander 2005, 23) in both the past and the present-day Caribbean (and well beyond), the insistent sexuality of these female characters presents an avenue of opposition vis-à-vis a policing communal order. Their sense of their erotic self incorporates a range of "deviant" strategies and practices—adultery, bisexuality, sadomasochism, bondage. Several of these women instrumentalize their sexuality, and all are perfectly capable of dissociating lust from love. Each of these works manifests a protective, if not survivalist, principle according to which love for self serves as the basis from which to claim, or at least to imagine, nonviolent and nonviolating love from others. Each stages the sticky question of agency in the context of vulnerability or abjection. Is it even possible for the Caribbean woman to be sexual—to be sexy—without also inviting or deserving violation? As Mimi Sheller affirms, leaning on Audre Lorde, "the erotic is a kind of pervasive energy that can be a source for social and political change"; nevertheless, "it remains hotly debated whether this [kind of] sexual performance is liberatory or not" (2012, 244, 42). Thus, while these women queer both the textual and extratextual worlds they inhabit, the challenge they propose is in many ways circumscribed and therefore ambivalent.[25]

This tension is starkly rendered in all of the works I discuss here. For the disorderly women of these novels, self-eroticization functions as an instinctive, unmediated, and unplanned refusal. It does not declare any fully articulated political objective, nor does it even always look like success. Ultimately, each of these women "merely" hopes to survive and to find freedom in accordance with her own definition thereof. Every one of these characters resists the incursion of those who would temper her sexuality or reduce her to the status of gift for exchange, yet none of them generates, in any sustained fashion, productive alliance or certain allegiance. While in each case the woman's very being may be oppositional with respect to an oppressive narrative community, not one of these heroines quite manages to abandon the subjugating template that contains her. Each wants very much in fact to fit in somewhere—to belong to a community—and so none of them comes out on the other side, as it were, to embrace a wholly (self-)satisfying liberation. Their narcissism is defensive, not triumphant.[26] Although their behavior challenges various forms of injustice, these women remain in many ways marginalized within their textual communities. They are willing to reveal and even to revel in their personal refusals, but their implicit critique of normative standards does not empower others of their race and/or gender. Their pain redeems no one. In this sense, these women remain outside of, and are difficult to recover for, any "respectable" ideology, political position, or even racial category.

The matter of race is an additional site of disruption these characters produce. Without exception, the women of my corpus disorder by the very fact of their racialized bodies: beyond what they do or do not do, there is the matter of who they are. All but one of them are mixed race—born directly of the gendered forms of brutality and coercion that mark encounters between powerful men and disempowered women in both the colonial and postcolonial contexts. Their ambiguously racialized bodies signal the historical violence of the colonial past-cum-present. "Thinking metissage," argues Françoise Vergès, "requires accepting a genealogy and a heritage. In other words, the recognition of a past of rape, violence, slavery, and the recognition of our own complicity with the wicked ways of the world" (1999, 11). At the same time, the concept has been deployed also as a means of eliding this violent past by reading the *métis*—especially the *métisse*—both as the exotic product of empire's "colonial family romance" (11) and as a symbol of its more harmonious, less "Black" postcolonial future. In this respect, *métissage* risks offering resolution of the colonial past via repression of its originary antiblackness and white supremacy.

The novels of my corpus do not allow for a "withering away of the memory of slavery" (Vergès 1999, 9) through sexy or celebratory evocations of métissage. Nor do they gesture toward "*métissage* as a concept of solidarity" or as solid "racial ground on which liberation struggles can be fought" (Lionnet 1989, 9). The racial ambiguity of their central female characters instead presents a consistent challenge to communalist alliance. More often than not, in discourse about ambiguously raced beings, "what has remained constant has been a suspicion about the loyalty of the metis because of their 'division'" (Vergès 1999, 10). Insofar, that is, as "oppositional racial politics are an intrinsic part of black discourse" (Edmondson 1999, 86), the racial opacity of these women precludes the tracing of clear pathways for coalition. It renders them inherently suspect, of uncertain allegiance. Their racial indeterminacy provides space within which their respective authors "challenge the idea that racial and cultural identities function as stable points of reference in our unstable world" and present race "as a figuration of crossing whose patterns of meaning emerge only in light of the crossing of other categories such as class, gender, nationality, and sexuality" (Mardorossian 2005, 3, 18). Distinct from the aspirational notion that Lionnet and other postcolonial theorists propose, wherein métissage refutes hypocritical European colonial desires for racial purity, the intersectional identities of these characters produce isolation and fracturing more so than they provide points of generative articulation.[27]

The ways in which the women featured in these novels trouble and are troubled by binaries of race and sexual orientation make them obliquely political creatures. At most, they are political "in the narrower sense of the term," insofar as they hint, yes, at ways "to defend and enlarge the space of freedom practiced against and within the disciplines in our societies and against other types of domination" (Vintges 2001, 177). Their subversion is initially without intent, becoming more politically articulate only once they realize, for some rather belatedly, that the world—their world—is in fact what's wrong. The majority of them experience their marginalization first and foremost as personally unjust, and only by extension, and limitedly, do they begin to consider issues of social justice more broadly, and this to very mixed results. As such, the objectives and behaviors of these female protagonists are contestatory but not necessarily constructive; their actions are reactive rather than proactive. Each of them comes to anchor herself in individualist apprehensions of the world. She more or less radically divorces herself from the community or communities whose ethical positions and social practices have wounded her, folding back on herself and refusing even to engage in any sustained participatory counterpolitics that might offer a sustainable platform or practice from which to be in solidarity or to engender reconstituted, ameliorated community. They offer refusal without promise. A praxis of "NO," full stop.

In this, they can be frustratingly unsympathetic and equivocal beings. They make choices that are hard to get behind. Plainly put, they can be very difficult to like. They occupy varying positions along the scale from healthy self-regard to pathological narcissism. Some of them seem merely self-indulgent, others self-involved. Several, it might be argued, are problematically self-focused. For others still, the safeguarding of the self comes with some of the clinical attributes of the extreme narcissist: a propensity for vanity or fantastic thinking, a need to be admired and desired, a tendency to arrogance or manipulation, a sense of self-importance or entitlement. In these instances, protective self-regard is matched to varying degrees by the more classically pejorative elements of narcissism, tendencies that emerge from a profound existential insecurity that is in large part a product of the literal, physical *non*security of their individual existence.

Thus, as tempting as it might be to place all of these women in Foucault's or Butler's ethico-philosophical embrace, so to speak—to characterize their self-centeredness as the noble precursor to radical political participation—I do not want to suggest this sort of progressive movement toward a redeeming moral good. I want to take seriously these women's self-distancing from a readily identifiable and satisfying counterpolitical stance. They do not necessarily engage in purposed, conscious technologies of the self in the ways that Foucault or Butler would have it—their self-regard does not signal resistance explicitly; it is unharnessed from any clear larger project of transformation; it does not acknowledge or offer platforms for solidarity. These women's antisocial existence inevitably refuses what Jack Halberstam calls the "liberal fantasies of progressive enlightenment and community cohesion" (2008, 143). Refusing to find and embrace the happy ending of community reborn, these disorderly women point to the recuperative snares inherent in any fixed discursive stance. They embrace what Vèvè A. Clark has named a "*marasa* consciousness"—a way of countering "the binary nightmare" (1991, 45) of colonialism and its aftermath by refusing categorization and engaging in unsanctioned racial and sexual interactions.

In every instance isolated from her community, each of these women is unable to abide that which would make her a part of the collective or is unwilling to suppress that which keeps her apart. Each and every one of the narratives I examine evokes the precise social risks assumed (with varying degrees of consciousness) by the woman at their center. Each one encourages a careful consideration of the extent to which that woman's narcissism might in fact be a justifiable response to and serve as a valuable indicator of the perils and prejudices of the existing communal order. The very fact that these women can or will not be incorporated ultimately exposes the ethical lacunae of their respective communities. As such, the self-regard presented in these works and through these women does not presume the impossibility or even the undesirability of identifying with a collective. Instead, it challenges the foundations and parameters of the communal as revealed in the experiences of individuals whose presence or performance is deemed irreconcilable with existing codes of inclusion.

In their refusal to participate unambiguously in any politics of solidarity, the "inappropriateness" of these characters' behavior extends beyond the frame of the texts that contain them. They disallow any symbolic repackaging of their discontent or their individual protest as a politics of resistance and thus push at the limits of our inclusivity as scholars. They oblige a questioning of our less questioned reading practices and perspectives. They are not disposed "to easy accommodation in the liberal compact of cultural, feminist, or African-American studies" (Dayan 1995, 70). They question whether our antinormative, progressive, womanist, antiracist, anti-imperialist, postcolonialist engagements with the world and its cultural productions are capacious enough to accommodate those who make the "wrong" personal choices. Are we able to tolerate refusal that does not result in the triumph of the subject or her community? Can we resist our tendency to cast defiance by certain kinds of subjects as a progress-directed first step toward a "better" normative order? Are we capable of enacting a reading practice that embraces individuals who "misbehave," even under conditions of relative freedom? Must the novelist appeal to the register of selflessness or solidarity in representing Caribbean womanhood? Must a novel about a woman—about a Caribbean woman—present her righteousness in order for her to be counted among rights-deserving human subjects? These narratives call on us to confront the expectations we bring to our objects of study. They call on us to broaden our understandings of what freedom looks like. They present characters who struggle mightily to refuse the judgment of their community and to hold themselves only to their own standards of being human. They propose to us an ethics of self-regard.

Each of the chapters of this study focuses principally on a single author and a single novel. The theoretical interlocutors and perspectives I bring to bear on my corpus are as geoculturally diverse as my authors are nomadic. In my first chapter, "SELF-LOVE | Tituba," I argue that Guadeloupean author Maryse Condé's disconcerting heroine, the Black "witch" Tituba Indian, subverts the cohering-cum-coercive inclinations of both literal and literary community. Condé's 1986 novel paints a scandalous portrait of a historical figure whose being and behavior are on many levels antithetical to rigid constructions of selfhood and community in the Americas, past and present. As Condé has imagined her, Tituba's steady commitment to self-love, and the erotic expression thereof, transgresses the multiple paradigms that would conscript her existence—at once those that function in the context of the colonial

Americas and those that comprise various contemporary postcolonial critical communities. This chapter asks how Tituba's disordering self-regard not only contradicts seventeenth-century Puritan religious precepts but also pushes against the puritanical leanings of nineteenth-century American abolitionist discourse, of twentieth-century Caribbean intellectual currents, and of so-called First and Third World feminism. Although in the considerable body of scholarship about the novel much rightly has been made of Tituba's empowered self-liberation through sexual adventure, I am interested in the arguably less digestible dimensions of her triply othered (nonwhite, female, foreign) narrative being. I think alongside Sheller's reflections on the circumscription of voices considered disruptive by conventionally progressive Global South perspectives—the voices of those subjects deemed marginal with respect to particular nationalist and postcolonial ideologies.

I am particularly interested in Condé's subversive engagement with the female slave narrative tradition engendered by Mary Prince and Harriet Jacobs and, further, in her subtle refusal of the recuperative tendencies of both antislavery rhetoric in the colonial Americas and current postcolonial and feminist discourse. I examine the ways in which Condé's erotic and ludic take on Tituba's misadventures disrupts the slave narrative in its reticence and the contemporary Black female neo–slave narrative in its insistence on abjection. Moreover, specific elements of the novel's provocations make it a veritable cipher for the works by both Jamaica Kincaid and Marlon James I discuss in later chapters.

Chapter 2, "SELF-POSSESSION | Hadriana," takes as its point of departure the substantial criticism generated by the Haitian writer, intellectual, and militant communist activist René Depestre's 1988 novel *Hadriana in All My Dreams* among Caribbeanist scholars. I dig into the specifics of critical discomfort with the novel through my examination of Hadriana's turn to practical self-regard in the face of a very literal situation of life or death. I argue in this chapter that Depestre's manner of representing Haiti to the wider world, fraying the line between parody and unironic celebration in its foregrounding of the supernatural and the erotic, justifiably provokes the anxieties of colonial mimicry. I acknowledge the legitimacy of the critical unease Depestre's novel has generated. I also highlight the less obviously subversive qualities presented by the young woman at the center of this Creole tale—the self-sexualizing, white French zombie Hadriana. In a context wherein the aspirational codes of the Haitian bourgeoisie and the idiosyncrasies of Haitian spiritual practices compete to restrict feminine destiny, what possible opportunities exist for a woman to possess or be possessed of herself?

In looking for answers to this question, I make use of an interpretive frame similar to that which guides my reading of *I, Tituba*, highlighting the means by which sexuality and selfhood are linked to effect a subversion of troubling communalist politics. Relying in part on Italian feminist philosopher Adriana Cavarero's exegesis of the Orpheus myth, I emphasize Hadriana's refusal of the pressures of belonging. I focus on Depestre's configuration of the Haitian zombie figure as a metaphor through which the novel dismantles—or at the very least meaningfully pokes fun at—the very gender and racial clichés it has been accused of promoting.

"SELF-DEFENSE | Lotus," this study's third chapter, calls for a critical rethinking of Haitian author Marie Chauvet's largely unexamined 1954 novel *Fille d'Haïti*. One of Haiti's most significant and mystifying writers, Chauvet has long been placed at a remove from her well-canonized predecessors and contemporaries of the mid-twentieth century. Though Chauvet is increasingly a subject of interest for scholars of Haitian women's literature and of Haitian feminism, her work is only very rarely considered alongside that of more politically explicit Haitian novelists like Jacques Roumain, Jacques Stephen Alexis, and, for that matter, Depestre. My analysis of *Fille d'Haïti*, Chauvet's first work of prose fiction, puts the author in direct dialogue with her male contemporaries yet moves away from her inclusion within a feminist version of political radicalism. I look at both Chauvet's life and her work to tease out the ways in which her disorderly feminine presence as a writer, a wife, and a citizen encourages us to think about the potential hazards of politicized intellectual community in Haiti vis-à-vis the individual feminine self.

This chapter argues that Chauvet's configuration of a changeable, self-interested heroine obliquely evinces the specific mechanisms and mistakes inherent in the rigid and divisive politics of 1940s and 1950s Haiti. Writing at a historical moment when community-based polarization was the order of the day, Chauvet's novel pushes against the binaries embedded in collective constructions of race, class, gender, and other totalizing systems. Beginning with a meditation on the constraints of both Black radicalism and elite feminism in 1950s Haiti and an analysis of Chauvet's self-telling correspondence with French feminist Simone de Beauvoir in the 1960s, I read *Fille d'Haïti* as a sharp denunciation of the gendered strictures of her time. What options does a woman have, I ask, within the militarized, masculinist context of nation-building? How must she—how can she—possibly defend herself against the incursions of both the state and its revolution-minded opponents? I engage queer studies, feminist, and critical race theorist Amber Jamilla Musser's insightful considerations of gender and power within the context of bondage/

discipline and sadomasochism; feminist political theorist Carole Pateman's perceptive unpacking of the "sexual contract"; sociologist Carolle Charles's analyses of gender realities under Duvalier; and postcolonial critic Homi K. Bhabha's theorization of the "in-between" to make plain Chauvet's audacious critique of the Haitian private and public spheres.

Chapter 4, "SELF-PRESERVATION | Xuela," presents Antiguan novelist Jamaica Kincaid's *The Autobiography of My Mother* (1996), arguably the most subversive work in the author's highly controversial corpus, as a work of philosophy—an extended meditation on the risks and perils of being nonwhite and nonmale in the Atlantic world. The chapter takes up Kincaid's fraught relationship to several prominent colonial, anticolonial, and postcolonial narratives of the self in community. Responding to Sylvia Wynter's call for vigilance regarding the presumed immutability of the postcolonial global order, I look at how Xuela's disorderly textual being and the novel's unsettling extratextual presence posit philosophically grounded possibilities for navigating an untenable social reality, contesting a traumatic history, and mounting a generative critique of contemporary community. With its supremely self-regarding Afro-Carib heroine Xuela, the *Autobiography* in many ways resembles Forbes's "individualist text." Yet the novel's deep engagement with community affirms the individual's inescapable attachment to the collective.

Examining this bind via Halberstam's theorization of the antisocial, I posit Xuela as a queering agent within the socio-ideological landscape of the Caribbean. I pay particular attention to Xuela's effort at the literal preservation of her self that claims indigenous American belonging to the island. Taking up Kincaid's engagement with the question of indigeneity, I argue that the *Autobiography* proposes a magnificently provocative intertextual response to William Shakespeare's *The Tempest* and Aimé Césaire's *A Tempest*—a response that foregrounds the complex position of the indigenous Caribbean subject at the extreme margins of postcolonial studies. I consider how, by underscoring the vulnerability of the native person as distinct from that of the Afro-diasporic subject, Kincaid marks her commitment to exposing intramural conflicts among nonwhite peoples of the American postcolony.

In my final chapter, "SELF-REGARD | Lilith," I turn to the 2009 novel *The Book of Night Women*, Jamaican writer Marlon James's harrowing deep dive into the experience of an individual, female, enslaved person struggling to survive in the Caribbean plantation universe. Among all of the novels I consider in *A Regarded Self*, James's narrative takes up the question of regard—self- versus external, internalized versus reflected—in a way that most explicitly outlines its attendant survival stakes. James's novel presents a heroine, suspected of possessing supernatural powers, whose ambivalent connection to both Blacks and whites renders her dangerously unreadable and unreliable with respect to both communities. That this enslaved woman somehow manages to conjure a space for passion and even romance in a context of abjection speaks, I argue, to the specific purchase of self-regard in the plantation context, wherein patriarchal white supremacy sets the terms of human value.

James's narrative insists that the reader come to terms with the complex subjects who experience antiblack violence as part but not all of who they are or will themselves to be. How, I ask, does this premise oblige consideration of what is perhaps the most fraught ethical question we pose about the Atlantic slave past: notably, whether it is possible, from the ostensibly removed space of slavery's long wake, to uncompromisingly represent the limitless violence of this history without becoming spectators to that violence or reproducing it through our narratives. Is it possible, that is, to tell the truths of slavery's horrors without tacitly facilitating transcendence, desensitization, or catharsis? Thinking with African Americanist scholars Stephen Best, Hortense J. Spillers, Saidiya Hartman, and Christina Sharpe, among others, I consider the ways in which James's heroine disallows unethical spectatorship and refuses the potential for pornotroping the experiences of the enslaved.

A Regarded Self, like the characters and the texts discussed throughout, lays out no new ideological program or political solutions. It does, however, propose opening up to reading old stories in new ways. It proposes a critical consideration of self-regard as a lens through which to rethink long-standing academic touchstones and ideological perspectives. Reading the five fictional women of this corpus in one another's company makes visible the provocation issued by marginalized individuals who negotiate national and transnational spaces. It does so, I hope, without consolidating their practices of refusal into newly constituted communities of activism or identity. The disorderly presence of these women in these texts provides a rich opportunity to query and to queer twentieth- and twenty-first-century constructions of a liberationist communal spirit in Caribbean literature as well as among Caribbeanist scholars. The insistent self-regard of these protagonists draws our attention to the constraints and insufficiencies of what we often presume to be radical or expansive categories. These women remind us that any commitment to inclusivity and justice must make room for wayward subjects.

Disorder implies an order. It reveals a norm that has been interrupted by behavior deemed pathological—that is, endangering of that order. Disorder is necessarily perverse. It commits to unsettling all things endlessly. In a critical context, disorder can be the means and the product of persistent vigilance regarding our own tendencies to resediment limiting notions of virtue. The socially, racially, politically ambivalent women characters I consider throughout this study encourage such vigilance. They struggle mightily to refuse the judgment of their community and to hold themselves only to their own regard. In so doing, they fruitfully upset understandings of the Caribbean and the human—understandings of the human from the space of the Caribbean.

Now, let us meet them.

1

SELF-LOVE | Tituba

The disorder unleashed in Condé's corporeal dramas leads away from an archetypal self to a multiplicity of selves.
—J. Michael Dash, *The Other America* (1998)

Maryse Condé is duplicitous.
—Raphaël Confiant in Chamoiseau et al., "Créolité Bites" (1997)

Guadeloupean writer Maryse Condé has been called many names: "inconvenient nomad," "postcolonial renegade," "recalcitrant daughter," and "iconoclast," to mention just a few (Cottenet-Hage and Moudileno 2002; Boisseron 2014, 59; Ngate 1986, 8; Hewitt 1995, 641). Whatever the particular wording, the various labels applied to Condé over the course of her long and successful career as a writer and an academic consistently point to her disorderly presence and her disordering effect on the worlds through which she has circulated and about which she has written.

Born in Guadeloupe in 1937, the youngest child in a prominent Black elite family, Condé enjoyed a comfortable existence in the bourgeois community of Pointe-à-Pitre. Like many of her social class, she migrated to France in her teenage years in order to pursue her studies, and it was during this period, as a university student in 1950s Paris, that Condé's life rather dramatically changed course. While studying at the Sorbonne, she began to associate with African and Caribbean students and came to experience something of a political awakening. She became deeply invested in global anticolonial struggles, ultimately marrying a Guinean man and moving with him in 1960 to sub-Saharan West Africa, where she intended to raise her four children.

The years Condé spent in Ivory Coast and later in postindependence Guinea were marked by a series of profound disappointments—personal, intellectual, and political. Condé had become a Marxist and a staunch Pan-Africanist while in Paris and, imbued with the perspectives and promises of Aimé Césaire's Negritude, expected to find her true home—and a home base from which to militate against colonialist racial capitalism—in Sékou Touré's Guinea. Not long after her arrival, however, it became clear that her esteem for Touré was ill founded: Touré's brutal treatment of political dissidents, among them teachers and students, gave the lie to his revolutionary Marxist platform and quickly revealed the autocratic nature of his regime.

Condé found herself equally disillusioned in her role as wife and mother, trapped by the gendered constraints of West African domesticity. By 1964 she had divorced her husband and left for Ghana, then a recently independent socialist republic led by revolutionary leader Kwame Nkrumah. She worked as a teacher in Accra until a military coup overthrew Nkrumah, sending him into exile in Guinea in 1966. Accused by the new regime of being a spy for Touré, Condé was jailed and eventually deported. For several years she moved between Europe and West Africa, returning in 1970 to France, where she earned a doctorate in Caribbean literature from the Sorbonne in 1975. After ten years spent in Paris, Condé relocated in the late 1990s to the United States, where, aside from two relatively brief attempted resettlements in her native Guadeloupe, she remained for more than thirty years, having embarked on a literary career that would make her one of the most prolific, versatile, and outspoken writers of the French-speaking Caribbean.

Condé's life story very explicitly informs her writing—her prose fiction, scholarly essays, and, of course, her memoirs. Throughout her diverse peregrinations, she has been constant in her critique of political, intellectual, and aesthetic ideologies that draw borders around racial, ethnic, and gendered identities and the performance thereof. Author of several novels, plays, children's books, and works of nonfiction, Condé has met with fierce criticism for her iconoclastic stance with respect to the postcolonial Caribbean literary institution. The virulence of this criticism often results from a tendency to conflate Condé the author with the various self-telling protagonists she configures in her fiction.

The publication of her first novel, *Hérémakhonon*, in 1976 marks a striking instance of this phenomenon. The book was widely condemned by reviewers from both Africa and the Caribbean owing to its perceived disparagement of Pan-Africanism. As Condé writes in her preface to the 1988 reedition, *Hérémakhonon* was initially met with "total unsuccess" (1988, 11), which she attributes in large part to the confounding of her authorial self with that of Veronica Mercier, the novel's disorderly self-narrating protagonist:[1]

> The narrator, Véronica—narcissistic, selfish, weak-willed, at times even spineless—is our witness to the drama. A witness who would prefer at first to remain indifferent but who little by little finds herself caught up in the heart of the action. Her petty little moods, her cynical, hateful, and often shocking reflections, parasitize the story, even exasperate the reader, who cannot help but want to tell her the right way to behave. On a psychological level, that of the portrait of a "lost" woman, as she herself claims to be, it was a complete success. So complete that hasty critics conflated me with my fictional character and chastised me because of it. It took a long time for their contempt to dissipate. And I suffered from that greatly. (12)

It was perhaps "too soon" to decry the failures of decolonization in sub-Saharan Africa, though, as Condé also remarks, her assessment was not wrong, merely ahead of its time: "If the denunciation of African independence, a cliché that only authors without any imagination dwell on now, and (in this moment where Patrick Chamoiseau insists on imposing the Creole language and the culture it subtends) the 'quest for an identity' are not both completely dated," she declares, "it is thanks to the character of Véronica" (12).[2]

These provocative remarks set the stage for Condé's later conflicts within the francophone literary community. Nearly two decades after the publication of *Hérémakhonon*, Condé engaged in an intense public dispute with the Creolists—writers Patrick Chamoiseau and Raphaël Confiant and linguist Jean Bernabé. The debate between Condé and this cohort of male Martinican intellectuals erupted upon the publication of the latter two's 1989 manifesto *In Praise of Creoleness* (*Éloge de la créolité*). Condé openly contested the manifesto, objecting to what she perceived to be its demarcation of a mythical and totalizing notion of what it means to be—and to write—from the Caribbean. In *Penser la créolité* (Thinking Créoleness), the 1995 volume Condé coedited with Madeleine Cottenet-Hage, more than twenty contributors reflect on the limitations of créolité as an ideological and aesthetic frame for Antillean cultural production. There and elsewhere, Condé is unsparing in her critique. Créolité, she argues, "presumes to impose a law and order" and "implies a notion of 'authenticity,' which inevitably engenders exclusion" (Condé 1998, 106).

Chamoiseau, Confiant, and Bernabé responded bitterly to Condé's criticism in a 1997 interview with Lucien Taylor, "Créolité Bites." In the course of this conversation, Chamoiseau argues that Condé's critique "makes no sense," given that she is "incapable of proposing any alternative," and he accuses Condé of "self-conscious cosmopolitanism" (in Chamoiseau et al. 1997, 150, 151). Confiant calls Condé "duplicitous" and "a prisoner of French" and implies that she is among those "deserters of development" who have left the Caribbean "to make a career for themselves where it pays well" (150, 152, 151). Throughout the conversation, the men persistently challenge Condé's loyalty to her island and to the Caribbean space more broadly, implying that her departure from Guadeloupe and her lesser command of Creole reflect both an indifference to and a discomfort with "locality" (150). This particular line of critique calls to mind Bénédicte Boisseron's observation that "nomadism always holds the potential of being inconvenient because by definition nomadism is meant to err and deviate from the assumed 'proper' location" (2014, 60). Condé, like her characters, it is true, deviates from the proper. Her characters, like her, suffer from that greatly.

In her 1986 novel *I, Tituba, Black Witch of Salem*, Condé paints a provocative portrait of the mixed-race Caribbean enslaved woman Tituba Indian, a figure whose very being is in many ways antithetical to rigid constructions of selfhood and community in the Americas. Compelled by the fact of Tituba's historical neglect to fictionalize the "Black witch's" post-Salem fate, Condé re-presents and recontextualizes the events of the 1692 trials by providing Tituba, at once the event's most central and most marginalized player, with a historical future. This gesture of recovery and representation situates Condé's novel solidly within the genre of the "historiographic metafiction," a genre of which the female slave narrative is a crucial exemplar.[3] Yet the insistent self-regard Tituba expresses throughout the novel resonates beyond the borders of the nineteenth-century Puritan textual community to vex present-day extratextual communities of scholars. Tituba's unwavering commitments to love and to the erotic expression thereof transgress not only the traditional female slave narrative genre but also Caribbean social and aesthetic movements, North Atlantic feminist ideologies, and postcolonial womanist understandings of freedom.

I am concerned in the pages that follow with the fervent self-love of which Tituba's disorderly sexuality is the most unambiguous expression. More specifically, I am interested in the ways in which Tituba's erotic self-regard places her outside certain of the representational norms governing Caribbean literary expression, past and present. Tituba's unfettered embracing of a defiant, individualist sexuality is legible, to be sure, as the counterdiscursive strategy of a marginalized Other confronted with an indisputably repressive Same—"the ultimate disturbance of patriarchal order" (Arnold 1993, 713). Yet this character's attitude and actions are in many ways difficult to assimilate. Although Tituba is very much self-aware, she is often stubbornly unwise in ways that confound attempts to recognize or claim her as wholly subversive.

It is certainly the case that *I, Tituba* jibes, for instance, with several of the most celebrated ethical and creative ideologies to have emerged from the French-speaking Caribbean in the twentieth century: Tituba's direct African descendance and her cultural retention of an African spiritual worldview, for example, evoke the tenets of Aimé Césaire's Negritude and Jacques Roumain's Indigenism; the very premise of Condé's narrative project "exemplifies [Édouard] Glissant's notion of Caribbeanness in that it fills in the blank spaces from lost history" (Scarboro 1992, 204); and her crafting of a reconfigured Caribbean past even affirms "the position taken by Jean Bernabé, Patrick Chamoiseau, and Raphaël Confiant in *Eloge de la créolité* who argue that historians need the support of writers of poetry and fiction to complete the process of revisiting and revising Caribbean history" (Mortimer 2007, 54). Despite these significant points of intersection, however, Condé explicitly keeps her distance from these ostensibly liberating iterations of Afro- and Creolocentrism, exposing the puritanical dimensions of even the most seemingly broad-minded among them.

Since the publication of *I, Tituba* in English in 1992, forewarded by Angela Y. Davis and back-cover-blurbed by Henry Louis Gates Jr., the novel has been identified with a hemispheric Black (and) feminist agenda—an agenda that means to interrogate and often contest the blueprints for freedom laid out within masculinist liberatory traditions. The novel is aligned, in particular, with the genre of the nineteenth-century female slave narrative, as well as with that of the twentieth-century female neo–slave narrative. Tituba's story certainly "has been enormously popular among U.S. feminists, multiculturalists, and francophone studies scholars," in that it "fulfills the desire for a first-person narrative by a strong Third World woman" (Moss 1999, 5). This being said, scholars have become aware of the many traps Condé sets for her readers—of the extent to which Tituba lampoons those for whom she has symbolized the empowering possibilities of "voiced" Black womanhood. Still, there has been little acknowledgment of the ways in which Tituba's emphatic desire to be seen sets her tale apart from those of even the most radical revisitings of the Black enslaved woman's experience. Tituba's consistent effort to refocus the gaze of others points to a form of freedom that aims at recognizing oneself—and being recognized—as a lovable being. By refusing to surrender to the vision others have of her, and insisting on her own regard as the sole frame within which she ultimately understands and loves herself, Tituba subtly upends long-standing conventions of both colonial and postcolonial feminine self-telling.

The Puritan's dilemma was that the way from self necessarily led through the self.
—Sacvan Bercovitch, *The Puritan Origins of the American Self* (1975)

Sexual excess was disturbing to the Puritan mind as a sign of disorder in the world.
—Kathleen Verduin, "'Our Cursed Natures'" (1983)

Condé's Tituba is born in Barbados of a Black slave raped by a white sailor during the Middle Passage. Upon her mother's death by hanging (for the "crime" of defending herself from being raped a second time by another white man) and her adoptive slave father's death by suicide, the seven-year-old orphan is driven off the plantation. De facto freed, Tituba begins a life in contented isolation, both literally and figuratively beyond the society of Man. She lives on the margins of the plantation universe, hidden away in a Creole garden where she develops her skills in African healing practices with the help of three "presences"—the spirits of her parents and of an old *obeah* woman called Man Yaya. This relatively peaceful life is dramatically altered when Tituba meets and determines to seduce John Indian, an enslaved man from a neighboring plantation. She soon leaves her home and garden to join the object of her desire. Upon marrying him, she effectively places herself in the service of his mistress, Susanna Endicott, although she never officially becomes the latter's property. When Endicott sells John Indian to the Massachusetts-bound Reverend Samuel Parris, Tituba again follows her man and consents to serve as the Parris family's (unpaid) domestic laborer. It is in this capacity that she becomes the catalyst for the Salem witch trials and is eventually imprisoned (this is the only element of the narrative that Condé takes from the historical record).

From this point in the novel on, Condé imagines Tituba in several other extraordinary situations: first as the slave and concubine of a widowed Orthodox Jewish merchant in Boston and then back in Barbados, where she first becomes the mistress of a maroon leader, by whom she becomes pregnant, before returning alone to her garden, intent on resuming the solitude she had left behind for John Indian. Once again, though, Tituba's plans are interrupted by—or, rather, Tituba interrupts her plans for—a man. She begins a sexual relationship with a young runaway slave with whom she organizes a rebellion. The local planters uncover this plot with the help of the island's maroons, including Tituba's former lover, Christopher. They execute the pregnant Tituba by hanging.

Beyond the obvious handicaps of her race and gender, Tituba's unremitting quest for love and tendency to erotic self-objectification make her a particularly suspect being in Puritan society. The veritable foundation of American identity from the mid-1600s well into the eighteenth century, Puritanism configured national selfhood as redemptive, exemplary, and prophetic—and church leaders rigorously policed the borders of this collective self.[4] Key religious and political figures of the period like Richard, Increase, and Cotton Mather, Thomas Hooker, John Williams, and Samuel Danforth lay out numerous strict social codes in their sermons, and sex figures prominently in their rhetoric. As Kathleen Verduin has observed, "sexuality, sometimes even within marriage, is treated with wariness, distaste, even horror, as a virtual invitation to damnation" (1983, 223).

The Puritanist doctrine at the root of the "New England Way" was based entirely on a communalist model of social organization reliant on the individual's voluntary submission to covenants with other members of the spiritual community and with God.[5] Marked by asceticism and conformity, the Puritan ethos inextricably wedded the individual's spiritual self to the communal self. "A truly virtuous person," it was understood, was one who "renounces all self-exaltation which sin, selfishness, and pride seek" (Lovejoy 1967, 233). Puritanism presented a closed social system in which "family and tribe, piety and politics, worldly hierarchy and spiritual democracy, all the cultural norms of the community were fused, for over half a century, with extraordinary success" (Bercovitch 1975, 97). For the Puritans, there existed nothing—no valid mode of being—outside the parameters of their collective faith. Steeped in an "eschatological consciousness" (Bercovitch 1975, 10) and "punitive worldview" (Verduin 1983, 228) that presumed the eternal damnation of all but those preselected by God for salvation, Puritans existed in a state of anxious "ambivalence toward selfhood" (Bercovitch 1975, 19)—what Michel Foucault (1988, 65) has called "the Puritan suspicion of self."

Spectacles of confession and narratives of conversion functioned to alleviate somewhat this persistent anxiety around humanity's "cursed Nature" (Verduin 1983, 228), but such redemptive opportunities "were typically gendered male and tended to exclude both women and minorities from participating in what was redeemed subjectivity" (Fessenden, Radel, and Zaborowska 2001,

6–7). Moreover, the specter of a distinctly feminized sexuality represented one of the principal threats to the integrated Puritan community. As Ed Ingebretsen explains, "framed through [the hermeneutics of Puritanism], unregulated sex, which was implicitly gendered feminine, signaled communal decline," and "sexual restraint was thought to set the Puritans significantly apart from the seeming sexual omnivorousness of the natives and from the alarming profligacy of other immigrant groups" (2001, 23). Any expression of sexuality in this context was to be sublimated in exaltation of the divine.

Given the highly conformist moral and political strictures of the American Puritan community, it is difficult to imagine what, who, or how an individual like Tituba could possibly have *been* in a world so defined. The answer is, of course, she could not. Be, that is. Tituba's foreignness, her religious independence, her ambivalent social status (as Condé has configured her, let us remember, she is not technically enslaved), her "witch-ness," all place her menacingly outside the purview of the communal. Insofar as Puritan New Englanders embraced the principles laid out by Governor John Winthrop's famous "city on a hill" speech, they understood their colonial community as a beacon of unified moral exemplarity for the rest of the world.[6] That said, and as historian Wendy Warren has argued, "emphasizing the communal aspects of the speech requires ignoring the exclusive nature of those crucial words 'we' and 'us.' Winthrop spoke to and for a self-selected group of religiously motivated colonists: 'members of the somebody,' to be sure, but not members of a universal body" (2016, 14).[7] These forms of subtle but absolute distinction would have been absolutely critical to constructing the notion of selfhood in the Puritan Americas.

Configured as a dialectical Other, Condé's Tituba has no access to the "aura of ascendant millennial splendor" (Bercovitch 1975, 157) promised to the regenerate Puritan self and so is expected to serve the community sacrificially. She is demonized, sequestered, and ultimately expelled as a convenient scapegoat upon which to project some of the Puritans' darkest (the pun is intended) existential fears. The men in power in Salem exploit her as they "*generate* the fantasy of transgression they intend to uncover." Tituba's wayward being enables them to "bolster [their] own authority, oddly by invoking the very disorder [they seek] to put down" (Ingebretsen 2001, 30).

It is ironic that, though she is a disorderly being vis-à-vis the New England Puritan community, Tituba very much embodies the original democratic and liberal principles of Protestantism. As Charles Lloyd Cohen has noted pithily, "Puritans may have thought of themselves as sinkholes of corruption, but sinkholes deserving of extended discussion; it is hardly coincidental that a great number of locutions employing 'self-' entered into English during the first half of the seventeenth century" (1986, 20). Tituba's spiritual "self-possession" (Ingebretsen 2001, 31) aligns with those individualist elements of Puritan doctrine that motivated the initial break with the Anglican Church and condemned the latter's residual papist tendencies. The foundational tenets of sixteenth- and seventeenth-century Puritanism asserted that God was the "ultimate authority" (Stout 1986, 23) over the individual and that the individual thus had a right to communicate directly with God without intermediary or interference. Tituba makes precisely this sort of claim to spiritual independence through her refusal to take confession from Samuel Parris. Insisting on a private spirituality beholden only to her own judgment, she asks, "Why should I confess? What goes on in my heart and in my mind is no one's business but my own [*ne* regarde *que moi*]" ([1986] 1992, 41; emphasis mine).[8] This affirmation of a private faith is entirely consistent with the Puritan principle of an individual relationship with the divine.[9] That Tituba is condemned for insisting on the sanctity of this relationship uncovers the religion's veiled hypocrisies and disquieting ambivalence.[10]

Tituba's threat to the order established by the Puritan authorities is most apparent in her interactions with Parris's daughters and their friends. As Mildred Mortimer affirms, by "creating an atmosphere of gaiety for the child despite the Puritans' religious prohibitions, Tituba unwittingly introduces a system of values that conflicts with the Puritan father's ideology. The African cultural legacy she generously shares with the children of Salem represents a subversive alternative to the Puritans' austere form of Christianity" (2007, 64). It is certainly the case that Tituba undermines the physical and social restrictions that determine (feminine) existence in seventeenth-century New England. It is not the case, however, that the challenges she issues are necessarily or primarily African. Rather, from her very first encounters with the Puritan girls to the moments where she finds herself at their mercy, Tituba contests the specifically sexual nature of the constraints placed on their emerging womanhood. She immediately identifies their malicious conduct as the expression of a pubescent sexuality that the girls are forced to keep hidden. Their restrictive clothing, pulled-back and covered hair, and shamefaced quietness are to Tituba the troubling indicators of a dangerous communal angst, and she empathizes with the girls as innocent victims of their perversely repressive society: "I pitied them with their waxen complexions, their bodies so rich with promise but mutilated like those trees that gardeners try to dwarf" (Condé [1986] 1992, 60).

Tituba does her best to help the girls—loosening their dresses, telling them fantastical stories, encouraging them to dance—even as she becomes aware of the threat they pose to her. And, of course, they do turn on her, convinced that Tituba's emotional and carnal nonconformity are so much evidence of her sinful nature. The pleasure they get from indulging in the forbidden activities to which Tituba has initiated them is matched only by their increasing feelings of guilt—guilt for dancing, laughing, and listening to her tales and then an even more pernicious subconscious guilt about their bodies and their budding sexuality. In the end, the girls reconcile these tensions by claiming to be possessed. Tituba observes during one of these displays, "How they burned with a desire to throw themselves on the ground, attracting the gaze of the entire assembly!" (76). In their roles as victims of witchcraft, the girls are allowed to scream and freely hurl themselves about, "afflicted by the most indecent convulsions" (75). They are granted access to a sexualized register of expression that has been denied to them as members of the Puritan social group.

As Boris Vejdovsky has helpfully posited, the "uncanny effects of witchcraft appear as sexual disorder and confusion caused by the devil who sexually possesses the witches," disrupting "the logocentric, economic, and sexual order of the domineering patriarchs of Puritan society: god, the minister, the husband" (2001, 63). The patriarchs of the Salem community are right to fear Tituba's power. She has placed herself in a maternal role, a direct counter to the Puritans' strict and sober God-patriarch and their "governing ideals of respectability" (Sheller 2012, 22). Likewise, as Doris Garraway reminds us, "If Christ was protected from evil and the devil by his masculinity and rationality, femininity, it was presumed, offered the devil an impressionable imagination and fleshly sensuality through which he could literally inseminate the world with evil" (2005, 187). The witch trials were thus the consummate "deflection of social anxiety through a gendered sexual narrative discourse" (Ingebretsen 2001, 35). Against this social backdrop, Tituba's adolescent accusers feign demonic possession so as to approximate from a position of victimhood the very physical, nonneurotic, sexually charged freedom Tituba refuses to relinquish.[11]

Whereas in the self-reflective writings of Puritan reformers, "self-examination serves not to liberate but to constrict" and "selfhood appears as a state to be overcome, obliterated" (Bercovitch 1975, 13), Tituba is perfectly comfortable with her body, without Adamic shame, and able to accept the consequences of her own fallibility. That she takes every opportunity to sneak off for a love-making session with her otherwise worthless husband, whose "main asset," she admits, "lay below the jute cord that held up his short, tight-fitting *konoko* trousers" (19), or that she is willing to quarrel about the joys of sex with her only friend, the well-meaning but repressed Elizabeth Parris—"I was annoyed: 'Goodwife Parris, all you talk about is malediction. What is more beautiful than a woman's body! Especially once it has been elevated by a man's desire!'" (43)—are among the imprudent claims to self-determination that put Tituba entirely at odds with the rest of the Puritan community. They are part and parcel of the guiltless appreciation of her own physicality in evidence from the very beginning of the novel, following her first encounter with John Indian:

> Up until then I had never thought about my body. Was I beautiful? Was I ugly? I had no idea. What had he said? I took off my clothes, lay down, and let my hand stray over my body. Its swellings and its curves seemed harmonious to me. As I neared my pudenda, it suddenly seemed like it was no longer my own hand but John Indian who was caressing me. Out of the depths of my body gushed a pungent tidal wave that flooded my thighs. I could hear myself moan in the night. (15)

Tituba uninhibitedly explores and takes pleasure in her own physical being, exhibiting a healthy autoeroticism in the face of the profound insecurity and "masculine paranoia" (Vejdovsky 2001, 67) of the Salem community. Her expressions of unrepentant sensuality epitomize what the Puritan authority condemns as so many "pagan tributes to the splendor of the human body ... and its extravagant claims for self-determination" (Bercovitch 1975, 10). Although—or perhaps because—such practices of loving self-adoration stake a goddess claim in God-fearing Salem, they are the behaviors that earn Tituba the label "witch."

Is all of this a narcissistic orgy centered on the pleasure of hearing one's story told? Is this perhaps an auto/biographical twist on typical modern individualism, in feminist clothing?
   —Adriana Cavarero, Relating Narratives (2000)

I look for my story in that of the Witches of Salem and do not find it.
   —Tituba Indian (in *I, Tituba, Black Witch of Salem*)

In his introduction to Adriana Cavarero's *Relating Narratives: Storytelling and Selfhood*, translator and literary theorist Paul A. Kottman lays out the stakes of naming and name-calling: "The pain caused by the word comes from ... the feeling that *who* one is, is *not* being addressed . . . from the fact that one's singularity, a singularity that exceeds any 'what,' is utterly and violently ignored, excluded from these semantics . . . the pain or shock we feel, that *what* we are called does not correspond with *who* we feel ourselves to be" (1997, xix–xx).¹² Condé is attuned to this question of semantic violence and makes it foundational to the arc of Tituba's tale. Early on—before leaving Barbados for New England, even—Tituba becomes aware of her vulnerability to interpolation by the Puritan community. On her very first day in the service of her husband's owner, Susanna Endicott, she finds herself the subject of cruel banter between her mistress and a group of lady friends. The women never address Tituba directly but talk freely and disparagingly about her among themselves. They objectify and degrade her, making plain their disgust and, more nastily, their indifference to Tituba's presence:

> What shocked and revolted me wasn't so much what they were saying, but the way they were saying it. You'd have thought I wasn't even there, standing in the doorway. They were talking about me, but at the same time, they were completely ignoring me. They'd crossed me off the map of the human. I was a non-being. Invisible. . . . I, Tituba, had no more reality than whatever these women saw fit to grant me. It was horrible. Tituba had become something ugly, vulgar, and inferior just because they had decided it was so. (24)

The women's gaze—or, in this instance, their refusal to see her—is an act of deliberate and violent disregard. And Tituba is wounded by this imposed transparency. Tituba recognizes viscerally the danger she faces—that of the community's power to strip her of her identity and even her humanity with its words. This is confirmed by the fact that, not long after this encounter, the psychological threat posed by the women's dehumanizing regard becomes literal. Susanna Endicott learns the circumstances of Tituba's "free" status and interrogates her—"Weren't you raised by that Nago witch they called Man Yaya?" (26). Tituba attempts to explain who she really is, to explain that neither she nor her guardian is a witch, but to little effect. The very next day, Tituba observes her mistress conferring urgently with the pastor's wife and quickly realizes that her very life is at risk:

> A plot was hatching.
>
> In court the word of a slave, even of a free black, didn't count. I could scream and shout as much as I wanted that I didn't know who Satan was, no one would pay me any mind.

> That's when I made the decision to protect myself.
> Without waiting another minute. (27–28)

The time has come, Tituba understands, for a different kind of self-defense. She understands, that is, that it is not only her sense of self that is at stake but her physical safety and her freedom; she understands that her regard for herself must be both existential and literal.

While Tituba certainly has the most to fear from the white slaveholding authority in Barbados, it is in fact the enslaved community that initially presents her with a demeaning image of herself that conflicts with who she understands herself to be. The very first time Tituba encounters a group of enslaved people, briefly having left the solitude of her garden to pursue some runaway livestock, she is astonished to discover that she is feared by her "own kind." More precisely, she is astonished to discover the disjunction between the fearfulness of those she considers her brethren and her own vision of herself: "The minute they saw me, everybody jumped into the grass and knelt down, while half a dozen pairs of respectful, yet terrified eyes looked up at me. I was stunned. What stories had they woven about me? They seemed to fear me. But why? Daughter of a hanged woman, left to live alone at the edge of a pond—should they not have pitied me?" (11–12). Although her pride is wounded, Tituba experiences the enslaved group's misrecognition as not only unfortunate but also unfair. She remains unconvinced by this inaccurate communal narrative of *what* she is and thus asserts the true story of *who* it is she sees when she sees herself: "Their terror seemed unjust to me. Ah! They should have greeted me with shouts of joy and welcome! They should have come to me with their illnesses, which I would have tried my best to cure. I was born to heal, not to frighten" (12).

Further, her beloved John Indian officially introduces Tituba to the term *witch* and makes her aware of the word's negative associations. Perplexed by this misconception, Tituba proposes a substantive revision of the word, again steadfastly refusing to cede to the disgrace it implies:

> What is a witch? I noticed that when he said the word, it was tainted with shame. But why? The ability to communicate with the invisible world, to keep constant connections to the dead, to care for others, and to heal—what is all that if not the ultimate gift of nature, something that should inspire respect, admiration, and gratitude? Consequently, shouldn't the witch—if indeed that's what the person with such a gift is to be called—be cherished and revered rather than feared? (17)

Aware of the extent to which *witch* has been misapprehended, Tituba invests in the term's disorderly capaciousness and insists optimistically—creatively—on its resemanticization. Finally, toward the novel's conclusion, after having been named a witch many times over and accused of and imprisoned for practicing witchcraft, Tituba makes clear that she still has not wavered from this original resistance to the community's distortive interpolation. She has attained a measure of clarity about the foundational expansiveness of the term *witch* as engaged by the various communities she has passed through, an expansiveness she determines to read as freeing. She attempts to articulate this to Christopher, her maroon lover. "Everyone gives that word a different meaning," she patiently explains. "Everyone believes they can mold 'the witch' to fit their needs, so that she can satisfy their ambitions, their dreams, their desires" (146). But Christopher cuts her off, uninterested in listening to her "philosophize" (146), and summons her to use her magic to make him invincible. When she explains to him the limits of her powers, he becomes disinterested in her, eventually insulting and dismissing her as valueless to the community.

That it is the enslaved people and maroons in her native Barbados who introduce Tituba to the vilifying label *witch* subtly articulates Condé's critique of Afro-communities traditionally understood to be sympathetic, inspirational, or otherwise "ideologically correct." The ambivalent portraits she paints of Black revolutionary masculinity and of the Afro-Creolocentric masculine intellectual tradition with which it intersects directly prefigure her groundbreaking theoretical invention in "Order, Disorder, Freedom, and the West Indian Writer," discussed in the introduction to this book. Condé's *I, Tituba* presents a radical transgression of this long-standing order. In her configuration of a female protagonist motivated by an open-minded and self-focused sexuality, Condé explicitly counters a number of the "rules" she attributes to her male predecessors and contemporaries even as she foregrounds the existence of such determining ideologies. Her heroine undermines and undoes the masculinist, heteronormative orthodoxies and injunctions of Caribbean postcolonialism at every turn. Distinct from the quasi-epic Pan-Africanist narrative of Negritude's male hero returning to vindicate his people, the mock-epic antiheroine Tituba tells a highly personal "her-story" that suggests her apolitical unconcern with, if not disregard for, the connections between her New World existence and an African past, despite her direct genealogical connection to that past. I am thinking in particular of her dismissal of Africa during her conversation with Hester Prynne—"We don't know anything about Africa anymore and it no longer has any meaning for us" (96), of her willing acceptance of Jewish suffering as greater than Black suffering in her conversations with the Jewish merchant Benjamin d'Azevedo—"He outdid me every time!" (127), and of her uncomfortable encounter with an "obeah man" in Barbados.

Furthermore, Condé provides a quietly ironic counterpoint to the emphatic coming to disalienated self and voice traced in Césaire's *Notebook of a Return to the Native Land* ([1939] 2013).[13] Tituba's concern with her own personal posterity—"And what about me? Is there a song for me? A song for Tituba?" (153)—contrasts markedly with Césaire's vision of the humbled hero standing hand in hand with his people and, ultimately, alongside an arisen and awakened collective. Through " a Tituba portrayed in parodic fury about her exclusion from writing" (Rody 2001, 188), Condé makes plain the intertextual presence of Césaire's canon-founding prose-poem, indicating at once her belonging to and defiance of the literary tradition Césaire initiates.[14]

Condé likewise troubles the discourse of antillanité formulated by Édouard Glissant, most pointedly through her damning portrayal of the maroon figure, the runaway slave who figures famously as Glissant's rallying point for a revitalized collective Antillean future. Whereas Glissant's work foregrounds the maroon as the shamefully neglected foundational figure of redemptive Caribbean identity, Condé's novel aggressively counters this construction.[15] Glissant insists that this figure of original resistance offers the most viable option for the establishment of a dignified, geohistorically grounded Antillean collective and laments the maroon's "tragic absence" (1981, 717) from regional consciousness. Condé's portrayal of the maroon leader Christopher as a collaborator with the island's white planters provocatively pokes holes in this image. As A. James Arnold convincingly asserts, "the heroic maroon is one of the myths dear to the hearts of West Indians that Maryse Condé skewers in *Tituba*. . . . As a woman writer, she cannot afford to reinscribe the maroon as the Hero of West Indian culture because of the gendered nature of this figure" (1993, 713).

Even more iconoclastic, though, than Condé's "skewering" of this postcolonial hero as traitorous sellout is the fact that she de-emphasizes Christopher's political identity and foregrounds his sexual relationship with Tituba. Though initially put off by the maroon leader's arrogance, Tituba ultimately finds herself unable to resist his "charms," as it were, and soon becomes his lover. In their very first conversation, it is Tituba who puts sex on the table:

Christopher entered [my hut]. . . . I sat up.

"What's the matter? Aren't your two wives enough for you?"

He rolled his eyes and I was immediately mortified by what I had said.

"Listen, I'm in no mood for sexual banter," he replied.

> "Well then, what are you in the mood for?" I asked flirtatiously as, despite all my misfortunes, I had not lost that deep instinct that makes me a woman. (145)

Indeed. Tituba herself seems surprised by the inappropriateness of her own behavior and is even slightly ashamed. Yet the reader can understand this behavior, which Tituba admits may be nothing more than "vanity ... a desire to arouse a keener interest in the eyes of this man" (144), as yet another effort to impose her way of looking at herself. Tituba's desire to make her self-regard correspond with the way in which others, men especially, regard her is the novel's central tension.

Once again, the terms of Tituba's self-regard are sexual. The vanity she succumbs to serves to counter the persistent attacks on her self-worth that threaten to devastate her completely. It is a question here, moreover, not of romantic love but of physical desire—of lust. Tituba admits, "This commerce only involved my senses. All the rest of me continued to belong to John Indian.... While Christopher writhed on top of me, my mind would roam and I would relive the pleasures of my nights in America" (152). Even her eventual discovery of Christopher's moral corruption is primarily a function of her relationship to him as an erotic partner rather than any sort of awakening to (Afro-)political consciousness. Tituba comes to see his flaws—not least of which is his treachery with respect to the island's slave population—foremost through the lens of a lover's wounded pride. Her precipitous departure from the maroon community happens on the heels of a domestic quarrel. In these ways relegating to the background the ideological canon undergirding francophone Caribbean letters, Condé privileges one woman's personal tale of emotional self-reliance and physical survival.

If the Tituba Condé has configured stands in ambivalent relation to Afro-Caribbeanist discourses, she is even more manifestly disordering with respect to the various communities of women that populate the novel. As Michelle Smith has argued convincingly, the narrative is largely structured by a series of circular echoes, among which is the bond of solidarity that unites Tituba and Elizabeth Parris in a parallel to the friendship between Tituba's mother, Abena, and her young mistress, Jennifer Darnell. This doubled affirmation of transracial, gendered solidarity, Condé's reminder that all women suffered the brutality of early American patriarchy, prefigures her staging of an encounter between Tituba and Nathaniel Hawthorne's complicated heroine Hester Prynne, an evocative intertextual moment that Smith calls "the most dangerous trap the novel lays for seekers of female solidarity" (1995, 603). The scene of the two characters' first meeting begins by establishing the ties that bind them as women, both victims of Puritan male hypocrisy. Brought together in a prison cell, where Tituba has been placed after her arrest for witchcraft and where the pregnant Hester has already been languishing for months, the two women fall immediately into a mutually sustaining, loving relationship that transcends the color line. However, Hester's passionate declarations of misandrist, militant feminism fail to convince or convert Tituba. There is no overlooking the ambivalent gesture by which Condé "[repositions Tituba] within an essentialist and exclusionary feminist rhetoric that [she] interrogates even as she articulates it" (K. Simmons 2009, 82).

It is crucial to look closely at the exaggeratedly lascivious nature of Tituba's counterassertions to the possibilities for female solidarity Hester proposes. Tituba's sexualizing of her personal worldview marks a fundamental refusal to be defined by constructions of herself as victim. While Hester orates impassionedly about gender inequality, Tituba interjects with playful asides that remain oblivious to—or undeterred by—the political content of Hester's discourse. In response to Hester's description of an imagined feminist utopia—"'The model of a society governed and run by women! We would give our names to our children, we would raise them alone'"—Tituba playfully reminds her, "'We couldn't make them alone, even so!'" Then, to Hester's mournful, "'Alas, no. . . . Those abominable brutes would have to share in a fleeting moment,'" Tituba responds with the suggestive, "'Not too short a moment! I like to take my time!'" Finally giving up on transforming Tituba into a recognizably political being, Hester concludes, "'You're too fond of love, Tituba! I'll never make a feminist out of you!'" (101). As Dawn Fulton has noted, "Hester's teasing reproach of Tituba implies an incoherence between sexual desire for men and the precepts of feminism" (2008, 54). Through her resistance to this moralizing, Tituba hints at the potential constraints of feminism itself. Her response to Hester calls for forms of feminism that provide space within which a woman can determine her own actions and not an externally determined script for women's (politically) correct behavior.

While it is true that Tituba resists Hester's (one-dimensional) feminist politics, countering it with her own claims to pleasure and human intimacy, Hester catalyzes a new, queer valence of Tituba's sexuality. From their first encounter in the bleak context of their shared prison cell, a deliciously sensual connection emerges between the two women. Each finds the other lovely. On seeing Hester for the first time, Tituba is enthralled: "The woman who had spoken was young, beautiful, and not more than twenty-three. She had thrown back her hood unashamedly and revealed a mass of thick hair, as black as a crow's wing, itself the color of sin for some people and worthy of punishment" (95). Similarly moved by Tituba's physical beauty—"She thought to herself out loud: 'How magnificent it is, that skin-color of hers . . . !'"—Hester establishes the terms of their alliance as sensual: "'You cannot have done evil, Tituba! I am sure of that, you're too beautiful! Even if they all accused you, I would defend your innocence!'" Tituba responds in kind: "I was so moved I was bold enough to caress her face and whispered: 'You too, Hester, are beautiful!'" (96). These moments of gentle, haptic relation blend the sisterly and the erotic. Although Tituba steadfastly refuses Hester's absolutist politics and communalist utopian imagining of "a world of women . . . more just and humane" (178), she nonetheless finds Hester otherwise seductive. Long after Hester's death by suicide, Tituba continues to invoke the loving presence of her sister-friend:

> That night Hester lay down beside me, as she did sometimes. I laid my head on the quiet water lily of her cheek and held her tight. Surprisingly, a feeling of pleasure slowly flooded over me. Can you feel pleasure from hugging a body similar to your own? For me, pleasure had always been in the shape of another body whose hollows fitted my curves and whose swellings nestled in the tender flatlands of my flesh. Was Hester showing me another kind of bodily pleasure? (122)

The two women never consummate their love on the material plane, but they remain beloved of one another through to the conclusion of the narrative. Hester's love is a sustaining presence for Tituba. It corresponds with Tituba's regard for herself but ultimately does not demand that this self be compromised.

Once Tituba has been released from prison, she moves on to a sexual relationship with her post-Salem master, Benjamin Cohen d'Azevedo. It is a relationship in which Tituba directly counters Hester's version of freedom with one of her own making. When d'Azevedo offers to emancipate her, Tituba refuses, thinking, "Hester, Hester, you would not be happy with me. But certain men who have the virtue of being weak truly make us want to be slaves!" (140). Bear in mind that, as with Christopher, Tituba does not actually love d'Azevedo: he is her stand-in for John Indian, as she is his for Abigail, his deceased wife. This ambiguously mutual amorous relationship between master/lover and slave/concubine more or less takes romance out of the equation as justification for Tituba's willingness to remain enslaved. In other words, Tituba's sexual choices make no satisfyingly overt claims to emancipatory feminist discourse, nor do they fit into the trope of an idealized romantic love. As such, if Condé's reader attributes any such intentions to Condé's character, she must put words in Tituba's mouth—a decidedly antifeminist move that would effectively render Tituba voiceless by disallowing her to mean what she says!

Tituba's resistance to Hester's ideological perspective—her inability to fully recognize herself in the elevated, educated arguments of this classics-reading, Mayflower-descended white woman—is Condé's at once oblique and over-the-top reminder of the specificity of Black women's oppression: the well-known schema according to which "European women have been constrained by patriarchy, African and Afro-Caribbean men by colonialism, and African and Afro-Caribbean women by patriarchy and colonialism" (Mortimer 2007, ix)—the phenomenon of double marginalization, in other words. From such perspectives, Condé's Tituba presents a wagging finger of absolute alterity with respect to naive or self-righteous Euro–North American feminism. As Bonnie Thomas asserts in her sophisticated and nuanced analysis of Tituba's ideological value, "for many scholars in the fields of francophone literature, feminism and multicultural studies, Tituba has become something of an icon, providing the voice of 'a strong Third World woman' which can be harnessed to aid in the empowerment of other oppressed women. Tituba's expression of her own point of view as a black, lower-class woman also encourages Western critics to examine their bias and reflect on their privileged position compared to women in other cultures" (2006, 50).

Marie-Denise Shelton similarly maintains that the "voice" of French feminists like Hélène Cixous and Catherine Clément "falters somewhat when contemplating the relationship of black women to the feminist agenda" and that "feminism as a concept remains for Condé and her heroine a foreign notion which is not quite congruent with the Caribbean woman's experience" (1993, 720). Elisabeth Mudimbe-Boyi explicitly recuperates Tituba for Afro-feminism, arguing that "although Tituba is speaking only of herself and recounting her individual life, her narrative also encompasses the story of many other black women who, like her, have been relegated to the margins of history, if not erased from it, reduced to invisibility and silence" (1993, 753). Similarly, Angela Y. Davis claims Tituba for an "other" or diversified resistance discourse, affirming that Tituba's "voice can be viewed as the voice of a suppressed black feminism." Tellingly, she concedes that "because of her sexuality, [Tituba] is reluctant to call herself a feminist," but then Davis does not allow this reluctance to stop her from recovering Tituba for a multicultural feminist agenda, insisting that "from our contemporary vantage point, feminists of all cultures may find enlightenment in her ambivalence" (1992, x).

By most critical accounts, then, Condé's Tituba is, like her nonfictional enslaved foremothers, "a political activist, a woman who spoke not simply on behalf of herself but also on behalf of a community of slaves" (J. Sharpe 1996, 40). Yet such eloquent and passionate assertions of Tituba's symbolic importance do not tell the whole story. Beyond this blatant parodying of Hester's militant feminism, Condé poses equally significant obstacles to any triumphant reclamation of Tituba for Afro-feminism. While it is certainly tempting to accept that "Tituba's whole essence is tied to a celebration of being a black Caribbean woman" (Scarboro 1992, 213), her privileging of erotic self-regard in fact disrupts the models of communal solidarity put forward by Mudimbe-Boyi, Davis, and others.[16] Condé effects, for example, a finely tuned interruption of womanist discourse by troubling the notion of the Black woman's empowerment as a maternal figure within the slave community, interrogating the claim that "the plantation space privileged women and feminine sensitivity, because black women had the work of creating the hearth and holding their society together" (Scarboro 1992, 188). Tituba embodies to an extent the expected characteristics of the Black woman as self-sacrificing, maternal, sisterly, and otherwise selflessly nurturing. Yet she often mobilizes these traits to serve the interests of the "wrong" people—the Puritan girls, the Jewish merchant's family, the fever-stricken white sailors aboard the *Bless the Lord*—while never becoming entirely integrated into any of the Black communities depicted in the novel. Even during her short-lived stay among the maroons upon her return to Barbados, or in her practice of using her healing gifts to treat the sick and wounded among the enslaved, Tituba remains at a distance from those presumed to be her people.

Always first feared as a witch, even by the enslaved she cures of sickness and injury, Tituba is never able to fully assume a caregiving role in the Black community. Her domestic prowess and commitment to nourishing family in the face of hardship, while very much highlighted throughout the narrative, manifest most explicitly with respect to the whites she serves. Thus, if Tituba bears out the claim that "women have shared the common goal of creating safety zones—physical, emotional, spiritual, and economic—for their communities and their loved ones" (Newson and Strong-Leek 1998, viii), she also problematizes such notions by the context within which she takes on these responsibilities (i.e., for inappropriate communities and loved ones). In the one instance where Tituba begins to establish a communal connection in accordance with her Black female identity, her sexual choices directly undermine the possibility of true solidarity: "When I was not treating the slaves on the plantations I spent time with the maroon women. In the beginning, they had treated me with the greatest respect," she notes. "Then when they learned that Christopher shared my bed and that, after all, I was no different from them, they became hostile" (153).

Tituba's story also pushes against the paradigm of matrilineal, transgenerational knowledge transmission that several Caribbean women writers have put forward as a departure from the Creolist model of the male storyteller.[17] Although Condé emphasizes the presence and impact of Tituba's African spirit guides—her mother, Abena; the healer Man Yaya; and her feminized (sensitive, maternal, gentle, etc.) adoptive father Yao—she consistently highlights Tituba's petulant and at times disrespectful attitude toward these should-be sacred beings.[18] Thus, while it can most certainly be argued that Tituba is a "character of extraordinary power" who "possesses a superlative degree of self-awareness," it is trickier to characterize her as an unambiguous "depositary of the wisdom of her ancestors" (Araujo 1994, 222). On the contrary, time and again Tituba dismisses the counsel and warnings of "her ancestors" when they conflict with her romantic or erotic objectives. She proves little more inclined to accept direction or constraint from these archetypal representatives of a feminine Afro-spiritual heritage than from the well-meaning but bitterly man-hating Hester. Tituba strategically affirms neither Black nor white sisterhood with any degree of reliability.

Most provocatively, *I, Tituba* draws on yet unsettles recognizable rhetorical topoi of sisterhood in the Americas through the novel's refashioning of the female slave narrative. Tituba's account of her life interrogates and shines light on the anxieties that mark the genre, complicating the relationship between sex and self embedded in such accounts yet only ever cautiously alluded to. Her story radically departs, in its substance, from the traditional female slave narrative but relies formally on the genre in its implication of certain recognizable tropes.[19] Whereas the chronicles of formerly enslaved women, most notably Mary Prince and Harriet Jacobs, were premised on their narrators' untiringly virtuous efforts to secure a liberated and enlightened future for themselves and others, the trajectory Condé traces for her outrageous heroine is decidedly unbound by predetermined models of freedom. Posing questions of Black female sexual agency within the largely unfathomable, ungendering context of enslavement, Condé makes visible those elements of the Black enslaved woman's experience that remain buried in the subtext of the traditional female slave narrative, revealing both its strictures in its time—that is, the contingency of collective abolitionist goals on exemplary individual Black enslaved female respectability—and the contours of its deployment in the contemporary moment.

Tools of abolitionism, the stories told by escaped female enslaved persons chronicle, by definition, the passage from servitude to emancipation. In addition, they describe the journey of a fall from the innocence of childhood to the corruption of sexual victimization, alongside a steady progression toward rehabilitated grace. These parallel narratives are supported by an account of evolving Christian faithfulness.[20] As Sandra Pouchet Paquet rightly posits, nineteenth-century self-writing women whose "literary production operates within the constraints of an Anglo-American cult of domesticity complicitous in the patriarchal or colonial project" fall prey to "strategies of self-erasure imposed and internalized by cultural practice" (2002, 16). It was understood that "the personal or inner self was not a part of the narrative's formula because that self had no currency in rhetorical value" (Mitchell 2002, 8). Neither Mary Prince nor Harriet Jacobs, for example, the authors of the celebrated chronicles *The History of Mary Prince* ([1831] 1988) and *Incidents in the Life of a Slave Girl* ([1861] 2001), respectively, can be explicit regarding her own sexual or romantic desires, knowing well that the "truth of [her] testimony depended upon demonstrating that she was a decent Christian woman" (J. Sharpe 1996, 32).

If Prince and Jacobs were compelled to "overcome the sexual stereotyping" (J. Sharpe 1996, 38) deployed by proslavery advocates to justify Black women's subjugation, Tituba's unabashed lustfulness would seem to contradict that generic convention directly. Yet, while Tituba recounts her experiences with an openness that her predecessors could in no way afford to indulge, her presentation of Black female sexuality as at once strategy and expression of genuine sentiment is a reminder that for women like Prince and Jacobs, too, "something akin to freedom" would have been possible within the context of enslavement.[21] We are invited to consider, that is, that sexual relationships between Black women and white men might have been spaces of either dehumanization or humanization—and, at times, both. We are called on to recognize that in circumstances wherein Black women's sexuality was disparaged and their capacity for love denied, to embrace either or both amounted to a veritable freedom cry.

Most radical with respect to the female slave narrative paradigm are the very premises of the in-credible plot Condé has configured—specifically, that Tituba resigns herself, on more than one occasion, to a state of bondage in the interest of assuming a freedom of sexual choice. This is crucial. Condé distorts the historical record, which, even if it tells us very little about Tituba Indian, confirms her enslaved status. We know Tituba to have been imbricated in the arguably more intimate but no less absolute chattel slave system that anchored New England within the Atlantic slave economy. That Condé places her in ambivalent relation to that system—coerced perhaps but not conscripted into it—emphasizes the unsettling disorderliness of Tituba's life choices (choices made, yes, under conditions of structural domination). Even though her prioritization of love and sex consigns her to a condition of servitude, Tituba pursues an existential liberation denied to her literary predecessors, who sought first and foremost to escape from one very specific type of bondage and to facilitate such a freedom for others.[22] In privileging her sexual selfhood, Tituba's narrative redefines freedom in terms that depart from the codes upheld by her literary foremothers. Because her objectives do not and never have included deliverance from slavery, she makes no concession to a dominant discourse (like abolitionism), nor is she obliged to convince anyone that she is worthy of emancipation. Condé's Tituba remains entirely unfettered by the moral constraints that bind the self-narrating nineteenth-century Black women she necessarily recalls. Any confession she does make—any shame she feels, that is—has only to do with her own moral code.

Tituba's primary aim in telling her story is to rehabilitate, in accordance with her personal ethics, an image she believes has been misrepresented by the sole existing piece of historical documentation concerning her life: the court transcripts of her false confession to having practiced witchcraft. She aspires only to set the record straight regarding her individual posterity and is far less concerned with the uplift of her "sisters who are still in bondage" (Jacobs [1861] 2001, 28).[23] Tituba has little interest in such assertions of selfless communal intention, an intention that ostensibly overrides the narrator's natural reticence. Mary Prince, for example, makes a veritable refrain of her pledge of communal solidarity—"I have been a slave—I have felt what a slave feels, and I know what a slave knows" ([1831] 1988, 11), she writes. She then later insists, "I have been a slave myself—I know what slaves feel—I can tell by myself what other slaves feel, and by what they have told me" (Prince [1831] 1988, 23). Harriet Jacobs expresses an even more explicit humility: "I have not written my experiences in order to attract attention to myself," she explains, "on the contrary, it would have been more pleasant to me to have been silent about my own history. Neither do I care to excite sympathy for my own sufferings" ([1861] 2001, 6). Both Prince and Jacobs narrated their lives in such a manner as to contribute effectively to subverting the system that had kept them enslaved. Tituba's motivations for telling her story, by contrast, are very plainly personal ("And what about me? Is there a song for me? A song for Tituba?"). Tituba wants to be known as an individual presence in American history—to be remembered for who she was and how she lived. Her being and her behaviors remain candidly opposed to the regard of an audience that saw fit to oppress and forget her.

Condé's subversions of the nineteenth-century female slave narrative genre align *I, Tituba* with a host of mid- and late twentieth-century African American women's prose fiction works belonging to the neo-slave narrative genre.[24] According to scholars like Joycelyn K. Moody, Elizabeth Ann Beaulieu, and Angelyn Mitchell, works belonging to the genre are best described as "liberatory" or "freedom" narratives that foreground the reality of enslaved women as mothers and emphasize women's connections to their families and communities. "Each one is, at its core, the story of a slave mother's concerns for herself and her children as she attempts to escape to freedom," argues Moody (1990, 633). Beaulieu similarly attests, "Twentieth-century slave narratives by black women writers are not so much 'slave' narratives—narratives about slavery—as they are *freedom* narratives: stories that celebrate freedom from the 'soul-killing effects' (Douglass [1845] 1982, 58) of slavery, freedom from commodification, and freedom from the invisibility that has historically enshrouded the enslaved mother" (1999, 13–14).

On the one hand, like Toni Morrison, Gayl Jones, and Margaret Walker, among others, Condé engages in a process of "rendering the female slave experience visible and voiced . . . revising the male canonized view . . . creating meditations on her/story" (P. Barnes 1999, 193). Her novel similarly eschews "the portrayal of the objective conditions of slavery" and is "far more interested in disclosing the subjectivity and interiority of enslaved Black women and their worlds" (Mitchell 2002, 11). This being said, just as *I, Tituba* at once parallels and tracks away from antebellum narratives like those of Prince and Jacobs, the novel also plays with the conventions of their twentieth-century avatars. Tituba's story evokes the plight of the enslaved Black mother but is "skeptical of all easy maternal myths" (Rody 2001, 188). Motherhood ultimately is not as fundamental to Tituba's story as is her assertion of herself as a loving, decidedly non-procreatively erotic being. Her relationship with the merchant Benjamin Cohen d'Azevedo, noted earlier, is particularly marked by such ambiguities. In describing her self-interested desire to be purchased by d'Azevedo because of his ties to the native land to which she wants desperately to return, Tituba uses the language of the erotic. She admits, "His downright ugliness had become the most seductive of assets. Did he not symbolize the prospects I had dreamed of? . . . Hope and desire shone in my eyes" (120–21). Later, having become his mistress and servant, Tituba professes an affection for him more important than her freedom—"I don't want that freedom. I want to stay with you" (134). Such choices make it decidedly difficult to view Tituba's story as "describing how to achieve freedom" (Mitchell 2002, 4)—at least not a freedom easily recognizable as such.

Whereas neo-slave narratives make it a point to explore Black enslaved women's erotic lives, they are focused in large part on the violence and coercion that was an inescapable dimension of that historical reality as well as a continued traumatic echo into the present moment. Condé's configuration of Tituba's erotic life departs markedly from this frame. Tituba alone decides with whom she enters into sexual relationships, and she is uninhibited with respect to age, gender, race, and social status (free/enslaved). She does not ever suffer the ongoing sexual tyranny of a white master, nor does she express fear of being forced in the way Prince and Jacobs feared throughout their lives.[25] She counters the model of the enslaved woman's sexuality as dispossessed—quite literally owned by white male slaveholders as breeder and/or concubine and then also regulated and circumscribed discursively by white male and female abolitionists. Tituba entertains questions that haunt narratives like those of Prince and Jacobs, questions that remain taboo in most twentieth-century recoveries of enslaved women's experiences. She goes so far, for example, as to conflate her own first experience of sexual pleasure with reflections on the contours of her mother's trauma during the Middle Passage. In the wake of her first orgasm, that is, Tituba dares to wonder, "Was that how my mother had moaned despite herself when that sailor raped her?" (15). That this moment of onanistic self-discovery leads her to contemplate the uncomfortable possibility of con-sensuality in the absence of consent marks Tituba's refusal to be determined by a fear of sexual victimization—her insistence on seeing herself other than as an always potential victim of rape.

If it is the case, as Darlene Clark Hine asserts, that "every known nineteenth-century female slave narrative contains a reference to, at some juncture, the ever present threat and reality of rape" (1989, 912), Condé writes Tituba outside of this generic convention. Tituba's mother's experience of sexual violence is, yes, at the root of Tituba's own existence and is implicitly responsible for the initial tragedies that befall her, notably, the absence of her mother's affection and the loss of both of her parents following her mother's traumatized reaction to a subsequent attempted rape. Yet Condé's configuration of Tituba as an adamantly sexual being proposes a tricky pushback to the notion that Black (enslaved) women's lives have always been defined by their "sexual vulnerability and powerlessness as victims of rape and domestic violence" (Hine 1989, 912). If indeed rape as ever-present phenomenon has produced silence—a "culture of dissemblance" in which "the behavior and attitudes of Black women . . . created the appearance of openness and disclosure but actually shielded the truth of their inner lives and selves from their oppressors" (912), Condé's Tituba contradicts this portrait of selfhood in bondage. Although John Indian and others implore her to hide her true self from the community in the interest of self-preservation, Tituba refuses to compromise in this respect. She wants nothing more than to be known and understood, and she will not deny the extent to which sex is constitutive of the self that she loves—and that she believes deserves to be loved. Her erotic self-positioning unsettles broad assertions that "sex under [such] conditions of power inequity constitutes a form of rape" (Edmondson 1999, 132). And this unbinding of Tituba's sexuality from the fear of rape is among the most provocative elements of Condé's novel.

On occasion after occasion, Tituba preserves her sexual being in the face of the most extraordinary prohibitions. Having privileged libidinal satisfaction over social liberation not once but twice, Tituba ultimately constructs a notion of free will that nuances the strict model to which her foremothers adhere and that is sustained and confirmed through to the final words of her self-centered story. Even once she has become a part of the spirit world, that is, Tituba does not give up on the life-affirming commitment to love and pleasure that effectively brought about her death. In the end, it is Tituba's ghost who shruggingly acknowledges, "Me, I have loved men too much and I continue to do so. Sometimes I get the urge to slip into someone's bed to satisfy a bit of leftover desire and my fleeting lover marvels in his solitary pleasure" (178). With these words, which appear only a few paragraphs before the close of the novel, Tituba affirms that the geographic circularity of her journey reflects the constancy of her ethical sense of herself; she remains very much who she is from beginning to end. There is no narrative of progress and enlightenment here, no capitulation to any reader's expectations. She does not learn from her mistakes; she rarely heeds the counsel and warnings of the iconic feminine figures that surround her. This seeming nonevolution into an exemplary victim or unequivocally admirable survivor is a counterpoint to the narrative of progress underlying conventional identity categories in which the Black enslaved woman historically has been contained.

From that day on I drew closer to the plantations so that my true self could be known. Tituba must be loved!
　—Tituba Indian (*in* I, Tituba, Black Witch of Salem)

In her assessment of Tituba's agency and empowerment through sexuality, Michelle Smith points to what she considers the fundamentally paradoxical nature of Condé's protagonist. Smith writes:

> Tituba herself emerges as less a character with understandable motivations, and more a convergent essence of supernatural manipulation and

> sexual behavior. But although she may be (written as) the mistress of nature-as-cosmos, she feels "instill[ed] in [her] the desire to be a slave" to nature-as-(sexual) body (140). How can this circularity be rendered readable? I would begin to read it by proposing that we read Tituba's writing as her "conceal[ing] from [herself] the blinding evidence" of the meaning of her sexual being(-ness) so "that what is essential always eludes [her] so that [she] must always start out again in search of it" (Foucault 1980, 33). My larger point is that precisely because the evidence is "blinding," Tituba's continuing to miss it can only be a willful—but, importantly, uninscribed—act. (1995, 604)

Pushing back against Smith's suggestion that Tituba "willfully" makes unwise sexual choices throughout her life, I argue that Tituba does not at all "miss" or deny the link between her actions and their consequences. Her "sexual behavior" is not something whose costs "elude" her but rather presents an unfiltered manifestation of who she is. Her fall from her Edenic paradise is no accident. She leaves the blissful ignorance of her man-less garden despite the warnings of her gods, and with no intention of narrating her way to liberation and redemption, at least not in any traditional fashion. Nowhere is this more apparent than in her grappling with her very first decision to leave her world for her man:

> My mother had been raped by a white man. She had been hanged because of a white man. . . . My adoptive father had killed himself because of a white man. Despite all that, I was considering living amongst white men again, in their midst, under their domination. And all because of an uncontrollable desire for some mortal. Was that not madness? Madness and betrayal? That night, and for seven more nights and days, I struggled with myself. In the end, I confessed I was beaten. I wouldn't wish on anyone the torments I went through. Remorse. Shame. Panic. Blind terror. (19–20)

Tituba most certainly appreciates the "meaning of her sexual being(-ness)," and she is genuinely surprised at the many obstacles to its full expression. Although she experiences moments of doubt and frustration, at no point does she ever sincerely consider abandoning the desires that sustain her. In the instances in which she questions her decisions with respect to men, she consistently makes a clear choice to follow her heart or, more frequently, her libido.

In the end as in the beginning, Tituba privileges her sexual autonomy. This is Condé's most trickster-like move. Tituba's perception and knowledge of the world come through sexual intimacies that may look like promiscuity but in fact run absolutely counter to the perversions of intimacy inherent to New World slave society. Although in many ways trapped within a historical context that "excluded women, dependents, slaves, former slaves, and servants precisely because their bodies were stigmatized as overly sexual, emotional, and incapable of the higher rationality of disembodied objectivity" (Sheller 2012, 25), Condé's Tituba leans into these stereotypes and refuses their stigmatizing effect. As Lillian Manzor-Coats has so eloquently affirmed, "Tituba constitutes herself as a desiring subject, her otherwise despised black body becoming a desirable body, a body she can enjoy and a body that permits her the intimacy between two human beings which both the plantation society in Barbados and the Puritan society in Salem prohibit" (1993, 742). While the master discourse—or the discourse of those who would be her masters—may read her as a slave, Tituba persists in seeing herself as empowered and of value. Her initial decision to join the world of men is made once she pronounces the words, "I want this man to love me" (14), and this mantra governs her actions through to the narrative's conclusion.

That despite the absolute trauma of her experiences in Barbados and New England Tituba is capable of evoking the pleasures of having been "suffocated in love" (Condé [1986] 1994, 152) provocatively posits the possibility of both true love and unregenerate desire—for oneself and for others—under slavery. In the face of multiple physically, emotionally, and psychologically violent assaults on her person, Tituba's willingness to "risk the body is [not] a gratuitous celebration of eroticism" (Dash 2003, 314). It is an insistence on the right to vanity, to lust, to love, to imperfect humanity, and to self-regard. In a dehumanizing legal context that "dictate[d] that women, as objects of violence, function under fear, becoming subjects of fear" (Manzor-Coats 1993, 740), Tituba's embracing of love and lust is a testament to her refusal of such a fear-based existence; her sexual choices—even the awful ones—defy the rape that always threatens. Despite the myriad trials and tribulations she suffers, Tituba is fully reassured by the permanence of her sexual self.

Writing of Condé's configuration of "The Artist," Lydie Moudileno posits that for Condé artists function "to unveil the dynamic of their communities" in their "individual and collective illusions, fantasies and phantasms" (1995, 626). While Tituba is not an artist *sensu stricto*, she nevertheless takes on a similar role, allowing Condé to reflect on her own relationship (as an artist) to communities "whose heritage [s]he shares" (Moudileno 1995, 639) but whose ideological parameters she is compelled to resist. Through Tituba, an enslaved woman who chooses love and sex over conventional forms of freedom on more than one occasion, Condé taps into the anxieties produced by feminine desire, inevitably allegorizing her own experiences and frustrations as a politically nonaligned, postcolonial woman writer. Beyond merely tweaking convention for its own sake, Condé makes plain her refusal of the constricting expectations of solidarity latent in even the most ostensibly liberating Caribbean discourses. Subtly resisting appropriation by politicized communities that have imposed insidious moral constraints on sexualized female selfhood in the Caribbean and beyond, Condé fictionalizes the historical Tituba's destiny so as to engage with phenomena of coercion at work in present-day Afro-Caribbean literary and ideological communities. She thus proposes Tituba's nonheroic, unassailable self-love as an ethics in its own right.

2

SELF-POSSESSION | Hadriana

The militant, the warrior, the politician, shed their arms before the writer, who finds the necessary fulfillment in his own art.
—Katell Colin-Thébaudeau, "René Depestre" (2005)

For a literature defined by the near-unanimity of its voices agitating, analyzing, narrating and narrativizing political projects of emancipation and antiracism, too great an attention to delight and joy and happiness seems a political betrayal.
—Darieck Scott, *Keeping It Unreal* (forthcoming)

A Haitian writer—a man—living in the south of France publishes a novel about a beautiful young French woman living in Haiti who gets turned into a zombie on the day of her wedding. The French literary establishment goes wild. The novel, *Hadriana in All My Dreams* (Hadriana dans tous mes rêves, 1988), sells nearly 200,000 copies and wins several awards, including the prestigious Prix Renaudot, and the press just can't seem to get enough.[1] The response of many literary critics in the academy, however—Haitianist, postcolonial, feminist—is remarkably different. The very terms used by the French reviewers and award givers to extol the virtues of the novel become the terms of engagement for its sustained academic critique—a critique that had already begun to attach to Depestre and his writing on the publication in 1981 of his prizewinning collection of short stories *Alléluia pour une femme-jardin* (Hallelujah for a Garden-Woman).[2] To think carefully about the nature of scholarly responses to Depestre's fictional writings provides a crucial opportunity to consider what it is precisely, albeit tacitly, that (we) Caribbeanists want—even expect—from Haiti and its authors.

At issue in critical analyses of the novel is a deep-seated concern with long-standing and fraught questions of authenticity, community, and political solidarity—or, put otherwise, with exoticism, individualism, and betrayal. It is certainly true that *Hadriana* foregrounds the marvelous and the erotic within a frame that opens onto the Atlantic world from an idiosyncratically Haitian perspective. The women are beautiful, the landscape is lush, and "magic" infuses the quotidian. This manner of representing Haiti to the wider world has garnered *Hadriana* the most intense criticism from scholars. Charged more and less directly with having abandoned his commitment to a political praxis, with exoticizing and thus exploiting Haitian culture, and with eroticizing and thus exploiting his central woman character, Depestre has been taken to task by some of the most insightful and important theorists of Haitian, Caribbean, and postcolonial studies. Founded on what are, without question, attentive and sophisticated readings, these critiques situate the novel within the wider context of Depestre's projects as both a politically engaged social actor and a writer of poetry and fiction, and they find *Hadriana* problematic with respect to both roles.

Depestre is perhaps particularly vulnerable to critical interrogation along such lines given that—from his very first forays into literature—he proclaimed an inextricable link between his creative and political praxes. As a young writer and political dissident among Haiti's post–American occupation intellectual community, Depestre self-published the poetry collection *Étincelles* (Sparks) in 1945, a text that unexpectedly made him famous at the age of nineteen and, true to its title, lit something of a fire under the Haitian people. With the money earned from sales of the volume, Depestre founded the Marxist newspaper *La Ruche* (The Beehive), along with Jacques Stephen Alexis, Théodore Baker, and Gérald Bloncourt. This cohort of university students welcomed exiled surrealist poet Andre Breton to deliver a series of lectures in Port-au-Prince in December 1945. The French intellectual's impassioned discourse on surrealism and revolution, in which he lauded the inherent radicalism of the Haitian people, directly inspired Depestre and his coeditors to call for the "liberation" of Haiti from what they perceived as its alienating cultural self-loathing and internal political repression. Their declaration was taken seriously by President Elie Lescot, who seized the offending issue of *La Ruche* and arrested Depestre and his coeditors. This act of repression quickly backfired: the incarceration of the student leaders inspired a student strike that transformed within days into a nationwide strike, which toppled Lescot's government. These events marked what was arguably the most impactful instance of popular revolt in Haiti until the ousting of Jean-Claude "Baby Doc" Duvalier in 1986 (see Nicholls 1974; Parkman 1990; and M. J. Smith 2009).

Depestre was at the forefront of this popular political movement and very much came into his own in this moment as a militant and a poet. Yet this first political triumph was to prove fleeting, as Depestre soon found himself a persona non grata in Haiti, considered a troublemaker and "urged" into an exile disguised as a government scholarship to study in Paris. This departure was to be the first in a series of successive exiles that stretched from 1946 to 1986—from France to Czechoslovakia to Brazil, Argentina, and Chile, back to France briefly, to Haiti even more briefly, then to Cuba (with forays to China, Russia, and Vietnam), and, finally, to permanent settlement in France. Arguably the most significant period in this forty-year displacement throughout the Atlantic world and beyond began in 1959, the year Depestre left Haiti for good and settled in Fidel Castro's socialist Cuban state. Depestre had returned to Haiti in the early winter of 1957, following a tenuous sojourn in Paris, optimistic about the election of Black nationalist leader François Duvalier to the presidency. Duvalier had at first welcomed the celebrated young poet, inviting him to serve as his minister of culture. But the tenor of Duvalier's politics quickly became clear, leading Depestre not only to refuse the appointment but to speak out against Duvalier's increasingly repressive state apparatus. These actions led to threats, surveillance, and, ultimately, imprisonment within his own home.

Depestre was, in a sense, saved by the Cuban Revolution of 1959. Having published a passionate article in support of the revolutionary government only days after Castro's march on Havana, Depestre was invited to Cuba by poet Nicolás Guillén "to come speak about Haitian poetry" (Couffon 1986, 60). Depestre took the opportunity to escape Duvalier's Haiti. He settled permanently in Cuba and dedicated himself to supporting the ideology of the revolution in various capacities: as a journalist; as a literary advisor to the Cuban National Press, to the National Cultural Council, and to the Casa de las Américas; as a broadcaster at Radio-Habana-Cuba; as a professional translator; and as a professor at the University of Havana. During the two decades he spent in Cuba, Depestre witnessed and contested the unrelenting international pressure on the country, the political and economic isolation, the sporadic military aggressions. Yet, while he continued to believe firmly in the underlying values of the socialist experiment, he became all too intimately aware of the limitations of Castro's revolutionary agenda. In an uncanny echo of his experience in Haiti, Depestre found himself increasingly at odds with the regime, monitored by government agents and effectively decommissioned from his various professional activities. Thus, in 1978, having more or less fallen out of favor with Castro, Depestre left for France, where he has remained ever since. Over the decades following this final exile, Depestre explicitly renounced radical politics in multiple forums, from the 1992 poem "Adieu à la révolution" ("Farewell to the Revolution") to the 1998 essay collection *Ainsi parle le fleuve noir* (So Speaks the Black River) and elsewhere.

Depestre's highly visible and vocal geopolitical trajectory, his celebrity within the metropolitan French context, and the extent to which—timing-wise—the latter flowered following his break with militancy and definitive relocation to France have made him to a certain degree suspect. The harshest critical assessments of *Hadriana* posit that, in the wake of his disillusioning experience in Cuba, the once-political Depestre resigned himself to the insufficiency of revolutionary politics and has since become lost in fantasies of his native land, content to bask in strategically garnered postprize acclaim.[3] Several scholars have evoked more and less virulently the coincidence of Depestre's abandonment of the socialist revolutionary political project and his heightened success in France. His very displacement to a space outside of the Caribbean, it has been suggested, is of a piece with his treacherous willingness to offer Haiti up for North Atlantic consumption.[4] What to make, they wonder, of the presence of the overtly (excessively) sexual and the overtly (excessively) tropical in his representation of Haiti from the space of luxurious exile in southern France, given especially the fraught nature of that particular moment in Haiti's history?[5] "Does Depestre, because he is Haitian though Frenchified to the bones, have a responsibility to present Haiti in a way that resists mythologizing?" asks Colin Dayan. "Has Depestre been zombified by French fame?" (1993, 167, 175). Or, as Jean-Marie Salien wonders, "At this critical moment, could Depestre legitimately withdraw into a Nietzschean pursuit of personal accomplishment (erotic, aesthetic), losing sight of any moral obligations, especially given that, as a famous writer, he had publicly identified himself with this country?" (2000, 87).

The question of context—literally, where Depestre is writing from and, metaphorically, what his location signals regarding his politics—is at the heart of such critiques. This is evidenced, for example, by the fact that while

Depestre's earlier novel *Le mât de cocagne* (The Festival of the Greasy Pole, 1979a),[6] similarly eroticizes elements of Haitian popular culture, it has never been subject to the same condemnation. This, I would argue, is due both to the fact that Depestre wrote and first published the novel in Cuba and to the immediate legibility of its political register. *Le mât de cocagne* is a "dictator novel," a thinly veiled allegory of François Duvalier's régime in all its violence and perversion. The novel features a lone Marxist hero struggling on behalf of the people against a corrupt totalitarian authority. It also contains a number of graphic sex scenes and portrayals of Vodou ritual. Indeed, Depestre's commitment to writing both Vodou and *l'érotisme solaire* (solar eroticism) has been a constant in his work.[7] This proclivity did not begin with his departure from Cuba. The critical outrage sparked by *Hadriana* would seem, then, to have a great deal to do with Depestre's political self-positioning, both at the time of its writing and in the decades since. The principal offense Depestre has committed in *Hadriana* seems to come back to the question of what he owes Haiti as a writer: "Can one at once be from a suffering island like Haiti and dedicate one's literary praxis to nothing more than an unbridled praisesong to pleasure and the body? Is there not some kind of contradiction—some kind of paradox there?" (Colin-Thébaudeau 2005, 50).

Indeed, there is no shortage of scholars who have condemned Depestre's move away from explicit revolutionary politics following his departure from Cuba in the late 1970s. Lamenting Depestre's later-life embracing of Europe, both as geographic and ideological sanctuary (ironically via a reference to two canonical European thinkers), Silvio Torres-Saillant, for example, identifies *Hadriana* as the turning point in Depestre's trajectory of deradicalization: "*Hadriana* marks what Althusser, in examining the development of Marx's thought, referred to as an 'epistemological break.' . . . The novel exhibits a departure from the major ideological tenets evident in Depestre's previous works" (2013, 228). Others who have proposed a similarly periodized reading of Depestre's literary career include Philip Kaisary, who argues that "renouncing revolutionary politics coincided with being lionized by the French literary establishment." Kaisary continues, "Depestre is now a Gallimard-published author who is regarded as a key Franco-Haitian spokesperson for *la francophonie*" (2014, 73). Earlier, in a study framed as a consideration of the "properly political" (2) in postcolonial studies, Chris Bongie writes scathingly of Depestre's "slack postmodern stance" and "fawning enthusiasm for *la francophonie*" (2008, 329). And in an essay that sets out to defend Édouard Glissant's later work from accusations of depoliticization (levied by Bongie), Charles Forsdick offers up Depestre as a handy counterexample. Glissant's "late style" must be distinguished, he argues, from the "disenchanted lateness of a near contemporary from the francophone Caribbean such as René Depestre, who has emphatically eschewed the revolutionary politics of his youth in favor of exoticist *métissage* and apologies for *la francophonie*" (2010, 123).

Though the tone may vary, the underlying preoccupation is consistent: Is it permissible for a Haitian writer to eschew the explicitly political? This is the question and these are the stakes that have underpinned critical reception of *Hadriana in All My Dreams* from 1988 to the present moment. Looking closely at the language of expectation that has framed such critical analyses of Depestre's fiction reveals, in fact, ways in which the novel stages the most fundamental point of criticism lobbied against the whole of Depestre's post-Cuba writings: that is, that Depestre turned his back on his original revolutionary political imperative, and has since left his readers to "wonder what has happened to the apocalyptic social visionary" (Dayan 1986, 583).

Taking Dayan's loaded wondering as an earnest query rather than a rhetorical gesture, I propose a counterreading of *Hadriana* that pays close attention to the structural choice made by Depestre in the novel. *Hadriana* is a work in three distinct parts—three movements, to use Depestre's terms. The first movement describes one weekend in January 1938 in Jacmel, Haiti—the three days that span Hadriana's death, zombification, and disappearance. This first movement is narrated by Hadriana's godbrother Patrick Altamont: it presents the adult Patrick's recollections of this capital event in his childhood, told from what the reader later learns is a significant temporal and spatial remove. The second movement is situated similarly within the space of Patrick's memory but relates events that occurred in the late 1970s. Also told by Patrick in the first person, the chapters of this second part describe the narrator's attempts to come to terms with the traumatic loss of Hadriana and the extent to which her disappearance from Jacmel has haunted his wanderings around the Caribbean and the wider world. The third and final movement is a repetition with a difference. Anchored also in the time-space of memory, it retells the story of those same three days in Haiti in 1938. But in this instance, those days are recounted by a different first-person narrator—Hadriana Siloé herself.

The most strident critiques of the novel tend to focus almost exclusively on the first and second movements of *Hadriana*, those presented by Patrick. Referencing a fairly fixed selection of passages, these critiques point to what they argue is the author Depestre's misogynistic fetishization of white womanhood; his alienated, francophilic, exoticist exuberance; and his devaluation of Haiti's revolutionary history. I push against such readings of *Hadriana* and propose, even, that Depestre himself may be making these very same critiques, relying on the distance between his authorial self and his narrator Patrick. Though I recognize the excesses of Depestre's decidedly priapic literary imagination, I nonetheless question condemnations of Depestre's highly erotic portrayal of his heroine. I argue that Depestre ultimately empowers the self-telling Creole Hadriana, though not, as is claimed, at the expense of the novel's Black Haitian population.[8] I look at gender clichés in the novel (particularly those gender clichés that stage women's association with or integration into a nationalist imaginary) as the springboards from which Depestre dismantles—or at the very least meaningfully pokes fun at—the very stereotypes he has been accused of promoting. In this, I posit *Hadriana in All My Dreams* as a highly sophisticated work of social criticism.

My analysis does not delegitimize existing critical perspectives on the novel but provides, rather, an opening onto what I believe is also legible in Depestre's text. To be clear, I am not interested in proving whether Depestre is or is not a consistently Marxist revolutionary writer. My discussion is meant as neither a defense of nor an apology for Depestre qua political being. It is undeniable that Depestre's late twentieth- and early twenty-first-century politics depart from his earlier commitments to radical revolution. There are ways, yes, in which the sixty-, seventy-, eighty-, and ninety-year-old man who moved to France, became a citizen, and has since devoted himself exclusively to writing may seem to have broken with his younger self. The socialist militancy that not only informed Depestre's writing during the first half of his adult life but also absolutely determined the contours of his existence is very much a thing of his past. There is little trace of the fiercely radical young man who bounced around the world in service to a dream of global revolution that never came to pass. That being said, I would suggest that Depestre's well-earned frustration with the limits of radical politics might better (more generously, more fairly, more logically) be understood as a former revolutionary's brokenhearted reassessment of socialist ideology, rather than as an old writer's cynical late-in-life bid for fame and fortune. Moreover, there is greater coherence in Depestre's literary project than certain critical voices have acknowledged. If Depestre has renounced and even denounced the exuberant political radicalism that once defined him, he nonetheless has remained steadfast in his commitment to a utopian worldview wherein art, love, and desire serve as the most reliable tools of human transformation.

Scholarly discomfort with Depestre's investment in the aesthetic of the erotic in the absence of explicit politics has, I argue, obscured readings of

Hadriana's incisive and highly provocative humanist assertions, among which is the affirmation of individual investment in the self in the context of coercive community. I focus here on the extent to which Depestre's writing accounts for yet avoids any fixed hierarchization of the constituent parts of his political and creative evolution and ultimately reflects an eclectic but fundamentally coherent vision. In giving text to this vision, Depestre foregrounds issues of race and sex in ways that present a real challenge to extratextual social and political ideologies, maintaining the ambivalences and unresolved tensions that are part of the Haitian and the human real.

Unaligned with the racialized and otherwise communalist projects espoused by influencers throughout the Caribbean political and intellectual spheres, Depestre embeds his work in Haiti's foundational cultural realities and risks exposing their "tropicality"—a collage of postcolonial Haitian and more broadly Caribbean idiosyncrasies that many critics appear to be uncomfortable addressing. These idiosyncrasies include, notably, the persistent fetishization of whiteness and bourgeois French culture, the hypereroticism (especially of the feminine principal) and attention to the corporeal that mark Afro-spiritual practices across the Americas, and the prevalent belief in the supernatural as constitutive of real social phenomena.

What do you mean, a poetic revolutionary, a meditating gunrunner?
Audre Lorde, *Sister Outsider* (1984)

In an interview for the now-defunct radical Texas-based activist journal the GAR, Depestre offers some reflections on erotic love and the inconsistency of the "I," matters he admits to have been grappling with in his debut prose fiction writings—"I speak of love as it can be lived in the Caribbean, in Brazil, without it being necessarily autobiographical" (Depestre 1979b, 20).[9] In the course of this response, Depestre pointedly names himself an artist:

> Parallel with the phallic adventure of the Haitian tyrant, I evoked what an erotic relation could be between a man and a woman consumed by fires of love. There is in my book a love story treated with the freedom of expression found in *Alléluia pour une femme-jardin*. The heroine of my novel is also a woman-garden. To the eyes of this poet there are ordinary women, real, worthy of praise, and there are woman-gardens [*femmes-jardin*], the truest, the most seductive, allied with the sun, the moon, the natural cycles of life. It's a literary myth. Every writer has the right to invent his myths to attempt to express human truths. (20)

Depestre has evoked Haiti and its political realities several times by this point in the interview, yet here he seems to want to make clear an equally essential dimension of his writing praxis. He gestures beyond the specific concerns of the Haitian political context to evoke broader literary questions. Given this, interviewer Hal Wylie's follow-up to Depestre's assertions of artistic freedom and investment in the erotic is particularly revealing: "Since you are speaking of Haiti," Wylie posits leadingly, "what do you think of the Haiti of today? *What are you doing for the liberation of Haiti?*" (Depestre 1979b, 20; emphasis mine).

Now to be fair, there is no doubt that Wylie—at that time a long-term friend and admirer of Depestre, the "troubadour activist and wandering knight" (Wylie 1981, 285)—offered this statement-question from a place of deep appreciation.[10] The interview took place in Havana, Cuba, where Depestre had been living since joining Castro's revolution in 1959 and where Wylie had been invited to participate in a meeting of the United Nations Special Committee against Apartheid. Wylie was well aware of Depestre's long-standing commitment to anticolonialism and to fighting all forms of social injustice in the international arena and in 1976 undoubtedly viewed Depestre as a similarly politicized brother-in-arms. Over the course of the interview, Wylie shows himself to be perfectly comfortable exploring the erotic dimensions of Depestre's fiction as a manifestation of the latter's politics. All this to say, the tone of the question must be understood as contextually neutral: neither "What are *you* doing?" nor "What are you *doing*?" Nevertheless, in seguing from Depestre's broad humanist aesthetic reflections to a—to *the*—question of political engagement suggests a desire on Wylie's part to guide the conversation toward and ultimately conclude with a clear assertion of Depestre's political groundedness. What strikes me in this conversation is the extent to which, even in this context where Depestre's political commitment and revolutionary credibility are not at all in question, the interviewer's impulse is to reconcile explicitly the political and the sexual and to articulate plainly the primacy of the former. Embedded in this moment is a concern with articulating the Haitian writer's commitment to a legible political praxis. In this respect, the question offers a prefigurative view of *Hadriana*'s reception just over ten years later.

I want to note also the biohistorical significance of the context in which the interview took place. For Depestre, 1976 was a decidedly transitional moment, both politically and aesthetically. As already noted, during this period Depestre's increasingly vocal frustration with Castro's government and his subsequent relegation to a toothless professorship at the state university in Havana were making it increasingly apparent that he had overstayed his welcome and that his Cuban sojourn would end imminently. Indeed, only two years later, Depestre left Cuba for what would be his final exile and retirement in France. This interview also took place three years after the release in Montreal of *Alléluia pour une femme-jardin*, a collection that had been refused publication in Cuba. It came also just one year after the publication—in Spanish with a Cuban press—of the aforementioned *Le mât de cocagne*, which Depestre describes in the interview as both a "political fiction" and a "love story" (1979, 20).[11] One might argue that 1976 was in many respects Depestre's watershed moment. It marked the apex of the period during which he came to realize the impossibilities of his nationalist political beliefs—his "heroic dreams of modernism" (Bongie 1998, 354)—and to embrace the possibilities of his humanist prose imagination, what Martin Munro calls the "particularities of his own creole identity" (2000, 165).

Yes, Depestre was very much in transition at this point in his political, literary, and personal trajectory; this was the beginning of a deliberate, active practice of self-reconstruction within all three contexts. I would disagree, however, with any description of this transition as Depestre's movement away from "public interest" (Salien 2000, 87) in favor of an onanistic solipsism. Rather, Depestre's post-Cuba turn is marked by a continued effort to integrate the personal and the political, the individual and the community—to interrogate the personal *as* political, the individual *in* community—through literature. *Hadriana* is the risk Depestre takes in laying bare this process of reconciling the troubled self with a troubling world.

I have foregrounded my consideration of Depestre's novel with this extensive discussion of an interview that precedes the novel's publication by more than a decade in part to note the extent to which the marriage of the erotic and the political has been a long-standing subject of critical inquiry with respect to Depestre's work. It is also to note that from his very first works of prose fiction, Depestre has been well aware of the dangers of using the "I" in ways that encourage a conflation of his authorial position with that of his narrators. "The writer's 'I' is a plural 'I,' an imaginery [sic] 'I,'" he insists in his conversation with Wylie (Depestre 1979, 20), in what serves as a prescient response to criticism that would come much later. This question of the "I" is the point of greatest interest to a reading of *Hadriana* in the context of critiques of the novel. It is truly striking, that is, to note the critical tendency to conflate Depestre's authorial "I" with that of his male narrator. Yes, several elements of the narrative link the character-narrator Patrick Altamont and the author René Depestre. There is, however, ample room for understanding that blurred boundary as deliberate and meaningful rather than alienated or naive. Insofar as Depestre is a "trickster" (Benedicty-Kokken 2015, 199), his "I's" must be appreciated as multiple, unreliable, and provocative. Or, as Derek Walcott has pithily declared, "Every 'I' is a fiction finally" (1990, 28).

The "I's" of *Hadriana* might be considered first through the lens of surrealism, one of the novel's many diverse interpretive prisms. From the outset, *Hadriana* directly encourages the reader to acknowledge a surrealist undercurrent to the narrative. The second line of the book's two-sentence dedication reads: "To the memory of André Breton and Pierre Mabille." The following page offers an extract from a poem by French surrealist René Char. The final paratextual offering assures the reader that "Jacmel, folklore, history, and mad love have inspired the characters of this novel," thereby gesturing unambiguously to Breton's 1937 novel *L'amour fou* (Mad Love). This being said, and as Munro has laid out beautifully in *Shaping and Reshaping the Caribbean: The Work of Aimé Césaire and René Depestre* (2000), Depestre's relationship to surrealism, though long-standing, has been by no means constant. The author's evocation of surrealism in *Hadriana* marks the tempered and ambivalent refashioning of an aesthetic from which Depestre had maintained something of a distance during much of the period preceding the novel's publication.

Indeed, almost immediately following the optimistic moment of poetry-inspired revolution in which Depestre and his colleagues had been implicated in Haiti in 1946, Depestre was forced to acknowledge the limits of poetry's ability to effect lasting political change (see Depestre 1974, 204–13). The generative alliance of politics and poetics—of Marxism and surrealism—had been ephemeral, and a disillusioned Depestre eventually turned in the 1950s and 1960s toward a revolutionary aesthetic more aligned with the social realism of staunch Marxist writer Louis Aragon than with Breton's formal experimentation. This period in Depestre's writing life marks a crucial first movement in my consideration of the writer's struggle with community and has everything to do with his self-definition as an artist. I am referring to an incident in which Depestre was accused—by no less than Aimé Césaire—of a lack of individualism, of conformity to a French poetic ideal that denied the specificity of and even betrayed his Black Haitian poetic self.

The context was a series of articles published in 1953 and 1954 in the Marxist literary journal *Les lettres françaises*. In these essays French surrealist communist writer Louis Aragon had launched an unequivocal call for the end of formal individualism in poetry and a commitment to revolutionary communist ideology at once national and international. Depestre was by that time very much disheartened by the failures of post-1946 Haiti. He had become convinced that a revolutionary politics should take precedence over the tribulations and desires of the poet, and he published these thoughts in an open letter, which appeared in *Les lettres françaises* in June 1955. In this letter Depestre announced that Aragon's social realist aesthetic had been of great help with respect to the political and aesthetic issues he had been grappling with in the years since his departure from Haiti. The influential Pan-Africanist journal *Présence Africaine* published extracts from Depestre's letter that same year, positioning the young Haitian's remarks as the point of departure for a debate on the question of national poetry in the Afro-postcolonial context. This debate was immediately taken up by several Afro-francophone intellectuals, among whom were Aimé Césaire, Gilbert Gratiant, Léopold Sédar Senghor, and Amadou Moustapha Wade. It evolved into a heated polemic in which Depestre found himself standing—writing—in opposition to key figures in the ostensibly liberal and progressive mid-twentieth-century francophone Pan-Africanist community. It is not an exaggeration to say, as has Maryse Condé, that Depestre's remarks "set the francophone world ablaze" (2001, 177).[12]

Césaire led the charge against Depestre with the brief and excoriating "Réponse à Depestre poète haïtien" ("Response to Depestre, Haitian Poet" [1955a]), later published in a volume of Césaire's collected poems as "Le verbe marronner" ("The Verb 'to Maroon'"). This eloquent, if tightly wound, poem is categorical in its chastisement of Depestre. Césaire suggests that Depestre's exile from his home country has diminished his sense of an Afro-self: "Is it possible / that the rains of exile / have slackened the drum-skin of your voice?" Césaire asks rhetorically—accusingly—of the formerly "valiant knight of the tam-tam" (1955a, 113). Using language meant to evoke a specifically Afro-Haitian ("some macumba," "a powerful Vodou," "the valiant tam-tam") revolutionary (Boukman, Dessalines, Vertières) heroism that Depestre has betrayed, Césaire exhorts the poet to "maroon" the Frenchman Aragon as exemplar and to heed instead the call of his African blood.[13] In condemning what he names Depestre's "detestable assimilationism" in a subsequent essay, Césaire centers the debate on questions of poetic responsibility, authenticity, and Afrocentricity (1955b, 39). At issue, ultimately, is Depestre's loyalty to a Haitian identity or, put otherwise, Depestre's betrayal of his obligations as a Haitian (ergo) revolutionary writer. This public quarrel took place, it should be noted, during what was at once a critical moment in Césaire's evolving personal perspective on political community and a time of fervent international debate around issues of race and colonialism—a period marked by Césaire's increasing ambivalence toward Marxism and, ultimately, his resignation from the French Communist Party in 1956.[14]

Also in 1956, *Présence Africaine* organized the First International Congress of Black Writers and Artists in Paris, which both Depestre and Césaire attended. While this reunion of Black intellectuals from across the globe in many ways highlighted the diversity and contradictions of the so-called Black experience, support for Césaire's denunciation of Depestre in the months leading up to and during the congress was nearly unanimous. In a series of passionate essays published in *Présence Africaine* in 1955 and 1956, a veritable who's who of Black intellectuals joined Césaire in admonishing Depestre for his willingness to adopt a French poetic form. As scholar Anne Douaire-Banny (2011) has noted in her astute analysis of the stakes of this debate at the time, harsh criticism was issued by several of conference's "heavy-hitters," "all in line with Césaire, all for the cause of poetry emerging from the primordial darkness rather than from an anesthetizing formal practice." The debate finally closed in December 1956, by which time, as a result of the September congress, Depestre had come around, or so it was claimed, to the prevailing opinion. The editors write, *"It is the experience of the Congress that has allowed Depestre, among others, to go beyond the contradictions still visible in his analysis of the* Haitian *basis for realism in poetry"* ("Conclusion" 1956–57, 100).

Whether the "prodigal son" (Douaire-Banny 2011) was genuinely convinced by the arguments put forward by Césaire and the other contributors to the debate, or whether he was worn down by a coterie of intellectual strongmen, what is most interesting to me in this Afro-intellectual conflict is its irony—that while calling for Depestre to assert his independence from the dictates of the French, each of Depestre's Pan-Africanist detractor-interlocutors insists that he should conform to the poetic intention they have set. Indeed, young Depestre was more or less cowed in the face of an insistent collective condemnation of what was perceived to be his betrayal of Haiti and its revolutionary principles, of Black Africa and anticolonial politics, and of his responsibilities as a Third World artist. Moreover, the tenor of Césaire's admonishment and the subsequent rallying around Césaire seem, in the personal and emotional nature of their arguments, to prefigure uncannily the tone taken by much later critics of Depestre's literary choices in the name of other progressive agendas.

Over the decade following this public debate, Depestre, from his home in communist Cuba, continued writing poetry and also published his first prose fiction works. He had abandoned the surrealism of his youth in favor of a more rigorously political poetic intention. At the same time, however, he was gradually becoming conscious of the dangerous limitations of Caribbean socialism. As already noted, Depestre had come to realize, during his final years in Cuba, the impossibility of an uncompromised integration of his personal poetics and an ideology-driven politics. During this period he authored his first collection of short stories, *Alléluia pour une femme-jardin* (1973), and his first novel, *Le mât de cocagne* (1979a). Both of these prose fiction works are marked to an extent by surrealism—"the notion of the sovereign rights of love, of desire as the catalyst of a liberated self" (Jones 1981, 27) and l'érotisme solaire—but on terms that situate Depestre's aesthetic very clearly in the wake of a diversified experience of creative engagement.[15] Already in these first fiction writings, the political dimensions of the poetic self are less starkly asserted. The erotic is foregrounded without the slightest restraint, and Haitian spiritual practices take center stage.

This hypervaluation of sex and Vodou in *Hadriana* has drawn the most critical fire. Several scholars have argued that the novel's foregrounding of the erotic comes at the expense of dealing properly with the complexities of Haitian historical reality: both J. Michael Dash and Martin Munro accuse Depestre of "escaping history" (Dash 1998, 125) in *Hadriana*, the latter positing that the "stark differences between the politically engaged parody of *Le mât de cocagne* and the escapist, fantastic images of the homeland in *Hadriana dans tous mes rêves* bear testimony to the radical changes in Depestre's political sensibility" (Munro 2007, 132). Lizabeth Paravisini-Gebert faults the novelist for having written a text in which the "intertwinings of zombification and the erotic seem aimed at emptying Haitian history of its content." Depestre has crafted, Paravisini-Gebert argues, what amounts to "a somewhat peculiar meditation on Haiti's history that succeeds only in denying the significance of the devastating chronicle of its people's fate through its subordination to the narrator's single-minded quest for erotic fulfillment with Hadriana" (1997a, 47).

Even critics arguably less put off by Depestre's discursive turn away from militancy posit a rigid binary distinction between René Depestre, the nomadic revolutionary poet, and René Depestre, the sedentary *homme de lettres*: "When *Hadriana* was published," writes Jean-Marie Salien, "Depestre was in the midst of a transition from writer of public interest (decolonization, Marxism, anti-imperialism) to a writer of private interest (eroticism, aestheticism)." Salien allows that "[it] is possible that, subconsciously, [Depestre] remained attached to the militantism of the preceding years and that, by force of habit, he continued to serve a public interest" (2000, 87). While far more sympathetic—or less condemning—than Dayan, Paravisini-Gebert, and others, Salien similarly presumes that the distinction between politics and the erotic, between ideological and aesthetic principles, lines up neatly with that between public and private interest. Depestre's *Hadriana* is, however, a risky refusal of such binaries. The novel reflects Depestre's commitment to a deeply eclectic imaginary—an uninhibited reliance on a constellation of nonideologically grounded perspectives on love, sex, spirituality, and death.

The fully realized person of individualistic or communistic humanism is the dead person.
—Jean-Luc Nancy, *The Inoperative Community* (1991)

A goddess was born on the soil of Haiti who has no precedent in Yoruba or Dahomey. Far more specific in her attributes than Oya, Yemanja, or Oshun the Ezili (whether Ezili Dantò, Ezili Freda, Ezili-je-wouj, or Marinèt) recalls the violent yoking of decorum and lust.
—Colin Dayan, *Haiti, History, and the Gods* (1995)

We have been raised to fear the yes within ourselves, our deepest cravings.
—Audre Lorde, *Sister Outsider* (1984)

Hadriana in All My Dreams tells the tale of a small Haitian community's efforts to cope with the zombification and subsequent disappearance of one of its most beloved members, the eponymous Hadriana Siloé. A beautiful and wealthy young Creole adolescent, the blond-haired, green-eyed Hadriana enjoys a seemingly perfect existence in her community. As the "tutelary fairy of Jacmel" (52), she is cherished and adored by all, and her upcoming wedding to a local boy from a prominent Haitian family is considered a blessing on the town. On the morning of her marriage, however, Hadriana's dream life abruptly becomes a nightmare. Having imbibed a mysterious potion just before embarking on her wedding march, she collapses at the altar at the very moment she pronounces her vows. She is transformed into a zombie, and her wedding day becomes her funeral. She is buried by the town and revived by an evil sorcerer; she then escapes and evaporates into popular legend, never to be seen in Jacmel again.

Hadriana's plot indeed suggests that Depestre has distanced himself from the explicitly political fervor of his years in Cuba. The narrative is erotically driven and draws from the Haitian popular imagination. The formal and thematic elements that mark Depestre's earlier works are deployed in *Hadriana* with both greater nuance and greater ruse. The novel's plot is inspired by a well-known incident in Haiti that has been fictionalized in texts ranging from Jacques Stephen Alexis's short story "Chronique d'un faux amour" to numerous Hollywood screenplays.[16] *Hadriana* diverges significantly from other zombie stories, however, in its presentation of the perspective of and choices made by its zombified heroine—in the fact and the implications of Hadriana's escape from zombification. As mentioned earlier, this novel is a telling and retelling of the events surrounding Hadriana's transformation into a zombie. Importantly, while the first version is told in the third person by the male narrator Patrick Altamont, Hadriana's godbrother and greatest admirer, the second, corrected version is told by Hadriana herself.

The first to assume the role of narrator and direct witness to the events in question, Patrick relates the story of Hadriana's false death and disappearance at a remove of several decades. Over the course of his narration, he describes himself as dreamy, impressionable, and sexually curious—in a nutshell, a teenage boy. In thinking about the adolescent Patrick's impressions of the events of that January weekend and about the narrative choices he then makes in the second movement as a middle-aged man, it is helpful to return to our earlier discussion of Depestre's history with surrealism. Patrick puts surrealism on the table from the very beginning. Setting the stage for his narration with a description of moments in his childhood, he recalls, "I used to take my sorrows out for a little air on the balcony of [my aunt and uncle's] wood-frame house. I'd wait there for something to catch my eye, to distract me enough for my imagination to wander off into daydreams [*surréalisme quotidien*]" (Depestre [1988] 2017, 25).

Depestre's direct evocation of surrealism in the first paragraph of the novel is telling. It is a hint to the reader that Patrick's journey in *Hadriana* might be viewed, at least in some measure, as a surrealist inquiry into the nature of his individual being. The quintessential Bretonian question "Who am I?" (Breton 1964, 9) animates Patrick's desire to tell Hadriana's (and his own) story, and this unabashedly individualist call for rooting in the self draws heavily on the sexual and the sensual as crucial influences on Patrick's processes of self-interrogation and self-construction. With this brief early evocation of surrealism as an aspired-to state of being for Patrick's adolescent self, Depestre winks affectionately at and perhaps even makes peace with surrealism as part of a young man's cherished past, "far from the real world," yes, but nevertheless foundationally constitutive of an adult self. In other words, Depestre presents Breton's surrealism in *Hadriana* as formative and foundational but operative primarily within the romanticized context of nostalgia. In this respect, that Patrick is besotted with Hadriana—"the ideal of French beauty that had set my young life on fire" (61), as he declares—and that she is described as something of a personal muse for him in both of the two movements he narrates can be read perhaps as Depestre's parodying of such an adolescent relationship to the feminine and the corresponding naive belief in the seamless integration of Eros and revolution, rather than as an instance of the author's "objectifying the object of his [own] desire" (Dayan 1993, 170).

There are other indications in this first movement that a distanced parody-cum–social critique is Depestre's intention—instances in which Depestre at once stages and interrogates the clichéd objectification of women. One of the most provocative of these instances is the tale of the sex-crazed butterfly-man Balthazar Granchiré, the tale with which the entire novel begins. This local legend is obliquely but, as it turns out, mistakenly linked to the zombification of Hadriana. Patrick introduces the story but then cedes the storytelling role to a local hairdresser and notorious fabulist, the evocatively named Scylla Syllabaire. With this narrational sleight of hand, Depestre offers this story within a story as another wink at his reader. First, the framing of this anecdote from Jacmel's past does the metatextual work of reminding the reader to be always vigilant about the instability of narrative authority overall. That is, almost immediately after transferring the storytelling role to the hairdresser, Patrick proceeds to marvel at the fact that "Scylla Syllabaire's detailed account of the events . . . ended up being accepted as the official truth," even though, "from the very beginning, [Scylla's] story didn't match up with what I had so excitedly seen with my own two eyes" (32, 34). Patrick continues to poke holes in Scylla Syllabaire's account all the way through to its conclusion, bookending most of the hairdresser's claims with an "according to Scylla" or "Scylla claimed" and an "In reality" or "Scylla similarly distorted" (34).[17]

Beyond this trickster's call to the reader to be alert to the subjective nature of narrative truth, the content of the story of Balthazar Granchiré is itself unsettling, to say the least. For several theorists it is an example "of the deeply rooted sexism that pervades the text" (Paravisini-Gebert 1997a, 50). Granchiré is a young man who has been turned into a sexually insatiable giant wood moth by the sorcerer Okil Okilon. He is burdened with an outsized penis and is prone to drugging and penetrating members of Jacmel's female population while they sleep:

> He would wait until nightfall to slip into a bedroom and then hide out under the bed. Once his prey had fallen asleep, he would fill the air with his aphrodisiac exhalations. A few minutes later, breasts would be popping the buttons on nightgowns, bottoms bursting the elastic of underwear, enflamed thighs opening wide, vaginas, fascinated, crying out with thirst and, above all, hunger. At that point, all Balthazar would have to do was launch his campaign. Superb adolescents, having gone to bed virgins, safe

within the cocoon of the family, would awaken dismayed, with blood everywhere, brutally deflowered. (39–40)

Just as troubling as Granchiré's violent predation is the narrator's description of the women's reactions to his nocturnal assaults:

> On those mornings, the dreams that permeated the sleep of the victims generally involved an episode of fabulous flight. Everyone remembered having flown in an airplane at low altitude over the bay of Jacmel in an uninterrupted orgasm. . . .
>
> Lolita Philisbourg felt as if the folds of her own soft lips, open to the exact size of the skies above the bay, were violently enveloping the rest of her body. Her sister Klariklé felt her love tunnel open up beneath her like a trap door while her own father whispered in her ear that she should not have forgotten her parachute at home. Sister Nathalie-des-Anges saw her very Catholic cavern-of-the-Good-Lord impetuously competing with the frothy waves bubbling on the surface of the sea. Such was the calling card that Balthazar Granchiré left between the sheets.
>
> Hoping to catch the incubus before his assaults, vigilant mothers sat at their daughters' bedside, armed with steel mesh. The following morning they would discover to their dismay that they had succumbed, without even putting up a fight, to the same witchcraft as their innocent progeny. They, too, remembered flying just above the waves, whisked away by an orgasm that could only be described as miraculous.
>
> Mrs. Eric Jeanjumeau confessed to Father Naélo that she had had six orgasms in one minute. Mrs. Émile Jonassa had come furiously thirteen times in a row. The widow Jastram's rapture had been a true classic of sensual pleasure: she promised herself to hold onto it beyond the dream so as to include it later in a sex education manual. (40–41)

Some critics of the novel maintain that these descriptions of the aftermath of Granchiré's violations—the notion that the women actually took pleasure in being attacked while asleep—are even more egregious than the attacks themselves. I would like to take something of a risk here, however, and propose that a consideration of the context within which the Granchiré affair emerges leaves room for an alternative reading of this ostensibly misogynist episode from "Jacmel's imaginary."

Depestre makes it a point in this first movement to paint a very particular portrait of Jacmel as a largely—an aspirationally—bourgeois community. Peppered with doctors, lawyers, shop owners, and low-level bureaucrats, the townspeople strive to maintain an air of Gallic respectability in the face of the pervasive influence of various popular beliefs and practices. Several Catholic characters and institutions figure prominently in Patrick's narration of his boyhood—Fathers Naélo and Maxitel, the Saint-Rose-de-Lima convent, the Friars School—as do bourgeois touchstones like the Cercle Bellevue social club and the Meyer holiday resort. Considered against this demographic backdrop, the fantastic legend of Granchiré becomes differently legible. That the reports of the butterfly's "rape rampage" (Paravisini-Gebert 1997a, 50) include parodically explicit details of the intense and unprecedented multiple orgasms experienced by Jacmel's should-be chaste female population may be read as something other than an "unfortunate reprise of the 'every girl wants to be raped syndrome'" (Dayan 1993, 170).

It is possible, that is, that Balthazar at once represents a form of collective hysteria and functions as something of a scapegoat, enabling the otherwise policed women of Jacmel to circumvent the bourgeois strictures imposed on their sexuality.[18] It is no coincidence that Granchiré's putative victims are nuns, adolescent private-school virgins, and married high-society mothers. Claiming to have been violated by a giant butterfly while unconscious might be a handy way of masking consensual acts like premarital sex and masturbation—or of explaining the kind of naughty dreams that would make a woman cry out in the night and leave her more than a little disheveled in the morning.

Moreover, this account of the horny lepidopteran is embedded in yet another story—that of the even more legendarily erotomaniacal Germaine Villaret-Joyeuse. Grande dame of Jacmelian society and godmother to both Patrick and Hadriana, Madame Villaret-Joyeuse is famous for her miraculous "genital apparatus" (42)—her seven loins, to be precise—and she proves more than a match for the cursed butterfly. Her voracious sexual appetite, which sends two of her three husbands to the hospital and succeeds ultimately in taming the black-magic man-moth, challenges the claim that Granchiré's tale "objectifies female sexuality and is built on male-centered fantasies of erotic dominance" (Paravisini-Gebert 1997a, 50). Depestre's depiction of the erotic goings-on in Jacmel is thus decidedly ambivalent. In light of what we later learn from Hadriana—and given Patrick's insistent reminders that narrative truth is by no means certain—it is possible, if not imperative, to spend time unpacking Depestre's provocations.

The story of Granchiré reveals a preoccupation with respectability among the people of Jacmel that enormously impacts on Hadriana's fate. In effect, this first movement exposes a vision of Hadriana that is shared by the entire community. Hadriana is heralded as "the princely gift that the French nation of Debussy and Renoir has given to our country" (52), object of the town's admiration for all things French. She is the veritable patron saint of Jacmel and symbol of its "natural filiation between the real and the supernatural" (161). Munro is right to contend that there "are obvious traces here of . . . francophilia" (2007, 126), but I argue that this alienated love of France is staged and parodied by Depestre, not embraced. Hadriana's marriage to a Haitian—which has been planned as the kickoff to the carnival season and to which all members of Jacmel have been invited—fully implicates the community. The ceremony is described as "a veritable public bacchanalia," "an unprecedented carnival celebration," and is intended "to reunite Jacmel with the rhythms of life through dance and fantasy" (51, 52, 51). In essence, Hadriana's wedding is viewed as an offering of herself—of her self—to the entire village.

It is, therefore, quite fitting that Hadriana should die at the high point of the marriage ceremony. These last moments of Hadriana's life (in Jacmel), as recounted by Patrick, resemble nothing so much as a virgin sacrifice. Dressed in white and followed by her wedding party, the young bride-to-be passes through a crowd of admirers in a slow procession to the church. There are hints that this is problematic, that getting married might not be as much of a happily-ever-after for Hadriana as for the wider community. For instance, one of the young girls breathlessly watching the wedding procession bursts into tears on seeing the bride approach, aware despite the joyfulness of the occasion that these were the last moments during which Hadriana would possess "that freshness that marriage permanently takes away from us women. More than any other young girl in Jacmel," she laments, "Nana Siloé had a paradise to bury" (63). With the zombie poison already flowing through her veins, Hadriana walks to embrace her death in a scene that perfectly evokes the performance of a ritual sacrifice. When the priest calls upon her to pronounce her vows, she crumples to the ground at the foot of the altar but not before consenting to her own martyrization with what Patrick describes as a "staggering 'Yes' of distress" (64). Expiring in the same breath with which she affirms her commitment to Jacmel, Hadriana enters irreversibly into popular memory as the virgin bride, unsullied even by her legitimate spouse and thus fixed in an eternal purity—a Creole Eurydice.[19]

What follows Hadriana's dramatic death continues Depestre's work of parody and critique, as her value and service to the community of Jacmel remain very much in play. Because Hadriana's marriage to Hector was meant to usher in the carnival season, her death poses a logistical problem: "What was to be done about the crowd of merrymakers who had not stopped singing and dancing beneath the windows of the manor?" (72). How, in other words, could the community be expected to forgo its long-awaited collective jubilation? It thus becomes immediately apparent that the symbolic resonance of Hadriana's marriage will have to be redeployed via an appropriation of her death. As such, a traditional wake for her family and close friends, "conducted 'in the manner of the French-from-France,'" becomes unthinkable. Her initial sacrifice is only the beginning; it is determined that Hadriana still owes something to Jacmel, even in death. "Should the bride's body be displayed? In the Siloé's sitting room, in the communal space of the town hall, or in the prefecture?" (72).

After much discussion, Hadriana's open casket is placed in the town's central square. But in the course of making the decision to display the young girl's lifeless body and thus make it available to the Jacmelian community, another issue arises: that of keeping her virginity intact. "In the case of a death like this one, isn't properly deflowering the victim the very first precaution to be taken?" (73) asks the Siloés' neighbor, "reputed to be something of a *mambo* [Vodou priestess]" (68). A debate ensues as to whether such measures are necessary for the daughter of a "prominent French—and Catholic—family" (73). With this question Depestre makes plain that the town's investment in its "dearly beloved fairy" (76) is very much contingent on her chastity.

In the context of the discussion of how Hadriana's death might be appropriated to sustain the life of the community as a whole, Depestre places the question of Haitian popular spiritual practices squarely on the table. "From that moment on," recalls Patrick, "there began a pitiless battle between the two belief systems that have long gone head-to-head in the Haitian imagination: Christianity and Vodou" (67). In effect, this comical—and arguably tropicalizing—discussion regarding whether and how to safeguard Hadriana's innocence from the "devastating erection" (75) of whatever evil spirit had brought about her untimely death is one of the ways in which Depestre stages the class and culture issues surrounding Haitian Vodou. There was, as scholar Bridget Jones reminds us, "a particularly clear polarity between the Catholic Church and vaudou during Depestre's formative years" (1981, 27), and the complicated relationship of the Haitian intellectual—particularly the Marxist and exiled Haitian intellectual—to popular religion underpins much of the nation's literature.[20]

Fascinating in Depestre's approach is the deployment of his characteristic tricksterism. The polarizing dispute between the town's Catholics and Vodouisants is by no means B/black and white: the race of several of the interlocutors who participate in the conversation regarding Hadriana's funeral (like Father Naélo, the doctors Braget and Sorapal, and Hadriana's childhood friends, the

Philisbourg twins and the Kraft sisters) is left deliberately ambiguous. Class lines, too, are slippery and unclear.[21] At no point, then, do the poles of the debate align neatly with social standing or color, a meaningful ambivalence to which I return later in this chapter.

In the end, although a compromise is reached "between the rites of Catholicism and those of Vodou, those two rivals fighting bitterly over the young girl's body and soul" (72), Jacmel's Hadriana drama continues. Already distraught by her tragic death, the community bears the further insult of Hadriana's zombification. Following the opening carnival festivities, on the day after her funeral, it is discovered that her grave has been disturbed and her coffin emptied. Hadriana's body is nowhere to be found. And so the book's second movement describes the devastating fallout from Hadriana's disappearance: "Time, hope, doubt, reason, compassion, tenderness, and even the will to live had all evaporated from Jacmel along with the beauty of [Hadriana]," Patrick affirms (147). In this movement, an older, more circumspect, now well-traveled Patrick presents a hodgepodge of texts that reflect his efforts to work through the tragedy of Hadriana's prolonged absence. From the dreamy, fantasy-based perspective of the innocent Haitian teenager, the narrative segues to the nostalgia-driven reflections of a middle-aged man. An intellectual and writer at this point in his life, Patrick informs the reader that he has been grappling for forty years not only with the loss of Hadriana but also with the question of the zombie myth in Haiti. Thus, once the object of an adolescent crush and local Jacmelian celebrity, Hadriana has assumed the role of Patrick's full-blown muse—"the cross I bore throughout my years of exile"—and the source of Jacmel's collective social and economic downslide. She has become even more symbolically powerful, though no more individually empowered than before her zombification.

Embedded in this second movement is a collage of supporting materials that escape Patrick's strict chronicle of events: a 1972 newspaper article in *Le Monde* describing the decline of Jacmel, Patrick's imagined supplementation of the article via a personal interview with the reporter, and an anthropological sketch of the zombie phenomenon in Haiti that describes the myth's relevance to a humanist understanding of history and the world. The former texts—the article and interview—detail the collective depression, or "Hadriana-ache" (145), that overwhelmed Jacmel in the absence of Hadriana. They rehearse and parody utopian, prelapsarian narratives of the Haitian past—the "rituals of nationalism and loss" (Dayan 1995, 87) so often deployed by unscrupulous politicians and well-meaning intellectuals. The third text, titled "Prolegomena to a Dead-End Essay," is of an entirely different nature.

Deeply informative and scientific in tone, it makes a number of substantive claims regarding the connections between the zombie myth and other global social phenomena. The zombie, Patrick writes, is "a perfect fit in the gallery of the wretched of the earth that the writings of Sartre, Memmi, Fanon, and Simone de Beauvoir, among others, have collaged together from various portraits of the colonized (black, Arab, yellow)—not to mention women and Jews" (169). Patrick's "dead-end" prefatory remarks thus announce a fascinating treatise on the "racializations of colonial conflicts" (170) and the concomitant "mythological and semiotic vulgarization" (171) of human reality by exploitative imperialist interests.

By the conclusion of this second movement, the reader is resettled firmly within the space of Patrick's soul-searching adventure. Patrick has relocated to Kingston, Jamaica, and relaxed into a peaceful and relatively happy existence teaching classes on Caribbean aesthetics at the University of the West Indies. There, he explains, he has managed to "make [his] peace with the natural, the comical, the playful, the sensual, and the magical aspects of Jacmel's painful past" (171) and to write the chronicle of those three days in January 1938 (the first movement of *Hadriana*). And there, on "Wednesday, May 11, 1977, at six in the evening" (180) the would-be bride Hadriana walked into his classroom and back into the rest of his life. Their reunion is "an explosion of joy" (182); they have incredible sex throughout the night, and the next morning Patrick recounts, "I let her read my tale of her extraordinary past" (183).

Hadriana responds by handing him her book.

[question] How can the woman turned muse step down from her pedestal and write words of her own? . . . As pretext for an experience that transcends her, as source for the man's divine afflatus, how could she presume to be anything more than diverse forms of beauty fixed in the eternal project of her male admirer?
Colin Dayan, "'Hallelujah for a Garden-Woman'" (1986)

[answer] "Hadriana's Tale"
René Depestre, *Hadriana in All My Dreams* (1988)

Colin Dayan posed the questions above in 1986, two years before the publication of *Hadriana*. They neatly encapsulate her critique of Depestre's *Alléluia pour une femme-jardin* and, especially, of the short story "Mémoires de géolibertinage," Depestre's ribald paean to the joys of commitment-free sex with bright young things from around the world, conveniently available in the dorms of a Parisian university campus for his lusty pleasure. Dayan foregrounds the matter of the political and the personal, arguing that in substituting sexual satisfaction for political action, Depestre exploits the eroticized feminine not as "an inspiration for revolutionary engagement, but an excuse for self-indulgence" (1986, 582). Her conclusions are compelling. The women who circulate in the collection are indeed, on the whole, fairly one-dimensional beings. It is worth considering, however, that Depestre may be offering something of a corrective to this earlier vision of the feminine in *Hadriana*. Thus, while the tone of Dayan's interrogation is rhetorical, here, as earlier, I read her remarks as sincere and discerning queries, in that the answer I have somewhat cheekily supplied in the epigraphs is precisely the issue I grapple with in the final pages of this chapter. "Hadriana's Tale," the novel's third movement, proposes real answers to Dayan's exasperated questions. These answers may fall to a degree on the side of parody and provocation, but they nevertheless very much affirm Depestre's commitment to reimagining both the feminine and the authorial "I."

Taking over from Patrick as narrator in this third movement, Hadriana revisits and reconstructs nearly all of the events that her long-suffering admirer has described in the first and second movements. Hadriana's tale is posed in dialogic relation to Patrick's account; it demystifies and effectively corrects his version of events. The fracturing of the narrative "I" into this third valence is an iteration of the marasa epistemology undergirding the whole of the novel.[22] It moves beyond binary structures in favor of sustained and generative irresolution.

In telling her tale, Hadriana takes on extraordinary powers. Beyond the obvious though by no means unimportant fact that she has been granted narrative control, Hadriana enjoys the unique position of bearing witness to—of living—her own death in community (the silver lining of zombification?). Of all the characters in the novel, she knows the most, has the most answers, and gets the last word on what happened to her. Foremost in Hadriana's corrective agenda is to set the record straight regarding her sexual self—to proclaim, that is, the sexuality that had been consistently denied her by the people of Jacmel. She reveals, for example, that while lying silent and paralyzed at her own wake, alive but trapped within her immobilized body and subject to so much debate, she had been both shocked and amused to hear the many evocations of her saintliness. Hadriana insists that her image as virgin saint had little to do with her real-life woman's experiences. She confesses to having indulged in numerous sexual encounters before her wedding day—including one that implicates Patrick himself:

> Me, a saint? You know, I managed—not once, but twice, Father—to offer my body, eyes closed, to another being, well before the lifting of the "not-until-marriage" bond: Patrick was but a single blond hair away from getting over the paralyzing fact of his awkward adolescent hand on my ripe almond and taking a proper manly dip in the passionately consenting waters of my womanhood. With Hector, from the very first night, it was the same scenario: my box of dreams had been ready and willing to reveal the last of its virgin secrets. A saint—really? Reverend Father, excuse me, but I have sinned! Another time, one overheated August afternoon, with the door to the balcony flung wide open against the sky above the bay, I was nude in my bedroom with Lolita Philisbourg. The black and purple coal of my seventeen-year-old sex cried out in the burning embers of her caresses. I was electrified by her mouth on my peach, riper than any other fruit in season, be it Haitian mango or French melon. It was incredible, Father, hearing the song of the birds outside as Lolita cultivated my springtime garden. It was wonderful, delivering my enflamed Creole flower, my untamed love box, to my best friend's tongue, as she brought me dizzyingly to seventh heaven with three, five, up to seven orgasms in a row on that blessed day. (207–8)

Using language that seems to have been taken straight from the pages of a Harlequin Romance, Hadriana reveals an eroticized being that is very much at odds with Jacmel's phallocratic collective construction of her individual identity. In her recollection of the debate over whether or not to deflower her before burial, Hadriana laughingly details her own efforts to dispose of her virginity with Patrick:

> Patrick very well could have been the one to open me up. It was the summer before I met Hector. At a holiday resort in nearby Meyer one night, we had wandered away from the others down a path that led to the beach. I was his for the taking. Would he be the one to penetrate me? His hand trembled between my legs. We had run down the hill in the light of a gentle moon that loomed over the empty sea. He had complete liberty to plunge into the mysterious waters of my flesh. He caressed me gently, with the amazement of a teenager who could not believe his clumsy hand was actually lying there, star-struck, on the mound of my ripe almond! (200)

That Patrick froze when offered the chance to have sex with Hadriana and that he expressly omits this incident from his own narration so as to preserve Hadriana's saintly image (knowing full well there was far more to her than that!) again serves to remind the reader of the contingency of his storytelling.

Hadriana goes on to relate yet another thwarted attempt to shed her innocence, implicating in this instance her then-fiancé Hector:

> From the very first night he, too, could have opened me right up—to the point where I had come to think of my virgin's ripe almond as Hector's very own box of dreams. But he dreamt of an act of love blessed in a church, by Father Naélo. And now he was in the hospital in a state of shock, with me walled up in my false death. Fate was punishing me for a sin I had not even committed. Hadriana knocked out, down for more than ten seconds on the church floor at her own wedding, disqualified from the spectacular combat of her honeymoon, from the work-of-the-flesh-only-after-marriage, as Hector had wanted it. Ashamed of his apostolic aviator's erection, he had placed a small hand over it, scared stiff by the possibility of committing a mortal sin. He was afraid to dirty the white skin of the French fairy, Creole daughter of a prince of mathematics and tobacco. (204)

Thus, we learn in Hadriana's tale that if she was still officially holding on to the title of virgin on her wedding day, it was by no means for lack of trying to shake it off. In fact, there is a decided disconnect between the heteropatriarchal preoccupation with Hadriana's virginity qua nonpenetration and the various workarounds Hadriana manages to sort out for herself. Given this, the reader must understand her emphatic "*Yes*" at the altar as, more than anything else, an embracing of the much-anticipated opportunity to finally—unfetteredly—have the sex she had long been waiting for. Although her death is read as the apotheosis of her virgin sacrifice to the community, Hadriana experienced it as something very different:

> I felt as if I were swimming desperately in viscous, bituminous water toward the most fantastic object in the world: my fiancé Hector Danoze, just to my right, his flesh turned shapeless and phosphorescent. He had become nothing more than three giant letters that spelled out YES. My frantic swimming sought only to reach that goal as it first came close, then moved away, liquefied into a stream of lava that enveloped Hector, the priests, the altar, the hymns, the decorations, the attendees, the sky beyond the apse. This empyreumatic sound-light-body, on one of its backward surges, suddenly threw itself at me. It lodged itself in my genitals. And my genitals came together as a final sigh that began climbing up through my body

like the rising mercury of a barometer. I felt its upward movement in my guts, then in my digestive tract. It left a strange emptiness in its wake. It stopped for a few moments at the level of my heart, which was barely beating. Was the sigh of my sex going to take its place? I felt it rise up through my throat. It nearly choked me before finally settling its burning weight on my tongue. With the four lips of my true mouth I screamed the ultimate *Yes* of life to my Hector and to the world! (192–93)

There is a radical intention in evidence here. Hadriana does not in fact "[open] up to the magic of Eros only when she has fallen victim to the zombi potion" (Dayan 1993, 168). On the contrary, she has sought out, been the agent of, and experienced her sexual awakening well before this trip down the aisle. For Hadriana, marriage will mean, above all, no more obstacles and no more hiding. No more pretending a butterfly did it. And given these revelations about Hadriana's myriad sexual exploits, it is hardly imaginable that the fifty-six-year-old woman who walks into that classroom in Jamaica had remained chaste over the four decades since leaving Jacmel, waiting for Patrick "in order to do the sex she had only envisioned" (Dayan 1993, 172).

With these revealing accounts of her own sexual agency, Hadriana dramatically interrupts Patrick's and Jacmel's mythmaking efforts. Over the course of her narration, she makes clear that the Jacmelian community's love for her, as well as the life of ease and privilege this communal adoration afforded her, came at a great price and was actually experienced as an increasingly stifling objectification. She is able to articulate that "the correlation between her whiteness and her continued role as desired virginal (white) erotic object" (Paravisini-Gebert 1997a, 51) is in fact a burden to her, a burden she refuses in escaping Jacmel.

Hadriana admits that she herself became fully conscious of the extent to which she had been exploited and constrained by her community only after being turned into a zombie. She tells Patrick of how she awoke in the cemetery, in her coffin, only to find herself in the hands of the evil *bokor* (Vodou priest) Papa Rosalvo Rosanfer, who had caused her zombification in the hopes of turning her into his concubine. Hadriana relates how she initially had managed to flee the sorcerer and his henchmen at the cemetery and then returned to town hoping to find refuge. With Rosanfer on her heels, she recounts, she had knocked desperately on door after door. But neither family nor friend, nor any of her many devotees, had answered. Were they afraid? Yes. But not so much of the zombie, I would argue, as of what Hadriana might have insisted on knowing—or perhaps what she might have figured out already about their complicity in her dispossession. As a community, the people of Jacmel could not afford to be contaminated by this woman reborn, and so they ignored her cries, seeing in them potential demands for accountability.[23] This collective refusal of her unsacrificed self, Hadriana explains, fully revealed to her the limits of the woman she had once been and the value of her escape and rebirth:

> To have had my horizon so frighteningly suspended between death and life would make my existence at once more dynamic and more sensitive to the delicately complex doings of my fellow man. My connections to the sea, the sky, the birds, the rain, the trees, and the wind had been forever fortified, just as my most vital senses had become better attuned to both animals and human beings. I'd do a far better job of listening to all aspects of my feminine voice, though always well aware, from that morning on, that while the natural woman may have been reborn from these trials more capable of fully savoring every moment, the woman I was in society would never completely recover from the wounds on her hands made by all the doors she'd knocked on that night. (244)

In other words, Hadriana's plan is to "begin to live from within outward, in touch with the power of the erotic within [her]" (Lorde [1984] 2007, 58). Henceforth she will refuse the implicit zombification that determined her social life long before the physical zombification that initiated her social death. She begins the process of reinventing herself according to her own desires. In a sense liberated by her false death, she rejects the fundamental impotence of her prezombie life. She renounces all ties to Jacmel and leaves for Jamaica, never to return to Haiti.

Just as tracing and telling the contours of her sexuality allows Hadriana to upend Patrick's and Jacmel's fantasy-driven configuration of her self as presented in the first movement, her decision to leave Jacmel rebuts the nostalgic fallacies Patrick constructs in the second movement. In having Hadriana leave Haiti, Depestre departs from the "gendered use of the landscape" (Francis 2010, 7) whereby "women appear as elusive figures who represent cultural loss" and are thus denied "a sense of identity separate from that of island nations" (Chancy 1997a, 107, 108).[24] Rather than reading "Depestre's representation of the devastating impact of Hadriana's death on Jacmel" as "ironic and illogical the moment it is revealed that through the decades of Jacmel's sorrowful decay Hadriana was . . . alive" (Paravisini-Gebert 1997a, 48), I understand this construct as entirely consistent with Depestre's project. It makes perfect sense, that is, that the independent existence Hadriana has carved out for herself would in no way impact Jacmel's communal fate: her implication in Jacmel's destiny is the town's collective *myth* and not her individual *reality*. Depestre insists on this disjunct by indulging Patrick's clichéd masculinist nostalgic longing for Woman as fantastic personification of the homeland, only to have Hadriana refuse that fantasy with the narration of her own material truth.

Depestre ultimately makes no attempt at "sublimating and denying the violence perpetrated against women in both 'public' and 'private' spheres" (Chancy 1997a, 107). On the contrary, Hadriana relates in exquisite detail the social and physical violence that constitutes her experience of zombification. Quite literally dying to live and decidedly more jaded than before, Hadriana has learned a lot and is justifiably angry. By no means innocent, sexually or otherwise, Hadriana has come to understand. And she has determined that Jacmel's desire for her sanctification will no longer be her weight to bear. The self-narrating ex-zombie she has become is ready and equipped to navigate the coercions and constraints that conditioned her belonging. If she is to be a goddess, she will not be ill served.

On that night back then, in the depths of everyone's conscience, we all just wanted to keep our distance from the young zombie bride, brutally abandoning her to her inescapable fate, seeing her as a danger for the whole of the Jacmelian community. That's what happened.
—Patrick Altamont (in *Hadriana in All My Dreams*)

That self-connection . . . that deep and irreplaceable knowledge of my capacity for joy comes to demand from all of my life that it be lived within the knowledge that such satisfaction is possible, and does not have to be called marriage, nor god, nor an afterlife.
—Audre Lorde, *Sister Outsider* (1984)

Through Hadriana's recounting of her political self-awakening, Depestre effectively offers a provocative critique of race and gender norms and expectations within Haitian communities. He does not shy away from the less-than-ideal realities embedded in the nation's cultural idiosyncrasies. As eminent scholars of Haitian Vodou Patrick Bellegarde-Smith and Claudine Michel have pointed out, the "world of deities in the metaphysical plane may be half female and the majority of priests may be women, but the Haitian scene in the physical plane remains unapologetically macho and sexist" (2006, xxiii). Karen McCarthy Brown similarly notes, "Haitian culture is a misogynist culture. The ideology of male supremacy is fierce. Haitian humor is rife with anti-woman jokes, and domestic violence is a frequent occurrence. Vodou has not escaped the influence of this attitude." At the same time, she continues, "Vodou empowers women to a larger extent than the great majority of the world's religious traditions" (1991, 220).

Depestre romps around in the ambivalence these scholars evoke. He does so, in particular, via an engagement with two specific Haitian cultural configurations of the feminine, one "high" and the other "low." That is, Hadriana is in meaningful intertextual dialogue with two vital figures of Haitian womanhood: Jacques Roumain's Annaïse and the *lwa* (spirit) Ezili-Freda.[25] Within this engagement, questions of Depestre's responsibilities as a Haitian writer come very much to the fore, as does the matter of women's obligations to Caribbean community. At stake in considering these two avatars of Haitian womanhood, as with Depestre's heroine, is the extent to which women in Haiti are able to navigate "the forces that define and confine them" (Brown 1991, 221).

Roumain's *Masters of the Dew* (Les gouverneurs de la rosée [1944] 1988) is the urtext of Caribbean community.[26] It is the model and the standard for the social and moral transformation of an unenlightened and oppressed, but ultimately noble and potentially progressive, collective into a politically conscious and industrious whole. The novel is mythical and allegorical. It is unabashedly Marxist. Considering *Hadriana* in *Masters*' light—considering, that is, Hadriana in Annaïse's light—reveals much about our critical expectations of Haitian writers. Criticism of Depestre's novel reveals a desire, that is, for Roumain's tragic fairy-tale ending.

There is much to suggest that Depestre crafted Hadriana as, at least in part, a provocative counterpoint to the "ideal of the perfect community" (Britton 2011, 23) presented in *Masters*. The points of similarity between Depestre's novel and Roumain's are perhaps not obvious, but they are nonetheless significant. In both texts, an exceptional insider-outsider in a blighted community is configured as the determinant of that community's fate. In both texts, the sacrifice of the exceptional individual is positioned as the prerequisite for a nostalgia-driven restoration of lost collective harmony. Yet where *Masters* proposes a binaristic and coherent novelistic universe with a clear moral imperative—"Put aside your differences and unite in recognition of my sacrifice"—the conclusion to *Hadriana* amounts to the simple exhortation, "I won't be who you think I am, so I'll be on my way." Put otherwise, whereas for Roumain's male protagonist, Manuel, "what counts is the sacrifice of a man" (Roumain 1988, 181), Hadriana invests in her own resurrection as woman. Hadriana's story of herself interrupts, challenges, and undoes the myth advanced by *Masters*, in that it divorces individual sacrifice from collective rebirth.

Given the extent to which *Masters* has been critiqued for its patriarchal treatment of the central woman character, Manuel's beloved Annaïse, it is significant that the novel has figured, with varying degrees of subtlety, as a counterpoint to Depestre's novel. Evoking *Hadriana*'s "joyous eroticism," for example, J. Michael Dash writes, "The drought, decay, and human waste that afflict Jacmel cannot be solved by another *coumbite*, as was the case with Fonds-Rouge, but by the return of a nubile, white Erzulie" (1998, 125). Dash continues, "It is as if the grounded Annaïse of Roumain's earlier political parable had been transformed into the groundless Hadriana of Depestre's novel, written four decades later and enacting a desperate, late phase of Caribbean modernism" (126). Dash positions the particular model of Caribbean Afro-womanhood that Annaïse represents as somehow indicative of a political optimism that Depestre no longer possesses. He posits the pregnant, widowed Black Annaïse as the community-reproducing predecessor-avatar of the libertine Creole Hadriana, so much evidence of Depestre's post-Cuba feeling of "impotence" (130). These comments are interspersed throughout Dash's analysis of the "erotic vein" in Depestre's prose fiction and are meant to support his broader contention that a postrevolutionary Depestre turned to sex as "compensatory fantasy" (125) in the face of political impossibility. Dash closes his argument by distinguishing between Depestre's apolitical, "harmlessly ludic enterprise" (126) and the work of other Caribbean writers (C. L. R. James, Ina Césaire, Kamau Brathwaite, Wilson Harris, and Earl Lovelace, among others) who, he notes, demonstrate "an immensely creative interest" in carnival as "a master trope of Caribbean literature equivalent to the use of the *coumbite* in Roumain's novel" (127).

Less pointedly evoking *Masters*, Paravisini-Gebert is nevertheless similarly convinced that Depestre's enactment of "narcissistic revenge" (Dash 1998, 126) in *Hadriana* represents a missed opportunity for political engagement. She reads Depestre's focus on the white "virgin" zombie Hadriana as a "peculiar meditation on Haiti's history that succeeds only in denying the significance of the devastating chronicle of its people's fate through its subordination to the narrator's single-minded quest for erotic fulfillment" (Paravisini-Gebert 1997a, 47). She offers Mayra Montero's short story "Corinne, muchacha amable" (Corinne, A Sweet Girl) as an example of a more responsible representation of the Haitian community. Yet, in so doing, Paravisini-Gebert puts forward a somewhat troubling critical binary that seems to celebrate the very martyrization of the individual—especially the individual woman—that Depestre's *Hadriana* in fact refuses. Paravisini-Gebert notes approvingly that "Montero never dwells on the pathos of Corinne's situation; no sentimentality is wasted on the fate of the brave young girl. . . . Her individual fate is not Montero's central concern; it is depicted as bound to that of the Haitian people" (52).

Paravisini-Gebert goes on to evoke Pierre Clitandre's *La cathédrale du mois d'août* (Cathedral of the August Heat), similarly extolling its configuration of a community redeemed by the suffering and death of an individual. She contrasts Clitandre's valorizing narrative choices with Depestre's "exploitative" parody of the carnivalesque and his "subsuming of Haitian political history to an erotic quest that privileges the white woman as innocent victim" (1997a, 56). Clitandre's novel, she insists, "is above all a metaphorical tale of a lost people's desperate struggle to recover their history and, with it, the source of precious water that can restore them to fertility and bounty" (53). Thus placing Depestre (and Clitandre) in the shadow of Roumain, Paravisini-Gebert's critique implicitly reinforces the community-good/individual-bad binary according to which the erotic is understood as antithetical to politics. Thus, while scholars would almost certainly agree that it "would be wrong to expect the Caribbean author to be constantly 'saying something' about his situation" (Munro 2007, 132), critics of *Hadriana* seem to find themselves in an uncomfortable bind in this respect. Responses to the novel suggest a visceral and adamant desire for Depestre to be saying something different—or at the very least differently.

A number of highly charged word-concepts are embedded in the critiques of *Hadriana* outlined by Dash, Paravisini-Gebert, Munro, Dayan, and others. I mean specifically the imbricated evocation of, on the one hand, Ezili-Freda and, on the other, Hadriana's whiteness. As I have already noted, that Hadriana is white is "a thing." Not only is it "a thing" for the people of Jacmel, it is also "a thing" for reader-critics of the novel. Pointing to Hadriana's European origins as so much evidence of Depestre's racial betrayal, certain critics of the novel posit Hadriana as an outsider to the wider Jacmelian community. Ignoring that Hadriana was born in Jacmel and that she is deeply integrated into its racially diverse elite community, such readings ultimately fail to take into account the "literally revolutionary" Vodou frame that structures the novel (Tinsley 2011, 418)—the extent, that is, to which it "invites us to imagine beyond the binary" (Clark 1991, 43). Understanding the novel through the prism of the marasa principle makes plain how Hadriana embodies the "transformation of cultural oppositions in plantation societies," the rendering of racial categories beyond oppositional constructions of blackness and whiteness (Clark 1991, 45).

The ways in which Hadriana's whiteness disorders and disturbs extratextually is most evident in discussions of the moment when Hadriana leaves Jacmel—the moment when "Depestre abandons the inhabitants of Haiti to their fate" (Dayan 1993, 174).[27] This moment suggests yet another point of distinction vis-à-vis *Cathédrale*, insofar as "this depiction contrasts sharply with the struggle of Clitandre's people to regain their precious source of water" (Paravisini-Gebert 1997b, 227). In this comical scene, having escaped all of her zombifiers and arrived at the end of her ordeal, Hadriana comes across a group of Haitians at the seashore preparing to migrate to Jamaica in search of work. The little group immediately takes her for the water deity Simbi-la-Source (a spirit linked to one aspect of the spirit Ezili) and enjoins her to accompany them on their diasporic voyage.[28] Hadriana leaps at the chance; unlike Manuel, she decides not to stick around to be sacrificed for some greater good. This is, in and of itself, a purely self-regarding decision: she leaves the community and effectively takes the source with her! She accepts without hesitation the title the group has granted her, fully aware of and able to articulate the regrettable geopolitical reality that undergirds this final phase of her adventure:

> These are the circumstances in which I arrived in Port Antonio, at dawn on February 3, 1938, having made the decision to cut all ties with my Jacmelian past. It was the first time that Immigration Services in Jamaica had ever seen a young white woman disembark with a bunch of Haitians, veritable pariahs of the Caribbean wherever they migrated in search of work. Profoundly flustered by my presence, the British agents pretended to believe the story my travel companions had already been spreading: I was Simbi-la-Source. The gods of Vodou had charged me with the task of escorting a handful of Jacmelian emigrants to Jamaica. Goddess or whore, I wouldn't have had any trouble obtaining a lifetime resident's permit in any island of the archipelago. In those days, white skin and blond hair, better than any diplomatic passport, were worth as much as a visa of divine right. But that is a whole other story. (249)

The phenomenon by which whiteness is fetishized across the Caribbean is decidedly not "presented for the most part without irony in the text" (Paravisini-Gebert 1997a, 51). Quite the contrary. That Hadriana's color is the basis for her deification—not only in Haiti but also throughout an American hemisphere in which Haitian blackness is unwelcome on foreign shores—is Depestre's engagement with a rich and tricky line of inquiry. That she is white and a zombie is a provocation but by no means a gratuitous one. Depestre exposes a fundamental ambivalence that marks both Haiti and the broader Caribbean, and he does so by drawing on the Haitian vernacular context—specifically, the cult of the goddess Ezili—in ways that critically evoke Haitian color politics and the bourgeois strictures regarding feminine respectability in the postcolonial Americas. He digs into a set of linked phenomena—constitutive of that "whole other story"—that mark Haiti as profoundly as does the nation's history of anticolonial resistance. He invites a critical interrogation of the very bones of what is arguably Haiti's most authentic cultural practice: Vodou.

On the one hand, Depestre's novel encourages a reading of Hadriana's whiteness and the quasi-devotional fetishization of that whiteness by the people of Jacmel as linked to ritual worship of the goddess Ezili-Freda. Hadriana, like Ezili in certain of her aspects, embodies a hyperbolic perfection. She is, like the goddess, depicted as extraordinary in her beauty and elegance. According to anthropologist Maya Deren, "in Erzulie, Vodoun salutes woman as the divinity of the dream, the Goddess of Love, the muse of beauty. It has denied her emphasis as mother of life and of men in order to regard her ... as mother of man's myth of life—its meaning. In a sense, she is that very principle by which man conceives and creates divinity. Thus, to man himself, she is as mistress"—she sanctions freedom from "the flat weight, the dreary, reiterative demands of necessity" (1953, 83). Yet to understand Ezili in this single dimension, as Dayan argues that Deren does, is to misunderstand and underestimate the goddess. Far more than a tropical translation of the Western Venus or the Virgin Mother, though she is certainly connected to both, Ezili is an exceptionally iterative spirit. Capacious, if not to say schizophrenic, she "recalls and replays all the uses, pleasures and violations of women in Haiti, from colonial Saint-Domingue to post-Duvalier Haiti, whether they be slaves, free coloreds, or white Creoles" (Dayan 1994, 16). For Dayan, Ezili is most fascinating and most useful for comprehending Haitian culture and society in the multiplicity of her aspects and in the corresponding fact of her profound ambivalence.

Unquestionably linked to Ezili, one of many spirits in Vodou "who model and mentor the divinity of gender and sexual nonconformity" (Tinsley 2018, 19), Hadriana embodies this same multiplicity and ambivalence. As Alessandra Benedicty-Kokken has astutely noted,

> Hadriana is troubling because she represents too many identities: in her whiteness, she signifies colonialism; in her familial upbringing, she is the product of progressive republican values of cultural tolerance; in her young late adolescence, she is engaged and married to a member of the Haitian elite; and in her childhood and young adulthood, she is Haitian of a more common order, baptized alongside other Haitian children, including Patrick; and most importantly, she is abducted, possessed, and zombified as a Haitian by a *bokor*. (2015, 213)

In her own recollection of the ordeal that followed her "pronouncing that formidable, famished *Yes*" (206) at the church altar, Hadriana makes clear the extent to which, like her divine avatar, "she subverts the roles she affects" (Dayan 1995, 63). She has done her very best to seduce and be seduced across lines of class, race, and gender, but she has been denied satisfaction by her potential lovers Hector and Patrick (and who knows how many others) because of their adherence to bourgeois moral conventions regarding purity and respectability. The people of Jacmel have failed to recognize Hadriana's multidimensionality, deifying her in "an exuberance of devotion" (Dayan 1995, 63) that limited and constrained a spirit they themselves had summoned into being. Thus, Hadriana's "aborted marriage begins a non-heteronormative characterization ... that continues throughout her spiritual evolution" (Strongman 2008, 15). This evolution, along with what Hadriana reveals to be the truth of her life before walking down the aisle, can be appreciated within what amounts to a "queer Caribbean Vodou epistemology" (Tinsley 2011, 419).

Once the narrative's world opens up to and through Hadriana's perspective, the full force of her connectedness to a Haitian spiritual identity is implicated. Out of zombification Hadriana manages to wrest something of an initiation. During her wake, for example, Hadriana catches a glimpse of another "young girl in a wedding veil ... a very beautiful black girl" (214), whom she recognizes as her own double. This unnamed woman had already appeared in Patrick's narration of the same scene. He describes her as having been suddenly possessed by "the goddess Erzili, guardian of the freshest and clearest waters" (104). Hadriana's physical yearning for this dark-skinned doppelgänger is a first step toward her imagining, and ultimately seizing, a similar freedom: "She bent over me and let her breasts hang above me. I wanted to bite into their vivacious feast: huge breasts swollen with life and lyricism, round, firm, suspended above my famished abyss. I recognized my own breasts disguised in the bosom of this black girl participating in my marriage carnival" (214).

After several hours of lost consciousness following this out-of-body experience and the subsequent funeral procession and burial service at the cemetery, Hadriana awakens underground, sealed within her coffin. At first overwhelmed by the suffocating emptiness that surrounds her, she gradually becomes aware of a "cosmic whispering—the throbbing of the nearby sea" (226). This moment marks the beginning of the second, most critical phase of her spiritual awakening. From this point on, that is, the bay of Jacmel becomes a motivating force allowing her to retain a selfhood untouched by the zombifying poison. In this moment Hadriana begins in earnest the work of literally getting her self together: "It was the mysterious call of the bay of my childhood, an indescribable summons to travel, to hope, to act. The sea of Jacmel was driving me secretly back toward the luminous space of everything I was this close to losing forever. Victory was still possible over the diabolical forces that had zombified me" (226).

That Hadriana's mounting refusal of her zombification is directly facilitated by a relationship to the water gestures evocatively toward one of Ezili's spirit kin, the lwa Lasirenn.[29] Generally depicted holding a mirror in Vodou cosmology and thus associated with self-reflection, Lasirenn offers "self-affirmation through looking in, a personal process which takes place independently of skin color or class status"; the lwa opens the metaphysical door to a "rebirth of the self with a more realistic self-awareness which is grounded in situating oneself within a cosmic structure" (Szeles 2011, 195, 200). Embodying the same inclusivity and fluidity as Ezili, "Lasirenn is never one, but more: two races—black and white; two sexes—male and female; two sexualities—straight and same-sex loving" (Tinsley 2018, 19). In these attributes as well, the connection to Hadriana is remarkable. Such descriptions of Lasirenn resonate profoundly with the process of Hadriana's escape from zombification. Holding fast to the vision of "the dense blue waters of the bay of Jacmel" (227), looking inward to the reserves of sensual and sensory feeling she has accumulated over the course of her young woman's life, Hadriana is able to project herself beyond the confines of her coffin and to access the psychic "freedom of movement necessary for survival" (Szeles 2011, 199). Thus, when Papa Rosanfer eventually comes to extract her from her grave, he finds himself facing a most recalcitrant zombie. Now (em)powered entirely from within, Hadriana refuses to be ex-posed (posed in exteriority) any longer. She decides to run for what is left of her life, declaring, "At that exact moment, I looked at myself *in my inside mirror* and said: Let's go, Hadriana!" (238; emphasis mine).[30]

Considering the terms of Hadriana's rebirth, it is by no means unreasonable that Hadriana decides to leave Haiti and never look back. Her transformation from deity to flesh-and-blood woman is a revolution. Having thus evolved from unwitting to unwilling to self-serving goddess in the novel, she takes advantage of her privileged status as a white Creole to effect her own empowerment, escape, and rebirth. Yet this charged conclusion does not necessarily represent an instance of Depestre and Hadriana/*Hadriana*'s "betrayal" (Paravisini-Gebert 1997a, 56) of the revolutionary narrative according to which Haitians are imminently capable of "transcending a history of colonialism, slavery, postcolonial poverty, and political repression" (Paravisini-Gebert 1997a, 49). Hadriana's departure need not be understood as a suggestion that "all that remains of his Haiti is a portrait of black, poor, apathetic husks of humanity, who can never awaken into freedom" or as an implicit claim that "being white, beautiful, and rich, [Hadriana] can quickly recover her will, whereas the Haitian people, because they are black, gullible, and poor, are trapped in zombiedom forever" (Paravisini-Gebert 1997a, 49).[31] For Hadriana is not just white. Her cultural métissage evinces an ambiguity that, not unlike Ezili, colors outside the lines of race. Moreover, Depestre has taken great pains to establish that the inhabitants of Jacmel are decidedly not a homogeneous group of impoverished Black sufferers. They are socially and racially diverse, self-reflective, and wholly articulate regarding the challenges and the concerns they face as a community. But they are wrongheaded in their belief that Hadriana owes them her life.

The terms in which Hadriana frames her departure from Jacmel and Haiti thus do not posit the essential impossibility of Black self-determination or an equally essentialist white superiority. Rather, the figurative-cum-literal deification of the white "virgin" Hadriana stages a very different critique. It simply is not a critique of the usual suspects (France, colonialism, the United States, or any other of the known enemies) and concomitant glorification of Haitian resilience in the face of North Atlantic oppression. Linking specifically Haitian social constructs to a broader question of community and individualism, Hadriana's experience is both a commentary on the alienated underpinnings of colorism in the Caribbean context and a bold expansion of the zombie metaphor beyond the cliché of the "black, gullible, and poor." Her escape from Jacmel and from zombification has to do primarily with resistance to collective conformity from an individualist perspective at odds with any and all manifestations of coercive community.

To love oneself entirely immunizes the self-lover from the accident of being killed by anyone else's love. Therefore, regarding the self is, in a word, IMMUNITY and not a narcissistic disturbance.
—Iké Udé, "The Regarded Self" (1995)

There is no gift for the beloved. The lover alone possesses his gift of love. The loved one is shorn, neutralized, frozen in the glare of the lover's inward eye.
—Toni Morrison, The Bluest Eye (1970)

Eurydice dies; Orpheus seeks consolation in his art. . . . As the symbol of the poetry of love, Orpheus inaugurates the stubborn tradition, which wants the loved woman to be a dead woman.
—Adriana Cavarero, Relating Narratives (2000)

In a chapter titled "Lovers," part 3 of her manuscript *Relating Narratives: Storytelling and Selfhood*, feminist philosopher Adriana Cavarero offers a series of intriguing reflections on the myth of Orpheus and Eurydice. She situates this tale of perfect, tragic love with respect to the question of relation—relation as being-in-common, relation as storytelling (the act of relating). Cavarero argues that, largely thanks to—or perhaps merely first articulated by—the Orpheus myth, lovers "risk remaining entrapped in the tragic emphasis of a literary imagination that has for centuries celebrated the *authenticity* of love precisely in death. The death of the other, as the highest figure of un-relation [*irrelazione*], becomes the horizon in which love sustains itself" (2000, 101). Cavarero suggests that Orpheus—and thus poet-lovers in the Western tradition ever since—values the silent but adored Woman more as a source of poetic inspiration than as the material woman he loves and who loves him back:

> Founded as it is on the triad—love, poetry, death—the myth [of Orpheus] makes evident and instills in the Western imagination the great pathos of the lack of relation [*l'irrelazione*]. In other words, its fascination lies above all in the *mise en scène* of the separation of the two lovers; and in the absolute impossibility of bridging that separation . . . because she is dead, she is not there, she is unreachable, lost forever. Drawing his inspiration from the now-dead Eurydice, Orpheus sings *of* her but not *to* her.
>
> Perhaps this is why he mischievously turns around. . . .
>
> If he had turned around afterwards, along with an improbable happy ending, we would have been able to enjoy a love brought back to the narrative scene of the relationship—a banally happy love, a love accessible to all. Instead, as we know, he turned around *before*: pushing her back in order that he enter into the myth. (101)

What Cavarero describes here certainly could have been—but ultimately is not—what happens to Hadriana. Hadriana does not suffer the "crushing loss of presence" (Dayan 1989, 50) that so often characterizes the feminine in the literature of the Caribbean and elsewhere, although those are her narrative beginnings.[32] Rather, she asserts a counterdiscursive authority that calls into question all of the silencing tropes and conventions that mark the first two-thirds of the novel. She "force[s] the reader to know violently the implication of being or being told to be pure and unstained" (Dayan 1994, 7).[33]

Having staged the Orphic myth, Depestre proceeds to undo its tenets in illuminating ways. He configures Patrick as Poet and Hadriana as Woman-too-beloved-to-live-in-this-world, but then refuses the paradigm whereby the death of the narrated subject serves as the ideal condition for narration. Thus, if for decades Patrick persisted in living Hadriana's death, the tale she offers him is sensuously, sensorially, the tale of her birth. "Desperately, passionately, fatally in love with life" (249), as she proclaims in the very last words of her story, Hadriana defies the "logic of unrelation" (Cavarero 2000, 99) that would relegate her to the idealized space of perfect and perpetual absence by reducing her to the self-sacrificing role of immortal beloved. Hadriana survives, and she writes. She simply will not be the "woman who is born to die" (Sartre 1964–65, 40), nor will she be the "non-literate muse who suffers most extremely the curse of idealization" (Dayan 1995, 131). In his trickster fashion, Depestre positions the reader to imagine Hadriana as this traditional figure—"muse of the writer in search of his voice," "feminine instrument of inspiration . . . only there *for* the poet" (Cavarero 2000, 105)—only to reconfigure that image more than halfway through the narrative. Subtly mocking how masculinist expressions of adolescent desire and middle-aged nostalgia too easily flatten Woman into a symbolic tool and literary stereotype, he gives us *one* woman—Hadriana—and a love story wherein both of the central characters truly grow up across the time-space of the novel. Both Patrick and Hadriana literally write the story of their maturation into liberated beings.

Patrick resumes narrative authority in the final section of *Hadriana in All My Dreams*. The chapter reads, in its entirety: "Having told our two tales, Hadriana and I could have added, as an epilogue to the memoirs brought together here, the story of the ten years we've since spent as a happy couple. Yet, although not entirely convinced, we've decided to take it on faith that the travails and the splendors of love have, in fact, no story . . ." (250; ellipsis in the original).

In a way, this brief epilogue leads us to the less-referenced "redemptive coda" (Silverman 2009, 5) Ovid proposes for Orpheus in *The Metamorphoses*. Kaja Silverman's elegant exegesis of Orpheus's return to the underworld following his own death further enables us to recognize Patrick's narrative arc as meaningful humanist evolution:

> Orpheus is killed and dismembered by a group of women, who resent his misogyny, and death transforms him. When he arrives in Hades, he sees again what he has seen before, but now he sees it differently. He also looks for Eurydice, and when he finds her, clasps her "tightly in his loving arms" and acknowledges her *ontological equality*. Sometimes they stroll "side by side" through Hades. At other times she walks ahead and he follows, or he walks ahead and she follows. (2000, 5; emphasis mine)

Patrick similarly finds—is found by—Hadriana after years of bumbling searching. He similarly confronts his misguided desire to recover his beloved to the story of Jacmel and to his story of himself, and he similarly prepares to embark on a life of more perfect relation.

Patrick's epilogue is also a winking refusal to make his and Hadriana's story vulnerable to the coercions of the world outside their relationship. It announces a narcissistic retreat into the lovers' respective relating "I's." Depestre takes pains here to propose a more ethical way of loving—a way that pushes against what Anne Anlin Cheng describes as the "ineluctable complicity between love and consumption" (2009, 97). Cavarero is helpful to thinking this moment as well: "As many have noted, the language of lovers is anti-social," she writes, "because society . . . is perhaps the greatest impediment to the inborn [*in-nata*] self-revealing of uniqueness. Within the social scene there appears in fact only the *what* of the protagonists, never their *who*" (2000, 110). What Patrick asserts in the two sentences of this last chapter is a measure of protection for two individuals who, having escaped the tyranny of the "we," plan to enjoy—without exposing—the sharing "I/you" of their couple. Patrick does not push Hadriana back into the darkness for the sake of his love song of himself, nor does he indulge any prolonged story of love requited. His final words propose instead an oddly precise answer to Cavarero's call to imagine alternative narratives—a "different outcome"—in that what remains for the reader of Depestre's novel is an image of "the lovers, together once again, enraptured in the delight of a reciprocal tale" (Cavarero 2000, 110, 109).

Hadriana in All My Dreams ultimately traces a beautiful young girl's transformation from a community's *what*, trapped within a symbolic order that requires her death, to the self-narrating *who* of a love story. From her emplacement at the heart of carnival—a space that itself affords a limited but recurrent "critique [of] patriarchal heteronormativity"—to her resuscitation and rebirth through communion with the sea, to her reincarnation as a masculine water deity, Hadriana challenges the "dictates of gender and sexual norms" (Strongman 2008, 18, 19) by embracing a self-actualizing Vodou erotic. Depestre's investment in the erotic thus must not be seen merely as a flight into "a narcissistic space, outside time and history" (Munro 2007, 132). On the contrary, an incisive critique lies at the heart of *Hadriana*. If the novel reflects in some measure Depestre's disillusionment with collective political or social agendas, it is because such agendas too often imply the sacrifice of individual liberty in the name of arguably progressive community. Depestre asks that the reader consider whether a collective that imagines its fulfillment on the back of any one of its members can be considered truly progressive. Can it be considered an ethical body? As Celia Britton reminds us, the "attempt to convert an individual's death into an edifying meaning that reinforces the immanent community can be seen as one example of the role of myth-making in common being" (2011, 13). So, just as Hadriana's narration interrupts Patrick's desired fiction, Depestre's novel interrupts Roumain's founding communalist, national narrative.

A Eurydice who refuses to evaporate into the lofty silence of the eternal muse, Hadriana very plainly challenges a community whose coercive adoration threatens her freedom. Yet in abandoning this community, Hadriana does not exact any sort of revolutionary vengeance, nor does she inspire or prefigure collective action. Hers is a coming to self-consciousness, and a subsequent act of self-empowerment, in the face of a community that—across class and color lines—has betrayed her. The people of Jacmel created, then abandoned, the zombie in their midst. The town's gradual degradation and ultimate passage into a permanent state of neglect present an appropriate conclusion to this cautionary tale. In the end, Depestre takes this postcolonial community to task for its willingness to sacrifice—twice over—one of its own for the purposes of maintaining collective harmony.

Thus, while it may seem logical to assess Depestre's artistic trajectory as a lamentable devolution from engaged revolutionary poet to self-indulgent, apolitical narcissist, *Hadriana* might be better understood as Depestre's evolution toward the writing of a more fully realized female character. Distinct from the hypersexualized handmaiden Elisa Valéry, auxiliary to the heroic Marxist hero Henri Postel in *Le mât de cocagne*, and from the myriad muses and objects of desire that figure in Depestre's poetry and short-story collections, Hadriana Siloé is the crafty young virgin who crawls out of the volcano. No stand-in for Woman, Hadriana stands up for her Self. She is a specific being in relation.

Bridget Jones is absolutely right to stress "the vulnerability of a *machismo*, however revolutionary, to criticism from a feminist point of view" (1981, 21). The matter of how to deploy "Comrade Eros" once the undermining of the bourgeois order via sexual liberation has become cliché is complicated to negotiate. Given *Hadriana*'s movement from adolescent idealization to middle-aged nostalgia to feminine voice, is there a way we might read this novel as Depestre's self-reflexive call to grow up? Is it possible that whereas certain of the author's writings have shown "little strain in blending the pursuit of liberated love and the rhetoric of action" (B. Jones 1981, 27), the later *Hadriana* might reflect in fact a certain circumspection—a questioning of naive fantasies of transgression and transformation on or through the body of a woman? To claim *Hadriana* as a feminist text may be a bridge too far, but the novel's self-serving, pleasure-focused protagonist nevertheless presents a fine avatar of her community-wary creator. After all, to whatever degree readers accept a conflation of Depestre with his first-person narrator, must they not also read the authorial "I" into all the "I's" of *Hadriana*, including that of Hadriana herself?

Hadriana's eroticized nature marks a sustained belief in the subversive power of individual human sexuality that aligns, yes, with the philosophy of the revolution-seeking surrealists and with Depestre's own érotisme solaire. It also resonates with the "erotic impulse" (Dayan 1995, 128) that animates so many literary configurations of Haitian Vodou, and of Ezili in particular. The staging and parodying of these phenomena in *Hadriana* also underpin a broader humanist intervention, staking a bold claim to valorize "that which is female and self-affirming in the face of a racist, patriarchal, and anti-erotic society" (Lorde [1984] 2007, 59). In effect, the echo of a queer utopianism resonates throughout the novel. Hadriana/*Hadriana*'s literal and literary queerness leads us to José Muñoz's optimistic exhortation to "dream and enact new and better pleasures, other ways of being in the world, and ultimately new worlds" (2009, 1).

Hadriana comes to learn, the hard way, that her world is not enough—that her life in Jacmel was ultimately a lethal illusion. Being left for dead by her community is a revelation; it marks a dramatic "initial encounter with her own mortality" (Silverman 2009, 27) that brings an end to the "infantile narcissism" that lasted until her wedding day. Hadriana's experience of actual and social death allows her to embrace a mirror-searching, Fanonian, narcissistic self-possession. It inspires her to refuse the Jacmelian fairy tale wherein "her value is created by the patriarchy, whose discourse she becomes" (Froula 1983, 335).

While Hadriana's experience serves to point to and challenge conventions regarding race, class, gender, sexuality, and the so-called folk that pervade Haitian society, in particular, the narrative also makes a calculated move outside the specificity of the island. Depestre acknowledges the tragic fact of a world in which the "West is the norm, whiteness the standard" (Bellegarde-Smith 2006, 25). He writes explicitly of the origins and persistence of Francophilia in Haitian culture but embeds and critiques it in his narrative, refusing to silence Vodou and other complex Haitian social realities. If Haitians have long had to contend with the presumption that they do "not provide the world any of its definitions, not even those applied to Haiti" (Bellegarde-Smith 2006, 25), Depestre proposes Hadriana as a rebuttal. By placing a self-telling, white-Creole-French woman zombie at the center of this Haitian tale, Depestre articulates the zombie's vast metaphorical potential as a Haitian lens through which to reflect on matters of respectability and marginalization, individualism and community.

As noted at the beginning of this chapter, *Hadriana*'s critical reception and garnering of prizes and praise from a French reading public, along with the "absence of any residual postcolonial opposition to France" (Munro 2007, 126) in the novel, have been read as so much proof of Depestre's too-cozy exile in a North Atlantic space hungry for sexy tropical tales. I would argue, though, that Depestre's eroticism serves at once to caricature a bourgeois cult of feminine respectability and to provide heft to individualist affirmation in the face of repressive, if not overtly violent, community. *Hadriana in All My Dreams* is indeed deeply marked by the objectification of a woman. But an analysis of the novel must not end there: Patrick's and Jacmel's objectification of Hadriana is contested by Hadriana's self-objectification—the rendering of her/self as an object of narration. Insisting that the reader confront her multiple entombments, Hadriana refuses Patrick's love story until her own story becomes known. She takes the narrative power she has been granted by Depestre and writes—rights!—her story in history. Her escape from zombification and from Jacmel thus traces an instance of resistance to gendered self-sacrifice. Depestre's nonengagement with the classic postcolonial battles is not, then, an indication of apathy and self-indulgent storytelling. It is a provocative invitation to a richly layered conversation.

3

SELF-DEFENSE | Lotus

My mother repeated too frequently for me to forget: "I will never align myself with any group. I abhor all indoctrination and all dictatorship."
—Erma Saint-Grégoire, "Interview" (1992)

But women are not born free; women have no natural freedom.
—Carole Pateman, *The Sexual Contract* (2004)

In her 1981 study *Visages de femmes, portraits d'écrivains* (Faces of Women, Portraits of Writers), scholar Madeleine Gardiner opens her discussion of Haitian author Marie Chauvet (1916–73) with a question at once bewildered and indignant in tone. "Why this voluntary omission," asks Gardiner, "of a woman whose entire life has been a long quest for justice, liberty, and fraternity, which is ostensibly the dream of all our men of action—our poets, writers, and politicians?" (1981, 110-11). Why, indeed? Despite having produced a rich and varied body of work that grapples with issues central to social and political identity construction both in Haiti and in a more broadly postcolonial space, Chauvet has been decidedly marginalized with respect to the nation's pantheon of engaged writers—those "men of action" so widely celebrated for their commitment to radical politics in the years before and during the repressive regime of François "Papa Doc" Duvalier (1957–71).

Since the early 2000s, there has been growing critical interest in Chauvet's contributions to Haitian letters, and concerted investigation into the reasons for her relative silencing in the past. Women scholars and writers in particular have taken up the task of establishing Chauvet's place in the canon, offering sophisticated articulations of the challenges her writings present to Haiti's national narrative(s). As celebrated Haitian writer Yanick Lahens has insisted, "undisputably, Marie Chauvet opened the way for the modern novel in Haiti, even if, unfortunately, she has remained completely misunderstood in her own country" (1993, 85). Theorists like Kathleen M. Balutansky, Myriam J. A. Chancy, Colin Dayan, Régine Isabelle Joseph, Ronnie Scharfman, Marie-Denise Shelton, Elizabeth Walcott-Hackshaw, and Clarisse Zimra, among others, have highlighted the extent to which Chauvet's work pushes against the frames put in place by her male predecessors and contemporaries. Caribbeanists, too, from J. Michael Dash to Valerie Kaussen and Raphael Dalleo, have acknowledged Chauvet's resonance in the wider postcolonial Americas. Building on the work of these scholars, I examine Chauvet's radically subversive creative praxis in the context of her first published novel, *Fille d'Haïti* (Daughter of Haiti, 1954). While Chauvet's later works, especially the 1968 trilogy *Amour, colère et folie* (Love, Anger, Madness) and her work of historical fiction *La danse sur le volcan* (Dance on the Volcano, 1957), are increasingly studied and celebrated, far less attention has been paid to this first work of prose fiction. This has to do, I argue, with the ways in which the novel disappoints the constituency of readers seeking a politically radical text. As with scholarly perspectives on Depestre's post-Cuba writings, much academic appreciation of Chauvet's early work conveys its critique in the revealing language of insufficiency and betrayal.

I frame my reading of *Fille d'Haïti* within a collage of texts authored by Chauvet—specifically, interviews she granted in the Haitian press and a series of letters she wrote to Simone de Beauvoir in the months surrounding the publication of her trilogy. When one looks at these instances of Chauvet's self-expression, it becomes clear to what degree she not only subverts the gendered expectations of both the Duvalierian state and the Haitian bourgeois class but also proves difficult to incorporate into any liberatory extratextual narrative of "collective... revolutionary movement" (Kaussen 2008, 149) or even womanist solidarity. Tailoring at once Jessica Benjamin's and Amber Jamilla Musser's respective theorizations of bondage/discipline and sadism/masochism (BDSM) and Carole Pateman's analysis of the sexual contract to the sociopolitical context of midcentury Haiti, I argue that *Fille d'Haïti* presents an audacious critique of the paternalism and patriarchy that undergird the Haitian private and public spheres. I look at the novel's protagonist, moreover, as a veritable template for the psychologically and ideologically conflicted heroines featured in all of Chauvet's subsequent works.

In his 2009 study of Haitian radicalism, *Red and Black in Haiti: Radicalism, Conflict, and Political Change, 1934-1957*, historian Matthew J. Smith paints a rich portrait of the transformations of the Haitian state and nation following the 1915-34 American occupation and preceding the advent of Duvalier's suffocating authoritarian regime in 1957. Chronicling the rise and fall of the multiple intersecting radical groups that dominated the political landscape in these years, Smith presents an elegant chronicle of the ideological divisiveness, violence, and ultimate failure of radicalism in mid-twentieth-century Haiti, weaving together a complex narrative that evokes all the key players, the intrigue, and the betrayals—in short, the politics—that undid the best efforts of Haiti's postoccupation radical reformers. In telling this story, Smith has generated productive discussion among Haitianist scholars. All heartily agree that this neglected period in Haiti's history must be thoroughly accounted for to truly understand the political, social, and economic issues that have faced Haiti well into the present day.

While Smith's book references such prominent writer-intellectuals of the period as Roumain, Depestre, and Alexis, no mention is made of Chauvet. The writers Smith recognizes as "committed" are deemed so by virtue of their political activity.[1] Their literary contributions are celebrated, yes, but it is tangible political engagement that qualifies them as radical intellectuals: Roumain's founding of the Haitian Communist Party; Depestre's positioning at the vanguard of the 1946 student strikes that resulted in the ousting of despotic president Elie Lescot, as well as Depestre's later militancy in Cuba; and Alexis's involvement in multiple syndicalist movements and, ultimately, his torture, imprisonment, and murder on Duvalier's orders in 1961. In each instance the writer's radical credibility, so to speak, is linked explicitly to his performance of a decisive politics—a readiness to fight, quite literally, and even to die in the practice of his political beliefs.

On the one hand, Chauvet's work explicitly raises concerns similar to those of her male counterparts—"concerns over U.S. economic penetration, dictatorship, class issues" (M. J. Smith 2009, 6), among others. Her fiction perfectly illustrates many of Smith's claims regarding the nuances of political affiliation in midcentury Haiti, particularly as regards the ambivalent role played by color in relation to class. Unaffiliated, though, with any of the Marxist, syndicalist, and/or nationalist groups active during the period, and not writing for any of the radical journals in circulation, Chauvet remained firmly at a distance from organized politics. Although such issues as political freedom and social justice are at the very foundations of her writing practice, Chauvet was no political animal. As sociologist Carolle Charles has pointed out, "praise of Chauvet, which comes from many corners, is paradoxically not based on her own political engagement. Rather, her association with some form of radicalism is based on the revolutionary nature of her literary works" (2014, 66). It is perfectly reasonable, then, to omit her from the historical narrative of Haitian radicalism. Smith's parameters are clear: he is interested in tracing the political activities of ideologically based groups competing for state control—groups that were overwhelmingly male in leadership and constituency.

Given all of this, one might be tempted to imagine that it was Chauvet's gender that kept her from performing her politics in the manner of certain male writers of the period. Gender justice is one of the primary preoccupations manifest in Chauvet's fiction, and even the most progressive political platforms in Haiti—past and present—have tended to overlook the particular circumstances and needs of women and children. As Haitian writer, activist, and scholar Myriam J. A. Chancy has so eloquently affirmed, "nationalist agendas, focusing as they do on 'the people,' have, by and large, been gendered as male even as they espouse gender-neutral politics" (1997a, 39). In the Haitian context in particular, nationalist discourses of communal solidarity have been, historically, overwhelmingly androcentric, with women "embodying both the conflicts and the fragmentations experienced during the establishment of a national, masculinist identity that is willing to sacrifice women to its cause" (Lee-Keller 2009, 1296).

Yet the question of Chauvet's silence arises in the feminine political sphere as well. Chauvet is glaringly absent, for example, from the roster of the Ligue féminine d'action sociale (Women's League for Social Action) and never wrote for its literary-political journal *La voix des femmes* (The Voice of Women). The Ligue was a Haitian women's organization whose initiatives during the late 1930s and early 1940s resulted in beneficial legislation for Haiti's most marginalized. Their journal explicitly called on members of Haiti's bourgeois class, women in particular, to "become conscious of their responsibilities as citizens to the impoverished classes" (Chancy 1997a, 41) and drew attention to the disenfranchisement of women of every social stratum within the existing sociopolitical structure. Formed in 1934 and active until its transformation— its crippling, more accurately—into a charitable organization under Duvalier, the women of the Ligue campaigned fervently for access to higher education, children's rights, social assistance, increased literacy among both urban and rural populations, and women's citizenship rights, obtaining suffrage for women in 1957.

Of a kind with the bourgeois, intellectual leftist groups active during the period, the Ligue consisted primarily of elite women who, entirely conscious of their own privilege, sought to create a site of community unconstrained by color or class. A member of Port-au-Prince's bourgeoisie, daughter of a senator and ambassador, the privileged and accomplished Marie Vieux certainly fit the profile for the politicized upper-class feminine community the Ligue represented. She attended the Annexe de l'École Normale d'Institutrices (Annex of the Normal School for Teachers), an institution for the training of elementary-school educators, and received her teaching certificate in 1933 at the age of seventeen. After completing her studies, she married and had three children with her first husband, the successful doctor Aymon Charlier. She later divorced him and wed the travel agent and minister of tourism Pierre Chauvet, to whom she remained married until her exile to New York in 1968.

Throughout more than three decades spent in Haiti, Chauvet dedicated herself fully to writing—short plays to start and then several novels, making her the most prolific and most well-known woman writer in Haiti at the time. In addition to writing, Chauvet was *grande amie* (treasured friend) and hostess to a cohort of politically engaged, celebrated male poets known as the Haïti Littéraire (Literary Haiti) group, for whom she hosted a regular salon at her home in the affluent suburbs of Port-au-Prince.[2] She published her first three novels in rapid succession—*Fille d'Haïti* in 1954, *La danse sur le volcan* in 1957, and *Fonds des Nègres* (Negro Bottom) in 1960. Each of these early fiction works takes up issues of class, race, sexuality, and gender with daring incisiveness and is replete with thinly veiled allegorical references to the corruption and brutality of the Haitian state. Together they set the stage for the explosive *Amour, colère et folie*, an unequivocal denunciation of totalitarian state violence and of its particular impact on women—the last of her works to be published in Haiti and the last in her lifetime.[3]

Considering Chauvet's politically grounded attentiveness in her prose fiction to the neglect and victimization of women, it is curious that she claimed no affiliation with the Ligue, the most visible and recognizable channel for women's activism in her day. Her predecessors and contemporaries, among them the writers Marie-Thérèse Colimon, Annie Desroy, and Cléante Desgraves Valcin, actively linked their creative endeavors to political activism, but Chauvet developed her writing practice from a position of relative remove.

Literary historian Jasmine Claude-Narcisse notes Chauvet's refusal as a young woman fresh out of teacher's college to follow the traditional path expected of a woman of her social position and with her education—"the 'rite of passage,'" that is, that would have her performing charitable works for those less fortunate than she. "Much later," Claude-Narcisse explains, "the charming and lovely young woman she was to become would not count herself among the militants for women's causes, nor would she join any of the bitter political struggles that so dominated contemporary events" (Claude-Narcisse [1997] 2002). Chauvet makes her position clear in a 1953 interview with the Ligue Féminine d'Action Sociale Committee, published in the Haitian daily paper *Le nouvelliste*, following her naming as First Laureate of the Alliance Française. Having welcomed the women of the Ligue into her home, Chauvet is perfectly gracious during the conversation—"simply welcoming and charming in her mid-afternoon dress, rose-colored and embroidered in white" ("Marie Chauvet" 1953, 1). She is also resolute in her claims to political independence:

> —What do you think of feminism?
>
> —Only good things. That said, although I profoundly admire the Ligue Féminine d'Action Sociale, I really do not see myself participating in the feminist movement. Given how much social injustice truly disgusts me, you could say perhaps that at my core I am a fanatically revolution-minded feminist. Nevertheless, I prefer to remain independent and not to belong to any group. ("Marie Chauvet" 1953, 1)

Claude-Narcisse describes Chauvet's rejection of feminist political community as the expression of her "phobia regarding any form of association, which, to her mind, could only lead to an execrable enlistment" ([1997] 2002). To this I would add that Chauvet was arguably more radically minded than the reformist Ligue, as evidenced by the fearless condemnations of social injustice and foregrounding of individual liberationist action—as opposed to collective political efforts—that mark every one of her novels. The world Chauvet presents in her fiction is generally too far gone to be legislated into decency.

Chauvet's resolute nonalliance was not, then, a function of an irrational or disproportionate fear, as the term *phobia* might suggest, but of a reasoned perspective on the state of community—at least of the communities on offer—in the years following the American occupation. Inasmuch as political activism depends on some measure of politically motivated group identification, organization, and advocacy, Chauvet's isolation is meaningful. Her reticence to join any organized struggle was, at least in part, an expression of her profound wariness with respect to community in Haiti. This self-positioning independent of political identity has made her a real challenge to situate within Haiti's radical tradition, though her literary works propose a radical critique of the sides-taking and politicking that overdetermined the atmosphere in which she lived and wrote. That she is marginal with respect to the narrative of Haitian radicalism and without a definitive presence in Haitian feminist circles necessarily raises questions about the possibilities for political engagement available to women in Haiti.

Chauvet's writing life in Haiti was bookended by periods of particularly intense social tension between color- and class-based communities. It was also marked by heightened militarism in the political arena. From Dumarsais Estimé's election to the presidency in 1946, "when the electoral battle clearly took on the aspect of a color struggle" (M.-R. Trouillot 1994, 162) and when Chauvet's first play, *La légende des fleurs* (The Tale of the Flowers), was published, to Duvalier's election in 1957, Haitian politics was continually derailed by anxieties around ontological and ideological blackness. According to Haitian sociologist Michel-Rolph Trouillot, "extraordinary resentment among urban noirs, particularly those of the middle classes reached its height in 1946" (1994, 160). Not since Jean-Jacques Dessalines's 1804 declaration of Haiti's status as a Black nation had racial identity been so purposefully conflated with political identity. A century and a half later, polarizing constructions of racial community were having devastating material consequences for Haitians of all colors.

The expediency of racial categories belied the complexities of broadly disenfranchising political agendas. In reality, several would-be heads of state, be they "Black" or "mulatto,"[4] sought to consolidate political power in the hands of an elite at the expense of the majority, giving the lie to any strictly color-based class distinction.[5] Chauvet would have seen clearly and felt keenly, then, the corruptibility and dead-endedness of organized politics.[6] She would have witnessed the manipulation of the Haitian people by unscrupulous and charismatic political power-mongers and observed firsthand how certain of Haiti's post–American occupation leaders promulgated racial hierarchization and discord rather than attending to the needs of the nation's most disenfranchised.

These phenomena took on mythical proportions during Duvalier's regime (1957–71). The cynicism of racialized political divisiveness was the very foundation of a political platform wherein appeals to rural and urban underclass populations vilified mulattoes as responsible for the perpetual subjugation of Blacks. Perverting the Afrocentric, pro-peasantry cultural agenda of Indigenist ideology, Duvalier combined racial mystification and authoritarianism to produce his discourse of *noirisme*.⁷ This doctrine of essentialist Black power valorized Haiti's African roots exclusively and posited absolute racial purity as the foundation for a national identity. Duvalier even went so far as to declare Haiti's mulatto citizens enemies of the state, thereby concretizing the racial and class enmity that had marked the republic since its beginnings (see M.-R. Trouillot 1994, 146–74). Manipulating and exacerbating the striking, largely race-based social schism between the island's population of light-skinned haves and the masses of dark-skinned have-nots, Duvalier's noirisme emerged as a pointed response to the historical injustice perpetrated by Haiti's minority urban mulatto elite on the rural and proletarian Blacks who comprise the bulk of the population. With the acute suffering and disenfranchisement of the poor rendered all the more stark by the bourgeoisie's enjoyment of seemingly unlimited privilege in Haiti, the populist Duvalier had little difficulty rallying support for his ostensibly pro-Black politics.⁸

The racism and corruption that informed the Duvalierian state very much mirrored, then, the discriminatory practices that had long been in place in Haiti, and Duvalier's color-based fracturing of the nation quickly revealed itself as yet another iteration of the scenario whereby wealthy urban insiders exploited the largely impoverished *moun andeyò*.⁹ Moreover, Duvalier's discourse of divisive community and racial hierarchy was subtended by a climate of absolute terror. The state's arbitrary violence created a crisis of national dysfunction that suffocated political and creative expression in Haiti for nearly thirty years. The Duvalier regime relied on an all-encompassing brutality—a dramatic expansion of the parameters of victimization. Targeting religious groups and sports clubs, schoolteachers and priests, Duvalier's personal police force, the *tonton-macoutes*, operated without logic or sanction: "What the Duvalier regime created and promoted in its culture of terror was an arbitrariness that prevented any social group from feeling that it would be excluded" (Walcott-Hackshaw 2005, 43).¹⁰ State violence permeated every level of society, and the nation's writers and artists who chose—dared—to remain and create in Haiti during this period were harassed, censored, and even killed. Absolutely no one was exempt from persecution by the state, including women and children, and rape was commonly employed against the wives and daughters of Duvalier's political enemies.¹¹

Duvalier implicated women in national politics in accordance with a very specific model of femininity, constructing women "not only as mothers of the nation but also as important political actors" (Fouron and Schiller 2001, 147). He appointed, for example, a woman as warden of the infamous detention center and torture facility Fort Dimanche and, later, to the position of national commander of the macoutes. He also created an all-female unit of the macoutes named after the legendary rebellious slave woman Marie-Jeanne. In every way, "the Duvalierist state focused on a 'patriotic woman' whose allegiance was first to Duvalier. Any who did not adhere to these policies became an enemy subject to political repression" (Charles 1995, 139). This coercive "state feminism" perverted any preexisting women's movements to fit its aims, such that women's activist organizations were entirely co-opted for the agenda of national liberation.[12] However, "while Duvalier reenvisioned women as political agents, the nationalism he promoted did not challenge the upper-class ideal that the respectability of a family is judged by the behavior of its women" (Fouron and Schiller 2001, 147).

As a bourgeoise, a mulatto, a woman, and a writer, Chauvet found herself at the very center of the sociopolitical storm that was Duvalier's Haiti. The danger inherent in such an identity under Duvalier was dramatically made plain for Chauvet in 1968. In this year, over the course of six months, Chauvet wrote *Amour, colère et folie*. She submitted the manuscript to celebrated French feminist intellectual and writer Simone de Beauvoir, and the latter's endorsement led to the novel's acceptance by the prestigious Parisian publishing house Les Éditions Gallimard. While Chauvet's previous works had won regional prizes, and while she already enjoyed a certain celebrity in Haitian literary circles, Gallimard's publication of her trilogy would have all but guaranteed her immediate international celebrity and definitively inserted her into both Haitian and extra-insular literary canons. Would have. Instead, Chauvet's success was thwarted by Haiti's political reality in the late 1960s—a reality wherein a sociopathic state "Papa" presided over a dysfunctional national family.

Given the pervasive repression and violence directed largely at Haiti's putatively former elite during this period, Chauvet's husband convinced her that allowing the novel's distribution would put her family in grave danger. His fears were by no means unwarranted. Chauvet's father had been exiled for his political activity, and two of his brothers arrested in his place; one of Chauvet's nephews had been arrested and disappeared in 1968, and two others had been murdered. Pierre Chauvet thus enjoined his wife to purchase Gallimard's entire stock of *Amour, colère et folie* upon its release and to prohibit further printings, which, in a dramatic act of self-censorship, she did. The family subsequently destroyed all copies of the trilogy and for decades refused to allow its republication. While a scant number of clandestine copies remained in circulation, the novel was officially rereleased, by a different publishing house, only in 2005.[13] In the wake of this demoralizing experience and still faced with the very real danger of reprisals from the Duvalierian state, Chauvet divorced her husband—once again leaving a marriage "at a time when women of a certain milieu did not divorce" (Saint-Grégoire 1992, 464)—and went into exile in New York City, where she was married a third time, to a white American named Ted Proudfoot. Between 1971 and 1973, she wrote her fifth and final novel, *Les rapaces* (Birds of Prey), before succumbing to a brain tumor. *Les rapaces* was published posthumously in 1986.

This book has to sell, to help me survive, to hold on!
—Marie Chauvet, letter to Simone de Beauvoir (1968)

Chauvet's exile—both from the geographic space of Haiti in the last years of her life and, for nearly half a century, from the discursive space of the Haitian literary and intellectual canon—must be understood as a consequence of her disorderly being and behavior with respect to two distinct, though interrelated, Haitian communities: Duvalier's monstrous national "family" and the bourgeoisie of which her actual family was a part. To write for Chauvet was to write (in her comfortable house, in her fancy suburb) in opposition at once to a brutalizing, authoritarian government and to models of elite female subjecthood in Haiti. The initial request by Chauvet's husband and the subsequent disappearing of *Amour, colère et folie* by her family were motivated not only by fear of Duvalier's violence but also by profound discomfort with Chauvet's disparagement of the Haitian bourgeois class. In effect, the "suppression of the trilogy exemplifies the institutionalized marginalization and silencing faced by women in a male-dominated literary tradition" (Kaussen 2008, 50). Chauvet's accounts of color anxiety and racism, of sexual perversion and abuse, are as condemning of Duvalier's government as they are of the alienation, greed, and cynicism of the Haitian bourgeoisie. Feminist scholar Clarisse Zimra rightly argues, "Had [Chauvet] not been a woman who dared write out of our deepest desires, that is, in an 'unladylike' manner, one might wonder whether Chauvet's relatives would have dared suppress her last book with such single-minded determination. They behaved not only as embarrassed blood-kin but, as well, as members of a complacent class under attack in her novels. One might also wonder whether her contemporaries would have dismissed her as a minor writer, as did Pradel Pompilus, for example" (1993, 77).

The disorder Chauvet produced with respect to the Duvalierian state and the elite Haitian nation—the disorder she very much meant to produce—is poignantly legible in an as yet little-theorized corpus: the letters she wrote to

Simone de Beauvoir between 1967 and 1973.[14] Written during the period surrounding the publication and silencing of *Amour, colère et folie*, this rich and intimate correspondence amounts, in and of itself, to an extraordinary literary project. The letters convey Chauvet's sense of her role and responsibility as a writer in a context of political terror in the public sphere, and they lay out the concerns and limitations that marked her domestic existence as a wife, a mother, and a woman in Haiti's bourgeois elite.[15] At the heart of this epistolary undertaking is an articulation of the ethical, political, and logistical parameters of her individual freedom.

A persistent critique is embedded in Chauvet's communications with de Beauvoir. This critique hinges on a valorization of the individual writing self and a condemnation of the domestic and political impediments to the liberation of that self. The letters reveal Chauvet's understanding of the ways in which the private and public spheres align to produce the conditions of constraint under which the Haitian nation and the individuals who comprise it must exist. And while Chauvet identifies Duvalier as Haiti's most obvious and categorical monster, embodiment of the "hideous dictatorial regime" against which she is determined to "scream the truth" (April 16, 1967), she also identifies other, personal-and/as-political adversaries she means to fight as a writer and in her writing.[16] The great majority of her letters aim to impress upon de Beauvoir, whom she positions as both benefactress and confidante, that the publication of *Amour, colère et folie* will be transformative for her, as an individual being at once physically, socially, and professionally inhibited by her status as a wife: "If you only knew everything this publication will mean for me! An end to this life of routine and resignation, escape to a foreign country, *independence* through work. You can see that this is not about vanity for me. To obtain an exit visa, one first needs marital authorization and then, after that, official authorization" (December 23, 1967; emphasis mine). In this early letter, Chauvet makes three elements of her situation very clear: first, she is suffocated and constrained by her existence in Haiti; second, she intends to write her way out of these constraints; and third, these constraints are at once domestic and political in nature—that is, the patriarchal controls of marriage and the state operate in tandem to inhibit her freedom. Chauvet goes on, in a follow-up letter written just a short time later, to provide de Beauvoir with a further glimpse of what the marriage contract looks like in Haiti:

> I am so worried that I won't have enough money to travel to Paris. I was, in fact, counting on an advance from Gallimard to make this possible. My

husband could help me, but I don't want that. We are not on very good terms and I have been living off of him for 20 years. My pride rejects the idea of being in debt to him for the publication of these books, too. I do not mean to be ungrateful. Thanks to him I have had material security. But I impatiently await the moment when I can live by myself and achieve my *independence* through the only thing I truly love: writing. (January 5, 1968; emphasis mine)

Over the next several months, Chauvet continues to expresses similar sentiments.[17] Then, as publication of her manuscript becomes imminent and she has received a contract and a small advance from Gallimard, her letters to de Beauvoir change somewhat in tenor. She describes in detail, and anguishes over, the risks that publishing her book represents for her and her loved ones—"'they will kill every single person I count as family" (July 6, 1968). Yet, at the same time as she depicts the corruption and violence of the Haitian state, she also points to the more localized authority with which she must contend: "My husband, a charming man, is transforming with age into a veritable slot machine. Duvalierism has this disconcerting side effect—it transforms the best men into atrocious maniacs. I've made the decision to publish my books. It goes without saying that my husband is against this publication" (August 22, 1968). Writing at one point from New York, where her children already reside or soon will and where she has more or less gone into exile in anticipation of the trilogy's release, Chauvet explains at length her disappointing negotiations with Gallimard and muses on the ways in which her perceived class status and her gender have placed her at a real disadvantage in dealing with the press:

I am truly humiliated by Gallimard's refusal to assist me. I am no businesswoman and was not at all sure of what the advance should be when I signed the contract. Perhaps Claude Gallimard realized this right away. Perhaps he did not believe me when I wrote to tell him how cornered I am. He saw me in Paris with an impressive diamond on my finger. Alas! All that means nothing. My husband is a big travel agent. He insists that his wife do him justice and dresses me accordingly—and the ring is his mother's and he put it on my finger the day of our marriage. That is all. *He made a deal with me*: either I stay quietly at home and give up on publishing books that could turn the Haitian government against him and me, or I settle somewhere out of the country without his help. He made good on that threat when he learned of my decision. (September 4, 1968; emphasis mine)

Important in this letter is the semantic slide Chauvet puts into operation. Her phrase "He made a deal with me" bridges two distinct contexts—one past and the other present, one private and the other public. To what deal is she referring? To the contract by which she bound herself in matrimony to a man who would thenceforth impose himself as her political surrogate? Or to the deal this man, her husband, had offered her in exchange for giving up Gallimard's contract: publish, and you're on your own financially and socially; don't publish, and I'll continue to "protect" you (as per our marriage contract)? Chauvet keeps her intended context deliberately ambiguous, deliberately capacious. She establishes both of these events as existing on a continuum that consistently renders her the less powerful party in a series of exploitative and coercive contracts.

The letters tell us that, just a few months later, Chauvet had been pressured into intervening with Gallimard, imploring the press to retire the trilogy from circulation. We learn that her husband had in fact gone to Paris, planning to speak both to Gallimard and to de Beauvoir herself, prospects Chauvet found "humiliating." As a result of his intervention, there would be no reedition. Practically all copies of the book remaining unsold he eventually bought and destroyed. Gallimard abandoned her, undoubtedly frustrated by her "drama" and its impact on book sales. Fully disillusioned but not yet resigned, Chauvet is unsparing in her outrage:

> If I have taken roundabout ways to scream the truth, I had hoped at least to awaken the conscience of my compatriots and to make them truly feel their cowardice and their concupiscence. Four million terrorized, four million unclean. That is what we have become. All our values have been destroyed by 11 years of tyranny. I have lived enough to witness the transformation of the honest man my husband once was. Long live money! Let's kill one another but make as much as possible! That is our motto these days. He has worked very hard, it is true; he never stole, never killed, never made any official deals with the government, but he is also guilty of boasting our country's charms, of swearing that everything is going just fine, although so many have been murdered, beaten, tortured, imprisoned. A wide trench now separates me from him, and I am considering divorce very seriously. (November 16, 1968)

These are, of course, much more than the words of a woman complaining about her unhappy marriage. Here, as throughout the corpus of Chauvet's letters to de Beauvoir, Chauvet reveals herself as a social theorist acutely aware of the extent to which the Duvalierian state relies on the complicity of elite members of the nation, those who "continue to cover their eyes, mouth, and ears so as to live peacefully in a state of terror" (November 16, 1968). Over the first two years of her correspondence with the French feminist de Beauvoir, it becomes increasingly clear that the other "monstrous" figure that determines the boundaries of Chauvet's being in society is her husband—her husband as a stand-in for the whole of the patriarchal social and political context of her oppression—the "bathtub of resignation and humiliations" (January 29, 1968) in which she feels she has been drowning. If she has remained steadfast in her commitment to "denounce everything that's been going on here for the past 11 years" (November 16, 1968), just as urgent throughout the letters is her condemnation of Haitian society more broadly. This fundamental critique is, of course, at the foundations of Chauvet's entire prose fiction corpus, beginning with *Fille d'Haïti*.

> *What can it mean—the existence in a healthy society of a woman without faith? A woman who lives alone in her house, plagued by boredom, obeying only the perversity and hollowness of her own instincts? A woman who has never truly been anything clear-cut—at once a quasi-virgin adrift in the brothels of Carrefour, a half-hearted revolutionary, a cheating lover, a patroness of some sort performing charitable acts behind only the thinnest veneer of respectability. . . . All to say, Marie Chauvet has not yet managed to express her own truth. . . . Marie Chauvet seems, up till now, to be torn between two extreme visions that she attempts to reconcile through her equivocal creatures. Marie Chauvet should pick a side, dare to portray coherent characters—characters she can observe from the inside and then present in a less diffuse, more stable universe. Marie Chauvet must try to simplify her vision, to use her not insignificant talents to choose between the opposing natures she grants her characters.*
>
> —Ghislain Gouraige, *Histoire de la littérature haïtienne* (1982)

Haitian literary scholar Ghislain Gouraige made the preceding remarks in 1960 concerning Chauvet's first published work of prose fiction, the 1954 novel *Fille d'Haïti*. I have quoted from his commentary at length because, leaving aside its paternalistic tone, Gouraige's remarks—among the very rare critical analyses of the novel—reveal much about the expectations surrounding literary production in mid-twentieth-century Haiti and touch on the elements of Chauvet's prose fiction writing that in fact define her bold contributions to Haitian letters. What Gouraige undoubtedly meant to be constructive criticisms of Chauvet's nascent prose-writing praxis essentially articulate the stakes of her ambitious intention in this early novel and lay out the questions that animate the whole of her literary project. That his criticisms are echoed in more recent scholarly approaches to Chauvet's work attests to the coherence of this project and of its disordering impact.

Chauvet did not end up following this critic's advice. She did not ever "simplify her vision," nor did she make any attempt to provide less "equivocal" or more "clear-cut" characters. On the contrary, the complexity and instability that mark *Fille d'Haïti* are at the heart of Chauvet's entire oeuvre. Writing in a historical moment when polarization was the order of the day, Chauvet never stopped refusing the binaries embedded in social constructions of race, class, gender, and other totalizing systems. She never committed to "picking a side." This being said, there are many ways in which Chauvet might be said to adhere to the literary script of her time. From this first novel through to her very last, all of her narratives are at once anchored in and pointedly distinct from the modernist tradition of twentieth-century Haitian letters: they are realist, they are set in Haiti, they criticize political life, and they vividly describe society and its mores. Nevertheless, the intensity with which her works foreground "the interaction between the psyche and social life" (Benjamin 1988, 5) marks them as radically different from this tradition.

Chauvet engages head-on with the multiply contested belonging of women in patriarchal community and does so in full knowledge of the kind and degree of intervention she has made:

> One day I received a magnificent letter from a certain prominent literary critic in which he told me that I was a born novelist. . . . However certain of the scenes with Lotus had terrified him. He didn't deny it. I happily made the formal revisions he suggested, but I kept my complete independence with respect to my ideas. . . . In the end, everything that comes out of my books is absolutely personal to me. Independent, I rarely let myself be influenced, and the only corrections I accept have to do with stylistics. ("Marie Chauvet" 1953, 6)

As with the protagonists in all of her writings that follow, *Fille d'Haïti*'s protagonist, the beautiful and headstrong Lotus Delgrave, is difficult to place in any stable identity category. The orphaned "illegitimate" daughter of a wealthy mulatto prostitute and a French naval officer, Lotus exists entirely on the margins of society, alone aside from the company of a maid who despises her. The gated mansion in which she lives, the fruit of her mother's labors, is set physically apart from the dilapidated shanties on the other side of its walls, and the young woman's relatively comfortable existence behind its gates contrasts starkly with the desperate poverty of her neighbors.

Lotus is at once implicated in and marginal to the social and political communities vying for power in postoccupation Haiti. As a fair-skinned woman of some means, she meets certain of the phenotypic and economic criteria required for belonging in the local bourgeoisie. Her less-than-respectable lineage, however, precludes her acceptance by the Haitian elite. Ostracized by both the mulatto and the Black communities, the materially advantaged and disadvantaged, she is an uncomfortable misfit with regard to the normative—and polarized—identity categories that determine social existence in mid-twentieth-century Haiti, and her every social exchange foregrounds this issue of her nonbelonging.[18]

A woman whose "opposing natures" never entirely resolve into a coherent, recognizably correct political stance—at least not equivocally so—her positioning at the heart of the narrative has made *Fille d'Haïti* vulnerable both to criticism and, perhaps more perniciously, to critical dismissal. Just as contemporaries like Gouraige have scorned the novel as "a testament to the imprecision of [Chauvet's] as yet unformed talent" (1982, 447), later critics also tend to relegate *Fille d'Haïti* to the status of a less-than-successful first novelistic effort. Colin Dayan, one of Chauvet's most astute and insightful readers, asserts that, unlike in her crafting of the heroines of her later fiction, "when Chauvet wrote *Fille d'Haïti*, her mulatto heroine Lotus carried on the tradition of women standing by their men that had already been established by Roumain and Alexis" (1994, 23). Clarisse Zimra similarly casts the author's debut novel as the relatively toothless precursor to the more powerful works of her later corpus. Zimra characterizes *Fille d'Haïti* as "Chauvet's own romp through the negrophobic narrative convention, that self-indulgent side of the mulatto convention usually dealing with a (barely) colored woman too beautiful and too intelligent to be content with her inferior station." Zimra concludes that Chauvet must have been "trying her hand at all the conventional plots before trusting to her own instincts" (1990, 145).

On the whole, *Fille d'Haïti* has been relatively neglected, remaining in the shadow of the famously resurrected, now much-celebrated and analyzed *Amour, colère et folie*.[19] The exception to this long-standing critical indifference has been Valerie Kaussen's analysis in *Migrant Revolutions: Haitian Literature, Globalization, and U.S. Imperialism*. Kaussen places *Fille d'Haïti* within a wider, masculine tradition of politically informed Haitian fiction. She describes the novel as a "rewriting of engaged early indigenist fiction" and characterizes Lotus as a "modernist intellectual who resembles the troubled soul-searching young men" (2008, 148) that people works by Roumain and other midcentury Haitian novelists. Kaussen is perfectly right to evoke this particular literary lineage in reading *Fille d'Haïti*. However, Chauvet's Lotus does not replace the male hero of the Indigenist novel—she exists alongside him and is rendered incisive in her difference. Lotus is the prism through which the reader is afforded glimpses into the limitations of the male revolutionary hero and of his political project.

I want to pick up where Kaussen left off and take seriously *Fille d'Haïti* as a work of substantive social critique—a critique Chauvet engages in her sophisticated grapplings with the physical and social in-between. Whereas Kaussen positions the novel as a more or less straightforward account of its heroine's transformation into "a tireless defender of the masses . . . and an enemy of the system that oppresses them" (2008, 148), I insist on the ambivalence of Lotus's political self and leave room for the tongue-in-cheek dimensions of Chauvet's intervention. I also pay close attention to Chauvet's provocative exploration of the connections of power, politics, and the erotic. Chauvet's narrative plays at the edges of the model established by the explicitly social realist novels of canonical male writers like Roumain, Alexis, Edris Saint-Amand, and others—a model wherein the happy ending consistently appears, even in tragedy, via the political awakening of a transcendent peasant or proletarian Black male hero and/or the consolidation of a politically enlightened community. Chauvet's tale borrows from but pokes at this narrative frame. If Gouraige and other of Chauvet's contemporary critics were troubled by or disappointed in the novel, and if more recent scholars have tended to dismiss it, this critical fate has to do primarily with the illegibility, if not to say the perversity, of its heroine.

Might as well admit it straightaway, it is not without a certain pleasure that I evoke these memories and try to bring back to life that strange little girl, who was me.
—Lotus Delgrave (in *Fille de'Haïti*)

The more O submits, the more recognition she gains.
—Amber Jamilla Musser, "BDSM and the Boundaries of Criticism" (2015)

"My name is Lotus." These are the first words of *Fille d'Haïti*, and they make up the whole of the novel's opening paragraph. Spoken by the self-narrating central character, the Haitian daughter of the title, they hint at the solipsistic frame within which the entirety of the narrative unfolds. *Fille d'Haïti* is presented as a memoir and, as such, is necessarily egotistical in its self-telling—singularly focused on an individual being who has made an implicit claim to her own narrative worthiness and who is hyperaware of the reader's presence. All events, thoughts, emotions, and deeds are filtered through the lens of hindsight by this narrator-protagonist and have been arranged so as to tell a particular story in a particular way. There is, then, at the very foundations of the telling, the explicit fact of intent. What, the reader must ask, has this narrator-protagonist decided to let us know—about her story and about the world in which it is embedded? What does she believe is remarkable enough to merit telling?

In this respect alone, the novel presents a disordering counter to the contemporary Haitian literary canon—a canon wherein women most often stand in the shadow of a singular male hero. The female characters of Haitian novels of the 1940s and 1950s, especially, are largely without interiority, relegated to a romanticized supporting role. They are caught up in their social and political context and subject to events that occur all around them, but their individual experiences are subsumed within those of the collective.[20] As scholar Anne Marty has written, "the subjection of the narrator to the 'we' hindered the appearance of an original feminine consciousness" in Haitian letters. Chauvet, she argues, was the "first author to have explored a relatively autonomous 'I' with respect to a 'we'" (2000, 98, 111). Similarly, Chauvet's contemporary Frankétienne affirms that Chauvet was "the first Haitian writer to have used the technique of interior monologue in a novel" (2016, 83).

Both Marty and Frankétienne made these claims in reference to Chauvet's trilogy. This is consistent with the general tendency to overlook *Fille d'Haïti*, the work that, as discussed here, most legitimately lays claim to being "the first Haitian novel to show evidence of having taken the psychoanalytic into consideration" (Marty 2000, 126). The story of Lotus Delgrave presents an in-depth exploration of the psyche of an individual character suffering from what Marie-Denise Shelton calls a "sociogenic" illness, "rooted in the island's class/color hierarchy" (1990, 350). Lotus's internal disorder—the tension between her conscious and unconscious thoughts and feelings, between her individual desires and the expectations and constraints of her community—is the explicit result of a precise constellation of social-cum-familial trauma, a trauma Chauvet presents as markedly gendered. In this respect, *Fille d'Haïti* reflects the broader midcentury interest in psychoanalysis as a tool for understanding women's role in patriarchal society, a notable dimension of Simone de Beauvoir's work (see Tidd 2002, 359–69). Lotus is the psychological product of a father she never knew and an at-first distant and withholding, then absent (because dead) and haunting, mother figure. Moreover, she is heir to her mother's traumatic experiences of sexual exploitation and consequent mental disorder. Profoundly lonely and consumed by painful memories of her unhappy childhood, Lotus falls prey to her subconscious, besieged by the words, phrases, and images she is compelled to trace on the walls of her bedroom: "I would like to be a painter so as to create the image of a woman—eyes empty, hands dangling, and one foot suspended above an abyss. Her face would be stupid, so very stupid, and I would call that image: Life" ([1954] 2014, 46). She dismisses these uncanny musings as so much psychic detritus issuing from her "futile woman's little brain" (45). Nevertheless, the resonance of these mental ephemera is certain.

Lotus is especially tormented by the uncomfortable "dialogue of her heritage"—the "intimate little duel" (44) between her Black and her white ancestry, constitutive elements of her identity that she refuses to deny. Her phenotypical ambivalence, along with the fact that her mother has left her enough resources to survive without having to work, places her in a far better material condition than the impoverished slum dwellers who live just outside her gated villa. Given this privilege, Lotus's Black servants and neighbors fundamentally distrust her, associating her with a corrupt ruling class that has long kept them in their wretched circumstances.

The local bourgeois community proves equally hostile toward Lotus, whose lineage they disdain. The parents of her closest girlfriends presume her essential disrepute and thus bar their daughters from being in her company. Although Lotus makes every effort to belong, excelling in school and hosting lavish parties for her bourgeois classmates, she is never invited into her friends' respectable homes in return, and she eventually concludes that her many houseguests amount to little more than "a bunch of sluts and their men who, no sooner than out of my house, [see] fit to thank me by directing the very worst insults my way" (49–50).

From the very first pages of her story, Lotus lays out the basic elements of a fraught social identity that "cannot be understood outside of Haiti's repressive social and political institutions" (Shelton 1990, 353). The events of the novel mirror those of the period preceding the 1946 overthrow of elite mulatto dictator Elie Lescot by a tenuously (and temporarily) linked cabal of populist leaders, *noiristes* or *authentiques*, Marxists, and bourgeois students and the subsequent accession to power of nationalist Black president Dumarsais Estimé, Haiti's leader until 1950. The novel looks back to the final months of Lescot's repressive regime and the rise of colorist conflict that followed his removal from power.[21] Set against the backdrop of this moment of potential in Haiti's history, a period Matthew J. Smith characterizes as "Haiti's greatest moment of political promise" (2009, 2), *Fille d'Haïti* also anticipates Duvalier's ascension to power as the self-proclaimed legitimate heir to Estimé.[22] The novel evinces the specific mechanisms and mistakes inherent in the divisive politics of 1940s and 1950s Haiti and affirms the inevitable failure of a "Black republic" that has never come to agree on what *Black* actually means.

Alienated from both of the castes that make up her local social world, Lotus is utterly without an interlocutor. This physical and social isolation leaves her trapped in her own head, vulnerable to paranoia and misjudgment, and given to sudden, unpredictable expressions of a damaged psyche. She is, Gouraige is correct, "equivocal," both internally and in many of her relationships with those around her. She is, moreover, at once agent and victim of communal power structures, occupying "simultaneously the positions of mastery and subjection" (Garraway 2013, 205).[23] Inasmuch as Lotus suffers the violence and loneliness of her existence in society, she is also indifferent to and at times even responsible for the suffering of others. She periodically lashes out in uncontrollable rages, for example, berating her maid, Gertrude, for the slightest perceived offense. Envious that her servant, though Black and poor, can claim to be "useful for something" (41), Lotus leans into her own economic and color-based privilege: "Standing looking at this face, in all its silent impertinence, I felt my rage increase ten-fold. . . . I kept on making a scene, throwing any and everything within reach at her, purposely fixing my eyes on her bare feet and her ash- and mud-stained dress—just to humiliate her" (75–76).

Inevitably, following these instances of senseless misbehavior, Lotus is consumed with guilt. This then compels her to tolerate Gertrude's shows of disrespect, convincing herself that she deserves and even needs her maid's contempt: "Perhaps things had to be this way; after all, her hatred was as good a way as any of helping me see clearly who I really was. . . . I came to understand that the suffering her presence caused me was indispensable to my development" (91). This pattern of alternating abuse explicitly prefigures the sadomasochism that undergirds so many of the relationships in which the heroines of Chauvet's later novels are embroiled, relationships in which "there is a constant interplay between the two postures of domination and submission, pleasure and pain, and in which each position has the potential to change into its opposite" (Garraway 2013, 210).

Lotus's relationship with this servant woman, who lives in her home and is at her disposal yet by whom she feels constantly ridiculed and judged, has an unmistakably sadomasochistic cast. The dynamic of dominance and submission at play in this domestic realm carries over into Lotus's other interactions. This is nowhere more evident than in the peculiar erotic relations she indulges in with men of the local elite. In the absence of familial love, Lotus seeks some measure of empowerment by playing games of seduction and refusal with young men whom she loathes but who represent the social security to which she aspires. "I just loved that air of perfumed luxury they carried with them," she explains, "exciting in me, as it did, an attraction that showed how different they were from me, as far as society was concerned. Their company flattered me and I was somehow proud to offer them my kisses" (57). Reenacting with a twist the cynicism of her mother's profession, Lotus invites these anonymous young men into her bedroom for amorous romps but always stops short of the act of penetration, enjoying a few kisses and caresses before callously dismissing her frustrated would-be lovers: "From one dandy to the next, I reached my twentieth year without a single one of those little losers being able to flatter himself at having made me lose my head" (22).

This behavior earns Lotus a reputation for being at once promiscuous and a tease, trapped within the "obscure and improbable life of a virgin whore" (Shelton 1990, 350). It also results in her near-rape on two separate occasions. She describes her very first paramour as having for his "sole virtue" the fact of "having been intelligent enough to not make me have to chase him away that one day when, alone together, he tried to rape me." It is no surprise, then, that she understands romance as a literal battlefield. Although in this encounter she concludes blithely, "Even physically, I'm sure I was the stronger one," Lotus nevertheless learns that her defenses must be ever ready: "All these men's desires, rather than flattering me, seem to me to be, on the contrary, so many traps that have been set for my womanly weakness" (22).

These defenses are as much bodily—on another occasion, struggling with a suitor who refuses to take "no" for an answer, Lotus is obliged to "dig her nails into his eyes so ferociously that he immediately released me" (64)—as they are psychological. Even more troubling to her than the idea of being physically overpowered is the possibility of relinquishing emotional control to a man. When she considers, for instance, the likelihood that she will eventually lose her virginity, she draws up what amounts to a basic battle plan: "What am I waiting for? . . . I know perfectly well I'll choose one of them someday, maybe even the one I like the least, just to be contrary. I'll tell him: 'yeah, go ahead, you can have me.' Like that, at least, he won't get the idea he's conquered me" (39-40). Lotus's articulation of the real stakes of these erotic power plays foreshadows and mirrors the increasingly high-stakes relations between the sexes that ultimately play out in public spaces beyond her bedroom.

The connections between these domestic scenes and the realities of the public sphere first become manifest as Lotus enters into a romantic relationship with self-styled revolutionary Georges Caprou, an educated, left-leaning mulatto hero crafted on the model of the student militants of 1946 (one of Kaussen's "troubled soul-searching young men"). At first, Georges is merely one among the many suitors for whom Lotus's bedroom door is always more or less open. She desires him physically, even objectifies him—"I find him handsome, with his supple muscles, his Hindu prince's coloring, his seductive smile, and his long tender hands" (37). She discerns something special about him and vaguely admires his political commitments. This singularity initially piques Lotus's particular interest in him as a romantic target (note: not partner): "He pleases me a bit more than any of the others I've entertained, though—and it seems to me I've done everything in my power to seduce him, tried everything I can think of to get him hooked on me, risked everything to make him my slave" (37). Georges's attraction to Lotus is similarly perverse, and he also seems to view their entanglement as combat. He comes to her reluctantly, drawn to her almost as if against his will, and so makes it a point to insult and belittle her, making sure she understands that he views her as "nothing more than a wind-up doll to provide him with a bit of pleasure here and there" (37). Lotus is well aware of Georges's ambivalence toward her, and this only serves to heighten her desire to win (him over).

> "Is it possible that I disgust you?"
> He didn't answer, but turned his head away so disdainfully that I felt ashamed.
> "But what do you want—what do you expect of me?" . . .
> "You grant me your kisses—am I not the happiest of men? You, the beautiful Lotus with the little aristocratic nose, the haughty bearing, I'm your chosen one for the moment. What more could I ask of you? What you're offering is already so much [. . .]"
> Then abruptly changing his tone, and almost violently:
> "But I can be demanding [. . .]"
> "Exactly what I like."
> "We'll see about that. Ah! to mold you, to mold you as I please [. . .]"
> "Careful," I said to him then, "I'm not easily molded" . . .
> But as he kissed me, I felt a strange sort of regret tug at my heart, shrinking it to the point where it was barely beating. It was the first time a man had ever made me so weak by holding me in his arms, and *I let myself go.* . . . (38–39; emphasis mine)

The two lovers continue their battle of the sexes in this mutually suspicious manner, and the nature of their engagement becomes increasingly violent—"'If you're playing the tease, I'll never come back,' he said coldly. 'I'm not one to be toyed with [. . .]' Hatred and desire shone in his eyes, his nostrils trembled, and I could tell he was resisting a strong urge to slap me" (52)—but it soon becomes apparent that Georges has gained the upper hand. He develops a singular quality that makes him more attractive to Lotus than any of her other partners: he begins to disregard her. An advocate for the urban proletariat, Georges comes to prioritize his political commitments over his and Lotus's affair. He visits her less and less frequently as tensions escalate in Port-au-Prince and at one point breaks off their relationship altogether, having come to view her as a distraction from the real work of revolution that needs doing. Georges's love is contingent: if Lotus is to win him over, she will have to submit to his ideological principles. She will have to prove to him her capacity to conform to an idea(l) of womanhood. She will have to make herself available and committed to his politics.

Understanding the stakes of Georges and Lotus's relationship is helped by a turn to Amber Jamilla Musser's compelling work on literary representations of masochism. Specifically, Musser's analysis of *L'histoire d'O* (The Story of O), French writer Pauline Réage's erotic novel, published, like *Fille d'Haïti*, in 1954, provides insight into the questions of women's self-fashioning within the bounds of an inherently violent midcentury patriarchal order. Réage's "narrative of singular devotion and exclusivity" (Musser 2015, 132) unfolds within an erotic landscape of bondage and discipline and sadomasochism (BDSM). The novel is a Sadean vision of absolute female surrender to male control presented via the perspective of the woman in question, the eponymous O. Beautiful and financially independent, O embarks on a journey of self-discovery through increasing submission to the psychosexual demands of her lover, René. Over the course of the narrative, O gives inexhaustibly of herself in exchange for loving recognition (love *and* recognition, love *as* recognition) from her man. This relinquishing of her self is effected through a series of very conscious choices. She consents, verbally and explicitly, to each new physical degradation—each stripping, whipping, piercing, branding, beating, and penetrating—and its concomitant psychological undoing.

Musser convincingly reads "O's role in her own transformation as a Foucauldian technology of the self" (2015, 127). According to Michel Foucault, Musser reminds us, technologies of the self are practices wherein the individual seeks to realize a better, happier, more coherent version of the self, either alone or with the input of other people. These practices are so many pointed efforts to self-fashion and self-improve, and in this they necessarily reflect one's regard for oneself. At the same time, however, technologies of the self often reflect, if not require, self-abnegation in service to externally generated models of selfhood in community. This is the case in Réage's novel, wherein O's "relationship to the male gaze also calls attention to the ways in which technologies of the self interact with other technologies, namely those of normative femininity" (127). Yes, O is in control of her self-annihilation and may even be said to desire it. But how must this desired loss of self be understood given the "paucity of choices available to women" (127) within the sexual and other social structures of patriarchy?

Although BDSM is by no means an explicit dimension of Chauvet's novel, the parallels between the two mid-twentieth-century texts are striking. Most significantly, the protagonists of both narratives are prepared to give up everything in exchange for recognition, what psychoanalytic theorist Jessica Benjamin defines as "that response from the other which makes meaningful the feelings, intentions, and actions of the self" (1988, 12). In Lotus's case, emotional neglect by a psychologically broken mother and abandonment by a father she never knew, coupled with her social isolation from her immediate community, have left her with a deep feeling of unsettledness and incoherence. Before falling for Georges, her life had been devoid of the intimacy that would have allowed for recognition. Deprived of love from her earliest childhood, Lotus readily accepts the strictures of Georges's conditional affection. By positioning his gaze—his attention, his regard—as a prize not easily won, Georges (inadvertently?) provides the frame within which Lotus's submission becomes meaningful to her and useful to him.

As Benjamin explains, following Sigmund Freud and Georg Wilhelm Friedrich Hegel and prefiguring Judith Butler, it is through recognition by an Other that the individual is able to believe in the fact and the value of the self. The defining, sanctioning external gaze allows the self to "realize its agency and authorship in a tangible way" (Benjamin 1988, 12). In a situation of erotic domination and submission, this basic facet of human relation is amplified. The submissive partner becomes reliant on the lover to "[recognize] her acts, her feelings, her intentions, her existence, her independence. Recognition is the essential response, the constant companion of assertion. The subject declares, 'I am, I do,' and then waits for the response, 'You are, you have done'" (21). This dynamic best characterizes Georges and Lotus's perverse love story. Lotus makes more and more dramatic efforts to impress Georges as a potential partner; Georges responds to her efforts with alternating punishments and rewards.

Perhaps the most successful technique of discipline and control Georges deploys to establish his domination over Lotus is depriving her of his presence. He disappears for weeks or months at a time without ever telling her if or when he plans to return. He leaves her to wonder what it was she might have done to make him abandon her and what she can do to bring him back. Each time he does this, Lotus loses—gives up—something of herself: "I felt any pride I had just disappear" (64). She allows herself to be disciplined, rebuilding herself according to Georges's specifications—specifications that amount to an increasingly explicit demand for her erotic self-effacement and selfless political performance.

The first time Georges disappears, he stays away for more than a month, and his absence triggers Lotus's first, most dramatic act of self-erasure: having her houseboy paint over the many drawings with which she has covered the walls of her bedroom:

> Right there in front of me he killed off all my old friends, whose presence amounted to so many sketches of my dreams—dreams that I still don't know, to this day, if they were the involuntary expression of all that was tragic and untapped within me. . . . Like a new bride, the room sparkled in its new clothes. Brightened up, transformed, it seemed completely different to me and I felt like an intruder in the midst of my own furniture. (70)

Reborn, virginal, and cut off from her original personality, Lotus notes—but quickly accepts—these beginnings of a new self. She awakens the next day refreshed and at peace with her first steps toward self-erasure and happily anticipates the true start to her love story with Georges: "It seemed to me that I had broken with a whole world of unpleasantness and I felt as if a weight had been lifted. . . . Having donned my most beautiful dress, I waited for Georges" (72).

Her lover does not come that night, or the next, or for several more after that: "Thus did I come to know the anguish of unreciprocated feeling. I loved him and I wanted him to love me. I looked for ways to deserve his love" (72). Her plan: to prove to him that she is not the spoiled and fickle rich girl he believes her to be but a strong and reliable woman of the people, capable of both sexual and political fidelity. She cuts off her dalliances with other men, committing fully to her chaste vigil. She lowers her remaining defenses and slips ever more irremediably into a submissive position: "Everything I did from then on had only one purpose: to please Georges. I styled my hair for him, dressed for him, bathed for him, and read the things he liked" (74). Thus, even in his absence, Lotus grants Georges full control over her self. Even in solitude, she performs a version of her self that she imagines Georges will desire.

Lotus also resolves to go out and earn a living, having "always heard him praise women who work" (72). But after just one morning at her job as a typist, she decides she is being exploited and quits in protest, carelessly encouraging the other secretaries to do the same and imagining that Georges will be impressed by her act of revolt. Of course, all the women are expendable and are quickly replaced—but while Lotus is able to resume the relatively comfortable life she has always known, her momentary sisters-in-arms find themselves among the swelling ranks of the city's unemployed. This political failure is what finally succeeds in bringing Georges back. He shows up at her home and insults her—"Stupid, stupid, stupid, brainless little woman" (84). Lotus relishes the attention: "I loved his anger and appreciated him for insulting me—for treating me the way I deserved. I turned my too-calm face toward him and I saw him tense up, his hands trembling, ready to strike me" (84).

Georges refrains from hitting her (this time), instead leaving again and propelling Lotus into an immediate state of mental incoherence. Conveniently, though, she is able to recover from this breakdown thanks in part to her more evenly matched sadomasochistic relationship with Gertrude. In Georges's absence, that is, Lotus practices "seducing" Gertrude, her former sparring partner: "By suppressing my revulsion and my hatred, without knowing it I was honing feelings that, little by little, were developing to the point that I was becoming *a new person*" (91-92; emphasis mine). Despite Georges's resolute silence and prolonged absence, Lotus continues her journey of self-transformation and remains explicitly accountable to him: she writes him letters daily, offering a detailed report of every moment of every day, confiding everything, hiding nothing, until finally he comes back to her.

Once he does return, he and Lotus quickly fall back into their familiar routine. He insults her—"I'd forgotten that you're nothing but a foolish, superficial little girl" (103)—and she responds with a provocation. This time he does strike her, and they resume their positions in the erotic power play:

> "Don't go, don't go!"
> He picked me up and carried me up the stairs, the gentle weight of my body in his arms.
> Then, laying me delicately on my bed:
> "Farewell, Lotus," he said.
> "Take me, Georges."
> "Farewell, I don't like virgins."
> "Do you really find me that disgusting?"
> "You please me more than you know. But I don't like little girls telling me what to do. I'll take you in my own good time, Lotus." (104)

In other words, she must be patient. She knows the rules. Her reward will come.

Another month passes before Georges returns. She attends to him silently, earnestly, pleased merely to be in his company: "That night, he was particularly disagreeable with me. . . . I tried everything to please him, but in vain"

(115). But then just as she prepares to give up, she finally gains some clarity—as does the reader—regarding the specific nature of their relationship:

> He seemed to be battling with himself, as if he feared giving in to my charms. When he spoke, I knew that his ego had been the sole cause of his attitude toward me. But tired of constantly struggling, his pride had been vanquished at last, allowing him to give in to his desire, freeing him, humiliated, to accept my love.
> "When a woman pleases me, I don't share. . . . I like exclusivity in everything I possess, understand?"
> With that, he pounced on me, seizing me in his arms. He carried me to the bed [. . .] and that night, he only left at dawn. (116)

Thus does their relationship arrive at a sort of happy equilibrium, a literal win-win that exemplifies the "masochist/dominant's mutual dependence" and complicates "the power binary" (Musser 2005): as long as Lotus remains within the bounds of the womanhood Georges has prescribed, she enjoys his recognition and even a measure of control. Having realized this fully, she takes up almost *too* flawlessly the mantle of femininity as articulated within the Haitian nationalist frame: she sets up a small, informal school for poor neighborhood children, inviting them into her home and teaching them to read and write.[24] Georges's values have become her own, and she reaps the prize for her performance of virtue: "Ever since I began giving free lessons and surrounded myself with poor little children to whom I made myself useful by teaching, I saw Georges's love for me grow stronger. It was the most beautiful reward life could have offered me" (162). Though she has perhaps lost "any pride she had" before beginning this love affair, Lotus is content to replace her self-regard with that of her lover: "This is a good start, Lotus," Georges tells her after watching her read to her students. "I'm proud of you" (163). Like Réage's O, Lotus "submits so that she can receive love," and the fact that receiving this love requires her submission emphasizes, of course, "her very gendered precarity" (Musser 2015, 127). Georges's mounting control and presumptuous judgments of her being and behavior are so many instances of the way in which masculinist politics relies inextricably on practices of "regulating intimacy" (Francis 2010, 2).

The blissful coherence that results from Georges's loving approval transforms all aspects of Lotus's life. She becomes reconciled to the memory of her mother, and she plunges headlong into politics: "I begged him to use me as intermediary between him and his friends" (179). Despite some initial reluctance, Georges takes Lotus up on her offer. In fact, he goes on to presume her endless devotion, no longer seeing any boundary between his needs and her will. He turns her villa into a sort of headquarters, thus metonymically lending her out to other men. At first, his friends and coconspirators turn up on her doorstep expecting her to hide them, which she does. Soon enough, the men begin holding meetings in her home, meetings from which she is at first excluded before eventually being merely tolerated. Notably, Lotus's willingness to harbor political dissidents has everything to do with her romance/battle with Georges. "I want to serve your cause," she tells him, "not like a child you entertain, but like a woman who risks everything" (198).

The magnitude of the risk Lotus takes becomes apparent soon after she makes this declaration. Out on a mission with Georges and his coconspirators, she ends up being shot, but because they are hiding from the police, she cannot cry out: "As if already grown used to suffering, I felt like I was feeling the pain less and less" (201). Lotus's considered stoicism in the face of excruciating pain aligns neatly with her submissive's willingness to bear anything for the sake of earning Georges's love. As Benjamin points out, referencing de Beauvoir, "real masochism consists in wanting the suffering of pain not for its own sake, but as proof of servitude" (1980, 156). As Georges and Lotus's affair progresses, it becomes clear that she is, indeed, always meant to prove her worth, always on trial, always subject to Georges's demands. And, again like O, Lotus "did not wish to die, but if torture was the price she had to pay to keep her lover's love, then she only hoped he was pleased that she had endured it" (Réage). What, in other words, won't she do for love?

Soon after Lotus commits to sheltering Georges's collaborators, she gets her reward: a promise of marriage. This is a reward Georges rightly presumes she desires, although he has neither asked her if this is the case nor in fact asked her to marry him. He announces their future union matter-of-factly, as a shortcut to introductions on the occasion of his bringing five additional men into her home (also without asking her permission): "I present to you the mistress of the house. She'll soon be my wife" (182). The pronouncement is hurried and offhand, but its implications are consequential. For there is a contract embedded in Georges's promise; it reposes on the well-worn "conflation of property with marriage" (Alexander 2005, 35). That is, if Lotus is the mistress of the house and Georges is her soon-to-be husband and already-master, then Georges's promise announces that his and Lotus's existing erotic bonds will culminate in a future contract—a contract that legally will transform a woman and her property into *his* woman and *his* property.

Here again, the correlation with sexual submission is significant. In the case of exemplary submissive O, for example, the defining avowal of her subjugation to her lover-master and his associates is that she has consented to being always physically available to them, partially undressed and exposed for penetration, without boundary or barrier hindering access to her most intimate bodily self. Lotus has similarly consented to place her home at Georges and his comrades' disposal, leaving her intimate space exposed and vulnerable. She has lowered her defenses.

Through his declaration of marriage (his declaration of Lotus's dependence), Georges definitively moves Lotus's villa into the public sphere, and Lotus herself into the crosshairs of his political enemies. That he has designated her home his safe house proves deeply ironic. For it is as a proxy for Georges that Lotus is brutally assaulted in her home. Before the physical violation, her rapist at once disarticulates and conflates sex, humiliation, gender, and power: "'Right now,' the man said to me, 'you have a choice. Either you hand over your boyfriend or you have sex with me.... What I'm about to do here is only to prove to you that I detest you with all my strength and that women like you aren't worth much at all, despite your arrogance and your petty prejudices'" (264–65). He continues, "'In times of war, some things are difficult to explain. Well, we are more than at war now; we are in a time of hate. I'm looking for your boyfriend and I've *made a deal* with you'" (265; emphasis mine). That her attacker lays out the terms of Lotus's subjection with such pitiless clarity is crucial here. It establishes both his absolute control and her absolute object status, his dominance and her submission. Once again, analysis of O's experience provides insight. As Benjamin explains, the men who subjugate and debase O are careful to insist on her virtual irrelevance as a subject: "What they do is 'more for her enlightenment than their pleasure'—even in using her they do not need her. Rather their acts express a rational control, a rational violation through which they objectify their rational intentions. Each act has such a goal or purpose that asserts their mastery" (1980, 157). Like O, Lotus is but a means to an end that does not take her subjectivity into consideration. At best, she will learn something in this "exchange."

The violence of this rape is not entirely unfamiliar to Lotus. Rather, it is an extension of the "rational violence" that has been a part of her relationship with Georges all along. She has effectively been groomed—trained to expect violation—and she has already proven her "willingness to receive pain without resistance" (Garraway 2013, 217). Even the way in which her rapist plays out the ritual of Lotus's consent—"you have a choice," "I've made a deal with you"— recalls Georges's pedagogical/disciplinary strategies. Her rapist's justification (his *rationale*) for assaulting her holds to the tenets of BDSM, which "employs the will or volition of the violated and demands the rational control of the violator" (Benjamin 1980, 166). Of course, the stakes of this incident extend well beyond the interpersonal and intersubjective realm of erotic relations. That is, insofar as the objective of Lotus's humiliation is really Georges's submission, it is above all the psychosexual politics of patriarchy embedded in processes of nation-building that Chauvet means to interrogate. This foreshadows the explicit configuration of womanhood under Duvalier, discussed earlier. What happens to Lotus is consistent with Chauvet's insistence, throughout her corpus, on the likelihood of a woman serving as the "scapegoat for community in crisis" (Garraway 2013, 212).

At stake in the battles being waged all around Lotus, both within and beyond the borders of her home, is the question of civil freedom—the parameters that determine which citizens are afforded the protections of the state. That Lotus's sexual subjugation is articulated by her torturer as collateral damage in the real war being fought is Chauvet's reminder of the uneasy relationship between the social contract sustaining the civil rights of the modern citizen and the "sexual contract" sustaining the power of men over women in even ostensibly liberal or liberationist contexts (Pateman 2004, 6). Chauvet suggests that Georges and his comrade's struggle for civil freedom ultimately does not aim to acquire freedom for all members of the polis but rather only the male members. As Carole Pateman argues, "women are not party to the original contract through which men transform their natural freedom into the security of civil freedom" (2004, 6). They are merely the spoils of war among would-be patriarchs and their rebellious male progeny.

Given this, Lotus's rapist's discourse can and should be understood within the context of Georges's similarly masculinist assertions and behaviors, his threats and acts of violence and his disregard for Lotus's autonomy. Prefiguring the gendered violence that runs throughout Chauvet's trilogy, the violence Lotus endures in *Fille d'Haïti* confirms that the objectification of women is independent of ideology, cutting across the whole of the political spectrum; it is *not* incidental but essential to the functioning of nationalist politics.[25] Lotus's experiences attest to the reality of a social climate in which male sexual rights—"men's domination over women, the right of men to enjoy sexual access to women"—are not called into question. Both Lotus's lover and her aggressor, acting in the private and the public sphere, respectively and inextricably, function in accordance with an order in which "women's relations to the social world must always be mediated through men's reason" (Pateman 2004, 101–2)—in which paternalist political right equates with patriarchal sex right. Both sides of the political fence share a "base in male homosociality" (Boehmer 2005, 18) wherein "the privileged national agents are urban, male, vanguardist, and violent" (McClintock 1995, 96), and men's right to women's bodies in the context of revolutionary political action—the overthrowing of the father by the son, as it were—is left intact. Having no actual father to protect her from the incursions of the outside world or to filter that world's demands, Lotus is (perceived as) up for grabs.

Lotus's rape confirms, moreover, the particular danger of her ambiguous social situation as "the mistress of the house." She has basic financial independence, yes, but this independence equates with vulnerability, not freedom. Her villa is a dangerous place, the site of repeated threats to and assaults on her physical and psychological being. It is not a place where Lotus is at home. Rather, it is the place where she is most at risk. It epitomizes what Homi K. Bhabha, leaning on Freud, has named the space of the unhomely, space within which one finds oneself "taking the measure of [one's] dwelling in a state of 'incredulous terror'" (1994, 9).[26] Lotus is literally terrorized by and within her home: the "traumatic ambivalences of [her] personal, psychic history" indeed come to occupy the same physical space that houses (pun intended) "the wider disjunctions of political existence" (Bhabha 1994, 15). Lotus's villa is the spatial manifestation of her "borderline existence" (Bhabha 1994, 19)—of her defenselessness in the face of a sociopolitical community that considers her single-womanhood suspect. She is unprotected in her isolation, called upon time and again to defend herself both literally and metaphorically. And to the extent to which Chauvet's later, more celebrated heroines are similarly obliged to negotiate ambivalent social identities within the confines of unsafe domestic spaces, Lotus is worth paying attention to. Her insecurity within the personal space of her home tells a story about women's value to men in society—the political, public nature of what can never be their individual, private selves.

Fille d'Haïti's two-page epilogue confirms this explicitly. The chapter begins, just like the novel's first chapter, with the words "My name is Lotus." The reader learns that two years have passed, and in that time Georges has died in sacrifice to the cause of racial harmony. In the wake of Georges's martyrdom, Lotus, too, has achieved a measure of apotheosis: "I finally found peace *by letting go of myself*," she confesses (285; emphasis mine). By the end of *Fille d'Haïti*, Lotus has given herself over entirely to the cause of social justice. She has been transformed into a political being, fully awakened to the corruption of the elite and ready to resist the systems of exploitation by which the powerful maintain their privilege. She has been shot and sexually assaulted as a consequence of her revolutionary activities, so much proof of her devotion to Georges and of her willingness to put herself in danger for the benefit of the suffering masses. Georges dies a hero, having martyred himself by saving a young Black girl from being hit by a car, but not before giving Lotus her final instructions: "My beloved [...] continue my work. Stay on the right path" (282). And she does just that. She adopts a baby (named Georges), product of a mulatto woman and a Black man. She turns her villa into a school for women and children, thereby turning herself into an immaculate mother and transforming her lonely, unhomely house into a space of healthy community.

This conclusion would appear in many respects to support a definitive understanding of *Fille d'Haïti* as the straightforward account of one woman's moral and political conversion. It is true that Lotus comes to exhibit a "gathering commitment to social revolution," becoming an increasingly "useful comrade and advocate of the masses" (Kaussen 2008, 149) over the course of the narrative. Yet there is something of the parodic to Lotus's trajectory—something both unsettling and implausible about the tied-up-with-a-bow neatness of this utopian ending. The final moments of Lotus's story slyly echo those of Jacques Roumain's foundational fiction *Masters of the Dew*.[27] As in Roumain's novel, it is the community-cum-nation whose fate is in question. *Masters* ends with the hero's sacrifice and the literal and metaphorical commitment of "his woman" to engendering a better world in his name. The novel amounts to the "construction of a national romance, in which a purposeful, heterosexual coupling is used to represent allegorically the author's idea of the new and improved Haitian state"; it suggests that realizing this ideal state requires "a redirected physicality, a taming of desire, and the ideal of requited love" (Dash 2003, 310).

Chauvet's narrative alludes to Roumain's chaste nationalist script but also interrogates the timeless fact that "female autonomy seldom enters the narrow gate of Marxist paradise" (Zimra 1990, 150). The very last words of *Fille d'Haïti* confirm that the displacement of Lotus's "I" has successfully made room for her man's dreamed-of nation: "Hatred has finally ceded its place to brotherhood. Georges is resuscitated in this rediscovered unity and peace" (287). The state of blissful selflessness (and sexlessness) to which Lotus has at long last acceded mirrors the utopian peace that has descended on the whole of the country. And her domestication is literally state sanctioned: in appreciation of her public service, the new head of state gives her "a gold medal with the words 'Honor and Merit' engraved upon it" (287).

What emerges from Lotus's story of herself certainly might be read as the tale of one troubled woman's political evolution and attainment of social belonging. But *Fille d'Haïti* also chronicles this woman's coerced loss of self, her neutered adherence to patriarchal convention and "hypernormative modes of respectability" (Sheller 2012, 240). At the beginning of the narrative, we encounter a Lotus who, while isolated, politically indifferent, and arguably narcissistic, is also willful, curious, and sexually unconstrained. Lotus's original sense of who she is and how she should behave was contingent only on her self-regard—before meeting Georges she had defended her actions in accordance with her own objectives; she had refused to conform to the "ideal of virginity" or to concern herself with the "curse of promiscuity" (Dayan 1994, 26). She had refused, in other words, to participate in the cult of respectability that determines the parameters of feminine existence. In the end, however, loneliness, isolation, and the desire to be loved end up getting the best of her. Gradually abandoning herself to the gendered social "norms by which recognition is conferred" (J. Butler 1999, 3), Lotus ultimately replaces her imperfect original self with an externally generated ideal self—an elided feminine "I" devoted to and inseparable from a patriarchal "we." *Fille d'Haïti* is the story of this self-effacement.

Thus, if Chauvet seems to have configured Lotus as one of those Haitian heroines who "serve to take up the mantle of the fallen hero, to maintain the glimmer of [their] hopes and dreams" (Marty 2000, 97), she does not let such configurations remain unexamined. Lotus adheres to the stand-by-your-man model to a degree, yes, but she also undermines the image of her man's perfect heroism. Moreover, she takes up all the psychological space. Chauvet has shifted the narrative balance of power away from the novelistic model wherein a third-person omniscient narrator brings a woman character into focus only to reflect or support the efforts of a male hero. By allowing Lotus to tell her own story, Chauvet walks us through an instance of exactly how and why such selfless women might come to be.

For let us recall the narrative's formal conceit, that it is framed as a memoir. And let us further recall what Lotus announces as her project—her "pleasure"—to "try to *bring back to life* that strange little girl, who was me" (10; emphasis mine). Having "let herself go"—a sacrifice to the order required by her lover and the community he has died to create, Lotus nevertheless proposes her story as a modest act of self-defense, literally the defense of a self that once was and maybe still or again might be. *Fille d'Haïti* is a curated account of a woman's life, and everything we know about that woman is no more than what she tells us; she makes us privy to everything she does not get right and is harsh in her judgment of her own failings. Anything we read is presented from the perspective of this highly conscious, self-regarding first-person narrator, a narrator who is well aware of the offensiveness of her own behavior and who analyzes that behavior within a social context she also reveals. If we know Lotus to be capricious and changeable, weak and bratty, it is only because she has confessed these things to us. She is merciless in her self-criticism, as disposed to admit to her basest thoughts and most disappointing actions as to acknowledge her accomplishments and successes.

In revealing the ups and downs of her story, Lotus traces an evolution that contradicts broad and deeply embedded presumptions regarding women's civil consciousness. Whereas, "according to Jean-Jacques Rousseau and Freud, women are incapable of transcending their sexual passions and particular attachments and directing their reason to the demands of universal order and public advantage" (Pateman 2004, 102), Lotus presents overwhelming evidence to the contrary. Whether or not Chauvet means to tell an earnest tale of one bourgeois young woman's awakening to a mission of social justice, by highlighting her character's blurred edges and existential uncertainty, as well as that character's awareness thereof, Chauvet affirms women's capacity to think and to critique the public sphere.

The entirety of *Fille d'Haïti* chronicles Lotus's negotiation of her liminality in a society built and rebuilding itself on polarizing absolutes. As such, rather than read Lotus's indeterminacy as a reflection of Chauvet's limitations as a writer, I read a deliberateness in her characterization of this daughter of Haiti who, in her equivocality, anticipates the better-known Marie-Ange, Minette, Claire, and Rose.[28] Lotus's frustrating inconsistency—her ambivalent being (neither white nor Black, neither rich nor poor) and her ambivalent behavior (complicit with the repressive social order but also victimized within it, a promiscuous "virgin," socially conscious but loath to suffer the inconveniences of social equality until a handsome Marxist prince helps her see the light)—is not a function of Chauvet's incompetence as a writer. Rather, it offers a nuanced platform for social critique. It proposes "the transgression of a gentility that pretends social relations are personal and private rather than public, political, and class-based" (Sheller 2012, 224). Lotus's character is unstable but by no means sloppily so, as Gouraige would have it. Her equivocality makes a point. It is a function of Chauvet's brand of realism. Physically unsafe and, consequently, figuratively insecure, Lotus incarnates the absurdity and outright danger to the individual within a state that fantasizes the alignment of class, color, and moral right. Chauvet's heroine is, Gouraige is correct, deeply flawed, but her flaws make sense within the context of the social pathology that dominates both within and outside of the domestic space. Given her endangered existence, Lotus's behaviors present a reasoned self-defense as well as a mimetic reflection of her social world.

Writing of *Amour, colère et folie* in 2014, sociologist Carolle Charles takes issue with the absence of a consistent political intention and praxis among the heroines of Chauvet's literary fictions. Charles laments that while Chauvet the author may evoke the harsh realities of social life in Haiti, the "occasional posturing of the main characters never really offers alternatives to these hierarchical structures and the violence embedded in these social relations" (2014, 67). Like Gouraige, Charles finds Chauvet's heroines lacking—incoherent and insufficiently revolutionary in that they "never violate the norms and constraints imposed by these hierarchies." They are, she writes, "contradictory because they reproduce the essentialist reasoning that their narratives supposedly dismantle" (68).

Such criticisms of Chauvet and her work presume her obligation both to illustrate the failures of justice and human rights in Haitian society and politics and to resolve those failures through her writing. This is an obligation Chauvet starkly refuses. As a woman whose personal and political life became dramatically intertwined, whose sacred domestic space was so devastatingly encroached upon by the profanity of the political, Chauvet resolved only to illustrate and thereby critique the costs of patriarchal nation-building for women in the Haitian community. She was steeped in the revolutionary poetics and politics being espoused by the most important intellectual voices of her time but nevertheless situated herself outside the overtly political realm, even in its most progressive iterations. The vision of political community she presents in her fiction is best described as cynical. This cynicism is manifest in the story Lotus tells. Although, in the end, Lotus's choices may not "challenge gender norms that assume a naturalized feminine submission, [Chauvet's] act of authorship does" (Musser 2015, 123). Having written a narrative wherein coercive, ideologically opposed communities make binaristic affiliation a matter of life and death, Chauvet highlights the permeability of the boundary that only very tenuously separates women's personal lives from men's political world. She calls attention to the violent encounters that take place in intimate spaces—unhomely, domestic, feminine spaces—inhabited by changeable, individual, and, yes, even perverse women characters. This was radical in its time. It remains so.

4

SELF-PRESERVATION | Xuela

> *In traumatic times like ours, when reality itself is so distorted as to have become impossible and abnormal, it is the function of all culture, partaking of this abnormality, to be aware of its own sickness. To be aware of the unreality of the unauthenticity of the so called real, is to reinterpret this reality. To reinterpret this reality is to commit oneself to a constant revolutionary assault against it.*
>
> —Sylvia Wynter, "We Must Learn to Sit Down Together and Discuss a Little Culture" (1968)

Readers tend to take Jamaica Kincaid very personally. And this is arguably Kincaid's own fault. Kincaid speaks the stories of her life publicly, in print, more than most authors. These stories, as she tells and retells them, are not very pleasant. Kincaid describes the place where she was born and raised, the British Caribbean island of Antigua, as a bleak and self-hating colonial community, corrupt and degenerate. She describes the woman who raised her there, her mother, as unloving and shortsighted. Sent away from this cruel place by her cruel mother at the age of sixteen, Kincaid has explained, she relied on her talent to turn her banishment into an escape. She cut ties with her family and, after three years spent employed as a domestic worker in a wealthy New York suburb, made her way briefly to college and then to New York City, where she rather quickly became a published author.

Having since attained international celebrity, Kincaid is—she has made herself—particularly well known for her anger. She seems, despite her great success, never to have forgiven what she characterizes as the profound failings of her home and her family. She is categorical in her condemnation of the place and people she came from. Kincaid returns constantly to the details of her past not only in her essays, memoirs, and other nonfiction writings but also in every one of her prose fiction works, generating what amounts to a "serial autobiography" (Gilmore 2001, 98; Paquet 2002, 65). She has unabashedly mined the particulars of her past for names, places, relationships, and events, scattering them throughout her novels and short stories as so many easily referenced points on the road map of her life. From her troubled relationship with her mother to her ambivalence toward her much younger siblings to her abandonment by her father and her fury at her island, personal experiences plainly serve as a crucial source text for Kincaid's fiction—so many building blocks in the foundation of an "ongoing self-representational project" (Gilmore 2001, 97).

In the countless interviews Kincaid has given, she confirms the autobiographical dimensions of her novels. Unsurprisingly, then, the story of Kincaid's own life figures prominently in scholarly approaches to her work. Kincaid herself has cultivated the phenomenon. She presents her painful past as the emotional impetus for the anger that infuses her writing and that animates her unforgiving heroines. "We are disturbed by the arrogant voices of Kincaid's protagonists," writes Louise Bernard, "annoyed by her apparent love of unpleasantries and her uncompromising world-view" (2002, 134). Lizabeth Paravisini-Gebert confirms that the "prevalence of her self-contained, ruthless heroines has shored up the Kincaid myth of the author as outspoken, dauntless, quasi-shrew—an image that Kincaid appears to enjoy perpetuating.... She seems to enjoy making people uncomfortable" (1999, 17–18).

But Kincaid has long been playing tricks on her readers. Though her tales of herself tell a consistent basic story—Antigua is a narrow and loathsome place; her changeable and withholding mother endlessly broke her heart—the details are so many building blocks that Kincaid arranges and rearranges at will. She claims one thing in one interview, its opposite in another, and then something else still via the various "I" narrators whose stories she peppers liberally with details from her own biography.[1] We, her readers, are so many pinballs jettisoned from memoir to interview to essay to novel, hoping to parse truth and fiction, flailing about as we contend with the "unpleasantries" she evokes so relentlessly. Taking up a constellation of concerns around gender, race, and postcoloniality over multiple narratives, Kincaid consistently projects, as Sandra Pouchet Paquet eloquently notes, "an independent female voice in a seemingly continuous monologue arising out of an environment that is hostile to women's self-fulfillment" (2017, 120).

Kincaid meets this hostility with her unsparing and often venomous prose—the "vituperative tone" and "profound dislike for her former homeland" that emanate from both her nonfiction and fiction writing (King 2002, 891, 898). This attitude qualifies her as "one of these few dissident authors with Caribbean pedigree whose deepest views of life are not in accord with Glissant's cautious optimism" (Penier 2010, 243). This has greatly frustrated, and even angered, many Caribbeanist theorists of Kincaid's work, several of whom suggest that Kincaid has herself adopted a colonialist viewpoint with respect to the Caribbean. In "A Small Place Writes Back," Jane King claims that Kincaid has been dangerously irresponsible, relentlessly "denigrating our small place in this destructively angry fashion." King continues, "Anger and insult have a real force in the world, and it is anger and insult and little else which Kincaid offers her native Caribbean" (2002, 899, 907). Veronica Marie Gregg similarly takes issue with Kincaid's disparaging portrayal of the Caribbean and its people. Gregg accuses Kincaid of having established her renowned authorial "I" at the expense of a "we" she misrepresents and disdains: "The individual 'I' is purchased in part with the currency of the distanced and denigrated West Indian people and place. . . . I think, therefore I am. They don't think, therefore, they are not quite human" (2002, 927). Such critiques contend that Kincaid's work paints an exaggeratedly pessimistic and grossly inaccurate portrait of her homeland.

Beyond the affective dimensions of these scholars' admonishments, the offense taken at Kincaid's perceived literary betrayals, the question of her political obligation to her place of origin also lurks. While "she is claimed by Caribbean, African American, and Euro-American canons . . . her work is consistently marked by refusal of allegiances of every kind except an allegiance to narrating the individual self" (Forbes 2008, 24). This "shape-shifting, protean, slippery unwillingness to be pinned down" (King 2002, 905), it is argued, permits her to rail against colonial and postcolonial evils without getting her hands dirty. Comfortably secure in the embrace of international celebrity, "she and her work remain in the network of colonial/imperial desires dictated by England's and, subsequently, the United States's historically gruesome relationships to Black and African peoples all over the world" (G. Thomas 2008, 921).

The perception of Kincaid's "dissident" perspective and "ardent individualism" (Bernard 2002, 116) as an artist and a woman echoes, with uncanny precision, critical perspectives on her fictional avatars, perhaps in no instance more so than with respect to Xuela Claudette Richardson, the first-person narrating protagonist of *The Autobiography of My Mother*. If any of the texts in my corpus might be said to be individualist texts on the model Curdella Forbes so beautifully lays out, it would be Kincaid's *Autobiography*, with its central character, Xuela. At least as plain-speaking, unbending, and furious as her creator, Xuela "understands and accepts that she was born into a legacy of defeat, and her answer to this fate is to construct a self that is insulated and self-serving" (West 2003, 3).

The critical response to this 1996 novel, Kincaid's third, has been to laud its finely wrought stylistics, to laud the originality and mastery of its formal qualities, while at the same time expressing deep discomfort with its content.[2] "Although most reviewers praised the novel for the piercing honesty, elegance, and brilliance of its prose, many also found its protagonist and narrator . . . a difficult, unsympathetic character whose defiant tale, its lyricism notwithstanding, was profoundly disturbing" (Paravisini-Gebert 1999, 143). Characterizations of the novel more and less subtly posit what it could or should have done, and these critiques tend to fall into two entangled categories: lamenting the novel's failure to envision or propose political alternatives and condemning Xuela's narcissistic self-containment. "What," asks Elizabeth J. West, "does a novel like Kincaid's *Autobiography of My Mother* offer its readers?" (2003, 10). Leaning on Black feminist critic bell hooks, West argues:

> Xuela's inconsistent narrative exemplifies a body of fiction by contemporary black women writers that critic bell hooks suggests is both powerful and problematic. This fiction is significant "in that it clearly names the ways structures of domination, racism, sexism, and class exploitation oppress and make it practically impossible for black women to survive if they do not engage in meaningful resistance on some level," but a prevailing shortcoming in many of these works is that they "fail to depict any location for the construction of new identities." This failing is evidenced in Kincaid's heroine, Xuela. (West 2003, 20, quoting from hooks 1992, 50–51)

In the eyes of many theorists, Xuela's evident failure is her extreme self-regard—her "twisted," "grotesque," "obsessive," "narcissistic" love for self (Bernard 2002, 127; Paravisini-Gebert 1999, 162; Schine 1996, 5) and attendant refusal to care for others.

The Autobiography of My Mother focuses primarily on this autonomous making of a self—and on telling that process of self-formation—and it does so through a decidedly provocative engagement with autobiography as a genre. The novel's oxymoron of a title, as well as the very fact that it is a work of prose fiction, announces it as something not quite an autobiography.³ In this respect, it instantiates the kind of tricksterism that permeates the whole of Kincaid's corpus. The use of the evocative descriptor "autobiography" in the title of a text that also includes the words "a novel" on its cover is meant to disconcert. Further, the title announces the impossibility/absurdity of the text it names, insofar as it flouts/disorders the autobiographical convention wherein author, narrator, and protagonist are one and the same person. The title is further misleading in that the eponymous mother is by no means the focus of the narrative—neither the narrating self nor the principal subject of the narration, despite Xuela's concluding claims to the contrary.⁴ The figure of the mother remains peripheral, albeit foundational, and she is without voice or physical presence in the story.

Not in fact an autobiography, the *Autobiography* is a work of philosophy. It is an extended meditation on being human in a postcolonial world. In laying out Xuela's strategies of self-preservation, the novel evinces a philosophical perspective. A counterdiscourse. A counterpoetics. Thus, while it is true that the *Autobiography* eschews political solutions and offers no redemptive conclusions, it cannot be said that it "is not a novel whose power derives from its ethical vision or its capacity for self-reflection" (Chang 2004, 122). On the contrary, Xuela's remarkably self-reflective narrative proposes a very clear ethical frame, albeit not an easy one to accept.

I propose thinking about Kincaid's novel and its devastating heroine as articulations of Kincaid's ethics of self-regard. Specifically, I look to Sylvia Wynter's radical humanist querying of the postcolonial world order—Wynter's call, that is, for sustained interrogation of and vigilance regarding our presumptions about the "'what is'—the epistemic 'vrai'" (1990, 364). How, I ask, do Xuela's disorderly textual being and the novel's unsettling extratextual presence propose philosophically grounded possibilities for navigating an untenable social reality, for contesting a traumatic history, and for mounting a generative critique of contemporary community?

Since I do not matter, I do not long to matter, but I matter anyway.
—Xuela Claudette Richardson (in *The Autobiography of My Mother*)

The *Autobiography* has been cast primarily as an expression of its protagonist's misanthropic rage, marked by Xuela's narcissistic indifference and "unrelenting harshness" (West 2003, 2). While such assessments are no doubt true, it is also critical to recognize Xuela's story as the expression of her sincere disbelief in—even her refusal of—the racist and sexist metanarratives that condition her reality. Fundamentally unwilling to accept that what *is* denotes what *has to be*, Xuela seems to want nothing more than to interrogate the whole world—to commit to "demystifying, or 'disenchanting,' the foundations" (G. Thomas 2001, 101) of an arbitrarily codified and unjust order. She is unintimidated by the status quo and wants to know how the normative came to be and whether it is likely to endure.

At every turn, in every interaction, with the impassivity and precision of a scientist, Xuela interrogates—people, their feelings, her feelings about their feelings, their feelings about her feelings, their beliefs, her beliefs, their behaviors, her behaviors. Rather than remain transfixed by the gaze of those who despise and would diminish her, Xuela positions herself as a scientific observer. She witnesses and describes the phenomena of alienation and bigotry she sees around her "for the pleasure of deconstructing them" (hooks 2003, 101). She then records in great detail just how the world looks from her perspective. Whereas "What makes the world turn?" (131) is the question the powerful have the luxury of pondering, Xuela wants to know, "What makes the world turn against me and all who look like me?" (132). She reconceives this "innocent" philosophical musing as a high-stakes provocation and, in so doing, effectively draws attention to the racialized and gendered fault lines of the what *is*. Her restaging of this basic human question effectively "exposes and cancels its embedded claims of universal humanism" (Gregg 2002, 932).

Importantly, at the same time as—in fact, because—Xuela recognizes her externally determined position within the category of the dysselected, she sets the sights of her refusal lower, closer to home, in a sense. While perhaps animated fundamentally by the imperative to be outside the broad postcolonial order, in oppositional relation to the prevailing set of codes and its corresponding hierarchical organization of human beings, Xuela is focused on the more proximate threat to her freedom. She is attuned to the ways in which the experience of dysselection has infected her immediate community—her family members, her neighbors, her lovers, her schoolmates, her instructors, and so on—and she is committed to somehow escaping what she recognizes as "the hatred and isolation in which we all lived" (50). Xuela is intensely aware that her community has become resigned to its status as a degraded by-product of Man's "ethnoculturally coded narrated history" (Wynter 2000, 198). She is aware that everyone around her has been perverted, poisoned, and bewitched by and within a toxic master code. She recognizes and unfailingly points out the persistent accumulation of minor humiliations as so many "everyday mundane horrors that aren't acknowledged to be horrors" (C. Sharpe 2010, 3).

Everyone in the universe Xuela describes suffers from a stultifying "autophobic aversion" (Wynter 1989, 643). "To people like us," Xuela insists, "despising anything that was most like ourselves was almost *a law of nature*" (52). Xuela refuses to be bound by that law.

Like countless characters in Caribbean fiction before her, Xuela is painfully aware of history's trap. Her schooling begins with a map—a map that confirms her defeat (and that of her island community) and places this defeat at the core of what she is supposed to understand about herself ever forward: "At the top of the map were the words 'THE BRITISH EMPIRE.' These were the first words I learned to read," she notes (15). The moment recalls classroom scenes played out in any number of postcolonial Caribbean texts before and since, European colonial education being, as Maryse Condé has written, "the global influence that one society exercises over an other that it seeks to integrate" as well as the frame within which is established the "relationship between an individual and her society's dominant culture, whose most crucial values, moreover, she adopts" ([1979] 2000, 8). Gathered together in a vestigial colonial space devoid of love or pride, Xuela and her schoolmates are trained in their own devaluation.

Kincaid's staging of this crucial moment of indoctrination through an institution that could only represent, as Xuela insists, "a source of humiliation and self-loathing" (15) propels the reader into a confrontation with what is arguably the ur-narrative of postcolonial identity formation: William Shakespeare's *The Tempest*. Specifically, Kincaid's evocation of a self-hating school official in her novel *Annie John* (1986), published ten years before *Autobiography*, stages an explicit engagement with Shakespeare's drama:

> The morning was uneventful enough: a girl spilled ink from her inkwell all over her uniform; a girl broke her pen nib and then made a big to-do about replacing it; girls twisted and turned in their seats and pinched each other's bottoms; girls passed notes to each other. All this Miss Nelson must have seen and heard, but she didn't say anything—only kept reading her book: an elaborately illustrated edition of *The Tempest*, as later, passing by her desk, I saw. (1986, 39)

This moment comes during a scene in which the eponymous heroine, Annie, and her classmates have been tasked with writing "something [Miss Nelson] described as an 'autobiographical essay'" (38). This hardly seems coincidental.

In this scene from *Annie John* as well as elsewhere in her corpus, Kincaid points to the fundamental coloniality of the West Indian educational institution—the extent to which the colonial-cum-national system sediments the internalized pathologization of the "Afro-" by the "Euro-."[5] Shakespeare's play in particular has stood, since the mid-twentieth century, as an exemplar of the mechanisms of collective alienation among nonwhite peoples of the Caribbean. The British playwright's depiction of the relationship between the all-powerful colonizing agent Prospero and the debased Caliban, the island native he has humiliated and enslaved, has made *The Tempest* a veritable founding fiction of Caribbean letters. The conflict between Prospero and Caliban is a trope that undergirds anticolonial and postcolonial narratives across the Atlantic world.

Male-authored New World refigurations of and writings-back to Shakespeare's text abound and have been much analyzed and celebrated by postcolonial scholars. Writers like Aimé Césaire, George Lamming, Roberto Fernández Retamar, and others have grappled with and contested Shakespeare's drama in their respective plays, poems, and novels, making of Caliban the "central anticolonial figure of the twentieth-century anticolonial nationalist period" (Bogues 2008, 172).[6] Europe's lingering and alienating linguistic-cum-cultural dominance lies at the root of anticolonial engagements with the play—"Prospero invaded the islands, killed our ancestors, enslaved Caliban, and taught him language to make himself understood. What can Caliban do but use that same language—today he has no other—to curse him? . . . I know no other metaphor more expressive of our cultural situation, of our reality" (Retamar 1989, 14). Common among these works is the imagining of "a Caliban who could stand as a prototype for successive Caribbean figures in whom cultural and political activism were to cohere" (Nixon 1987, 569).

Equally common in these defiant rewritings is the absence of any substantive role for women. Scholars like Sandra Pouchet Paquet, in her foreword to Lamming's *The Pleasures of Exile*, and Jyotsna G. Singh have pointed to the ways in which anticolonial responses to *The Tempest* tend to cast "Caliban as the prototype of a male revolutionary," facing off in existential battle with his tormentor in "a utopia in which women are marginalized or missing" (Singh 1996, 194). Postcolonial women writers, among them Elisabeth Nuñez and Paule Marshall, have responded to this gendered blind spot by writing Miranda into a more fully fleshed-out being in their own reworkings of Shakespeare's play and its anti- and postcolonial avatars.[7]

Unlike the works of the preceding authors, both male and female, *The Autobiography of My Mother* presents not a rewriting of but an intertextual engagement with both Shakespeare's play and Césaire's revision, *A Tempest* ([1969] 1992). Kincaid's reframing of both works in the *Autobiography* is unique in this literary landscape. The narrative never explicitly references a source text via the names of its characters or the restaging of specific plot points. Rather, it relies on *The Tempest* and *A Tempest* to ground multiple layers of refusal, and it does so in ways that depart generatively from both texts. The *Autobiography* decries the silencing not only of women but also of indigenous peoples in both imperialist and anti-imperialist renderings of the colonial encounter.

From the outset, Kincaid posits the vulnerability of the native subject to the treacheries of colonial discourse—just as in the critical early scene already described, in which Xuela evokes the cultural violence of knowledge imparted to/imposed on the native by the colonizer. Xuela's context is the colonial classroom, the space wherein her missionary-trained teacher's words "so often seemed to be a series of harsh blows" (22) couched in a charade of disinterested generosity. Like Caliban, Xuela suffers these blows immensely and comes to know herself as marked by "vulnerability, subject to the powerful whims of others" (17). Yet, whereas Caliban's only "profit" from the language he has been forced to learn is that he knows "how to curse" a tormentor he continues to serve (Shakespeare 1611, act 1, scene 2), Xuela instinctively understands that the process of accessing the would-be master's knowledge represents the beginnings of a way for the colonized subject—a way that, if not yet situated altogether outside of the epistemic frame, at least escapes that particular instantiation thereof.

Once she has acquired literacy, extracting a bit of power from a wholly disempowering context, Xuela begins to write letters to her father, letters that, in the position she "was expected to occupy—the position of a woman and a poor one" (18)—she was never meant to have even imagined writing. Yet, in writing these letters Xuela inadvertently engages in a tentative practice of refusal. That the letters are discovered and sent to her father, and that they spur him to rescue her from the slow degradation of her context, is a revelation to Xuela. "I had," she writes, "through the use of some words, changed my situation; I had perhaps even saved my life" (22). Newly aware of her power to shape her own experience, she begins to trace the contours of a possible personal freedom.

Xuela's stumbling yet resolute quest for ways out(side) signals what I would argue is Kincaid's Wynterian contention with Shakespeare's play. A consideration of her actions within Wynter's theoretical frame makes the nuances of Xuela's subject position most clear. Wynter's powerful essay "Beyond Miranda's Meanings: Un/Silencing the 'Demonic Ground' of Caliban's 'Woman,'" the afterword to the landmark anthology *Out of the Kumbla: Caribbean Women and Literature* (1990), proposes a number of tools that are useful for reading Xuela through Shakespeare's text, as well as for understanding Kincaid's ambivalent position as a postcolonial Caribbean writer.

It is no coincidence that, as with Kincaid's *Autobiography*, "Beyond Miranda's Meanings" has at once made Wynter a target of critique and provided the foundations of rich theoretical inquiry.[8] The essay takes Shakespeare's *The Tempest* as frame and lays out a speculative critique that posits the significance and signifying potential of a remarkable absence—a silence, a queer and demonic beyond—in Caribbean history. This absence, Wynter argues, is a woman. A native woman. Caliban's "woman." Caliban's "physiognomically complementary mate" (Wynter 1990, 360). Unspoken because unthinkable, missing but not missed from the chronicle of New World origin stories, Caliban's woman has not merely been overlooked; she has been disavowed. Although she is absent, she is a powerful force. Her very absence speaks to this power—a power to disrupt the order laid out not only in Shakespeare's imperialist European imaginary but also in Césaire's anticolonial revisioning of the Shakespearean worldview.

Thrillingly for Wynter, Caliban's woman dwells in a space beyond both the scope of these two foundational texts and the veritable edifice of critical discourse they have generated. The absence of Caliban's woman is, Wynter argues, "the most significant absence of all" (1990, 360), in that this figure points to "an alternative source of an alternative system of meanings" (360). Her territory is a "demonic ground" at once marginalized and rich with potential. In the case of *The Tempest*, her absence reveals the very foundations of a secular Renaissance colonial project that sub/un/consciously envisioned the extermination (nonreproduction) of the native populations of the so-called New World. Her absence from *A Tempest* suggests the subconscious confinement of Césaire's rewriting within a colonial script. In both texts, only Miranda stands as representative object of desire and voiced feminine being. The native island woman exceeds the frame.

In his field-transforming 1986 work *Colonial Encounters: Europe and the Native Caribbean, 1492-1797*, Peter Hulme helpfully signals the existence of a frame within the frame of Shakespeare's play—that is, a built-in provision for excess in the original work. "In a play where so much of what is crucial has taken place before the curtain rises," he writes, "we are obliged to ask who is telling us what and how they know" (1986, 114). Hulme continues, "We are made aware that Caliban has his own story and that it does not begin where Prospero's begins. A space is opened, as it were, behind Prospero's narrative, a gap that allows us to see that Prospero's narrative is not simply history, not simply the way things were, but a particular *version*" (124). What, then, might be that history or those histories "behind"—beyond—the play? This is the space that Césaire and others, in their attention to Caliban, have sought to explore.

In considering this space beyond the play through Wynter's lens, however, we are called on to use our imaginations—to be demonic in our explorations of this territory outside. During those moments wherein a trusting Caliban was being lured or seduced into Prospero's history trap, might another story have been unfolding? Might there also have been a native woman there, unlinked to the original Shakespearean trio? A witness, hanging back? A less trusting being, perhaps—a being uninterested in water with berries and other poisoned fruits proffered by the colonial machine, aware that the global tides of history are turned against her and her kind?[9] A being determined to survive and to not be complicit? And if there were that being, who might she have been? What might she have been like?

Might she have been something like Xuela?

Vulnerable yet ruthless, dysselected yet self-assured, silenced yet refusing, Kincaid's heroine offers a response to Wynter's call for an epistemic space unconstrained by existing qualifiers of human being—an incarnation of this absent-because-unimaginable player on the New World stage. If some have argued that Xuela is "unbelievable in her isolation and pain" (Paravisini-Gebert 1999, 36), that is perhaps exactly the point. Xuela's lack of precedent, her singularity, her unthinkability within the structures/strictures of a contemporary postcolonial frame "[draw] attention to the insufficiency of all existing theoretical interpretative models" (Wynter 1990, 363). That Kincaid has written Xuela into existence serves to "make thinkable the possibility of a new 'model' projected from a new 'native' standpoint" (Wynter 1990, 363–64). To see Xuela in this light recasts the *Autobiography* as something other than a "barren fictional landscape of death, absence, and loss" (Nasta 2009, 71). We also find there a conceptual space that escapes Shakespeare's design as well as that of its conscripted anticolonial interlocutors.[10]

Xuela claims outright her status as native woman, in defiant contrast to the white femininity with which Wynter argues that women of color must contend. Observing the white wife of her employer (and future husband), for example, Xuela observes, "She was a lady, I was a woman, and this distinction to her was important" (158). She continues, "A lady is a combination of elaborate fascinations, a collection of externals, facial arrangements, and body parts, distortions, lies, and empty effort. I was a woman and as that I had a brief definition: two breasts, a small opening between my legs, one womb; it never varies and they are always in the same place" (159). Aware that she is perceived as a body-bound Other, Xuela highlights the long-historical separation between the *"true* women of the colonizer/settlers on the one hand, and *nativewomen* on the other" (Wynter 2000, 174). She understands and even celebrates this presumed difference. Refusing to be trapped by the overdetermined category of Black female sexual waywardness, she owns her "venal embodiment" (Sharpley-Whiting 1999, 12) and exists "freed from the restraints of dignity" (Weheliye 2014, 129). Whereas the white woman's "situation was a climate she did not like, a place full of people she could never love" (157), Xuela knows: this island is hers by her mother.[11]

What is more, Xuela presents an avatar of Caliban's woman that escapes even Wynter's own schema. If "Wynter's new theoretical model ... creates a trope in which the Caribbean woman is still to be inscribed as Caliban's 'object of desire,' functioning as his sexual reproductive mate" (Balutansky 1990, 543), Kincaid circumvents this limitation by imagining Caliban's *counterpart* rather than his companion. She avoids the arguably heteronormative imposition implicit in Wynter's narrative of thwarted procreative pairing and instead crafts a powerful alter/native subject position. Reproduction is not Xuela's end goal—her aim is a nihilism not unlike that of Frantz Fanon's damned (*damnés*).[12] No children survive, thrive, or procreate in the microcosm of Xuela's entire family. Legacy is interrupted, as is any inheritance of pathology. Never would she allow Caliban to "people this isle with Calibans" (Shakespeare 1611, act 1, scene 2). Never would she bear children into the snare of the Americas. She would sooner "eat them at night, swallowing them whole, all at once" (97).

Xuela is her own woman—a woman who would no more be Caliban's than anyone else's. If, as Lamming would have it, "Caliban orders History" ([1960] 1992, chap. 7), Xuela disorders it. She is situated beyond Wynter's beyond. And this is attested to by her very name. Prospero named Caliban, just as Christopher Columbus named the "cannibals" he encountered in the Americas—Caliban "is the name for the colonized, a name provided by the colonizer" (Goldberg 2004, 16). Césaire addresses the alienation inherent in this imposition by having his Caliban demand to be called X.[13] Kamau Brathwaite, too, refuses to be named by the colonizer. In his poem "X/Self xth letter from the thirteenth provinces" ([1987] 2001, 444-56) he follows Césaire's lead and endeavors to subvert both colonial nomenclature and numeration. Both writers evoke the masculinist tropes of Black revolution through this gesture. "Xuela" is a name invented by Kincaid—it gestures to the "X" of Black radicalism and is opaque to the extreme. Xuela, like her name, originates in the demonic ground of Kincaid's imagination.

> *This island's mine, by Sycorax, my mother!*
> —Caliban (in Shakespeare's *The Tempest*)

> *I claimed my birthright, East and West, Above and Below, Water and Land: In a dream. I walked through my inheritance, an island of villages and rivers and mountains and people who began and ended with murder and theft and not very much love. I claimed it in a dream. . . . I dreamed of all the things that were mine.*
> —Xuela Claudette Richardson (in *The Autobiography of My Mother*)

Reading the *Autobiography* as intertextually engaged with both Shakespeare's and Césaire's plays requires an attentiveness to Xuela's Carib identity and then to the real history—that history in the gap—that this identity contains. Here, too, Kincaid's novel proposes a conceptual space beyond even the possibilities Wynter dreams up. Not so fast, that is, with the idea of "the rapid decimation of the indigenous Arawaks of the Caribbean Islands" (Wynter 1990, 363).[14] Whereas Wynter elides the distinction between transplanted Africans and American native populations, *The Autobiography of My Mother* digs into the historical commonplace of "aboriginal disappearance" or "aboriginal absence" (Newton 2013, 108, 109) and evokes the centuries of indigenous struggle against what was perhaps always the inevitability of defeat.[15]

Kincaid refuses the absorption of this still-present native history into a history of disenfranchised otherness writ large. In this, her narrative diverges from Wynter's engagements with indigeneity. Wynter's "native" is a metaphor, a category of deferent and deficient difference that applies as much to indigenous Americans as to New World Blacks—the "ontological 'native/nigger'" (Wynter 1990, 364). Both natives and Blacks, in her view, are peoples reduced to "labor-machine[s]" in the transatlantic slave economy (360). In collapsing these ethnoracial categories and their histories, "Wynter does not deal with the internal problematics of coalitions among non-white people. Her analysis is inadequate to the relations of Man's Others and the power dynamics among them" (Serynada 2015).

Wynter's position is by no means unusual. As Melanie J. Newton has written, "by the 1990s anglophone Caribbean philosophers and cultural theorists firmly identified Caliban with an Afro-Caribbean intellectual tradition and experience" (2013, 113). The notion of the Caribbean as a space of "modernity without aboriginality" (112) was foundational to Caribbean narratives of subjectivity and revolution and is apparent in canonical anticolonial and postcolonial works by Césaire, Lamming, Brathwaite, and others. A reading of these authors' writings might easily sustain the scholarly conclusion that "the original inhabitants of the Caribbean, were annihilated, and nothing remained but a blankness waiting to be filled by African slaves" (Dayan 1992, 125).[16]

While Kincaid does not necessarily escape the "aboriginal extinction narrative" (Newton 2013, 121), she does nuance it significantly.[17] She exposes the positioning of "us" and "them" in conflict, as it emerges even from within nonwhite community. The *Autobiography* presents an individual Afro-Amerindian woman who declares herself worthy of consideration but does not subsume her nativeness into her blackness. Xuela extricates blackness from indigeneity and places the two in contentious relation to one another. Yes, her isolation is in many ways of her own making but not entirely so. With her long black hair, sharp cheekbones, and slanted eyes, Xuela is presumed by many in her community to be Carib, though she is so only on her mother's side—her father being of both sub-Saharan African and Scottish ancestry. "My mother was a Carib woman," Xuela declares, "and when they looked at me, this is what they saw: The Carib people had been defeated and then exterminated.... The African people had been defeated but had survived. When they looked at me, they saw only the Carib people. They were wrong but I did not tell them so" (15–16).[18]

Whereas, to take a celebrated example, Fanon describes his initial confrontation with his deficient otherness as taking place only upon his displacement to Europe as a young man—"*Maman*, look, a Negro; I'm scared!" ([1952] 2008, 91)—Kincaid's Xuela faces racial pathologization in a *local* context and from her earliest childhood: "My teacher, who was trained to think only of good and evil and whose judgment of such things was always mistaken, said I was evil, I was possessed—and to establish that there could be no doubt of this, she pointed to the fact that my mother was of the Carib people" (16–17). Such moments excavate a more complex regional history. They declare the specificity of the Native American experience of colonial exploitation—an experience largely unknown to and overshadowed by the experience of enslaved Africans and their descendants.

At a pivotal point in the novel, as a grown woman, Xuela has a dream. She has the dream as she lies on the floor of a hut, passed out from the pain of expelling a fetus from her womb—a fetus brought into being as a result of her affair with Jack Labatte, her landlord and her father's business partner. Xuela dreams herself journeying across her island on foot, naming all the spaces of her "inheritance" (89) as she travels. One of the first sites she names is Massacre, a city located on the southwestern coast of Dominica, not far from the capital. "It was at Massacre," Xuela notes, "that Indian Warner, the illegitimate son of a Carib woman and a European man, was murdered by his half brother, an Englishman named Philip Warner, because Philip Warner did not like having such a close relative whose mother was a Carib woman" (87). This one sentence contains a whirl of history. It points to an incident in 1675 wherein an expedition led by Warner was sent into Dominica to pacify by force a population of Kalinagos (whom the English called Caribs). From their stronghold in Dominica, these natives violently resisted British incursion into their territories in the Caribbean, "[using] the island as a military base for expeditions against the English" (Beckles 2008, 88). Warner's troops massacred the Kalinagos, among whom was his half brother Thomas "Indian" Warner, a prominent chief and, as governor of Dominica under the English, "an important figure in the complicated and shifting alliances of the mid-seventeenth century Caribbean" (Hulme 2000, 206).

While this was one of several defeats of indigenous Americans by colonial forces, the event is nonetheless a reminder of a significant yet rarely discussed historical truth: the enduring, substantive, and resistant indigenous presence in Dominica, which "kept the Windward Islands in a marginal relation to the slave plantation complex of the North Atlantic system for two hundred years, and in so doing, made a principal contribution to the Caribbean's anti-colonial and anti-slavery tradition" (Beckles 2008, 90–91). Thus, while Kincaid proceeds from the contested notion of native genocide in the Americas, Xuela's allusion to Carib anticolonial resistance insists that native and African histories were and continue to be deeply intertwined.

Massacre has been evoked in other postcolonial literary fictions. Most noteworthy is its mention by Jean Rhys in *Wide Sargasso Sea* (1982). In an allusion as brief and as provocative as in *Autobiography*, Rhys's protagonist Antoinette returns to Dominica with her British husband for their honeymoon and lands at Massacre:

> "And who was massacred here? Slaves?" her husband asks.
> "Oh no." She sounded shocked. "Not slaves. Something must have happened a long time ago. Nobody remembers now." (65–66)

In *Remnants of Conquest: The Island Caribs and Their Visitors, 1877–1998*, Hulme takes a close look at this claim—"Nobody remembers now"—and draws attention to what Antoinette's dismissive account means to express, notably, the binaristic presumptions of white violence against Black slaves in the islands. Rhys, of course, knew full well what happened at Massacre and knew that this event would fall outside the colonial, anticolonial, and even postcolonial scripts by introducing native histories that otherwise have been buried or disremembered. The "a long time ago" confirms this, insofar as it gestures toward a so-called prehistory, that is, a history unrecorded in the narrative of the transatlantic slave trade and the birth of the modern Americas. The silence around this history has to do with its complexity—it distracts from the bigger story of long-term Black subjugation in the so-called New World and opens the door, perhaps, to questions of missed opportunities for solidarity among populations of the defeated, if only through more rigorous attention to the historical record.

Though the Caribs were ultimately conquered, "it was through no fault of their own that they had lost" (198), Xuela insists. This history animates her subconscious and reminds her of her belonging to—her right to be in—this space from which she has been ostracized and banished. It is her persistent remembrance of an alternative world order—one in which the Caribs' struggle attenuates the shame of their final defeat. It allows her to withstand, in part, the hostility of the African-descended community that has staked its putatively "post-" colonial claim to the island. Thus can we begin to understand Xuela's grappling with and eventual mourning of a future that ultimately was not—but that might have been and that fought to be. What kind of men were they who came and wreaked such havoc on a people they neither knew nor understood? This question also haunts Xuela. "Murder and theft," she dream-remembers. Césaire and others tell us that the "great majority of northern Europeans who crossed to the Caribbean in these centuries were adventurers—pirates, merchants, and later, planters and paupers" (Boucher 1992, 8).[19] We also know that the "'Caribs' owed their bad name principally to their fierce resistance to European conquest and enslavement" (9–10). Xuela knows these things, too, though perhaps she knows them and can claim them for herself—as her truth—only in a dream.

The anti-social dictates an un-becoming, a cleaving to that which seems to shame or annihilate.
—Jack Halberstam, "The Anti-social Turn in Queer Studies" (2008)

Voluntarily narcissistic, women writers are concerned only with themselves and their ancestry, without thinking of the heritage they leave behind. . . . Because the world ends with them, no need to think about what it is becoming or its possible transformations. We should see in this attitude the expression of a certain anguish in the face of the future and of their powerlessness to define it or to propose any kind of solution to the burning problems of the Antilles.
—Maryse Condé, *La parole des femmes* (1979)

> *I did not see the future, and that is perhaps as it should be.*
>
> —Xuela Claudette Richardson (in *The Autobiography of My Mother*)

What happens immediately after Xuela's dream-journey, in her conscious life, suggests that the dream marks—has precipitated, even—a pivotal moment in her personal evolution. The first step in her escape from what Caribbeanist philosopher Paget Henry describes as "the inherited world of the ego" (2000, 106), it begins a risky process of Orphic descent into and unmaking of a self that has internalized imposed pathology. Following her dream of self-repossession, Xuela begins to reinterpret reality—to refuse its damaging distortions and to engage in "a constant revolutionary assault against it" (Wynter 1968, 24).

Once Xuela has awakened and physically recovered, she returns to the home of Jack Labatte and his wife, Lise, although it was in fact this home—and all the sly obligations and expectations embedded within it—that she meant to reject by aborting the child she had conceived there. Originally, Xuela had come to the Labattes' household not against, but also not of, her own will. Her father had placed her in the Labattes' home as the most expedient solution to the problem of what to do with her in the face of his new wife's—Xuela's stepmother's—violent hostility: "That I might have had aspirations of my own would not have occurred to him," Xuela writes, "and if I had aspirations of my own, I did not know of them" (63). Xuela's father had handed her over to Monsieur Labatte and his wife—or, more accurately, to Madame Labatte and her husband—as a boarder and servant.[20]

This was not the first time Xuela had been given to strangers by her father. Following the death of her own mother in childbirth, which had left her just "a small child vulnerable to all the world" (4), Xuela's father abandoned her to the care of his laundress, Ma Eunice, a woman with six children of her own. Beaten down by life, impoverished and perpetually unclean, Ma Eunice was no more or less loving toward Xuela than she was toward her own children; she simply "could not be kind because she did not know how" (6), Xuela observes. From the outset, Xuela is able to pick up on the danger this substitute family poses to her, and she feels her vulnerability keenly while there. That Ma Eunice cherishes beyond all measure a china plate embossed with an image of the English countryside and the single word "Heaven" and that "none of Ma Eunice's girl children attended school" (12) are simple but unambiguous manifestations of the combined forces of colonialist and patriarchal ideology that structure this family.

These phenomena are not fully legible to the child Xuela as such, but they nonetheless make her wary and recalcitrant. When, for example, she (accidentally?) smashes Ma Eunice's beloved plate, somehow aware of its symbolic menace, she neither feels nor is willing to say she is sorry. She has begun to grasp "the relationship between captor and captive, master and slave, with its motif of the big and the small, the powerful and the powerless, the strong and the weak" (10), and to understand what her place is meant to be within this schema. The price of allowing herself to be mothered by Ma Eunice, she understands, would be her own submission; it would be to accept Ma Eunice's "power to make [her] feel helpless and ashamed at [her] own helplessness" (25).

More dangerous to Xuela than the atmosphere of alienation in which she lived with Ma Eunice was the bodily threat later posed to her by her father's new wife. From the moment of seven-year-old Xuela's careless insertion into his new household following her inadvertent letter-writing campaign, Xuela's stepmother appears to her as "the face of evil" (28). Not only does this substitute maternal figure not love Xuela, but she seeks actively to humiliate and even destroy her.[21] "My father's wife wished me dead," Xuela insists, and this certainty, borne out by actual events, makes Xuela feel constantly "so alone," "in danger," "threatened," vulnerable (30). Xuela's response to this mortal threat is to engage in a sort of narcissistic artfulness and thus to cherish—discreetly—her physical self:

> The world I came to know was full of danger and treachery.... So... I tried to cloak myself.... I was very careful... I calculated.... I did not seem to them to have any interest in the world of my body or anyone else's body. This wearying demand was only one of many demands made on me simply because I was female. From the moment I stepped out of bed in the early morning to the time I covered myself up again in the dark of night, I negotiated many treacherous acts of deception, but it was clear to me who I was. (41–42)[22]

These reflections culminate in an act of bodily self-love, one that echoes Tituba Indian's onanistic moment of self-awakening: "My hands... traveled up and down and all over my own body in a loving caress, finally coming to the soft, moist spot between my legs, and a gasp of pleasure... escaped my lips which I would allow no one to hear" (43).[23]

As with Ma Eunice, Xuela's stepmother's lack of maternal affection is not personal. It is a function of a communal, social order structured around filiation, patriarchy, and the accumulation of capital. At the beginning, her father's wife fears Xuela's role as firstborn, reminder of another woman who has already fulfilled the roles of wife and mother of his child. Then, once she has children of her own, thus assuring her own reproductive value, she comes to view Xuela as another sort of enemy, "like a thief in the house, waiting for the right moment when I would rob them of their inheritance" (52).[24] Given her father's rapidly increasing material wealth, Xuela represents a potential filial interloper. In mortal danger in her stepmother's house, Xuela is brought to live with the Labattes for her own safety.

Not long after being set up in the Labattes' household, Xuela enters into a decidedly ambivalent relationship with her hosts. She and Madame Labatte come to care deeply for one another, establishing something like a mother-daughter connection: "She . . . told me to make myself at home, to regard her as if she were my own mother, to feel safe whenever she was near" (66). At the same time, however, Xuela senses that this kindness is compromised by Madame Labatte's love for her husband and desire to accommodate him. In Xuela's eyes, Madame Labatte's wifely adoration had made her a "shadow of her former self" (66); it had broken her, drained her of her vitality and beauty, and left her at once pitiably defeated and threatening in her desperation. Xuela is immediately and viscerally aware that, differently perhaps but just as truly as Ma Eunice or her stepmother, Madame Labatte is a danger to her: "She wanted something from me, I could tell that. . . . This thought came upon me slowly. . . . She wants to make a gift of me to her husband; she wants to give me to him, she hopes I do not mind. . . . The vulnerability I felt was not of the body, it was of the spirit, the soul" (68–69). Xuela eventually does enter into a sexual relationship with Monsieur Labatte—"I spent the day with her; I spent the night with him. It was not an arrangement made with words" (74)—and she eventually becomes pregnant. Then she realizes what Madame Labatte really wants from her. Unable to bear children herself, Madame Labatte means for Xuela to stand in not only as her erotic proxy but also as her maternal surrogate: "She wanted a child I might have" (77). This would be the real price of her room and board—shoring up Madame Labatte's domestic security and participating in her pathetic family fiction.

However, by refusing to play her prescribed role in this drama, by refusing to bear Monsieur Labatte's child and thus to allow her body to be the offering of a defeated wife to her all-consuming husband, Xuela initiates a process of affirmative self-realization. In an act of absolute refusal, she turns to a bush doctor and rids herself, in "a volcano of pain," of the "black hole" (82) she believes a child would have made of her life. The near-death experience of her abortion reminds her that her survival as a self-determining being is at stake: "I was a new person then, I knew things I had not known before, I knew things that you can only know if you have been through what I had just been through. I had carried my own life in my own hands" (83). This refusal to mother is the premise of her dream; it catalyzes her repossession of her self: "Exhausted from the agony of expelling from my body a child I could not love and so did not want, I dreamed of all the things that were mine" (89). It is a forceful determining of her self by herself, and it is contingent on a rejection not merely of this one would-be child but of the whole of a domestic paradigm that ultimately would co-opt and crush her.[25]

It is on seeing the Labattes for the first time after the clarifying ordeal of her abortion that Xuela articulates to herself this process of adamant self-preservation. Newly without child, and having successfully defended herself against Madame Labatte's maternal hunger, Xuela has emerged better able to decipher her world and define her own place in it: "We stood, the three of us, in a little triangle ... a wordless trinity. And yet at that moment someone was of the defeated, someone was of the resigned, and someone was changed forever. I was not of the defeated; I was not of the resigned" (93). Identifying herself as the one "changed forever," no longer as one of the defeated, Xuela means for the rest of her life to be legible with respect to this period of rebirth. Not long after this capital moment of restaging, Xuela embarks on a more definitive journey of refusal, abandoning the Labattes for good this time and leaving behind the conditions of social inclusion they represent and would impose. She decides to burn down, uproot, and annihilate these conditions, unburdening herself of the very possibility of maternity. Xuela's declaration of independence is well known and worth citing in its entirety:

> I had never had a mother, I had just recently refused to become one, and I knew then that this refusal would be complete. I would never become a mother, but that would not be the same as never bearing children. I would bear children, but I would never be a mother to them. I would bear them in abundance; they would emerge from my head, from my armpits, from between my legs; I would bear children, they would hang from me like fruit from a vine, but I would destroy them with the carelessness of a god. I would bear children in the morning, I would bathe them at noon in a water that came from myself, and I would eat them at night, swallowing them whole, all at once. They would live and then they would not live. In their day of life, I would walk them to the edge of a precipice. I would not push them over; I would not have to; the sweet voices of unusual pleasures would call to them from the bottom; they would not rest until they became one with those sounds. I would cover their bodies with

diseases, embellish skins with thinly crusted sores, the sores sometimes oozing a thick pus for which they would thirst, a thirst that could never be quenched. I would condemn them to live in an empty space frozen in the same posture in which they had been born. I would throw them from a great height; every bone in their body would be broken and the bones would never be properly set, healing in the way they were broken, healing never at all. I would decorate them when they were only corpses and set each corpse in a polished wooden box, and place the polished wooden box in the earth and forget the part of the earth where I had buried the box. It is in this way that I did not become a mother; it is in this way that I bore my children. (96–98)

Much has rightly been made of the violence and the rage that pour out of this passage. It is arguably the most brutal portrayal of a *mère dénaturée* (deviant mother) in all of Caribbean literature. But the violence with which Xuela refuses motherhood is merited in the war in which Xuela knows she is engaged, a war within which there can be no solidarity, not even among women. Every encounter with other women, be they elders, mothers, or sisters-in-exploitation, proves to Xuela that the victims of patriarchy can just as well be its agents, just as the victims of colonialism can also be its instruments: "For, in fact, much of Xuela's anger derives from women's own reenactment of certain self-subjecting cultural expectations ciphered in the notions of sexuality and reproduction, as well as from the place she is assigned within these expectations" (De Ferrari 2012, 150).[26]

Xuela is aware that even her own dead mother, "a quiet, shy, long-suffering, unquestioning, modest, wishing-to-die soon person" (199), could only have been a danger to her had she lived. This woman whose name she bears but whose fate she refuses would have been, and would have raised her daughter to be, resigned: "her sadness, her weakness, her long-lost-ness, the crumbling of ancestral lines, her dejectedness, the false humility that was really defeat" (200), this was the sum of her maternal heritage. Xuela thus views her mother's death as the primary condition of her own freedom. "To say it makes me sad not to have known her would not be true at all," she writes. "I am only sad to know that such a life had to exist" (201). To refuse and replace this tragic maternal being is at the core of Xuela's reordering of her self in the world: "This is an account of the person who was never allowed to be and an account of the person I did not allow myself to become" (228).

Xuela directly links her rejection of maternity, moreover, to the original tragedy of her own mother's death, insofar as she implicates the traumatic loss of her mother in the impossibility of imagining her own successful maternity: "She died at the moment I was born, and though I can sensibly say to myself such a thing cannot be helped . . . how can any child understand such a thing, so profound an abandonment? I have refused to bear any children" (199). This connection recalls Tituba's refusal to bear John Indian's child. Having witnessed as a little girl the execution by hanging of her mother, Abena, Tituba reacts viscerally to the sight of an elderly woman's execution in Salem, which confirms for her society's cruelty and injustice with respect to its most vulnerable members: "It was as if I had been condemned to relive my mother's execution. No it wasn't an old woman swinging there. It was Abena in the flower of her youth and at the height of her beauty. Yes, it was she and I was six years old again. And my life had to begin all over again from that moment! . . . It was shortly afterward that I realized I was pregnant and I decided to kill the child" (49).

There is something more troubling to Xuela's rant—something even darker to be read there, too. Xuela's celebration of her death-giving power speaks also to pleasure and the sublime. There is unbridled, delicious sadism in Xuela's graphic infanticidal musings. Her rejection of motherhood is as fierce as it is categorical. Xuela is clear: this is not a question of merciful abortion. She would give birth to these children so as to torture and kill them. She would be a cannibal, even. Unredeemable, inhuman. She refuses nothing so much as she refuses redemption. Her words announce the defiant unmaking of a human being—a woman—with respect to the ordering codes of a hostile world that has sought to prescribe her existence. In this way Xuela not only breaks with a traumatic past but also forecloses its attendant future. She refuses a past defined by the dogma of coloniality and patriarchy attached to maternity—a reality steeped in the "pressure to perform reproductive heterosexuality as a form of national citizenship" (Sheller 2012, 239), wherein "the Antillean man continues to valorize children, to take pride in having abundant offspring" (Condé [1979] 2000, 45–46). Xuela's unwillingness to mother is a refusal of this order. It is, moreover, a refusal to believe in the possibility of a better future world—or, rather, a refusal to believe in her own capacity or in the capacity of those around her to create the conditions of such a possibility.

Xuela's refusal of maternity is also a refusal of "the kind of black liberatory time Fanon would have seen as possible in the mid-twentieth century, or the kind of utopian future envisioned by 1970s revolutionaries" (D. Thomas 2016, 186). She proposes a Fanonian nihilism without the optimism of a consequent political project. As Curdella Forbes has written in regard to another of Kincaid's protagonists, Xuela's "vision of the collective is not redemptive—there is no third element of dialectic in which she sees self and collective potentially reconciled. Rather the third element is the self, self-made and standing alone" (2008, 26). Xuela makes no "claims for political inclusion," well aware that "the expression of political subjectivity is also always a further inscription into the state order" (Sheller 2012, 9) of which she wants no part. "The present is always the moment for which I live. The future I never long for, it will come or it will not; one day it will not" (205), Xuela announces. She will inhabit only a rough present, one without community and its treacherous particular beings. Her only promise to the future is to not reproduce its pathologies. And also to save herself.

After leaving the Labattes and declaring her sublime refusal to mother children, Xuela cuts off her long hair, dresses herself in a dead man's clothes, and takes a job doing hard labor, all the while destroying any last traces of her social identity up to that point: "I did not look like a man, I did not look like a woman" (98–99), she declares. This effortful self-ungendering marks Xuela's doubly literal trans-formation. Her actions are legible, that is, both as a radical change of appearance or character and as the embodiment of what theorist Marquis Bey calls "fugitive identificatory demarcations" (2017, 276). From the outset racially ambiguous, and from the moment of her final flight from the Labattes ambiguously gendered, Xuela comes to exist within the demonic ground of trans-ness and blackness. In Bey's deft theorizations, both trans-ness and blackness propose fundamentally "fugitive, lawless" categories that denote at once the phenotypical "materiality of ontic subjects" and "para-ontological forces" that extend beyond the limits of attachment to "bodies said to be black and transgender" (278, 276). For Bey, trans-ness and blackness de facto designate a "modality of constant escape" (279). Xuela commits wholly to this permanent liminality. She remains rooted only in elusiveness and refusal—untethered and often indifferent to (the desires of) parents, siblings, and sexual partners, uninterested in any connection that would require constancy.

Xuela's explicitly queer moment of trans-formation proposes, then, an experiment in "queer unbelonging" (Caserio 2006, 819). Insofar as "conditions for belonging presuppose a raced, gendered, classed, and sexed body" (Francis 2010, 2), Xuela chooses the disorder of deliberate social undoing. Where Tituba believed that embracing normative femininity—cutting and "neatening" her hair, decking herself out in a dress and jewelry to attract John Indian—would get her the love she desired, Xuela takes an opposing route. She concretizes, via literal bodily display, the "rejection of futurity" and a "relentless form of negativity." She makes of her body a personal contestation of what

Jack Halberstam describes as the "forward looking, reproductive and heteronormative politics of hope" (2008, 141) so much a part of any given anti-cum-postcolonial liberation project. Writing of what he dubs "the anti-social turn in queer studies" in an essay of that title, Halberstam embraces the extent to which a quasi-nihilist practice of refusal "mitigates against liberal fantasies of progressive enlightenment and community cohesion" (143), and posits queerness as a refusal to believe the hype of any national narratives. To the extent to which futurity "signifies the nation, the divisions of class and race upon which the notion of national belonging depends" (Halberstam 2008, 147), Xuela's declaration—"I refused to belong to a race, I refused to accept a nation" (226)—is at once apolitical and revolutionary.

Bordering on resistance, adjacent to agency, Xuela's refusal is an "occurrence of freedom in a zone of indistinction" (Weheliye 2014, 2). It is a refusal to do the kind of affective labor expected of women of color, and a refusal to be reconciled to the epistemic fictions that nationalism and Black sovereignty never managed to disrupt. We can understand this refusal, along with the abortion of her fetus and the violent freedom-dream it inspires, as the culmination of the knowledge Xuela has gained about maternity, futurity, and community. She will not entertain the "possibility of community outside of or after the self" and "makes no gestures at all toward futurity" (Rody 2001, 129).

Because of these categorical refusals, her community perceives Xuela as a danger. If "loyalty to the nation as citizen is perennially colonized within reproduction and heterosexuality, [Xuela's] erotic autonomy brings with it the potential of undoing the nation entirely" (Alexander 2005, 23). If, that is, "all tragedy deals with a community threatened by a break in the chain of filiation, what better way of altering [disordering!] the system of filiation than to give birth to oneself?" (De Ferrari 2012, 177). Xuela's resolute refusal to perpetuate community and her exclusive commitment to self-creation can only be perceived by that community as disordering and tragic.

The mirror for the redeemed narcissist, is not a mere site at which [s]he can perform such base functions as decoration or adornment. Rather the mirror serves as a location that allows "The Regarded Self" a sacred and intense solitude by which [s]he can renegotiate and disclose [her] superior self at all costs.
—Iké Udé, "The Regarded Self" (1995)

I love myself. I am my god.
—Elizabeth Lunbeck, *The Americanization of Narcissism* (2014)

> *My face was beautiful, I found it so.*
>
> —Xuela Claudette Richardson (in *The Autobiography of My Mother*)

Giving birth to oneself is precisely what Xuela means to do. This is the only procreative labor she will perform. Immediately following her rejection of maternity and subsequent autoliberation from the most obvious markers of her gender, Xuela closes herself within a chrysalis of refusal—"I spoke to no one, not even to myself" (99). She spends her days as an anonymous manual laborer and her nights alone in her rented shack. Out of this isolation, she becomes reborn into utter self-regard.

> I came to know myself, and this frightened me. To rid myself of this fear I began to look at a reflection of my face in any surface I could find: a still pool on the shallow banks of the river became my most common mirror.... It was seeing my face that comforted me, I began to worship myself.... My own face was a comfort to me, my own body was a comfort to me, and no matter how swept away I would become by anyone or anything, in the end I allowed nothing to replace my own being in my own mind. (99–100)

This unmistakable staging of the emblematic scene of self-encounter is the beating heart of Kincaid's novel. It is a pivotal moment of narcissistic retreat—what Iké Udé describes as a "sort of sublime awareness of the self, inhabited by the self and nourished with appropriate fastidiousness" (1995, 17). Once Xuela has determined to be the unique arbiter of her own value, she makes it a point to query relentlessly. "What is the everyday? What is the ordinary?" (169), Xuela muses. She will take nothing for granted, nothing for absolute truth—nothing for anything other than the construction of dangerous "truth-fors" that can only be her undoing.[27]

Xuela gradually discerns that "to be a colonial was precisely to be excluded from all autonomous processes of decision-making with respect to one's fate as a *collectivity*" (Wynter 1989, 637; emphasis mine)—to accept a self-defeating conformity. She knows that her survival—her physical and psychological self-preservation—is contingent on recognizing and refusing the deep-rooted self-hatred that surrounds her, even if it means being alone. To cleave to her community—so burdened and so overdetermined by its colonial hauntings—would be to accept fundamental nonsovereignty. It would be to accept alienation by association. Engaged in "a struggle to the death for the life of the self" (Forbes 2008, 32), Xuela harbors no illusions about her safety among her people—"The world I came to know was full of danger and treachery" (41)—and she does not expect to be reconciled to her community in some ameliorated future.[28] So she carves out a space of self in direct contradistinction to that of the collective.

From this instinctively, if painfully, created safe space of "sacred and intense solitude," Xuela sounds her own depths and determines to "renegotiate and disclose [her] superior self at all costs" (Udé 1995, 17) She embarks on a process of what Henry calls "voidings" of the ego, leaving her self "exposed to experiences of nonbeing" (2000, 33). She risks this exposure of the self—the self standing outside the everyday and confronting itself—so as to achieve a state of authenticity, in the most philosophical sense of the term:

> The word we translate as "authenticity" is actually a neologism invented by Heidegger, the word *Eigentlichkeit*, which comes from an ordinary term, *eigentlich*, meaning "really" or "truly," but is built on the stem *eigen*, meaning "own" or "proper." So the word might be more literally translated as "ownedness," or "being owned," or even "being one's own," implying the idea of owning up to and owning what one is and does. (Varga and Guignon 2014)

This question of ownership, in particular, is foregrounded throughout the *Autobiography*. Xuela articulates it directly on multiple occasions: "I felt I did not want to belong to anyone, that since the one person I would have consented to own me had never lived to do so, I did not want to belong to anyone; I did not want anyone to belong to me" (104). Unwilling to pay the price of inclusion, Xuela embraces self-ownership—"at that moment my self was the only thing I had that was my own" (159); "I chose to possess myself" (174)—along with the vulnerability it entails.

Although Xuela's commitment to an exclusively self-regarding existence serves to insulate her, to a degree, from the insults and assaults of her narrative community, critical responses to the *Autobiography* reveal the risk assumed by the author Kincaid in configuring such a character. As already noted, scholars of Kincaid's novel in many ways echo philosophers who see in the notion of authenticity a dangerous solipsism: "A frequently mentioned worry with the ideal of authenticity is that the focus on one's own inner feelings and attitudes may breed a self-centered preoccupation with oneself that is anti-social and destructive of altruism and compassion toward others" (Varga and Guignon 2014). Yet, as we have seen, in the precariously "post-"colonial universe Kincaid presents, antisocial self-defense is the only logical response to the social absurdity of Xuela's community. Radical self-regard in this context is not merely a logical or reasoned response; it is a necessary condition of psychic self-preservation.

Understanding this allows us to read Xuela's narcissism in the original Freudian sense—as a mechanism through which to ensure individual survival.

Given the extent to which the odds are stacked against her, Xuela must be ruthlessly self-centered if she wants to live and to live free. These are the stakes, and Xuela is well aware of them. Despite her positioning as "of the vanquished . . . of the defeated" (215), she persists in fighting the image "presented to her . . . of her worthlessness" (Schultheis 2001). She fights to maintain "critical distance" from the "dominant fiction"—to disavow the legitimacy of her community's determining categories and to remain utterly disdainful of its obligations. She resolves not only to "put [her] own behavior under reflexive scrutiny and make it dependent on self-determined goals" but also "[to call] into question the reigning social order and public opinion" (Varga and Guignon 2014). She takes on the "virtuous" Butlerian project of giving an account of herself, issuing a de facto social critique in the process, but her efforts are no precursor to social transformation. Her sole aim is to perform self-work.

From her position on the sidelines, she becomes a spy, an investigative reporter, and a code breaker; she exposes, in Wynterian fashion, the repressive master code (the code of the repressive once-and-still masters) and its racial fantasies, and she ever more insistently rejects its hold on her self. Xuela foregrounds her own "truth-for," "history-for," and "beauty-for" over the claims of those who would ethno-humanistically deny her worth. Yet the question remains: "If, on a political level, subjectivity only makes sense in the ideologically-coded terms of . . . the dominant fiction, then how can a subject transform or even reject that which renders her own consciousness possible?" (Schultheis 2001). In other words, what route does Xuela actually take to get outside?

I used to stare at myself in a piece of broken looking glass . . .
Xuela Claudette Richardson (in *The Autobiography of My Mother*)

"What Xuela wants is to stand outside of any community" (Chang 2004, 122). This, of course, is impossible. Xuela cannot stand apart from her community. Like all maroons, she must always and carefully negotiate with the plantation order. This delicate operation Xuela manages through her narcissistic investment in constant self-scrutiny. She grapples with colonialism's lingering malignancies via explorations of the self that are at once psychological and sexual and that emerge from a foundation of preservationist self-love.[29] Turning inward with absolute interest in and regard for herself provides a path toward relative safety from psychic harm. To understand what I mean, let us here again think through the ways in which narcissism figures into the experience of self-formation. As noted earlier, Sigmund Freud asserts that every human being is born with a primary narcissistic impulse to protect the self with absolute self-love. In the course of normal development, this love for self, or ego-libido, develops into object-love via the cathecting of the libido onto the external figure of the mother. This transference of self-love to another being, by whom one is loved in return, forms the basis for healthy social relations—the distributing of self-love to other persons who restore that depleted ego-libido by offering their love. In the absence of this exchange of affection, secondary narcissism develops, and with it the potential for pathology.

Operational within a Western frame that accounts for neither the particular toxicity of colonialism nor that of racism, Freud's model can have only limited purchase with respect to Xuela's political and personal reality. To examine her life within this Freudian frame is to presume the very feasibility of "healthy social relations" in the world she describes. For Xuela to have hinged her self-esteem on parental idealization would have been profoundly self-destructive. Neither her biological mother nor any of her subsequent mother figures would have protected her from the colonial and patriarchal violence of her community. So, in this sense, maternal absence is the very condition of her psychological freedom. The same can be said of her refusal to mother. To become a mother would be to "cure" her narcissism via a turn to what Freud calls "love according to the masculine type" ([1914] 1957, 89), that is, a transforming of her "inappropriate" narcissistic love for herself—what Freud derides as "the feminine form of erotic life" (89)—into "appropriate" love for her child: self-love to object-love. Xuela evokes this precise psychoanalytic frame in her own, starkly lucid account of the derailed primal scene of her self-formation:

> Observing any human being from infancy, seeing someone come into existence . . . must be something wonderful to behold . . . so wonderful to observe, so wonderful to behold; the pleasure for the observer, the beholder, is an invisible current between the two, observed and observer, beheld and beholder, and I believe that no life is complete, no life is really whole, without this invisible current, which is in many ways a definition of love. No one observed and beheld me, I observed and beheld myself; the invisible current went out and it came back to me. I came to love myself in defiance, out of despair, because there was nothing else. Such a love will do, but it will only do, it is not the best kind. . . . It will do, but

only because there is nothing else to take its place; it is not to be recommended. (56–57)

Xuela is clearly aware that, absent the possibility of object-love, an "excessive" self-love is her only option for survival. Although "not the best kind" of love, it is the sole nonthreatening, uncompromised love available to a woman in her circumstances. It is the motive force behind her commitment to finding a way of "enjoying completely the despair [she] felt at being [her]self" (165). To accomplish this, Xuela makes of herself a beheld, desired, erotic being. She remains stubbornly unconvinced of the legitimacy of her dysselection. Although self-loathing is expected, Xuela reaches for self-love.

If "Caliban 'images' the human as pure sensory nature" and "enslavement to its own lower sensory nature" (Wynter 1989, 641), Xuela—a being beyond Caliban's woman—embraces these attributes and makes of them her strength. She locates her essential value in the sensorial: "The smell of my underarms and between my legs changed, and this change pleased me. . . . In private, then as now, my hands almost never left those places, and when I was in public, these same hands were always not far from my nose, I so enjoyed the way I smelled, then and now" (58–59). Thoroughly marginal and disdained, Xuela is free to sense herself. She masturbates constantly. She becomes the inexhaustible source of her own pleasure. This reliable, always-available transformation of sensorial stimulus into sensual satisfaction enables her both to behold and to love her physical self. "I began to worship myself" (58), Xuela insists. She makes a goddess-claim and adamantly blesses her own body:

> My human form and odor were an opportunity to heap scorn on me. I responded in a fashion by now characteristic of me: whatever I was told to hate I loved and loved the most. I loved the smell of the thin dirt behind my ears, the smell of my unwashed mouth, the smell that came from between my legs, the smell in the pit of my arm, the smell of my unwashed feet. Whatever about me caused offense, whatever I could not help, whatever was *native* to me, whatever I could not help and was not a moral failing—those things about me I loved with the fervor of the devoted. (32–33)

Whereas Fanon is compelled "to know his body *through* the terms of an always already imposed 'historico-racial schema'; a schema that predefines his body as an impurity to be cured, a lack, a defect" (Wynter 2001, 41), Xuela compares her body favorably to other bodies by "embracing precisely what has been reviled"

(Goldberg 2004, 5). Digging deeper than the Fanonian theory of alienation, wherein marginalization is first economic and then epidermic, Xuela takes the Wynterian position.[30] She invests in the notion that marginalization is fundamentally epistemic: "a crisis that stems from our failure to institute a new *episteme* in which we are not defined by a category of lack whose symbols and conditions of fulfillment are elsewhere" (Henry 2000, 136). Although Xuela is certainly subject to the forces of devaluation, she recognizes the shame and the suffering of those who would define her, and she refuses their judgment. Her aim is epistemicide.

Xuela's somatic experiences provide the point of departure for her self-formation, and this, too, signals her radical refusal. From the very beginnings of her social life, and then increasingly as she grows older, Xuela mobilizes her thoughts and actions so as to mitigate her vulnerability with respect to the sociogenic master code on offer. Her behavior accords, then, with a more generous understanding of narcissism's value to human social and emotional development. As she matures physically and considers her relationship to her changing physique, Xuela develops intellectual and emotional insight; her philosophical evolution is contingent, that is, on her physical being. Her audacious delight in her own body presents a "strategic occupation of narcissism as a site of pleasure and a form of resistance to assigned sexual and social roles, a way of transcending the 'unkindness of the real circumstances'" of her existence (Isaak 2005, 54).[31] She procures this pleasure not only by her own hand but also through those she takes as lovers. With her father's business partner, Jack Labatte, she is "quite sure of [her]self, knowing what it was [she] wanted"; "driven by curiosity," she sleeps with her sister's wealthy fiancé; she impulsively seduces Roland, a married stevedore she actually loves for a time; and, finally, she beds her father's friend "Philip, the man [she] slept with but did not love and whom [she] would eventually marry but still not love" (70, 126, 139). In all of her sexual encounters, Xuela is the instigator and the one in control, even though, according to the terms established by her community, each of her partners should hold the power. It is consistently Xuela who seduces and then manipulates her lovers so as to maximize her own "pure pleasure" (71). "The body of a man is not what makes him desirable," she notes the first time she has sex with the older, wealthier Jack Labatte, "it is what his body might make you feel when it touches you that is the thrill, anticipating what his body will make you feel" (70). Cheekily casting Xuela as a man-eater, Kincaid draws subtly on the racist stereotype wherein "the Carib body and the discourses of ferocious libidinal and anthropophagic appetite are made analogous" (Morris 2002, 958).[32]

Xuela's "narcissistic sexuality" (Morris 2002, 966) not only counters typical gender relations between women and men but also unsettles any presumption of female solidarity under patriarchy. Xuela sleeps exclusively with other women's men, and in describing her relationships with these men, she unfailingly extracts the physical: the "long sharp line of pleasure" (71), the "deep pleasure," the "ache of pleasure" (72), "the pleasure of his thrusts" (163). As she moves in and out of these affairs, she not only disdains the codes of respectability that determine relationships between men and women—"I did not look for a husband" (147)—but also is sincerely bewildered by the fact that other women accept those codes. "Why is the state of marriage so desirable that all women are afraid to be caught outside it?" (171–72), she wonders.[33] Xuela seeks only personal pleasure and is genuinely perplexed to witness the limitations other women place on their own freedom. "The impulse to possess is alive in every heart," she reflects, "and some people choose vast plains, some people choose high mountains, some people choose wide seas, and some people choose husbands; I chose to possess myself" (174).

Xuela's choices—so much evidence of her categorical self-containment—risk being misread, of course. Unreservedly, Xuela allows herself to enjoy that "most primitive and most essential of emotions, that thing silently, secretly, shamefully called sex" (163). In this respect (too), she is suspect. In the Caribbean context, "positioning black, mulatto, and white creole women as sexually insatiable effectively nullifies violence enacted upon their bodies" (Francis 2010, 17). That Xuela is sexually insatiable and sexually self-determining—rather than vulnerable and preyed upon—is thus disordering. If she resembles "Caliban's sister," the praiseworthy "black woman w/firm feet, sensitive/aggressive breasts and a space & plan if not always a room of her own" evoked by Brathwaite (1994, 316), then she is also subject to the feminist critique Brathwaite's formulation has inspired—the fact that "the nature of the sexualization . . . gives pause" (Goldberg 2004, 90). Yet Xuela loves her "sensitive/aggressive breasts" and in no way sees them as incompatible with exercising control over her contestatory individual subjectivity:

> My breasts then were in a state of constant sensation, the breasts themselves small globes of reddish brown flesh, the nipples a fruit purple and pointed; they burned, they itched, and this sensation ceased only when a mouth, a man's mouth, was clamped tightly over them and sucking; I had long ago come to recognize this as perhaps an unremitting part of the way

I really am and so I looked for a man who could offer relief from this sensation; I did not look for a husband. (146–47)

Neither coerced nor seduced, coercible nor seducible, Xuela relies on her bodily being as a means to ignore any "socially prescribed sense of the self" (Wynter 2001, 48). Her behaviors speak with Audre Lorde's voice: "In touch with the erotic, I become less willing to accept powerlessness, or those other supplied states of being which are not native to me, such as resignation, despair, self-effacement, depression, self-denial" ([1984] 2007, 90).[34] Self-beheld, Xuela is not beholden to male sexual desire, though she arouses it unfailingly. Her "urge to see her own sexualized image" simply presents a "manifestation of self-love" (Linton 2010). "Her sexuality is precisely the physical expression of the highest self-regard and, often, the *sheer pleasure* she takes in her own powers" (Spillers 2003, 167; emphasis mine). In this respect, she is the veritable archetype of the femme fatale, an enigmatic and seductive woman whose principal charm lies in her impenetrability to her lover's affections.

The femme fatale, not unlike Freud's narcissistic woman (or the child), is singular in her "self-contentment and inaccessibility" (Freud [1914] 1957, 89). Freud claims that "such women hold the greatest fascination for men" ([1914] 1957, 89) because they are fundamentally sufficient unto themselves. More recently, Slavoj Žižek has described the femme fatale by evoking similar attributes, among them indifference and auto-isolation. He argues that "what is really menacing about the femme fatale is not that she is fatal for *men* but that she presents a case of a pure nonpathological subject fully assuming *her own fate*" (1992, 66).[35] The fate the femme fatale assumes is "the imminence of her own death" (64). She "embodies a radical ethical attitude, that of 'not ceding one's desire,' of persisting in it to the very end when its true nature as the death drive is revealed" (63). Xuela displays an ease with Thanatos from the beginning through to the very end of her narration: "I long to meet the thing greater than I am, the thing to which I can submit. . . . Death is the only reality, for it is the only certainty, inevitable to all things" (Kincaid 1996, 228), she declares. This "unreserved acceptance of the death drive" (Žižek 1992, 63) produces a sort of irresistible self-containment. It is the source of her immense erotic power over her lover-cum-husband, the Englishman Philip.

Prospero you're a great illusionist: you know all about lies. And you lied to me so much, lied about the world, lied about yourself, that you ended up imposing on me an image of myself: underdeveloped, in your words, incompetent, that's how you forced me to see myself, and I hate that image! And it is false! But now I know you, you old cancer, and I know also myself.

—Caliban (in Shakespeare's *The Tempest*)

Oh . . . to be a part of anything that is outside history, to be a part of something that can deny the wave of the human hand, the beat of the human heart, the gaze of the human eye, human desire itself.

—Xuela Claudette Richardson (in *The Autobiography of My Mother*)

The final chapters of Xuela's life—and of her story—find her self-marooned in the Dominican hinterland with her much older husband, Philip Bailey. She has exiled the two of them to a wild space "between the developed world and that which exceeds its reach" (Halberstam and Nyong'o 2018, 459). She means to further her inquiry into what constitutes the human, isolated from and undisturbed by the normative structures that would otherwise determine their relation. As with her prior lovers, Xuela relates to Philip in a way that contradicts the social schema that would have him be her superior. He is English, a doctor, and her employer. He is also, according to Xuela, "a man who was in love with me beyond anything he could help . . . a man I ignored except when I wanted him to please me" (170). That she has agreed to marry him in the absence of any feelings of love is a testament at once to her narcissism and to her take-no-prisoners nihilistic resistance to the colonial order and its legacies. In this removed, closed, socially stripped-down space—"the land where my mother and the people she was of were born" (206)—Xuela proceeds to reorder the world. Having sequestered the two of them safely (for her) well outside and beyond a community that could only ever perceive Philip as belonging to "the conquering class" (211), Xuela proceeds to study and experiment on him at her leisure.[36] Whereas, historically, "'whiteness' has been presumed transparent, given, natural, neutral, or *nothing to be seen*" (Braziel 2009, 12), Xuela does not allow Philip to stand unraced or unexamined. She trains her ethnographer's eye on him and thereby refuses the script wherein the native is beheld by the colonizer's gaze. She submits him mercilessly to her own regard, judging him with scientific clarity and paradigm-busting disdain:

> His hair was thin and yellow like an animal's that I was not familiar with; his skin was thin and pink and transparent, as if it were on its way to being skin but had not yet reached the state that real skin is. . . . The veins showed through it here and there like threads sewn by a clumsy seam-

stress; his nose was narrow and thin like the small part of a funnel, and tilted up in the air as if on the alert for something. (216)

Ending Xuela's story à *huis clos* allows Kincaid to flesh out the conclusion to Césaire's *A Tempest* in her own fashion. At the end of the 1969 play, Caliban and Prospero remain alone on the island. Caliban laments his failed attempts to restore a pre-Prospero, preconquest past—to "regain [his] island and win [his] freedom back again"—and affirms his commitment to revolutionary futurity: "One day my fist, my bare fist alone will be enough to crush your world!" (Césaire [1969] 1992, act 3, scene 5; 65). Vengeful and overcome by hatred, Caliban fumes and rages and cries for freedom. He blames Prospero for having compelled him to accept his inferior status for so long. Prospero returns Caliban's vitriol. Intent on realizing his civilizing mission and undaunted yet (or because!) unaware of his own futility, he resolves to stay and do battle with Caliban. In the play's final scene, Prospero has become old and frail; he has been defeated but still struggles to defend himself and what he sees as his work. He is cold but incapable of building a fire. Césaire's ending puts a fine point on a critical element of the historical relationship between colonizer and native: the former's utter dependence on the latter's subjection. "Caliban is indispensable to Prospero, the usurper depends upon the usurped" (Hulme 1986, 127). Césaire reminds his audience that Prospero, the colonial master, "can do anything at all except what is most necessary to survive. In other words, there is a precise match with the situation of Europeans in America during the seventeenth century" (Hulme 1986, 128).

Xuela's marriage to Philip similarly stages the relationship between European agent of colonialism and should-be subordinate colonized. Kincaid's rewriting of this narrative explores the beyond of Césaire's play, describing the fate of both native and colonizer from an alternative perspective. Like Prospero, and "just like those guys who founded the colonies and who now can't live anywhere else" (Césaire [1969] 1992, act 3, scene 1; 65), "Philip belonged to that restless people unable to leave the world alone" (209), Xuela observes. "He had an obsessive interest in rearranging the landscape: not gardening in the way of necessity, the growing of food, but gardening in the way of luxury, the growing of flowering plants for no other reason than the pleasure of it and making these plants do exactly what he wanted them to do; and it made great sense that he would be drawn to this activity, for it is an act of conquest" (143).

Xuela seems to understand intuitively that "the singleminded conquest of Nature by Western Man ... began with the discovery of the New World" (Wynter

1970, 35)—that "the wild had become part of a colonial division of the world into the modernizing and the extractive zones" (Halberstam and Nyong'o 2018, 455). Yet, although that world has invested Philip, as a physician, with the authority of a scientist, Xuela recognizes his science as flawed and self-legitimating (sociogenic)—an error-ridden reflection of his truth-fors and a prioris. She also recognizes this science as among the pillars of her defeat as a Black woman and a native. As such, she knows she must be on her guard. "He was so sure inside himself that all the things he knew were correct, not that they were true, but that they were correct" (222–23), she observes. This certainty is Philip's weakness in the face of Xuela's scientific inquiry. It allows her to manipulate him without him suspecting it—without him imagining her capable of it: "He now lived in a world where he could not speak the language, I mediated for him, I translated for him. I did not always tell him the truth, I did not always tell him everything," she confesses. "I blocked his entrance to the world in which he lived; eventually I blocked his entrance into all the worlds he had come to know" (224). She is the very opposite of Prospero's naive and serviceable native guide.

Whereas Césaire's drama concludes with a doddering Prospero raging still against Caliban's brute resistance to his civilizing efforts, as Caliban cries freedom in the hills, Kincaid places her native subject in the foreground and does away with any dream of exultant liberation. Not only does Xuela not triumph in any recognizable way, but she does not expect to. She has never expected to. Like Caliban, Xuela certainly desired a different story, one in which she would not have been of the defeated—"only such a thing would satisfy me. To reverse the past would bring me complete happiness" (226). But she has come to terms with the impossibility of history's remaking. Xuela's final years are not devoted to any explicitly revolutionary bid for native freedom. Rather, they are a very personal indulgence marked by unrelenting practices of refusal. Having eschewed utopian futurity, Xuela means only to rescue the story of her own brown, female life from oblivion and to better understand and disrupt the privileged life of her white, male husband, the selected Other. For her "Prospero," the wildness of her island would not serve as "a resource, a genetic variant, or an indigenous remedy to be patented, transplanted, exploited, commodified"; it would not provide "a source of white renewal from the supposed excesses of civilization" (Halberstam and Nyong'o 2018, 455). On the contrary, it would make of him one of the defeated.

Xuela knows that individuals are and have always been undone by one another. Given this, Philip and Xuela's marriage stages a battle between narcissistic wills. In addressing the particular "fascination" the narcissistic woman represents, Freud argues:

It seems very evident that another person's narcissism has a great attraction for those who have renounced that part of their own narcissism and are in search of object-love. The charm of a child lies to a great extent in his narcissism, his self-contentment and inaccessibility.... Indeed, even great criminals and humorists, as they are represented in literature, compel our interest by the narcissistic consistency with which they manage to keep away from their ego anything that would diminish it. It is as if we envied them for maintaining a blissful state of mind—an unassailable libidinal position which we ourselves have since abandoned. ([1914] 1957, 88–89)

There is something of both Philip and Xuela in this portrait of the narcissist. Unwittingly, and like a child, Philip has placed himself completely in Xuela's hands: "I dressed him in the colors of the newly born, the innocent, the weak, youth" (218), she explains. This treatment is appropriate insofar as Philip's status as Man, in the Wynterian sense, has made of him a blindly naive and largely irresponsible being: "His life, the external part of it, was full of victories, hardly a desire that could not be fulfilled, and the power to make the world the way he wished it to be" (224), Xuela notes flatly. "He never grew grim, there were no hardships in his own life, his disappointments were not known to him" (227). Philip's trapping and preservation of small animals in glass boxes; his pointless "arranging, disarranging, rearranging the books on his shelf, volumes of history, geography, science, philosophy" (224); his bumbling, self-satisfied walks through the landscape are all evidence of his childlike narcissism. He is indifferent to the history that made him, comprising as it does the "successful disruption of other peoples' worlds, peoples whose reality he and those he came from could not understand" (224). He remains undiminished by this legacy. But Xuela holds Philip accountable for this blissful ignorance of himself. She finds no "charm" in his narcissism.

Philip, however, is utterly seduced by Xuela's "unassailable libidinal position." In the game of chicken that is love, he flinches constantly. Xuela's narcissism, calculated and hard-won, outstrips Philip's because he is entirely undone by—vulnerable to—his love for her. And Xuela is well aware of this: "He grew to live for the sound of my footsteps, so often I would walk without making a sound; he loved the sound of my voice, so for days I would not utter a word" (217–18). Xuela's considered recourse to silence is perhaps the most strident of her everyday refusals, and it is a refusal that largely tends to be discounted. It is our (especially feminist) critical propensity to theorize speech and voice as the vehicles of women's freedom and to view silence as indicative of powerlessness. Convinced, as we are, that inclusion in the collective is our principal social end as human beings and that communication is crucial to establishing collectivity, silence suggests privation or lack. In Xuela's case, however, to be silent is to retain a measure of power. Her silence marks her deviance from normative codes—its literal refusal to dignify those codes with a response, as it were. Though she is "portrayed as 'voiceless' from the very start" (Nasta 2009, 71), the willfulness underlying her mutism is worth noting. Xuela's silence is "a form of disavowal" and "a constant defiance" (K. Ferguson 2012, 71, 72). Crucial to her sadistic refusal of intimacy and connection, Xuela's deployment of silence in her relationship with Philip is the culmination of practices of quiet refusal throughout her life: be it her refusal to speak for the first four years of her childhood, her fiercely silent presence in her elementary school classroom, her failure to apologize to Ma Eunice after breaking her plate, or her staring indifference to the insults of her lover's wife, Xuela's silence is the mark of her absolute unwillingness to engage.

Most vitally, Xuela's insistent, silent withholding in her relationship with Philip is a narcissistic display of "reverence for the self that is self-owned" (Dumm 1999, 101, quoted in K. Ferguson 2012, 71), the starkest expression of her effort at self-preservation. Not only does Xuela refuse to renounce any part of her self-love in exchange for loving her husband (ego-libido for object-libido), but she turns Philip's love for her against him to lay bare the depth of his dependency on her: "Xuela perceives his love for her as a sort of glitch in the colonial matrix: by unexpectedly altering the dynamics of power, Philip's love for her allows her to play games with the inequalities proper to the contact zone" (De Ferrari 2012, 155). Xuela dominates Philip; he is her submissive. The current of BDSM that carries this relationship is explicitly sexual—"I would . . . stand before him and stretch my arms all the way up to the ceiling and order him to his knees to eat and there make him stay until I was completely satisfied" (145), "I made him stand behind me, I made him lie on top of me. . . . I made him lie in back of me. . . . I made him kiss my entire body" (154–55)—and this sexual dynamic is a correlate of the broader power imbalance between them. The erotic power plays at work between the Afro-Carib woman and her rich British doctor husband articulate and reconfigure the mutual entrapment of colonizer and colonized staged by both Shakespeare and Césaire: Prospero loves Caliban—perversely, to be sure. And Caliban loves him back—perversely, to be sure.

Xuela and Philip, like their intertextual avatars, are trapped. "He and I lived in this spell, the spell of history" (218), Xuela admits. "We were weary; weary of being ourselves, weary of our own legacies" (221); "we could not both be happy at the same time. Life, History, whatever its name, had made such a thing impossible" (227). Both Xuela and Philip suffer but for different reasons, and in their respective roles they iterate those of Césaire's Caliban and Prospero—the one painfully aware of history's trap and powerless to escape or undo it, the latter unsettled but insensate. Yet, unlike Césaire's furious character, as mightily as Xuela endeavors to hate Philip and to hold him responsible for the sins of his forefathers—"He did not look like anyone I could love, and he did not look like anyone I should love, and so I determined then that I could not love him and I determined that I should not love him" (152)—she must admit the persistent fact of his common humanity. With her unwavering honesty, she acknowledges that there is something more than history between them:

> I married a man I did not love, but that word, "love," that idea, love—what could it mean to me, what should it mean to me? I did not know, and yet I would have saved him, I would have saved him from death, I would have saved him from a death I had not sanctioned myself.... Was this, then, a form of love, an incomplete love, or no love at all? I did not know. (216)

This bind underlies the ambivalent success of Xuela's challenge to the colonial plot. On the one hand, she concedes that her "marriage represented a kind of tragedy, a kind of defeat" (212). Its lack of recognizable love, its weariness, and its tacit recourse to romance—"refuge of the defeated" (216)—are sources of shame for Xuela. They are reminders of the limits of (her) resistance. Yet, in admitting these limits and failings, Xuela admits also to harboring some small measure of future thinking. She allows, "In my defeat lies the seed of my great victory, in my defeat lies the beginning of my great revenge. My impulse is to the good, my good is to serve myself. I am not a people, I am not a nation. I only wish from time to time to make my actions be the actions of a people, to make my actions be the actions of a nation" (216). With this concession, Xuela nuances the antisociality of her otherwise "no future" stance. She reveals that her relentless observation and critique of her community have been so many acknowledgments, however modest and disheartened, of the "critical potential of refusal" (Rodriguéz 2011, 333). The very fact of her "wish" in the context of the "defeat" she perceives as inevitable marks "an insistence on critique that nevertheless points to a 'not yet' of possibilities"—a recognition of refusal as "an operative mode of analysis that demands, rather than forecloses, futurity" (Rodriguéz 2011, 333). This ever-so-slight acknowledgment of "an outside, a possibility for difference" (Ellis 2015, 3) subtends what amounts to a "disorderly enunciation of black futurity" (Campt 2019b, 30). It is as close as Xuela gets to the queer utopian optimism proposed by José E. Muñoz and others.

Xuela's position of resigned remove also comes close to what Heinz Kohut describes as "cosmic narcissism"—"the enduring, creative result of the steadfast activities of an autonomous ego" that "very few are able to attain." Kohut understands cosmic narcissism to be an elevated state that, along with humor, "permit[s] us to face death without having to resort to denial." Arriving at such a state is an extraordinary feat, according to Kohut, the end goal of every human life. It is an individual emotional acceptance of "quiet inner triumph with an admixture of undenied melancholy." If one "can truly attain that quiet superior stance which enables him to contemplate his own end philosophically, we will assume that a transformation of his narcissism has taken place," Kohut asserts, "and we will respect the person who has achieved it" (1966, 266–68).

What could possibly resemble this state of serene, if melancholic, self-sufficiency more than Xuela's retirement to a world of her own creation? Unvanquished, superior, and alone with her broken husband, orphaned of both mother and father, she comes to experience "at last a great peace" (223). She has made herself "the primary subject of her own invention" (Spillers 2003, 167). Her story chronicles her accession to power from a position of vulnerability, an account of her success in finding some bit of security despite the constraints of her community. She has raged, on a very personal level, against the colonial machine. Because of her, Philip ultimately dies "a lonely man, far away from the place where he was born" (206). In this respect, Xuela is victorious. Thus do the final scenes of the *Autobiography* stage the limits of Man's power and the space of possibility for Xuela's own.

The slave in A Tempest *is also left without his freedom but not because he doesn't desire it: he cannot create a world where he is physically and psychologically free from Prospero.*
  —Armando García, "Freedom as Praxis" (2016)

I'm interested in being free. Free, do you hear?
  —Caliban (in Césaire's *A Tempest*)

In *The Autobiography of My Mother*, Kincaid aims to do no less than "rethink the origins of the modern world, and with it, the origins of different categories of people" (Wynter 2000, 174). The novel answers Wynter's call to become aware of and make visible the sociogenic process, insofar as Xuela risks asking, "How can we think *outside* the terms in which we *are*? Think *about* the processes by which we institute ourselves as what we are, make these processes transparent to ourselves?" (Wynter 2000, 206–7). Like Wynter, Xuela is preoccupied with race as the construct that "explains the contours of modernity best" (Goldberg 2004, 68). The community she inhabits is a Wynterian dystopia, fully obedient to a master code whose principles mark it as lesser and lacking.

Xuela understands that she is of the conquered peoples of this world—"the forever humiliated, the forever low" (30-31); she knows she is dysgenic, dysselected, disdained. She knows that she is considered a pathological subject—a product of pathological relations, imminently vulnerable and ever misjudged. Xuela understands all of this to be the position of the world, as it regards her from the outside in. And yet she will not have any of it. Instinctively, Xuela recognizes the pathetic limitations of those in power, and, like Condé's Tituba, she refuses their judgment. She sees very clearly that "whiteness draws its meaning from the denigration of its Others" (Gregg 2002, 926). Though she offers no solution as she puzzles through the structures of her unjust world, in relating the narrative of her self-discovery and her vengeance, she allows us a peek behind the curtain. She exposes the workings of the machine—"the invention of Man and his human Others" (Wynter 2000, 176)—and she shares her insights, unfiltered, as she makes them.

In granting Xuela a demonic space outside the frame of the colonial and its many prefixes, Kincaid more or less sacrifices the whole world around her heroine. For this, she stands accused of having written "a text that intends to hurt rather than to heal its readers" (Chang 2004, 123). It is true: *The Autobiography of My Mother* offers neither palliative nor politics. Yet, by presenting in meticulous detail one woman's struggle to first understand and then refuse the self-annihilating pathologies of her insular Caribbean community, Kincaid's novel turns a needed sharp eye to the less obvious burdens on our elusively "postcolonial" future. Xuela is not the victim that certain revolutionary writers of the Americas would have a woman like her be, "impoverished, beaten down by labor, or forced into prostitution" (Goldberg 2004, 89), nor is she a sympathetic maternal avatar of Sycorax—inspired to take back her island in a glorious act of revolution or inspiring some progeny to realize this aim. She is an annihilator, not a builder. Though the undisputed master of the textual universe Kincaid has created for her, Xuela makes no effort to make anything better. She decides to opt out.

Although, like every other human being, Xuela is interpolated by those who make up her social world, she never offers a response to her community's call. She is free from any feminist or nationalist "need to reply" (Forbes 2002, 13). Throughout her life, those who surround her want her to be sorry;

they demand that she apologize for herself—for the very fact of her being. But she is not and will not be sorry. She will not be sorry for breaking that traumatic plate, for aborting Madame Labatte's would-be baby, for bedding another woman's husband, or for in any other way transgressing the norms of a collective she has diagnosed as deeply ailing. Though she is preordained to be shamed, unloved, and otherwise devalued, her instinctive physical and mental self-preservation spares her this fate. Disorderly and perverse, she resolutely disbelieves any "narratives reproducing her negation" (hooks 2003, 101).

If "discovery" of the New World brought the construction of the category of native-as-lack into being, Xuela's "ontological sovereignty" (Wynter 2000, 136)—her "cognitive autonomy" (Henry 2000, 142)—is a plot not within but beyond that plantation order. The *Autobiography* is an autoethnography—a self-generated representation of Xuela's thinking, desiring self that serves to counter those ethnographic texts "in which European metropolitan subjects represent to themselves their others (usually their conquered others)" (Pratt 1992, 35). Xuela's narrative refuses such discourses of definition and conquest. In telling her story of herself and, obliquely, that of her mother, she exposes the consequences of "long-term contact and intractable, unequal conflict" (Pratt 1992, 37) in the Caribbean. She chronicles her battles against the hierarchies that determine the quality of individual lives in the hemispheric American "contact zone" (Pratt 1992, 7), making plain that the region is also, more accurately, a combat zone. Having embraced her incommensurability, Xuela has sought only to inhabit demonic ground—metaphorically throughout most of her life and then literally in the end, via her displacement to a place of inverted sociality and geographic wildness. It is in this seeking that her threats to order emerge.

Xuela's invention of existence, her self-creative instinct—her unending becoming or endless unbecoming—these do not happen in a vacuum. She lays out in detail what it means to "make a life of freedom possible in the most wretched of circumstances," and she proves herself awesomely capable of seeing and defying the strictures of her reality; she declares through her person "that there is more than one way of being human and free" (Garcia 2016, 345). Though unwaveringly self-focused, Xuela's narrative presumes an interlocutor. Her story is not merely life-writing; it is a life writing back. An ethnographer in her own right, Xuela has reversed the colonial gaze and looked critically at the world around her. She has engaged radically in study. Considering her individual being with respect to the cultural and historical realities by which she is bound, Xuela has subjected herself and those around her to equal scrutiny.

She has examined her community, its mores, its ideologies, its practices, and she has examined herself in relation to that discursive and material context. She is ruthless in her observation, hiding nothing about her own behavior as she exposes that of others. In the end, she declares, "I had been talked about, I had been judged and condemned. I had been loved and I had been hated. I now stood above it all, it all lay at my feet" (206). Above it all, yes, and perhaps even beyond.

5

SELF-REGARD | Lilith

> *James occupies an interesting in-between position, neither insider nor outsider, perhaps a peculiar brand of exile.*
> —Michael A. Bucknor and Kezia Page, "Authorial Self-Fashioning, Political Denials and Artistic Distinctiveness" (2018)

> *The archive demands imagination.*
> —Treva B. Lindsey and Jessica Marie Johnson, "Searching for Climax" (2014)

In an essay titled "From Jamaica to Minnesota to Myself," which appeared in the March 2015 issue of the *New York Times Magazine*, Jamaican writer Marlon James came out of the closet to nearly fifty million readers. His star-making novel, *A Brief History of Seven Killings*, had been published just a few months earlier and had taken home several major prizes, including the 2015 Man Booker Prize, the first ever to have been awarded to a Jamaican writer. James's career had reached extraordinary heights, and in the *Times* essay, he offers something of a prehistory to the story of Marlon James, famous author. The piece concludes some years before James's rise to prominence in U.S. and European literary circles, and it paints a heartrending picture of an artist who almost did not make it out of a very dark and lonely emotional place.

As James tells it, the years he spent as a young boy and adolescent in and around Kingston, Jamaica, in the 1970s and 1980s marked a dangerous period in his life. At the time, he was terrified that his sexuality would become apparent to the many homophobic and otherwise bigoted forces surrounding him, and so he lived under constant duress. Anxious and relentlessly bullied throughout his high school years, James contemplated ending his life on more than one occasion. A measure of salvation came eventually in the form of his University of the West Indies classmates, long-anticipated peers whose interest in the world of the mind allowed James a reprieve from an environment he found otherwise hostile to the truth of his body and its desires. As he invested increasingly in literature during these student years, at first as a reader and then, tentatively, as a writer, James began to imagine alternatives to self-destruction or perpetual disgrace.

His encounter with Salman Rushdie's novel *Shame* some years afterward, in his late twenties, changed everything, according to James: "It made me realize that the present was something I could write my way out of . . . and I wrote myself all the way to a book tour of the United States" (2015). Visiting the United States, James recalls, he was able to begin the process of fully becoming and expressing his authentic self. He could walk the streets of downtown New York City wearing the clothes and the demeanor of a man he finally recognized in the mirror. From this moment on, it became clear to him that he "had to get out of Jamaica" (James 2015)—that he could neither write nor survive for long if he remained at home.

James's confessional was heralded as moving and courageous by the international press; his interviewers and reviewers decried the homophobia and anti-intellectualism of contemporary Jamaica and smoothly conveyed James's relocation to the United States as a hard-won and fortuitous escape to personal liberation. This was a comfortable and familiar narrative, of course: persecuted artist from the Global South periphery makes it to a metropolitan center in Europe or North America where she or he can enjoy a far better creative and material existence. Yet this oft-rehearsed chronicle of exile as liberation, no matter how accurate, is a necessarily troubling trope, especially for those who do not leave. Such tales of freedom attained outside the presumably alienated and constraining space of the island affirm home as uninhabitable, as antithetical to creative expression. Not surprisingly, then, James's story of his personal and professional struggles at home before achieving fame in the world beyond his island has been met with some ambivalence in Jamaica.

In 2017 a group of University of the West Indies scholars convened at a workshop organized by a pair of academics from the United Kingdom to discuss the response to James and his work among Jamaicans. In their introduction to the volume of essays that emerged from that gathering, editors

Michael A. Bucknor and Kezia Page acknowledge at once the legitimacy of James's unhappiness in Jamaica—"that now well-known discomfort with being from a society that is considered incapable of being a literary home"—and their own desire as Jamaicans to "claim him for a place that he feels rejects and denies him himself" (2018, ii). While they do not directly dispute the truth of James's "inability to live in Jamaica" (iii), they nevertheless subject this stated impossibility to some scrutiny. Bucknor and Page point, for example, to "certain slippages in James' narrative of himself" (iii), slippages that dovetail with the particular and consistent choices James has made in his literary depictions of his home country. The editors note that in both his autobiographical and his fictional writings, James presents excessive violence and pathological masculinity as the status quo in Jamaica. Such representations, they argue, are a significant factor in "how marketable his works are" (iv).

James consistently emphasizes the brutality of past and present-day Jamaica, and this violence tends to preoccupy critics of his work. Without exception, both academic and popular readers evoke the traumatic experience of confronting James's "bloodstained" narratives (Bucknor and Page 2018, iv). *The Book of Night Women* (2009), James's second novel, has garnered a great deal of attention in this regard. Two of James's most incisive critics, Curdella Forbes and Sam Vasquez—in their evocatively titled respective essays, "Bodies of Horror in Marlon James's *The Book of Night Women* and Clovis Brown's Cartoons" (2017) and "Violent Liaisons: Historical Crossings and the Negotiation of Sex, Sexuality, and Race in *The Book of Night Women* and *The True History of Paradise*" (2012)—attempt to reckon with *Night Women*'s graphic violence, pointing to its mimetic value as a call to examine the internal and external forces of global power that prey on the world's most vulnerable. Other theorists, however, denounce James's insistent representations of misery and suffering. Markus Nehl, for example, argues that "James's novel exposes the enslaved to a further act of violence [see Hartman, "Venus in Two Acts"] by presenting the (female) slave's experience of humiliation and sexual exploitation in an explicit, even pornographic, way" (2016, 162).

Whether James's work is perceived as boldly realist or irresponsibly sensationalist, critical response to and analyses of the representation of violence in *The Book of Night Women* reflect, above all, the uncomfortable fact that there really is no adequate way to write the stories of the enslaved. There is no way to account sufficiently for the horror of arbitrary and unremitting collective dispossession. If the monstrous reality of human bondage is deeply wrong, how can words ever be expected to convey this reality in a way that feels right? Slavery's truths are unfathomable—of a depth and a darkness that cannot be sounded.

That slavery in the Americas "defies representation" (Forbes 2017, 4) has not been, however, too great a deterrent for those committed to trying. Be it through the "objective" lens of history and its endless dance with the archive, the speculations of the literary theorist, or the unsparing imagination of the creative writer, there has been no end of effort to reckon with this particular—this peculiar—past from the vantage point of our peculiar present. Jennifer Morgan's and Marisa Fuentes's careful prying apart of the colonial archive, Haile Gerima's and Octavia E. Butler's speculative fictionalization of the Middle Passage and the antebellum Americas, and Saidiya Hartman's and Omise'eke Natasha Tinsley's embracing of "critical fabulation" (Hartman 2008, 11) as a strategy for reading the Atlantic are among the myriad examples of creative literary efforts to grapple with histories of abuse that continue to do harm in the present.

Effecting this temporal journey and salvage mission in the face of fundamental unknowability—unfathomability—is a necessarily unnerving and costly venture for those who undertake it. "How," as Hartman has so affectingly asked, "does one revisit the scene of subjection without replicating the grammar of violence?" (2008, 4). How do we subvert the "potential for pornotroping" (Spillers 1987, 67), whereby erotically charged, spectacular enactments of violence produce objectified Black (female) flesh? How do we ever represent a past whose contours are contingent on Black debasement, brutalization, and humiliation without re-presenting those forms of abjection as the very premises of a Black present?

To the question of "How?," Stephen Best has added the equally provocative and despairing question of "Why?" Why—to what aim—do we persist in probing this past? What are we hoping to retrieve? What are the stakes of that recovery? Best argues, convincingly, that since the publication of Toni Morrison's watershed novel *Beloved* in 1987, Afro-American cultural actors of all stripes have been committed to what he dubs an "affective history project" (2012, 466), a process of "historical recovery (or the attempt to solicit the past for present purposes)" (455). According to Best, contemporary engagements with the Afro-American past posit an "ethical relation" (454) to that past—one that presumes a seamless connection therewith. "The idea of continuity between the slave past and our present provides a framework for conceptions of black collectivity and community across time" (454). In such a frame, redress and redemption become objectives, and the living express a vested interest in unsilencing and, importantly, in rehabilitating the dead.

Whereas our instinct may be toward compassionate connection to enslaved individuals from the past, that instinct risks leading the contemporary reader into various traps. First, it tends toward privileging past agency and solidarity as unique points of departure for reclaiming present-day justice. This, Best argues, creates a situation wherein "scholars have staked their own critical agency on a recovery of the political agency of the enslaved, making the slaves' 'hidden history' a vital dimension of the effort to define black political goals in terms of a model of representation" (2012, 453). Second, it invites a "too-easy intimacy" (Hartman 1997, 20) vis-à-vis the enslaved, which is its own kind of violence.[1] This tendency to rehabilitation—this "impulse to redeem the past" (Best 2012, 456)—Best finds questionable or worthy of questioning. Insofar as a redemptive impulse implicates matters of community more broadly, I, too, find it worthy of questioning.

The Book of Night Women relates the story of Lilith, born into slavery at Montpelier, a prosperous Jamaican slave plantation owned by the Wilson family. She is born awash in the "too much blood" (3) of her thirteen-year-old enslaved mother, who has died giving birth but not before cursing both Lilith and the baby's father—Jack Wilkins, the drunken and sadistic white overseer who raped her, from whom Lilith has inherited "the greenest eyes anybody ever done see" (3). Because of her mother's curse and those cursed green eyes, no one will take the girl in—"As soon as Lilith born the womens regard her with fear and trembling because of those green eyes that light up the room, but not like sunlight" (3)—and Wilkins places her in the care of the decidedly uncaring prostitute Circe and her putative partner, the castrated "mad nigger" Tantalus (5). When Lilith turns fourteen, a Johnny-jumper (an enslaved male empowered to keep order in the cane fields) attempts to rape her, very likely with Circe's approval, if not facilitation, and Lilith burns and decapitates him in self-defense.

The circumstances of Lilith's birth and this incident establish at once James's willingness to present the extreme brutality of the plantation world and Lilith's willingness and ability to meet that brutality with equally extreme violence. Her act of refusal sets the entire course of her life at Montpelier. It earns her the attention of Homer, the enslaved head of the Wilsons' household and leader of the Night Women, a group that includes five additional enslaved women—Pallas, Iphigenia, Hippolyta, Callisto, and Gorgon—all of whom are also Wilkins's daughters. Intending to harness Lilith's capacity for violence in service of the island-wide revolt she and the women are plotting, Homer manages to cover up the murder and to protect Lilith from the vengeful Johnny-jumpers by installing her in the great house kitchen. Lilith, however, intends different things for herself. Ungrateful for Homer's protection and uninterested in any sororal alliance, she sets her sights on seducing the plantation master, Humphrey Wilson, a plan that goes painfully awry. By the narrative's close, Lilith has been beaten, raped, and humiliated. She has murdered an entire family of white planters. She has caused the deaths of several innocent enslaved men and women. Also, she has fallen in love.

James's novel in many ways brings *A Regarded Self* full circle. As with Condé's *I, Tituba, Night Women* is a neo-slave narrative, and its backdrop is the anglophone slave Americas. Like Tituba Indian, Lilith is a mixed-race woman-child, born of rape, orphaned early, and left during her childhood and early adolescence more or less to her own devices in a liminal space adjacent to and delimited by the order of the plantation. Beyond these framing similarities, however, James's novel arguably pushes further than *Tituba* in its challenge both to nineteenth-century generic conventions and to present-day readerly expectations.[2] Confined within the oppressive space of a West Indian sugar estate, *Night Women* paints an unflinching portrait of the extreme gendered violence that would have been inherent in this geohistorical context. It spares the reader no detail of the physical horrors perpetrated on Black women's bodies in every facet of that world.

Like the stories told by her forebears, Lilith's story is mediated and transcribed. But unlike the amanuensis contracted by Mary Pringle or even Tituba's sophisticated twentieth-century go-between, Lilith's storyteller censors nothing and writes in a voice like Lilith's own. And what a voice it is. As Elena Machado Sáez notes, James's novel "uses an invented patois to both defamiliarize and train" (2015, 113) his reader. The narrator assumes a "confrontational posture" (Bailey 2014, 89) from the very first paragraph, interpolating the reader directly and setting a decidedly combative tone that refuses any "facile intimacy" (Hartman 1997, 19) the reader might expect or desire: "I goin' call her Lilith. You can call her what they call her" (3). From this moment on, it's "nigger" this, "pussyhole" that, "shithouse" this, "bloodcloth" that. And these words are spoken not by slave owners to their human property but, overwhelmingly, by the enslaved to one another. A brutal faux-vernacular marked entirely by the violence out of which it emerges, the language of *Night Women* amounts to a relentless assault.[3] Thus, to Hartman's question—"How does one revisit the scene of subjection without replicating the grammar of violence?"— James responds that one does not. One does not elide or obscure it. One does not imagine alternatives. One speaks in its tongues, with its syntax and, yes, its grammar.

The "confrontational posture" assumed by *Night Women*'s narrator works to undermine the redemptive impulse and obliges the reader "to reckon with the true alterity of the past" (Best 2012, 465). Moreover, the fierceness of the novel's idiom directly conveys Lilith's combativeness and steady resistance both to being defined within her textual community and to being consumed (too easily comprehended/apprehended/beheld) by a presumably empathetic extratextual community of readers. James's prose seems intent on producing "a failure or short-circuiting of the redemptive function" (Best 2012, 465). If indeed there is merit and value "to clear[ing] some space for a black politics not animated by a sense of collective condition or solidarity" (454), *Night Women* offers an instance of what such space clearing might look like.

Even in the worse circumstances of domination, the ability to manipulate one's gaze in the face of structures of domination that would contain it, opens up the possibility of agency.
　—bell hooks, *Black Looks* (2015)

Ye must be something special.
　—Robert Quinn (in *The Book of Night Women*)

As pervasive and ever present as the violence at Montpelier are the all-encompassing mechanisms of surveillance and the atmosphere of paranoia this surveillance creates. Masters and overseers watch the enslaved so as to punish and control; the enslaved watch masters and overseers so as to navigate these forms of domination; the enslaved watch one another so as to identify allies or adversaries. Everyone is beheld. The stakes are survival for all involved. More explicitly than in any other of the novels discussed in these pages, the gaze functions in *Night Women* as a crucial source of power and site of subject formation.

　In this context, the immutable self-regard James accords Lilith is striking. From her dispatching, as a child, of her would-be rapist to her escape, as a full-grown woman, from the apocalyptic violence that destroys every one of her would-be sisters, Lilith always looks out for herself—and looks at herself with care. She refuses to be allied with the enslaved of Montpelier, just as her narrator provides little opportunity to imagine or "acknowledge any shared bond with her audience" (Sáez 2015, 117). As Forbes attests, "Lilith's struggle is first the attempt to erect boundaries of consciousness that produce an 'I-self' within acceptable systems of moral and psychic order that she has only imagined" (2017, 10). Like others of the women characters in my corpus but arguably more incredibly, given her social circumstances, Lilith stubbornly adheres to a sense of herself that reflects only her own ideas about the world—what it is and should be.

The gulf between who Lilith believes herself to be and what she is told she is or must be is vast. Animated by the unshakeable conviction that she is special and that she deserves better than others in her circumstances, Lilith has an expectation of love and, most unreasonably, of inviolability: "Lilith thinking 'bout her bush and how nobody tell her that is man who must decide what happen to it" (15), she reflects before killing the Johnny-jumper who tries to rape her. That she holds herself in such esteem is often and much to her detriment: she gets her body *and* her feelings hurt in this agonizing process of autopoiesis. Rather than be a "will-less object," Lilith is time and again a severely "chastened agent" (Hartman 1997, 80). She suffers repeatedly the consequences of misreading her world yet never relinquishes her commitment to, nor ever disbelieves in, her own value.

Lilith looks at herself constantly. Her self-regard is a praxis she enacts to counter the degrading ways she is beheld by others. As such, mirrors largely determine the contours of her being in the world. Lilith's contemplation of her reflection is evoked repeatedly throughout the novel. At first, she uses mirrors to establish a baseline sense of herself; she is intent on gaining some clarity around the physical transformations occurring in her body: "Lilith look in the old silver tray that the great house throw away. Lilith look down the well and the dead part of the river. Lilith watching Lilith and trying to see which part of her turn woman" (7). It is not long before this practice of literal self-reflection turns into an arguably narcissistic and ultimately risky practice of self-admiration. The exceptional circumstances of her birth and early childhood, along with her peculiar phenotype, leave her entirely certain of her singularity vis-à-vis the rest of the enslaved community. Having internalized an epistemology according to which the "arrow from ugly to pretty was from black to white" (181), Lilith looks in mirrors to locate a desperately desired space, ironically, "beyond the forms of alienation produced by the negating gaze of white supremacy, which can only image blackness as abjection or supplication" (Campt 2019b, 43–44). Mirrors confirm what she comes to recognize as her exceptional beauty. They reflect her green eyes—"eyes that seem robbed from white lady" (4)—and convince her that she deserves and can legitimately aspire to those things meant exclusively for white women. They convince her to insist on her own desires in a space unfit for such longings. Moreover, the beauty these mirrored surfaces reflect back to Lilith creates the context for an individual erotic agency that conflicts with the (ostensibly) solidarity-based liberation movement into which Homer seeks to conscript her.

Lilith's green eyes tell her she is special and lead her to believe she has a right not to suffer the humiliations and abuses that are the lot of the enslaved:

"I be different from them nigger bitches. Me smarter and prettier and me tired of the damn cellar" (45). She cleaves to this self-determined singularity, unmoved by the risks others have taken on her behalf ("she know the other house slaves hate her. They have to. For she was thinking that if she wasn't Lilith she would hate Lilith too"; 46) and entirely disdainful of those who share her lot ("Lilith ask Homer when she goin' be a proper house negro and clean upstairs and how come she can't serve food like the other negrowomens in the house, since none pretty or have clean fingernail like she"; 53). Moreover, the uncommonness of her green eyes, which should be the tie that binds her to her revolutionary sisters the Night Women, Lilith instead views as her personal ticket out of her abject status and beyond the need for solidarity with those as abject as she: "Lilith was in the cellar brushing cobweb from a silver tray. . . . She look at herself and know that she never come 'cross no other woman with her colour eye save for Gorgon and Hippolyta, and they both ugly. She start to believe that . . . the road set before her was going to wind a different way than most nigger. That make her walk straighter" (82).

Confident of her arresting physical beauty, Lilith is determined to impress and seduce Montpelier's master, Humphrey Wilson, and to thereby foil the plantation order—to set off on that differently winding way: "Lilith want him to take her up in the house and out of common negro life. Lilith hear about massas and they chere amie and she know she prettier than any other negro in the field or in the house" (84). Her desire to seduce Humphrey is explicitly legible, that is, as an instance of the phenomenon wherein enslaved women aspired to a measure of protection from violence or to other humanizing advantages via their sexual relationships with white men. Lilith lays this out plainly:

> There be two things that a white man can do at once. A white man can save her from the Johnny-jumpers and put her above other negrowomens. A white man like Massa Humphrey can also take her and hold her with the gentle hand that niggerman don't got and bury him head in her bosom and make him man sound and it wouldn't be like what she hear coming from Circe hut. . . . A white man can be a prince or a lord, and whether in the bed or by the pen can free a niggerwoman. (80)

Framed as a sensible strategy for a woman in her position, a woman who is property, Lilith's interest in Humphrey is in this way unremarkable. James plays, however, with the specific nature of Lilith's disorderly aspirations. Her designs on her master would seem to highlight the coercive circumstances that determine the sexuality of the enslaved. But there is more to it. There is—absurdly, inappropriately—a girlishness to Lilith's feelings for Humphrey, the naive fantasies of a teenager infatuated with a powerful and handsome older man:

> But there be what she don't know and would never say, why she need him to look at her but feel to run when he do, why she need him to say something but not to her. . . . Why when breeze blow through him hair she feel hot and why when he smile at a good working nigger she feel hate for that one so bad she could scratch her eyes out. . . . She watch the massa shiny boots and him breeches and the green waistcoat with flower trim. After that Lilith make every effort to see him, and that was not difficult. (80)

With passages like this one, James introduces—absurdly, inappropriately—a comic element into the tragic space of Montpelier, digging into a plot point that renders complicated and even laughable the figure of the enslaved woman. He makes clear that Lilith herself is aware of a disjunction between strategic aims and her googly-eyed lust: "Lilith tell herself she not no foolish nigger. She know what being the massa favourite mean in real speak. She know that a nigger who not uncommon should think and plot. But she also see him hair blaze afire and . . . everything come together and make her mind burn" (81). She cannot help herself. She desires Humphrey in the way any woman desires a man:

> Massa Humphrey. She see him plenty time from far but never look at him before. She look at him hair blaze. She lick her bottom lip until it soft, and touch her hair. Lilith look at him as he pace from one end of the kitchen to the next and she rip the breeches off him legs and watch him pacing again. Lilith regarding the massa like she never regard a man before. . . .
> When he laugh, she giggle like an agreeable girl even if she don't know what she laughing for. . . .
> Lilith watch him taking him shirt off all the time. Him chest rise and fall when he laugh and him nipples surround by delicious pink they way a nigger own surround by nasty black. Lilith see him smile and think nothing evil could come out of that mouth. (79–80, 84)

That Lilith develops what amounts to a crush on Humphrey, despite having witnessed the savage cruelty of his interactions with those less powerful than himself, is deeply unsettling. She has seen him attack Homer; she has been the target of his foulest language; she understands that every beating administered, every privation imposed on the enslaved at Montpelier, occurs ultimately at his command. Still she uses any means she can devise to attract his attention: "She bite her bottom lip and swing her hip and walk but when Lilith look up he not looking. That make her want to cease but it also make her want to go on"—"she did fix her dress so that her titties push up like fruit that sell in the market.... She wish she did have some beet to rub on her lip and her cheek" (81, 85). Even when she finally agrees to meet with the Night Women for the first time, it is to serve her own interest, to further her explicit project of "defining herself over and against others" (Ngai 2006, 127): "The things you say me must learn to put me over other woman, Lilith say" (99). Though her various attempts at seduction are certainly foolish, they point nonetheless to a crucial dimension of Lilith's self-regard, notably, that she sees her condition as mutable. Lilith is confident, that is, in the impermanence of her abjection.

It might be argued, and indeed it has been, that such unwillingness to accept or identify existentially with one's enslaved status underlies any and all individual and collective practices of radical refusal in the plantation Americas.[4] What is *marronage* or slave revolt if not the expression of selves imagined otherwise than within the limits of identities crafted by white supremacy? Yet, while this is certainly true, Lilith's commitment to performing a self beyond her station has to do with a somewhat different kind of freedom—a freedom she has deemed more desirable, or perhaps merely more attainable, than freedom from bondage: that is, "the possibility of personal freedom, and interior, imaginative freedom" (Morrison 2019, 318).[5] More than anything, Lilith desires visibility as a unique, individuated being, and this desire to be seen in her uniqueness is both the true motive force behind her struggle for recognition by Humphrey and the reason she refuses solidarity with her literal and metaphorical sisters.

Lilith's "scandalous desire to be left alone" given opportunities for alliance may be "understood as more than just a symptom of narcissism or individualism" (Ngai 2006, 120, 119).[6] Rather, her insistent detachment is a desperate aspiration to singularity—an aspiration that "cannot be satisfied as long as there are other beings" like her (Silverman 2009, 4). These other, too-similar beings risk reducing her to one among many in the broader category of the (green-eyed) enslaved. As such, they necessarily become so many "rivals and enemies" (Silverman 2009, 4) in her eyes. Insofar as Lilith fears nothing so much as "nondistinction," her would-be sisters are threats to her "individuality or separateness" (Ngai 2006, 118, 117).

The nature of Lilith's desires becomes most apparent in her relationship with Isobel Roget, the wealthy planter's daughter whom Lilith (absurdly, inappropriately, *aspirationally*) perceives as her rival for Humphrey's attentions. Miss Isobel is the quintessential white colonial woman. Blonde, beautiful, and privileged, she exists in a parallel universe to that of Lilith—Lilith who somehow imagines that only the thinnest of lines separates her from a version of herself that Humphrey might love: "If only she could say something un-niggerlike," she muses, *"Like a lady of good breeding and learning"* (81; emphasis mine). Isobel is that well-bred and learned being (although, as the reader later discovers, far from "un-niggerlike"), and so it is no coincidence that James apposes one of Lilith's schemes to seduce Humphrey to Miss Isobel's first appearance at Montpelier.

In the moments before Miss Isobel's arrival, Lilith has just managed to gain entry to Humphrey's bedroom. She comes upon him completely naked—"him body lean and dark on the limbs but white like porcelain in the chest, waist and hips. . . . Massa member swing low like it hanging from a red tree that burst into flame like the red hair on him head" (85). She was certain this would be her long-awaited opportunity to seduce him. But Humphrey is distracted—the dogs have begun barking outside at the sound of a carriage arriving—and he pays Lilith no attention: "Massa Humphrey brush past her and gone" (85) before she can make her move. He heads out of the room and outside—shirtless—to greet Miss Isobel's carriage. Lilith observes their exchange through the bedroom window.

> The woman in the carriage yell out, Master Wilson! When she see him naked hand waiting to help.
> —I daresay, Lord Wilson, that I shall not be seen speaking to a man in such scandalous undress! she say. Massa Humphrey look round himself 'cause he don't know what she mean.
> —Madam? he say, looking down on him breeches that button right and tuck in him boots that did shine only last night.
> —I repeat, the lady Roget shall not be manhandled by a man with no shirt on, sir, even if he is a gentleman, or claims as much, she say. . . .
> Massa Humphrey dress himself right in front of the carriage while the woman inside giggle.
> —A thousand pardons, ma'am, I trust I'm far more presentable now, he say and bow low and grin like little boy. (86–87)

Indicating her chaperone, Miss Isobel continues, "Surely you would not expect a lady to come to a gentleman's abode all by her lonesome, would you? That would be irredeemingly improper, she say" (87).

The scene is a hilarious contrast to Lilith's botched attempt at intimacy. With her perfect performance of feminine respectability, Isobel Roget brings down the full weight of her white Creole womanhood, offhandedly crushing Lilith's fantasy and rendering stark the contrast between her own value as a white lady and Lilith's insignificance as an enslaved woman.

Rather than take the lesson, however, Lilith accepts the challenge: "She try to fix her dress to show even more bosom" (88), undeterred in her belief in her own powers of seduction. Yet Humphrey's indifference to her becomes only more absolute: "Lilith come in just as he wake up with the bed linen in her hand and her bosom push up like she selling them. The massa walk right pass her and go to the privy. She watch him not watching her" (88). Discouraged but not yet defeated, Lilith bides her time and continues to reassure/regard herself in the mirror: "Lilith go back to spending much time looking at herself in the silver tray in the kitchen" (88), reminding herself of her beauty and its worth.

While Lilith spends much of the novel's first half looking at herself and looking at Humphrey (not looking back), there are others who have focused their gaze on her. Homer, for example, watches Lilith closely—too closely for Lilith's taste: "Every time she steal a glance at the skinny woman, she see Homer already looking at her. Even when Homer back turn to her Lilith still feel her looking" (53). From the very beginning, Homer shows herself to be well aware of Lilith's self-regard, and she recognizes it within the frame of narcissism: "Homer say, Pretty gal go a river and see herself in water. Pretty gal drown when she go down to kiss herself" (53). Homer takes up the task of retraining Lilith's regard. She tries to disabuse Lilith of the romance of her green eyes, revealing to her that the heartless Jack Wilkins—not Tantalus—is her father: "You didn't think it queer-like that you eye green? You who love look in silver tray at youself—oh yes, you think me never see you loving how you think you look. Where you think them green eye come from?" (68–69). She warns Lilith not to be too taken by her own reflection—"'Look beyond you mirror, chile'" (76)—and enjoins her to see the world through less selfish eyes.

Although Homer has been brutalized in the past of the narrative—severely beaten, raped, and robbed of her children—by the time we encounter her in the present of James's novel she has established herself firmly as "the head nigger in this bloodcloth place" (293). Born in Africa and versed in the healing and punishing arts of Myal, she is feared and respected by all the enslaved on the plantation.[7] The Wilson family fully trusts and depends on her to keep domestic order, blind to the fact that she is planning a woman-led, island-wide rebellion meant to end slavery in Jamaica. She is Lilith's self-designated protector. Having saved Lilith from the consequences of killing the Johnny-jumper and brought her, at her own peril, into the relative safety of the great house, she teaches Lilith to read and opens her eyes to the true goings-on at Montpelier. James presents Homer as the archetypal figure of the revolutionary slave woman so often silenced in histories of slave resistance, thereby pushing back against the "traditional masculinist associations" (Bailey 2014, 76) that characterize the narrative of freedom struggles in the Afro-Americas.

At the same time, however, the personal conflict between Homer and Lilith complicates this counternarrative. James's emphasis on the antagonism of their relationship presents another of *Night Women*'s disordering effects vis-à-vis the "affective history project" Best describes. The two women's very first encounter is violent: "Lilith get a slap from that thin house niggerwoman who smell of mint and lemongrass" (6) when she is just a child learning her place within the ecology/economy of the plantation. From this point through to the end of the novel, Lilith and Homer's relationship is marked by its own kind of "familiar and intimate violence" (C. Sharpe 2010, 3). This is James's reminder that the brutality of the plantation very likely would have seeped into interactions among enslaved women as much as between Blacks and Whites: "Me no forget how you slap me, she say to Homer" (74) several years later. As such, when Homer begins grooming Lilith for what she believes is her revolutionary destiny, Lilith responds with suspicion.

> Homer come in the dark to teach her to read but she look at her too long. And she keep wiping things off Lilith face, even sweat. And touching her face and giving her extra onasburg cloth for monthly blood and tea for when them days get heavy. And talking to her 'bout how she must take care of herself because she busting out of her dress. And talking to her like she be a young'un. Lilith start to wonder what Homer desire. (57–58)

Instruction in literacy, gentle touch, sexual education—such acts of kindness and care among women figure in most accounts of enslaved community as instances of human connection forged despite conditions of utter duress. James troubles this classic representation. Lilith's behavior contradicts both Tinsley's utopian imagination of women-loving women and Hartman's speculative evocation of sisterhood and friendship in the belly of the slave ship.[8] Not only does Lilith rebuff Homer's maternal attentions, but she does so with increasingly virulent homophobia: "You watch me plenty already. Morning, noon and night you in me business. Now you all coming down to the cellar, 'bout you teaching me to read. You must really be a sodomite" (72)—and later, "Me no have to tell you nothing, say Lilith. So keep you woman secret and you woman loving to youself" (74). Lilith casts womanly community as a site of perversion and in this way troubles the reader's presumption of and desire for nurturing (gender-based) solidarity among the enslaved.

Moreover, for Lilith, to accept Homer's strategic plans—learning her place and to "accept things as them be, like a good negro" (101) until, united with her sisters, the time comes to throw herself into the liberation struggle—would be incompatible with her desire for personal freedom. Although, as an enslaved woman, she is a quintessential victim and thus necessarily merits the reader's empathy, she is also something of a brat.

> —You hate me, you hate me just 'cause me soon be mistress favourite, Lilith say.—She pick me, even when you try to frig it up, she pick me. The mistress think me better to show off than you, so me no want to turn into you if is that you offering. Me hear you piss through you ears now that way down there shrivel up. . . .
> —What you think this is, stupid negro chile, play-play? say Homer.—You think you is the mistress favourite new dolly? Me see prettier than you get kill 'cause the tea too hot, one more dumb bitch who think she and mistress be combolo.
> —Y'all hate me because she think me pretty. (72)

More categorically, more aggressively than Hartman's call to resist the temptation to locate—or "fabricate"—either a "romance of resistance" or an "event of love," friendship, or sisterhood in the colonial archive (2008, 8), James asks us to confront the absence of tenderness, the possibility—even likelihood—of animosity and suspicion among enslaved women. "Your finger be the last thing me want in me pussy" (152), Lilith viciously says to Homer. Woman-love, it seems, has no place in Lilith's heart. Thus, while James unequivocally stages female political articulations and practices of radical freedom, he also insists that not all enslaved women sought alliance on feminist terms.

Womanhood is both the process of woman-making and the state of being woman.
—Carol Bailey, *A Poetics of Performance* (2014)

My black woman's anger is a molten pond at the core of me, my most fiercely guarded secret. I know how much of my life as a powerful feeling woman is laced through with this net of rage . . . a boiling hot spring likely to erupt at any point, leaping out of my consciousness like a fire on the landscape.
—Audre Lorde, *Sister Outsider* (1984)

Lilith's one-sided rivalry with Isobel Roget and her indifference to Homer's offers of kinship and alliance ultimately have radical consequences. Ever more intent on attracting Humphrey's attention and unwilling to heed Homer's cautions, Lilith makes a near-fatal mistake. She decides to impress Humphrey by dressing up and serving his guests at the Wilsons' annual New Year's gala, even though she is untrained and thus unfit to assume the role (a role she attains by literally eliminating her competition, another enslaved woman). Homer is well aware of the risks attendant in Lilith's naive exposure of herself to the island's slaveholding class during the ball and so makes a final effort to open Lilith's eyes—to convince her that she should be "in fear and in trembling" faced with the prospect. But Lilith steadfastly clings to her personal perception of reality: "She don't have no looking glass, but in the silver tray she lookin' just fine" (147).

Within moments of the commencement of the dinner, as she is in the very act of crassly refusing Homer's counsel—"Me not no fool, me can carry a tray" (152)—Lilith makes a mistake that nearly costs her her life. The silver tray she is carrying from the kitchen to the ballroom literally and figuratively turns on her, spilling two pots of boiling hot soup onto Isobel's elderly chaperone. Humphrey flies at Lilith in a rage, pummeling her savagely before leaving her to further punishment at the hands of a group of the plantation's slave drivers. She is further beaten, gang-raped, and left for dead. For weeks afterward, per Miss Isobel's instructions, she is strung up and whipped daily before the entire plantation. "Betrayed" by the white man she foolishly dreamed would be her savior, Lilith suffers explicitly the consequences of her nonsolidarity.

In the two pages of the novel that recount the beating and rape, Lilith loses her name and becomes "the girl." In this scene of absolute abjection, Lilith is divested of her inwardly generated sense of herself and re-created as dehumanized object-being: "The girl head jerking and blood running from her nose"; "The girl try to run but she weak and pain overpowering her"; "The girl feel the whole weight of the man crushing her chest and forcing between her legs"; "The girl on the ground in the stable not moving, the dust making more sound than her" (153–55). This shift in perspective—the undoing of Lilith's original self—continues for the next several weeks, as she is forced to appear naked to receive a daily whipping: "Massa Humphrey sitting on the terrace with Miss Isobel.... Work stop and all the negroes gather to watch.... Some people watch her face, watch her breast, and some watch her arse and pussy" (163). Dragged outside and subjected to the gaze of the entire plantation community, she is literally ex-posed, "'posed' in exteriority" (Nancy 1991, xxxvii)—made to assume a position that demands her realignment within the social system of Montpelier. Via "the involvement of other slaves as spectators" (Forbes 2017, 9), Lilith's whipping changes her status—"one or two nigger smile when they see Lilith back smooth for the last time" (163).

This public flogging also shifts the focus of Lilith's regard. The whip mars the beauty she has long cherished. Lilith has known since childhood that "nothing make a nigger more black than whip scars" (26). Yet, while Humphrey's attack, her assault by the slave drivers, and her subsequent regular whippings are transformative, they neither subdue Lilith nor convince her to fall in line with Homer's plans for revolt. These experiences of extreme violence do reframe, though, how Lilith looks—in both the active and the passive sense—and at whom. At this pivotal moment, Lilith begins to turn her regard outward. Rather than become resigned, that is, she becomes resolved: "Scar only make the skin stronger but there be no whip, in hands or in a pants, that goin' knock her down again" (167–68). Lilith has to remake herself after the rape and the whipping and the being looked upon. She begins this process by looking hard at Robert Quinn, the white overseer who sanctioned her abuse by the slave drivers and who supervises her whippings: "She used to look in the sky, but by the third week she look straight at Robert Quinn and watch him look away" (164).

Also immediately following these punishments, Lilith realizes that Isobel, too, has been watching her and in fact awaiting an opportunity to undercut and recondition Lilith's inappropriate self-regard. Having been granted permission by Humphrey to bring Lilith to her plantation, Coulibre, for "seasoning," Isobel makes her plan very clear: "I shall make a little lady of you. Aren't you thrilled to hear it, Lilith? she say. . . . I have been watching you, Lilith. Watching you very closely. . . . Of course you would never have noticed, occupied as you were, watching somebody else" (176–77). Critical to note here is that Isobel is gloating—gloating like a woman who has gained the upper hand over a rival. She continues, speaking about and through but not to Lilith: "That . . . dress she wore with her bosom all tumbling out and embarrassing decent people? Get rid of it. She's so clear to me she might as well be glass. A woman knows another woman's heart, eh? Well, Lilith, you failed, and it will be my task to remind you of that failure. And of your place. In quick time you will be my shadow, Lilith" (177).

This amounts to a shocking little victory dance. Shocking, that is, in that Isobel—wealthy, beautiful, white Isobel—admits that she has been paying attention to Black, enslaved Lilith, a being who never should have figured in her consciousness. The time Lilith spent looking surreptitiously in mirrors and longingly at Humphrey, Isobel spent watching her like competition—like "another woman." And Isobel's threat/promise to turn Lilith into a "little lady" and to make Lilith her "shadow"—these, ironically, are acknowledgments of precisely what Lilith already suspects: that the things ostensibly reserved for white women might be available to her, too. Homer evokes the blurred nature of the line between the two women, musing, "She be white woman so she get what she want. Not like black woman, eh? . . . Maybe is 'cause you part white you think you must always get what you want too" (121).

"Whether white, mulatto, or black Creole, to be colonial is to be indeterminate," writes Colin Dayan in her analysis of the Haitian lwa Ezili (1994, 46). This conclusion bears out dramatically in the relationship between Isobel and Lilith, highlighting the specifically gendered nature of this indeterminacy. As a Creole woman, Isobel is herself subject to the strictures of "iconic femininity, the European-derived models of good womanhood, which in the English-speaking Caribbean have been based mainly on Victorian ideals of decency" (Bailey 2014, 80). These models are categorically raced, of course, affirming white virtue and Black degeneracy. "The spiritualized—and de-sexualized—images of white women depended," that is, "on the prostitution or violation of the dark women in their midsts" (Dayan 1994, 8–9). These models regulated the parameters of self-construction for both white and Black, free and enslaved women. As early as the second page of the novel, James establishes the intersections between Lilith's precarious existence and that of Isobel, equally ambivalent if differently precarious (because performative):

> The white pickneys reach the age when they become white and nigger become black and they don't play together no more. Lilith know one in particular, the girl from Coulibre who use to grab her hair and call her black sheep and always want to go on quest past the ratoon fields, which was forbidden. The same girl Lilith call donkey cause she laugh like a hee-haw. Plenty time Lilith say, Let we be the wickedest pirates! And the girl would say, Aye! and she lead the white girl astray to plunder the booty, cherry or plum or banana. They would tie cloth over one eye and be Henry Morgan and Blackbeard. And they talk secret-like so the boys wouldn't know. The white girl call her lank chicken and Lilith call her rank goat and they scream and laugh, and the girl take Lilith hand and neither think it uncanny. Then one day the girl come to the plantation dress up in bonnet like her mama and bawl out, Mama, pray tell why is that nigger addressing me? Lilith get slap for that from a thin house niggerwoman who smell of mint and lemongrass. (6)

The reader does not meet Isobel for another eighty or so pages, on the day she shows up unannounced at Montpelier, clad in some version of that first bonnet and all the frippery that goes with it and primed for her hyperbolic performance of ladyhood—"I dare say, Lord Wilson"—with which she is meant to win the status of Humphrey Wilson's wife. Although the social chasm separating Lilith and Isobel is vast, James alludes nonetheless to commonalities in both women's accommodation of the wider patriarchal frame: "The lady wearing a wide blue bonnet with a cream bow tie under her chin. Some of her hair tumble out and it curly and yellow. Her dress match her hat, blue with short sleeve and *cut low in the front to show her bosom*" (87; emphasis mine).

Once Isobel brings Lilith to Coulibre, having seen to the permanent marring of Lilith's flesh and its concomitant transformation into an enslaved Black body, she embarks on the real work of reeducation—that is, the complete reduction of Lilith to an insentient, "ungendered" (Spillers 1987, 68), laboring dark "shadow" of herself. Best-laid plans. As it happens, the increased intimacy of the two women's association sets in motion an extraordinary process of reversal. It eventually becomes clear that Lilith's "improvement" occurs in chiastic relation to Miss Isobel's degradation.

I use this rhetorico-linguistic concept—chiasmus—to bring Hortense J. Spillers's articulation of an "American grammar" to bear on James's novel and to extend Spillers's U.S.-centric reflections into the wider Afro-Americas. In her groundbreaking 1987 essay, "Mama's Baby, Papa's Maybe: An American Grammar Book," Spillers begins by evoking the names with which Black women historically have been saddled—"'Peaches' and 'Brown Sugar,' 'Sapphire' and 'Earth Mother,' 'Aunty,' 'Granny,' God's 'Holy Fool,' a 'Miss Ebony First,' or 'Black Woman at the Podium'" (65). "Lilith" might certainly be added to that list of "overdetermined nominative properties" (65). Taking as her point of departure the violence and spectacle embedded in the naming process, Spillers considers the grammar of "declension" that estranges "white" from "Black" ontology in an absolute hierarchy of regard (regard as esteem or worth) and that establishes the contingent power/empowerment of the one, relative only to the impotence/disenfranchisement of the other. In *Night Women*, James amplifies this contingency through the relationship between Isobel and Lilith, configuring gender as grammar—a performance of unstable signifiers. In its most basic form, a chiasmus proceeds from the presentation of two clauses and then the re-presentation of those same clauses in reverse order. It summons the reader to reassess the connection between the two clauses and to examine the context of their syntactic rearrangement.

Lilith's posttraumatic remaking evolves, astoundingly, in a deviant inverse parallelism to what ends up being Isobel's debasement. The process of reconditioning to which Isobel subjects Lilith effectively has the opposite result—because the terms of its undertaking tacitly confirm Lilith's suspicions about her own power and potential. This chiastic structure builds subtly. Significantly, it first begins to play out before Isobel's bedroom mirror. As Lilith brushes her hair, Isobel indulges in little monologues, teaching Lilith her place and working to replace Lilith's self-regard with the force of her own gaze: "Lilith commence to brush Miss Isobel hair. She look up and see Miss Isobel staring at her hard in the mirror" (193). But during these conversations, Isobel often "catch herself chatting like nigger" (212), that is, using the Creole vernacular of the enslaved people she so despises: "I'm too much in the company of negroes, yes I am. Way too much. You have all but ruined me with your nigger ways" (199). Isobel's "ruining" takes increasingly dramatic form and happens as a more or less direct result of Lilith's actions.

That Lilith has so badly burned the chaperone at the ball, for example, leaves Isobel sexually unpoliced, or less policed, an unexpected but entirely welcome liberation: "Miss Isobel confess to Massa Humphrey that she was not even a little sad to be rid of her" (164). It is only a matter of time before Isobel begins having sex with Humphrey, and Lilith fully grasps the significance of this transgression; she knows "white lady suppose to lock it up till wedding ring come to open it" (212). "Bitch getting treat like nigger, Lilith say" (211), thereby expressing her increasing awareness of conceivable flexibility within the continuum from lady to woman.

It also becomes increasingly evident to Lilith that any "easy division between 'lady' and 'savage' was," as Dayan has noted, effectively "made impossible by the planters' wives and daughters, who could move from a lengthy tête-à-tête with their servants to flogging and spitting" (1994, 16). Seeing this phenomenon bear out in the actions of Isobel and her mother ends up providing the foundations of Lilith's true education at Coulibre. From the moment Lilith is brought into Isobel's home, she enters into a space of quotidian cruelty, particularly in her interactions with Isobel's stepmother. As a personal attendant to the elder Mistress Roget, Lilith is for the first time subject to the full scope of the "everyday intimate brutalities of white domestic domination" (C. Sharpe 2010, 9). She becomes the primary outlet for her mistress's unbridled and unrelenting rage—rage at her spoiled children's unmanageable behavior, at her husband's constant infidelity, at her own dependency on the very enslaved women her husband regularly rapes.[9] She expects Lilith to "work and work hard, harder than everybody else" (180), and subjects her to daily whippings meant to tame Lilith's "disturbing spiriteness" (206).

In addition to the constant abuse she suffers, Lilith observes a level of quotidian sadism, sexual and other, more extreme than anything she had witnessed at Montpelier. James certainly portrays Master Roget as an extreme sadist and a brute, but his configuration of the two Mistresses Roget provocatively considers the extent to which white women's inhumanity would have determined the lives of the female enslaved. When Mistress Roget whips to death Lilith's only friend and confidante—ostensibly for the "crime" of allowing goats to get loose in her flower garden but actually for the "crime" of having submitted to Master Roget's sexual assaults ("How dare you come in here stinking of that damn nigger's sweat, the mistress say"; 199)—this triggers something in Lilith. She begins to acknowledge the rise of a feeling at once familiar and unsettling:[10]

> Lilith start to imagine what white flesh look like after a whipping. What white neck look like after a hanging and what kinda scar leave on a white body after black punishment. She think of the little Roget boy, Master Henri, of tying and hanging the boy up by him little balls and chopping him head off . . . and she think of Massa Humphrey and of blood and what sound a white body make when he fall from fifty feet. . . .
>
> Lilith take her beating in silence. But fire going off in her head. Blood spraying and flesh tearing. Lilith can't sleep, not 'cause the cuts from the whip burnin' her, but because darkness burnin' in her own heart. Ashanti blood racing through her and she can't stop thinking about white people shedding theirs. Even the two young children. Lilith count how much lash she get each time and by who and she remember it. She think of Mistress Roget getting tie to a tree and getting whip till she raw. She think of dashing salt in her gashes until the mistress smell like corned pork. She think of a cornstalk thick like black man cock ramming up Massa Roget so hard that he piss blood in him own bath. (200, 206)

These "dark thoughts" (206) reflect Lilith's troubling internalization of the violence that surrounds her at Coulibre—the violence meant to keep her in line, to shore up the plantation order, and to ensure the inviolability of its white inhabitants. They are terrifying to Lilith, but they are also necessary for her survival. Lilith anxiously acknowledges that, despite her efforts to rein in her fury, "she still seeing blood. And the more they whip her, or she see somebody get whip, the more blood she seeing" (220). Lilith's increasing rage ultimately emerges in an act of murderous self-protection that is tremendous in its devastation: she murders Master and Mistress Roget, their two young children, and their enslaved nanny, and she burns Coulibre nearly to the ground.[11] She allows others of the enslaved to take both the blame and the gruesome punishment for her actions. If burning Isobel's chaperone was an inadvertent stage-setting for Lilith's gradual self-repossession, burning up Isobel's entire family is her apotheosis.

The annihilation of the Rogets is as much a point of no return for Isobel as it is for Lilith. It marks the apex of the women's chiasmic inversion, an inversion that Isobel asserts openly in her grief: "I wish I wasn't a lady or a woman, but a nigger like you. Can you imagine that? Can you imagine me envying a wretched nigger like you?" (235). Convinced that her family's death is (fitting) punishment for her transgressive sexual relationship with Humphrey, Isobel admits to the fundamental reality hidden beneath her frilly performance of ladyhood: "I'm just like them, you know. Did you know I was no better, Humphrey? . . . No better than a negro I am, no breeding nor bearing, no education on how one becomes a proper lady" (237–38).

Meanwhile, Lilith becomes Robert Quinn's "wife."[12]

Whether or not the captive female and/or her sexual oppressor derived "pleasure" from their seductions and couplings is not a question we can politely ask.
 —Hortense J. Spillers, "Mama's Baby, Papa's Maybe" (1987)

What kinda nigger rather be slave to free?
 Lilith (in *The Book of Night Women*)

Following the destruction of Coulibre, Lilith is returned to Montpelier, and she is a woman greatly transformed. It might be expected—and, indeed, Homer does expect—that Lilith's experiences of abuse and her subsequent act of retribution would have primed her to engage at last in the more radical project afoot. Yet this is not the case. The discovery of her "true womanness" (236) destabilizes Lilith profoundly. It obliges her to recalibrate once again her sense of her self, a great unsettledness that is evidenced by a dramatic change in her relationship to mirrors:

> Lilith walking down the corridor and pass a looking glass on the wall. . . . It didn't make right and the mistress keep it away from people. Lilith watch the looking glass looking at her. The looking-glass Lilith have a flat head top, a chin that point all the way to the ground and eye so big Lilith can see another Lilith in it. She looking at the looking-glass eye holding her secret and wonder if maybe anybody can find out if they look hard enough. (236)

No longer does Lilith's reflection offer her a self-satisfying confirmation of her beauty. Rather, it reveals to her the "true darkness and true womanness" deep-rooted in her name. "True womanness," she realizes, "be the seed of destruction like plenty whorish woman in the Bible" (236)—like one particular "whorish" woman, that is, the midrashic "female night demon Lilith" (Baskin 2015, 9), Adam's combative and self-sufficient first wife.[13]

Gone, from this point on, is the prideful reassurance Lilith once found in her reflection. Gone, too, is the privilege to which she earlier believed herself entitled by virtue of her white paternity and its irrefutable declaration, her green eyes:

> Lilith go to her room and look through her belongings for the piece of looking glass. The one time she go back to Coulibre after the fire, a time she go with Robert Quinn, she find it sticking out from ashes and ready to cut her foot if she did step without looking. Lilith pull out the looking glass in the dim light. She look at herself, at the one thing that make her not black. She not black, she mulatto. Mulatto, mulatto, mulatto. Maybe she be family to both and to hurt white man just as bad as hurting black man. Lilith wonder if green eye is the only thing she seeing that any good. Maybe she should use the piece of looking glass to cut her eyes out so that she can't see herself. (277)

In the surfacing of Lilith's blinding fury (the pun is intended), any scrap of innocence has been lost from Lilith's gaze. James brings to the fore all the violence inherent in Lilith's mixed racial identity and forces her to grapple with the unacknowledged monstrousness and sexual savagery of which she is a product, as well as with the pathology she is presumed to represent as the embodiment of disavowed transracial carnal encounters. He stages her confrontation with the horrors embedded in the crucible of her blood. Emphasizing Lilith's racial ambiguity in the wake of her vicious social transgression at Coulibre and her "reward" in becoming Quinn's mistress, James edges up to the trope of "monstrous female sexuality" (Garraway 2005, 232) that attaches to colonial fantasies of the enslaved female and of the "sexually predatory" "mulatto concubine" (232, 229) in particular. Yet, in granting us access to Lilith's inner turmoil, he counters such stereotypes of perversion.

Having succumbed to rage so entirely, Lilith comes to question whether or not she can bear to look at the woman she has become—or, rather, at the woman she has fully revealed to herself. She is horrified to realize the equivalence of her "true womanness" with the rage that led to the devastation of Coulibre and its inhabitants. In granting us access to Lilith's inner turmoil, James has us witness the cost to Lilith of inhabiting demonic ground. This cost is most visible in her postfire relationship with Isobel. Like Lilith, Isobel is resettled at Montpelier. Unlike Lilith, she quickly becomes undone. Orphaned and thus without paternal(-cum-patriarchal) constraint, Isobel abandons any pretense of Victorian feminine respectability—"I do not need to be comforted Humphrey Wilson, I need to be fucked. Rutted like a common cow. Does that shock you? Are you quite horrified? Do you find me improper?" (249). She becomes hopelessly addicted to laudanum, for which she prostitutes herself during middle-of-the-night excursions to an opium den. Dressed as a man and traveling on horseback, "Miss Isobel ride to Kingston like a demon chasing her" (344).[14] In a reversal of Isobel's original plan to "make a little lady" of Lilith, the two women's interaction has produced the unintended, opposite effect as well: Isobel becomes something else in the face of Lilith's survivalist self-regard, and Isobel becomes something of a Night Woman.

In an ironic inverse parallel to Isobel's irretrievable debasement, Lilith attains the privileged and protected status of a white man's "chere amie," although on terms very different from those she imagined in the days before Coulibre. She is taken in by Quinn, who has become deeply enamored of her, and set up in a complicated facsimile of domesticity. Her change in status is instantaneous and enormous, and it serves as confirmation that the self she believed in is a self she actually could become. Moreover, being Quinn's concubine provides Lilith with an alternative to leaning fully into her wrath—a different path toward rebuilding herself in the wake of both the horrors she witnessed and those she caused.

Most significantly, Lilith discovers that she has become inviolable. This changed status is explicitly affirmed in a scene that repeats, with a crucial difference, the circumstances of her gang rape following her drastic misstep at the Montpelier ball: the very same slave driver who had brutalized her that night comes to Quinn's cottage, intending to force himself on Lilith a second time—"We're pickin' up right where we left off on New Year's, darlin, innit? the man say" (280). In this instance, however, in dramatic distinction to the earlier event, Quinn defends Lilith. He shoots and wounds her attacker and has him run off the plantation. Of course, it is unclear whether Quinn means to defend Lilith's honor or to protect his own property—to declare Lilith's inviolability or the sanctity of his domestic space.[15] The blurriness between these two intentions—those of the lover and those of the master—conveys the fundamental ambiguity of Lilith and Quinn's relationship, perhaps an instance of "the way multiple intimacies . . . and the desire to be free require one to be witness to, participant in, and be silent about scenes of subjection that we rewrite as freedom" (C. Sharpe 2010, 23). There are, indeed, versions of both love and pleasure between Lilith and Quinn, but James insists also on the impossibility of disentangling coercion from consent, desperation from desire. Shamed and confused by her feelings for Quinn, unable to stop herself from fantasizing about "him damn *wanton ringlets down his back*" (207), Lilith is surprised to find "she want it too" (265). She does her best to hold on to enough hatred to maintain a safe distance from the terror he represents. But even her mirror cannot help her: "She look up and see him grinning at her. She remind herself that she supposed to hate him. She wish she could see her back in a looking glass. Anything" (265). Her self-regard has come to include a view of herself as a beloved and legitimately desired being.

The final third of *Night Women* includes multiple elaborate and graphic sex scenes that detail every sensation, every moment of pleasure Lilith feels as she holds and is held by Quinn, as he enters her and as she takes his "Irishman" in her mouth, as he tickles and caresses and even kisses her, and as she "lie down on him chest" (269). These moments, James suggests, defy white supremacist constructions of "black subjectivity as will-less, abject, insatiate and pained" (Hartman 1997, 87). To the extent that sexuality in captivity would have so often been an experience of profound and humiliating alienation—"a *theft of the body*—a willful and violent (and unimaginable from this distance) severing of the captive body from its motive will, its active desire" (Spillers 1987, 67)—then "to feel, to be felt, to have erotic sensations was to steal bodies back from masters" (Lindsey and Johnson 2014, 187). Through Lilith's fraught freedom-like counterclaims to intimacy with Quinn, James restores a measure of autonomy and even delight to the sensate enslaved female body. In ways very similar to Maryse Condé's characterization of Tituba, James imagines the possibility of Black female love and lust in a built environment that presumes only the fact of Black female exploitation—"organizing," as Jennifer C. Nash has proposed, "around the paradoxes of pleasure rather than woundedness or the elisions of shared injury, around possibilities rather than pain" (2014, 3).[16]

James resists the potential inclinations of the (neo-)slave narrative toward pornotroping, the voyeuristic figuration of the enslaved body's "sheer physical powerlessness that slides into a more general 'powerlessness'" (Spillers 1987, 67). The reader looks on Lilith's sexualized body, which bears witness, yes, to the coercions and violations it has borne but does so through the eyes of a woman who can also imagine and experience toe-curling pleasure. That Lilith has found a physical, social, and emotional sanctuary with Quinn—"a place, a space, away, for individual reclamation of the self"—is a worthy accomplishment; it "is a part, maybe the largest part, certainly the most important part, of the reconstruction of identity" (Morrison 2019, 319). By successfully managing "to get the love she want" (100), Lilith finally realizes her "status as unique" (Ngai 2006, 119). Quinn's devotion, however contingent, abates her fear of nondistinction. As his beloved, she experiences the profound delight of being the "'only one'" (Ngai 2006, 119), recognized finally as her singular self.

James's unabashed exploration of Lilith and Quinn's romantic and sexual partnership pushes at the limits of what we imagine about the coercive nature of interracial sex in the plantation Americas. As Treva B. Lindsey and Jessica Marie Johnson provocatively argue, "sexual freedom remains largely untouched as a critical space for understanding the lived experiences of enslaved people" (2014, 189). The reason for this tendency to prudishness is arguably no different in the present moment or recent past than it was in the context of the nineteenth-century female slave narrative. Then as now, the treatment of feminine erotic agency in circumstances of unfreedom is inherently suspect. Absent any "clear political goals," "it suggests collaboration with masters and overseers" (181). It suggests, troublingly, that regard for self may have hindered solidarity, blurred allegiances, and in other ways disordered political agency among the enslaved.

That Lilith tries to save Quinn from being slaughtered along with the other Whites during the uprising—as a result of the love-like feelings she has for him and despite the fact that "he be the cause" (264) of the quilt of scars on her back—indicates James's willingness to grapple brazenly with the "dynamics of enjoyment in a context in which joy and domination and use and violence could not be separated" (Hartman 1997, 81). The something-like-love story James introduces is perverse and unrealistic as far as any "resolution of difference" is concerned. The trauma and brutality that precede Lilith and Quinn's coming together make any family romance a near-impossible outcome.[17] Nevertheless, within the constraints of her largely wretched subjectivity, Lilith manages to carve out a condition that corresponds with her own view of herself—a condition that thus offers something akin to freedom.

But what would be the point of questioning the very grounds of freedom?
—Sheri-Marie Harrison, "Marlon James and the Metafiction of the New Black Gothic" (2018)

Is there a song for Tituba?
—Tituba Indian (in *I, Tituba, Black Witch of Salem*)

For much of *Night Women*, James seems to blame Lilith's disordering presence for undermining the should-be community of Montpelier's enslaved women. She is too insistently nonaligned to make common cause with her fellow oppressed, and many of her decisions stand "in stark contrast to the needs of the collective" (Harrison 2018, 11). Lilith's antipathy toward Homer seems particularly unwarranted, a reflection of her blind self-regard. It appears, indeed, that Lilith has turned her back on the enslaved of Montpelier, having grown comfortable with her privileged existence as Quinn's lover. Homer, in contrast, is initially presented as a tough but well-meaning matriarch. In addition to saving Lilith's life and keeping her from the cane fields and the vindictive Johnny-jumpers, Homer assumes both the responsibilities and the liabilities of mediating between the Wilsons, the overseer Wilkins, and the enslaved women under their control. She lies to protect those she considers her wards, standing when necessary between them and the white and Black men's fists.

As the narrative progresses, however, it is revealed that Homer's motivations for building and nurturing this community of women revolutionaries are far from pure. Although by the time she takes her place in Lilith's story she has ascended to a certain power within the social economy of the Wilson plantation, she very well might have been the heroine of a tragic tale of her own. It is revealed bit by bit that her past has left her with deeply traumatizing literal and physical scars and that this past has been suppressed but by no means overcome. The reader learns that Homer has survived violent sexual and other humiliations at the hands of the elder Master Wilson, his wife, the overseer Wilkins, and men of the local maroon population. Following an attempted escape, she endured "the worst whipping ever in Montpelier" (216) and was severely mutilated and twice gang-raped. The children she was forced to "breed" were taken from her immediately, sold away, and eventually died from the abuse they suffered. Lilith learns of this history in a rare moment of camaraderie between the two women. But instead of these tragedies bringing her closer to Homer, they convince Lilith that the older woman's plans for insurrection are fundamentally flawed:

> —Of course, Homer. 'Cause everybody listen to you. All of them want to get free so bad them don't even see that you not making no sense. Not one thing about this rebellion make sense—
> —What don't make sense 'bout it, you damn Judas nigger? If you love slavery so bad then stay.
> —Them dead, Homer. Too late now to try be a mother. (341)

Lilith is certain that Homer's embracing of the revolution has little to do with freeing Jamaica's enslaved population and everything to do with avenging her stolen children—and she realizes that this desire for vengeance endangers everyone. "Me don't know why everybody in this plan," says Lilith, "but me know why you in it and is not no freedom business. And everybody goin' get capture or kill" (339). Rather than support Homer, Lilith mercilessly undermines her authority. She evokes the older woman's all-consuming grief for her lost children as the reason to reject any alliance between them. And when Homer accuses Lilith of taking no stake in the liberation of her "own people," Lilith coldly counters, "Me know what moving you and you not out to build nothing" (375). While this lack of empathy and sisterly fellow feeling seems callous and cruel, it becomes clear in the end that Lilith was right all along. Irreparably broken by the traumas of her past, Homer anticipates no future freedom. She dreams of a reckoning, nothing more.

Though just a girl to Homer's old woman, Lilith knows far better—she knows firsthand—what such reckoning requires of the self. She has exterminated an entire family in blood and fire but irretrievably lost something of herself in the process. Having very literally taken the master's tools and dismantled his house, she has discovered, as per Lorde's oft-quoted caution, that such actions can bring about no "genuine change" ([1984] 2007, 112). She explains as much to Homer: "Me get me blood and see me here. Nothing different. Nothing better. Revenge don't leave me nothing but them burning skin smell that me can't blow out of me nose nor wash out" (341). Homer nonetheless is intent on harnessing and training Lilith's lethal rage for the sake of her own revolt. Lilith refuses. She understands viscerally that Homer's "hatred is a deathwish for the hated, not a lifewish for anything else" (Lorde [1984] 2007, 152). Though she has killed and killed to save herself from death, Lilith does not intend to let this murderous part of herself be the whole of who she is in the world.

By the conclusion of James's novel, the reader has gotten a glimpse of the personal tragedies that animate each one of the Night Women's revolutionary fury, the horrifying ways in which each of them has been violated—maimed and disfigured, humiliated and silenced. Each woman remembers and lives in her suffering. Each woman is scarred. The emotional and physical wounds left by their individual experiences of misery, James suggests, are so many obstacles to generative collective action. Each woman's singular trauma pulls her away from a relational "we" and risks isolating her in the pain of her separate, distinct, lonely "I." Each of the women wants bloody, personal revenge. While this does not necessarily diminish the legitimacy of the Night Women's act of total revolution, it presents a differently humanizing portrayal of enslaved persons in the Afro-Americas.

To turn to the archive of slavery and extract from it stories of nastiness and discord among those who should have been allies—those who we want to believe acted as kin—is James's disorderly maneuver. It is "the problem" he tackles, the risk he accepts in attempting to "take the imaginative power, the artistic control away from the institution of slavery and place it where it belongs—in the hands of the individuals who knew it" (Morrison 2019, 307,

309). James insists that we readers enact our own practice of refusal—that we acknowledge our "inability to judge" choices made by the enslaved and embrace "refusal, not to know, but to conclude" (Morrison 2019, 308). If we are determined to speculate our way around the archive, James implies, we must admit the possibility of finding things we do not like about those we have gone in ready to love. We must admit the bad and the ugly into our renderings of history.

James cautions us to refuse any neat continuum with struggles from our past as the foundation for feminist, antiracist, and other communities of resistance in the present. He writes the unseemly practices of everyday life in the colonial Americas and recognizes blemished humanity among the victims of history. James abandons any "'protectionist' reading of representation" and acknowledges the likelihood of "complex and sometimes unnerving pleasures" (Nash 2014, 3) between the enslaved and their captors. James makes uncomfortable demands of his readers. He in no way seeks "to gentle the reader's experience of the terror of slavery" (Best 2012, 461) and instead makes it a point to "enact the indecent and unveil the unspeakable" (Hartman 1997, 107), gesturing forcefully to the original enslaved women's narratives his novel revisits. James asks that we "confront the extreme and quotidian manifestations of human horror" but does so without offering "the reassurance of change and cathartic resolution" (Cheng 2009, 93). His refusal to propose a way out of this discomfort disrupts the tacit forms of judgment that inhere in our critical and creative relationships to the hemispheric American past.

The portrait James paints of Lilith is in many ways unflattering. Arrogant and misguided, narcissistic and often unkind, she is difficult to accept within nobler castings of enslaved female subjectivity. Lilith is a singular and uncommon being: she is so by birth but also wills herself so by her many demands and expectations—demands and expectations incompatible with her status as an enslaved woman. Lilith does not evolve from "savagery" to "enlightenment," abjection to grace. Rather, she comes to accept her "darkness" as a "technology of freedom" (Forbes 2017, 8) and mobilizes it in her own self-interest. This becomes the key to her survival in a society held together by chains. Lilith's insistent self-regard often has the effect, yes, of disregarding the needs and desires of her fellow enslaved.

Even the very way in which Lilith's tale comes to be told reflects the imposition of her self on the world. At the narrative's conclusion, James reveals that the entire story has been told by Lovey Quinn, Lilith's daughter: "Me was but nine year in age when me mother start to teach me how to read.... And she teach me how to write.... But she didn't teach me for me but for her, for when the time come to write her song she have somebody true to be her witness. Somebody who know that one cannot judge the action of a niggerwoman who only wanted to be everything and nothing" (416).[18] Lilith's autopoietic intent has an annihilating effect on her daughter-scribe, effectively forced to write the autobiography of her mother. "This was not the story me did plan to tell" (411), Lovey insists, but, duty bound, she has bent to Lilith's will.

Like Tituba, Lilith desires a song. She wants to be seen by history and to be seen on her own terms. Also like Tituba, Lilith allows herself to contemplate the true nature of the freedom claims she wants to make, and she allows love and lust to factor into those musings. In this fashion, she undermines the pornotropic foundations of slave society that would have her be no more than exposed and brutalized flesh. Through Lilith's insistent story, *The Book of Night Women* reaches for something more than the potentially too-familiar outraged display of abjected brown bodies. James is unsparing in his efforts to narrow the hiatus between his reader and the inhuman world Lilith inhabits, but in evoking its atrocities, he does not inure the reader to them. His explicitness serves, on the contrary, to confront us with the full force of slavery's hideousness—to *abnormalize* that which was at one time perfectly banal. He makes clear, too, that Lilith herself is always shocked and traumatized by the horrors she witnesses and into which she is conscripted.

In this dehumanizing context, in which Black and white, enslaved and free, are rigidly controlled categories, Lilith's self-determined individualist liminality places her only unreliably in solidarity with those who would revolt against white patriarchal and colonial injustice. In the end, she privileges her own romantic and erotic needs over and above those of the communities on offer in her world. Defiant self-regard marks her every interaction—be it with her masters, with her lover, or with the community of women who are her kin by blood but never quite her comrades-in-arms. She is a self-defending and self-loving being whose enslaved status never inhibits her from reaching for the version of freedom she imagines. Lilith is deeply flawed, it is true, and in her imperfection she reveals the moral and other failures—the suffocating rage, the sadism, the opportunism—of those she only reluctantly acknowledges as her sisters. Her refusal to turn on her man and join the Night Women's struggle may look at first glance like "hindrance" and "compromise" with respect to a "greater goal of freedom" (Bailey 2014, 113), but this is true only if freedom is conceived in a particular manner. In the end, Lilith lives to ensure that her story is told. And that story insists on the many possible ways of being both enslaved and free. "'You think you is woman,' Homer say. Me think me is Lilith, Lilith say" (341).

EPILOGUE

Sometimes it is enough and downright crucial just to acknowledge what is in order to understand what will be. In short, we may have to risk the aporia of political uncertainty in order to reinvent the possibilities of the social.

—Anne Anlin Cheng, "Psychoanalysis without Symptoms" (2009)

If the novel was good, it was because it was faithful to a certain kind of politics; if it was bad, it was because it was faithless to them. . . . In that no-win situation—inauthentic, even irresponsible, to those looking for a politically representative canvas; marginalized by those assessing value by how "moral" the characters were—my only option was fidelity to my own sensibility.

—Toni Morrison, foreword to *Sula* (2004)

This project originated from within the very core of my scholarly habitus. As a researcher and teacher of francophone and Africana literature and culture, I have long been attached at once to a particular corpus of texts and to a particular set of theoretical concerns. Both these texts and my critical approach to them turned around questions of race and gender in the geocultural space of the Caribbean and its diasporas. In grappling with the phenomena of inequality and violation attendant to these particular social constructions in this particular regional context, I had grown quite comfortable distinguishing the righteous from the despicable, the historical victims of abuse from long-standing perpetrators of injustice.

Many, if not all, of the works of my personal professional canon—those works I have taught and retaught as so many touchstones of my intellectual-cum-pedagogical inquiries—portray women compelled to navigate structures of domination that allow for, if not encourage, their abuse. Bound by the strictures of slavery, colonialism, and their long wake, the women in these narratives necessarily do battle with well-known forces of bigotry and gendered violence. They are survivors, heroic victims of history, meant to fit within the category of the righteous-because-abused. These are women defined, in large measure, by their opposition to or contestation of a racist and misogynist status quo and by their struggle to create alternative, improved conditions of being.

Among this group of superwomen, raging in their own ways against a political machine designed to relegate them to subhumanity, I have found myself dwelling most often on a select few—a handful of self-telling women characters who prove more difficult to accommodate within the category of "heroine." They are neither righteous nor even generous, at least not with any real consistency. They stand outside of communities with whom they ordinarily would be expected to identify, alongside or for whom they ordinarily would be expected to struggle. They are characters who, though violated within their social contexts and fundamentally disempowered, fail to elicit (my) full sympathy.

I am not alone in feeling unsettled by these women. They present a particular challenge to many of the theorists with whose work my own scholarship has been most often and most deeply in dialogue. As I have tried to show in these pages, it is primarily in the privileging of their individual selves over the interests of their communities that these women characters have issued their threat to order—first within the space of their narratives and then also, extratextually, within the space of Caribbean literature and its study. They have been largely misapprehended or ignored or have proven difficult to account for in scholarly projects committed to identity-based or ideological perspectives. In many instances, the authors of the narratives in which these women appear have been implicated in the critiques directed at their characters. Rules of reading have been broken. Real complaints have been lodged at fictional beings.

There are ways, that is, in which reactions to these characters expose just how we as scholars often enact the very practices of gendered constraint our work means to expose, if not combat. On the one hand, we are well aware of and we denounce situations in which an individual woman is forced into the role of "surrogate victim"—that of she "who serves as a substitute for all the potential culprits in the community and ensures the resolution of unappeased violence and the survival of the community as such" (Garraway 2013, 212–13). Yet in privileging certain representations of raced womanhood, we expect and tacitly enjoin some authors—very often people of color, very often women—to take up the role of healers or activists through their fiction. When they do not, such authors run the risk of being labeled fantasists—"indulgent, foolish, frivolous, merely escapist, naively utopian, in some way wrong—inattentive to the real, defiant of the realist" (D. B. Scott forthcoming). Never mind that defiance of the real through the indulgence of purposeful fantasy and other modes of refusal may be precisely what is called for. For if it is true that "we are each of us born into a world already enslaved by its realisms, by its versions of the real," perhaps a measure of freedom from subjugation by "the shackles of perceptual and political realism" (D. B. Scott forthcoming) is a "simple" matter of disbelieving perverse and biased truth-fors. Reliance on the self—on one's unique thoughts, feelings, and experiences as the truths that matter most—would then be an impressive counter to social constructions that can only ever wound that self. Relentlessly querying the strictures of the perceived real might very well be enough to count as freedom.

As I have argued throughout this study, particular costs are borne by women in the geohistorical spaces of the Americas, especially in circumstances wherein a woman says "no" to communal obligations that present a threat to her individual being. I have been interested not only in the blatant forces of oppression that determine the parameters of individual women's existence in the Caribbean but also in those restrictions that are not uniquely the product of phallocentric power. While the twin scourges of white supremacy and patriarchy are formidable adversaries in any quest for self-determination among those who are dysselected by virtue of their race or gender, white men are not alone in thwarting the desires of marginalized subjects. Beyond the vicious plantation masters and overseers, the corrupt neocolonial political and religious authorities, and the abusive heads of household that undermine women's efforts at self-creation, there are arguably subtler violators of individual personhood worth considering. I have examined, in my engagement with each of the works discussed here, those social forces whose offerings of love or alliance often comprise contingency and constraint.

To forgo love or alliance in contexts of violent domination or duress amounts, I have argued, to a practice of bold self-regard—a consideration of oneself or of one's own interests over and above all others. Whether we name this practice self-love, self-possession, self-defense, self-preservation, or, indeed, self-regard, the important question is not whether such self-interest can or should be deemed narcissistic. More crucial to understand are the endangering circumstances that oblige a radical and sustained turn inward as a means of protecting the self. For if colonialism, capitalism, and other hierarchizing ideologies of power have required the dehumanization of certain kinds of individuals, with special agonies reserved for women, self-regard in this context does not—or, in any case, does not merely—equate with vanity or inflated egotism. Following on Iké Udé, "I beg to differ from this mode of narcissistic taxonomy." The "victorian code of ethics" (Udé 1995) that is the edifice of this kind of moral judgment is incommensurate with the worlds described in these narratives, worlds that so readily abide the grievous injury of women and girls. The narcissism at work in each of the novels I examine is a defensive practice, not a character flaw. It is both weapon and shield in a battle for life and to the death.

There is something truly rare and mighty about self-regard, especially when it is somehow conjured by those who inhabit the space of margins. To love, to possess, to defend, to preserve, to regard oneself—to behold oneself in defiance of the gaze of more powerful others—must be recognized as an ethical practice. In the face of redemption withheld and redress foreclosed, the regarded self seizes the power of judgment from her community and nurtures it within herself. She shifts to an inside-in point of view and works at self-building within and despite the frame of a badly built world.

Trapped within communities that simply are not capacious enough to embrace certain forms of singularity, the women of my corpus are powerful, yes, but vulnerable. Both what is beautiful about them and what is abject assume the risk, in equal measure, of being commodified and devoured. In response to this constant threat of consumption, these women defend themselves and disconcert those around them by cultivating, with varying degrees of success, a resolute self-sufficiency. They query and ultimately queer a normative order that would perpetuate community via the policing of their beauty, their sexuality, and their reproductive capacity—valences of social relation easily manipulated to dispossess women of themselves. Each of these women struggles to achieve a self-containment that, to those around them, reads as callousness or impenetrability, waywardness or arrogance.

The women of these fictions are uncanny beings. Their experiences reveal inconvenient, not-so-secret truths that their communities would much prefer remain undisclosed. They expose, through their behaviors and in their persons, uncomfortable social realities—the autonomy of women's sexual selfhood, the long history of violation and unsanctioned intimacy embedded in racial mixture, the ungovernable fluidity of desire. They call for a measure of reckoning. Some among them are what Toni Morrison has called "outlaw women"—"naturally disruptive" because born "not under the rule of men" (2004, xiv). Others come into their disorderly selves later in life, more gradually, if not reluctantly. This is as it should be. All of these women have different destinies and certainly very different ideas about what constitutes a happy ending—or indeed about whether or not happiness is even a goal at all. While we may busy ourselves with questions like, "What does freedom or happiness really mean? What does it look like to be free/happy? How does one become free/happy?" (D. B. Scott forthcoming), the women of these fictions unsettle the preset correlation of such concepts.

These disorderly women leave us disoriented, but that is just fine. These times call for disorientation. Desiring, unruly, queer, and undeterred, these women make radical demands on our world but offer us no model for radical politics. They promise only to unsettle all things endlessly. They refuse despair but commit to nothing, make no assurance beyond "never again" and "no more." If we do not love them, that too is just fine. They love themselves enough instead—or they have an idea of how to get the love they want. No, it does not matter if we love or even like them. We have only to see that they are there, trying to *be* without restraint.

NOTES

Introduction

1. My project enters into conversation with a constellation of theorists all concerned with community as a fraught model for social being. "This rethinking of community not only marks a turn in the way we might conceive of the constitution of the idea of community, but also a shift in the way in which we might mobilise community as a means of rethinking the terms of solidarity" (Devadas and Mummery 2007).

2. Since 2015 I have had the opportunity and great privilege to be in sustained conversation with an interdisciplinary cohort of scholars as part of the Practicing Refusal Collective, convened by Tina Marie Campt and Saidiya Hartman. Our reflections in the context of this group have turned around an effort "to think through and toward refusal as a generative and capacious rubric for theorizing everyday practices of struggle often obscured by an emphasis on collective acts of resistance" (Campt 2019a, 80). "The practice of refusal invoked in the collective's name," Campt explains, "signals a rejection of the status quo as livable. It is a refusal to recognize a social order that renders you fundamentally illegible and unintelligible. It is a refusal to embrace the terms of diminished subjecthood with which one is presented and to use negation as a generative and creative source of disorderly power to embrace the possibility of living otherwise. The practice of refusal is a striving to create possibility in the face of negation" (Campt 2019b, 25). Campt's own theorizations of refusal underpin an ethos of community-building in the overlapping domains of Black feminist art, activism, and study. However, as she notes, refusal is a "capacious rubric" and, as such, usefully frames less overtly political modes of defiance like those I discuss throughout this book.

3. "behold (v.)" Old English bihaldan (West Saxon behealdan) "give regard to, hold in view," also "keep hold of; belong to," from be- + haldan, healdan. Online Etymology Dictionary. "behold (v.)." Accessed April 11, 2020. https://www.etymonline.com/word/behold

4. The formulation "healthy narcissism" was first coined in the 1930s by Austrian American psychologist Paul Federn, who believed narcissism should be recognized as a potential source of "positive investment in the self" (Lunbeck 2014, 104). Kohut brought this idea into the mainstream, condemning the conventional clinical-cum-moral presumption that object-love is good and

self-love is bad. Further, although at odds with Kohut on many specific points, psychoanalyst Otto Kernberg similarly recognized narcissism as a matter of "self-esteem regulation" (Lunbeck 2014, 108). All this being said, even though clinical understandings of narcissism move beyond Freud's largely misogynistic and homophobic condemnation, the popular association of this "disorder" with pathology has persisted.

5   "And there we are, in a hand-to-hand struggle with our blackness or our whiteness, in a drama of narcissistic proportions, locked in our own peculiarity" (Fanon [1952] 2008, 45).

6   Pointing specifically to Udé's "defiantly naming narcissism not only as healthy, but even heroic," and to photographer and videographer Lyle Ashton Harris's coining of the term "redemptive narcissism," Miller (2009, 245) acknowledges the permeability of the border between destructive and constructive self-focus.

7   Merriam-Webster Thesaurus, s.v. "self-regard (n.)," accessed April 11, 2020. https://www.merriam-webster.com/dictionary/self-regard.

8   For a deeply researched and compelling analysis of the latter phenomenon, see Vergès (2017), especially chap. 5: "Cécité du féminisme: Race, colonialité, capitalisme."

9   Bénédicte Boisseron writes insightfully about the (self-imposed) isolation of Caribbean authors who write outside of Caribbean community. Her study includes two of the authors whose work I consider here, Condé and Kincaid: "Though all these Creole figures have received international acclaim for their work, they also all share a noticeably ambivalent relationship with their background. . . . Their communities (broadly defined) have accused them, in one way or another, of being traitors, sellouts, or simply opportunistic writers who are oblivious to their origins. . . . All of these authors have been held accountable for their individual positions of enunciation, for allegedly thinking about themselves first, their freedom, their survival, and their autonomy. Their works, lives, or actions have occasionally been characterized as unsympathetic to their islands, individualistic, or plainly selfish and opportunistic" (2014, 5–6, 18).

10 Britton presents Condé as something of an outlier or foil in this schema.

11 Here Hall (1989, 75–76) cites Benedict Anderson and Edward Said, respectively: "Africa must at last be reckoned with, by Caribbean people. But it cannot in any simple sense be merely recovered. It belongs irrevocably, for us, to what Edward Said once called 'an imaginative geography and history,' which helps the mind to intensify its own sense of itself by dramatising the difference between what is close to it and what is far away (Said, *Orientalism*, p55). It 'has acquired an imaginative or figurative value we can name and feel.' (Said, ibid.) Our belongingness to it constitutes what Benedict Anderson calls 'an imagined community.' To this Africa, which is a necessary part of the Caribbean imaginary, we can't literally go home again."

12 The Caribbean Artists Movement (CAM) was a significant cultural phenomenon that emerged in London, England, and was active from about 1966 to 1972. Initiated by West Indian writers Edward Kamau Brathwaite, John La Rose, and An-

drew Salkey, the movement focused on the work of Caribbean writers, visual artists, filmmakers, and performing artists.

13 In a sharp critique of the literary culture of the French-speaking Caribbean published a year after Condé's essay, theorist A. James Arnold provides a thorough delineation of the literary lineage that produced the rhetoric of créolité: "The créolité movement has inherited from its antecedents, antillanité and Negritude, a sharply gendered identity. Like them, it is not only masculine but masculinist. Like them, it permits only male talents to emerge within the movement, to carry its seal of approval. And, like them, it pushes literature written by women into the background. This characteristic is not, however, unique to the French West Indies. It can be found, mutatis mutandis, across the Caribbean archipelago" (1994, 5).

14 Davies and Fido likewise posit first-person narration as a direct counter to the phenomenon of women's voicelessness that preoccupies so many of the contributors to their volume of essays (it is worth noting that only two of the seventeen contributors to *Out of the Kumbla* are men).

15 Here, I am thinking of Valérie K. Orlando's "Writing New H(er)stories for Francophone Women of Africa and the Caribbean" (2001).

16 Edmondson also notes that the "formulations of a feminist aesthetics vary greatly among its advocates: the American school presupposes a specifically female consciousness in its reading of canonical and noncanonical female-authored works while the French school privileges formal and linguistic experimentation. Nevertheless, the premises on which the formulations are based are the same: namely, that an essentially female/feminist discourse exists or can be created" (1999, 85).

17 Expectations of textual-to-extratextual/character-to-reader community-building are bound to the phenomenon wherein "voice is celebrated as the means through which an alternative truth can emerge through spontaneous expression and replace the lies of dominant representations. By extension, the character in possession of a narrative voice in fiction is traditionally the one with whom the reader identifies and the one who consistently moves closer to an 'authentic' self as the story progresses. We expect the narrator to work toward achieving full autonomous subjectivity as she successfully bridges the gap between speech and thought, representation and emotion" (Mardorossian 2005, 19).

18 For an insightful and wide-ranging study of the trope of madness in anglophone Caribbean prose fiction, see Kelly Baker Josephs's *Disturbers of the Peace: Representations of Madness in Anglophone Caribbean Literature* (2013).

19 In "Narcissism as Ethical Practice? Foucault, Askesis and an Ethics of Becoming" and in "'Must We Burn Foucault?' Ethics as Art of Living: Simone de Beauvoir and Michel Foucault," Elaine Campbell (2010) and Karen Vintges (2001), respectively, provide thorough accounts of the theorists who condemn Foucault's refusal of engagement as deeply unethical. Both Campbell and Vintges take issue with such characterizations of Foucault's

philosophy, suggesting that his engagement with askesis—the practice of self-formation—and autobiographical impulse must be understood as, if not political, then humanist and ethical.

20 Feminist theorist Adriana Cavarero formulates this concept of obligatory interhuman empathy as follows: "To the experience for which the I is immediately . . . the self of her own narrating memory—there corresponds a perception of the other as the self of her own story" (2000, 34).

21 Paraphrasing Theodor Adorno's claims in his 1963 lectures, *Problems of Moral Philosophy*, Butler foregrounds the suspicions regarding community that I am arguing are at the philosophical core of the works I look at here. She evokes Adorno's concern "that the collective ethos . . . postulates a false unity that attempts to suppress the difficulty and discontinuity existing within any contemporary ethos" (2005, 4).

22 Foucault asserts that "with the Greeks and Romans . . . it was necessary to care for the self, both in order to know one's self and to improve one's self, to surpass one's self, to master the appetites that risk engulfing you" ([1984] 1987, 116). He continues, "Liberty is then in itself political. And then, it has a political model, in the measure where being free means not being a slave to one's self and to one's appetites, which supposes that one establishes over one's self a certain relation of domination, of mastery" (117).

23 Forbes builds her discussion around two novels, Jamaica Kincaid's *Mr. Potter* and Colin Channer's *Waiting in Vain*, of which neither protagonist is an "I" or a woman.

24 The works I consider do and do not accord with Donette Francis's concept of the "antiromance." While these narratives similarly counter many of the coercive tropes that mark the literature and cultures of the Americas, they do not share the explicit political project Francis convincingly identifies in the texts she places in this category. According to Francis, antiromances "seek to bond an imagined transnational community of Caribbean people wherever dispersed. These multiple iterations of intimate violence call forth a radical, Caribbean, feminist agenda to understandings of female sexual citizenship for the new millennium . . . a cohesive literary project." To the extent that the novels of my corpus fundamentally question communalist agendas, they fall somewhat outside of Francis's description of "a cooperative project for literary critics and social scientists as well as novelists and social activists" (2010, 22).

25 Here I am thinking of Teresa de Lauretis's contention that "a queer text carries the inscription of sexuality as something more than sex" (2011, 244).

26 I am referring here to Freud's assertion regarding humor as a strategy of self-defense wherein "the grandeur clearly lies in the *triumph of narcissism*, the victorious assertion of the ego's invulnerability. The ego refuses to be distressed by the provocations of reality, to let itself be compelled to suffer" ([1927] 1957, 162; emphasis mine).

27 Here I mean to invoke Brent Hayes Edwards's and Stuart Hall's characterization of articulation as, respectively, "a process of linking or connecting across

gaps" (Edwards 2003, 11) and "the recognition of necessary heterogeneity and diversity" that permits "a conception of 'identity' which lives with and through, not despite, difference" (Hall 1994, 402).

1. SELF-LOVE | Tituba

1. Translations of quotations from Condé's preface are mine.
2. Let it be noted that *Hérémakhonon* presents a self-regarding feminine refusal of masculine social and literary orders and would be fitting for inclusion within the corpus of this study. I find, however, that I have little to add to Curdella Forbes's masterful reading of the novel in her 2012 essay "Between Plot and Plantation, Trespass and Transgression: Caribbean Migratory Disobedience in Fiction and Internet Traffic."
3. In her compelling essay "Postmodernizing the Salem Witchcraze: Maryse Condé's *I, Tituba, Black Witch of Salem*," Jane Moss qualifies Condé's novel as a "historiographic metafiction," a term she borrows from Canadian critic Linda Hutcheon. Paraphrasing Hutcheon, Moss describes the genre as one in which the author "lays claim to historical personages and events at the same time as it manifests a theoretical self-awareness of History and fiction as human constructs and questions historical discourse as a discourse of power (chs. 6–7)" (1999, 6). Moss goes on to argue, however, that the very premises of Condé's project are in fact misleading: "From 1692 on, Tituba does indeed figure in the historical record and also seems to have captured the imagination of some of our most prominent writers.... In short, Tituba is not the forgotten victim Condé makes her out to be" (9). To be clear, though, while Tituba's role in the witch trials has been documented by historians subsequent to the events of 1692, it is only in the fictional context that her post-Salem life—her historical future—has been imagined.
4. The cultural and political import of Puritanism, or the New England Protestant ethic, has been widely acknowledged by scholars, most famously by Sacvan Bercovitch, whose *The Puritan Origins of the American Self* convincingly "reveal[s] the complexity, the intricacy, the coherence, and the abiding significance of the American Puritan vision" (1975, ix). As the editors of the 2001 volume *The Puritan Origins of American Sex: Religion, Sexuality, and National Identity in American Literature* assert plainly, "the view that American history and culture must be viewed in relation to the rhetoric, ideology, and culture of Puritan New England articulated by *The Puritan Origins of the American Self* has become a dominant critical paradigm" (Fessenden, Radel, and Zaborowska 2001, 3).
5. The "New England Way" refers to the principles of communal religious governance outlined in John Cotton's *The Way of the Churches of Christ in New England* (1645), which was later retitled *The New England Way*. As Harry S. Stout has explained, "By locating power in the particular towns and defining institutions in terms of local covenants and mutual commitments ... which combined economic and spiritual restraints, New England towns achieved extraordinarily high levels of persistence and social cohesion" (1986, 23).

6 "City on a hill" references Winthrop's famous discourse, "A Model of Christian Charity." It was given aboard the *Arbella* in 1630 in advance of the English refugees' arrival on the shores of what would become New England.

7 On the Puritans' connections to the enslavement of both Africans and Native Americans and exclusion of such populations from the community of the fully human, see Warren's excellent study, *New England Bound: Slavery and Colonization in Early America*. Warren argues compellingly that "the New England colonies were intimately tied, early on, to English possessions where slavery was a central feature of the society, such as Barbados and, later, Jamaica.... New England's early colonists were no strangers to slavery. In fact, the region in many ways depended on plantation slavery—those plantations were simply offshore" (2016, 12).

8 While I rely for the most part on the English edition of the novel, I have made in some instances very slight alterations to Richard Philcox's translations.

9 It is just this sort of "spiritual self-possession"—Tituba's calm adherence to a code of ethics dictated by her personal relationship to her spirit guides—that "would have done away with ministers entirely. It was for this possibility, we recall, that Anne Hutchinson was banished" (Ingebretsen 2001, 31).

10 In focusing briefly on Reverend Parris's efforts to convert Tituba, Condé succinctly draws attention to the wider hypocrisy of Puritan America, notably, that the Puritans owned slaves and were by no means de facto abolitionist.

11 As Nara Araujo asserts, "those accused in Salem, young women caught in the asphyxia of Puritanism, find a way to satisfy frustration and discover sensations through hysteria" (1994, 222). I would simply point to Condé's emphasis on the specifically sexual dimension and highly calculated nature of the girls' psychotic episodes.

12 It is worth noting that the Italian title of Cavarero's study is *Tu che mi guardi, tu che mi racconti*, which translates literally to "You who look at me, you who narrates me."

13 In her insightful reading of *I, Tituba*, Mara Dukats (1998) notes specific intertextual allusions to *Notebook* in Condé's novel.

14 Condé also challenges the notion that the "native land" is the only valid spatial framework for the Caribbean novel. She moves her heroine beyond a bounded regional space into that of colonial New England—a textual choice that makes *I, Tituba* the first novel of the French-speaking Caribbean to link the British West Indies to the colonial United States and that echoes Condé's own positioning as a Guadeloupean writer exploring an anglophone Caribbean and American space.

15 The standard against which all the central characters of Glissant's novels are measured, the maroon serves as the central myth underlying the entirety of his fictional work—"the sole true popular hero of the Antilles ... incontestable example of systematic opposition, of total refusal" (Glissant 1981, 180).

16 In this respect, *I, Tituba* arguably prefigures the interrogation of Afrocentrism and (Afro-)feminism Condé enacts in *Les derniers rois mages* (Last of the African

Kings), published six years after *I, Tituba*. In this later novel, Condé mercilessly derides the obsessive Afrophilia of central character Debbie Middleton, an African American Black history professor whose desperate immersion in a largely superficial Africanness is obliquely responsible for the demise of her (sexual) relationship with her husband.

17 Gisèle Pineau's *La grande drive des esprits* (The Drifting of Spirits, 1993), Simone Schwarz-Bart's *Pluie et vent sur Télumée miracle* (Rain and Wind on the Miraculous Telumée, 1995), and Evelyne Trouillot's *Rosalie l'infame* (The Infamous Rosalie, 2003) are among the more prominent examples of this phenomenon. Bonnie Thomas remarks, "Schwarz-Bart insists on the active role of women in making history. She also draws attention to the importance of the grandmother in preserving these traditions, reinstating a figure frequently left in the margins of history" (2006, 36). As Mildred Mortimer asserts, "Caribbean women's writings also posit resistance by emphasizing the importance of female elders and their unique role in communicating the knowledge of healing arts, nurturing, memory, and survival skills to women" (2007, 24). Emilia Ippolito also claims that "women had a special role as bearers of fundamental elements of the native culture—the African folk traditions of storytelling, music, and songs" (2000, 4–5).

18 Frustrated at one point, for example, by what she interprets as Man Yaya's reluctance to help her in her relationship with John Indian, Tituba angrily mocks her spirit protector with the spiteful barb, "Do you mean to say there's a limit to your powers?" (19).

19 Lydie Moudileno asserts that *I, Tituba* marks "the appearance of the first slave narrative written in French" and lauds Condé's effort to provide a founding/grounding narrative for Antillean literature (2005, 480). She concludes her essay, however, with a questioning critique of what she perceives as the novel's limitedly disordering intervention: "The detour through an anglophone tradition leaves intact the logic of origins and canonicity that animates [Henry Louis] Gates's discourse, for example. In effect, why not invent a narrative for an enslaved francophone woman from Martinique or Guadeloupe? Why does the text's historicity repose on a literary legitimacy already conferred by American History? Can there be no other mode of literary and historiographical revenge for Martinican or Guadeloupean enslaved women—one that would not pass through the American model and would be, therefore, truly new?" (484).

20 My understanding of the conventions of the genre relies on Jenny Sharpe's discussion of Mary Prince in "'Something Akin to Freedom': The Case of Mary Prince" (1996), on Paula C. Barnes's research on the female slave narrative in "Meditations on Her/Story: Maryse Condé's *I, Tituba Black Witch of Salem* and the Slave Narrative Tradition" (1999), and on Charles Davis and Henry Louis Gates Jr.'s exploration of the slave narrative genre more generally in *The Slave's Narrative* (1985).

21 In presenting her decision to engage in a sexual relationship with "a man who was not [her] master" so as to escape the coercions of her owner, for example,

Jacobs admits, "Revenge, and calculations of interest, were added to flattered vanity and sincere gratitude for kindness" ([1861] 2001, 48–49).

22 In her discussion of the autobiographical writings of Harriet Jacobs and Zora Neale Hurston, Elizabeth Fox-Genovese convincingly posits the enslaved woman's conception of her self as distinct from her understanding of her material circumstances, or condition. "The self," Fox-Genovese maintains, "develops in opposition to, rather than as an articulation of, condition. Yet the condition remains as that against which the self is forged" (1990, 177).

23 Jacobs's full statement reads: "Reader it is not to awaken sympathy for myself that I am telling you truthfully what I suffered. I do it to kindle a flame of compassion in your hearts for my sisters who are still in bondage."

24 The most well-known of these narratives include Margaret Walker's *Jubilee* (1966), Octavia E. Butler's *Kindred* (1979), Sherley Anne Williams's *Dessa Rose* (1986), Gayl Jones's *Corregidora* (1987), Toni Morrison's *Beloved* (1987), and J. California Cooper's *Family* (1991).

25 That Tituba is assaulted with a crucifix by the three Puritan men in Salem and later has a nightmare in which John Indian participates in this violation might seem to contradict my claim that Tituba does not fear sexual compulsion. I would argue, however, that this instance functions outside of the erotic dimension that is so tellingly silenced or denied by Prince and Jacobs and reclaimed by Tituba. Tituba's experience of abuse alludes to but does not directly reflect traditional representations of coercive sexual intercourse between Black women and white men, in which the entire gamut of human emotion and power relations is implicated. Rather, Condé stages her assault as explicitly ideological and symbolic—implicated in the political and religious struggle taking place in Salem, specific to that context, and in this way distinct from the forms and scenes of sexual violence repressed in nineteenth-century female slave narratives or presented in those female neo–slave narratives that venture to depict the erotic lives of the enslaved.

2. SELF-POSSESSION | Hadriana

1 That same year, the novel also won the Prix du Roman de la Société des Gens de Lettres (Society of Letters Prize for the Novel) and the Prix de l'Académie Royale de Langue et de Littérature Françaises de Belgique (Belgian Royal Academy Prize in French Language and Literature), among other prizes. In her critical essay, "France Reads Haiti: René Depestre's *Hadriana dans tous mes rêves*," Colin (Joan) Dayan has compiled several of the most over-the-top contemporary French responses to Depestre's novel: "Critics warn that Europeans must 'let themselves go,' forget Descartes, and read themselves into the magic of Haiti, 'the land of zombis.' Jacques Folch-Ribas writes: 'The story is fiery, it reads well. You're seized from the first lines by the beauty, the suffocating heat, the music, the odors—like the tourist descending from the plane right into the Caribbean.' Seething with 'deflowerings, aphrodisiac emanations, sexual exploits, forbidden ecstasies, the text exerts an irresistible sorcery on its readers' (*Est. Éclair*,

1/17/89). 'Nothing seems to rattle the gaiety of the tropical man, even in those moments where Depestre sets forth grave deeds and theories' (*Public*, Lebanon, 11/88). 'What better escape from the woes of postmodernity than a return to the myth of the happy savage,' those 'who have nothing to lose or gain,' who 'live in a nearly perfect accord with the heavens and the earth' (*La Quinzaine littéraire*)" (1993, 164). Translations are by Dayan. (Unless otherwise indicated, all translations from the French are mine.)

2   Originally published and circulated on a limited basis in Canada by Éditions Leméac in 1973, this collection won the 1982 Bourse Goncourt de la nouvelle, following its 1981 publication in France by Gallimard.

3   Katell Colin-Thébaudeau is perhaps the harshest of Depestre's critics. She accuses Depestre of courting "a Western readership" and casts suspicion on the literary merit of the novel owing primarily to its success among a North Atlantic reading public: "To what possible expectations did *Hadriana* conform that earned the novel such an impact in the closed world of 'French' literature?"; "René Depestre wants to be read in Europe, in North America. . . . The insular reader, for his part, is neither interpolated nor implicated"; "He does his best to entice this foreign reader to the island of Haiti by reflecting back to him a host of delectable exoticist images"; "Depestre isn't far in his approach to writing and composition from launching himself, full steam ahead, into the clichés of facile exoticism" (2005, 43–46). Colin-Thébaudeau goes so far as to suggest that all of Depestre's theoretical writings on Haiti's popular culture are designed to mask and legitimize his troubling fiction writings: "Concerned about warding off criticism, he accompanies his fictional writing with theoretical and self-reflexive texts whose function consists primarily in affixing a seal of legitimacy to his formal practice" (46). Coupled with these claims regarding Depestre's exoticism in the novel is the contention that his treatment of women characters amounts to so much cheap eroticism: "*Hadriana*, in effect, is the site of carnality par excellence, a work saturated with exaggerated, foregrounded, celebrated corporality" (48).

4   See my article "'Blackness' in French: On Translation, Haiti, and the Matter of Race" (2019) for a full discussion of the perceived compromises inherent in the commodification of postcolonial literature. In that essay I reflect on *Hadriana* as a work of cultural translation and think through the novel's reception among both professional and nonprofessional reading audiences.

5   The year 1986 saw the overthrow of Haitian president-for-life Jean-Claude Duvalier and a subsequent crisis of extreme violence referred to as the period of *dechoukaj*. In a striking parallel to Depestre's experience in 1946, this moment of radical political refusal of dictatorship in Haiti was soon followed by an extended period of military repression.

6   Depestre's first novel was originally published in Spanish as *El palo ensebado* in 1975, and then edited and published by Gallimard in French in 1979.

7   Depestre explores this concept in his 1998 book of essays, *Le métier à métisser* (The Business of Mixing), in a three-part section titled "Vive l'érotisme solaire!"

(Long live solar eroticism; 124–30). Depestre describes *érotisme solaire* as a contestation of "the dolorous experience that has marked the historical adventures of Eros in the West." It refuses pornographic renderings of sexuality as corrupted by "shame, sadness, and guilt" (125) and anticipates claims made by, for example, Treva B. Lindsey and Jessica Marie Johnson (2014, 171) regarding the possibilities that emerge from considering enslaved and otherwise dehumanized or marginalized persons as "erotic subjects."

8   The term *Creole* designates, in this instance, a person of European parentage born in the Caribbean.

9   Although the interview took place in 1976, it was only published three years later, in 1979.

10 It is worth noting the arc of this particular interviewer-critic's evaluation of Depestre's work. Wylie next writes about Depestre in a 1981 essay in which he lauds Depestre's fully integrated political and creative practice. However, after Depestre's publication of the 1998 essay collection *Ainsi parle le fleuve noir*, Wylie writes an excoriating critique of Depestre—as writer and as political actor—that is deeply emotional in tone. Beginning with a blunt condemnation of the volume—"René Depestre's old age has given birth to a stunted child"—he writes about the book in ways that read as expressions of having been personally betrayed by Depestre's apparent depoliticization, concluding that "this writer who distinguished himself for many years as an engaged man of letters, defending a leftist ideology with carefully reasoned logic, resigns himself here to vague hopes and snap judgments" (1999, 378).

11 Given the timing of the novel's publication, it might be said to perform double duty: both an overtly allegorical configuration of the Duvalierian state and a critique of *castrofidelisme* and the toll it takes on the individual (artist).

12 Condé offers an insightful reading of the conflict between Depestre and Césaire. She presents the debate as a sort of David and Goliath narrative in which Césaire, "the Martinican poet who no longer needs any introduction," brings the full weight of his "unequaled" (2001, 179) poetic and political authority down on the younger, less well-known Haitian poet. Condé argues that in showing fealty to Aragon's prescriptions, Depestre created "a certain unease" (180) among his contemporaries as well as among present-day readers. She goes on, however, to insist that "it would be a mistake to see in Depestre's letter a pure and simple denial of his own personality"—to miss the extent to which the Haitian poet was offering "*avant-la-lettre* . . . the entire definition of what today we call *francophonie*" (180).

13 To "maroon" (*marronner*) has particular resonance in the Haitian context, where the maroon—the runaway from the plantation—stands as a symbol of the nation's revolutionary origins.

14 *Discourse on Colonialism* was first published by Réclame in 1950 and then reedited by Présence Africaine in 1955. It contains within it the seeds of Césaire's disillusionment with the ideology of the Marxist international left, which Césaire came to believe never could or would be sufficiently attentive to the particular

struggles of Africans and Afro-descended peoples. Césaire ultimately resigned from the party in the name of race-based communal solidarity.

15 "Throughout the 80s and 90s, his exploration of Haitian *réalisme merveilleux* offered him a new mode of expression once liberated from Marxism's austere control. In some ways, then, Depestre has come full circle; from one (European) form of Surrealism to Marxism back to another (Caribbeanized) form of Surrealism" (Munro 2000, 203).

16 As Paravisini-Gebert has thoroughly discussed, the event in question—the story of Marie M., or the girl from Marbial—has been evoked by figures ranging from African American writer-anthropologist Zora Neale Hurston to Swiss anthropologist Alfred Métraux to Haitian doctor C.-H. Dewisme to writers like Alexis and Depestre. In *Hadriana*, Depestre plays with all the ambivalent elements of the classic zombie narrative, "elements that are always present in accounts of the zombification of women: the coveting of a beautiful, light-skinned or white upper-class girl by an older, dark-skinned man who is of lower class and is adept at sorcery; the intimations of necromantic sexuality with a girl who has lost her volition; the wedding night . . . as the preferred setting for the administration of the zombie poison; the girl's eventual escape from the *bokor* [evil sorcerer] in her soiled wedding clothes (the garment of preference for white or light-skinned zombie women); her ultimate madness and confinement in a convent or mental asylum" (Paravisini-Gebert 1997a, 40).

17 "His evocation of Hadriana Siloé's appearance on the scene was even further from the truth than what I had seen with my own eyes"; "He had some gift for misrepresenting the truth! What a bald-faced rearranging of reality! . . . The hairdresser's mystically illuminated version won the day as far as Jacmel's imaginary was concerned. . . . He bent our minds to the will of his fantasies" (34, 46).

18 A connection can be made here with Condé's representation of the adolescent girls who initiate the witchcraft trials in eighteenth-century Salem, Massachusetts, as per my analysis in the previous chapter of this study.

19 "On the very night of her death, the Jacmelians who had loved and admired Hadriana like some kind of fairy princess integrated her into the vast repertoire of the country's folk imagination, in an utterly fantastic tale" (71). That the crowd bursts into "cries of joy" when Father Naélo leaves the church with the lifeless Hadriana in his arms, "thinking this was some impromptu add-on to the ceremony" (66), brings home the idea of Hadriana's death as the desire of the collective unconscious.

20 In the 1941–42 "anti-superstition campaign" in Haiti, Lescot's government and the Catholic Church made a violent effort to eradicate Vodou in Haiti (see Dubois 2011, 307–8; Ramsey 2011, 177–247). Many of Haiti's intellectuals, for the most part members of the national elite, relate ambivalently to the beliefs and practices of Haiti's nonelite populations. Although twentieth-century writers like Jacques Roumain, Jacques Stephen Alexis, Edris Saint-Amand, and others focus their creative energies on rendering Haitian peasant realities, for

example, their works reflect a certain distance-cum-critique of "unmodern" popular culture.

21 "The reader has only to note the social status of the characters who declare themselves practitioners of Vodou. These include the narrator, Patrick Altamont, his mother, a number of dignitaries and professionals from the city of Jacmel. . . . It is rare that a Haitian novel presents members of the ruling class as practitioners of Vodou, and even rarer that these figures are main characters fixed at the very center of the plot" (Salien 2000, 91).

22 According to the principle of threes embedded in the Vodou faith through the notion of the *marasa twa*, the sacred twins (*marasa*) find their completion in the child born immediately after them (*dosu/dosa*). The relationship between the twins and their younger sibling signals possibility for a "relief from contradictions" (Clark 1991, 44) and models the embracing of "rupture and continuity" (Pressley-Sanon 2013, 119) useful for survival in plantation societies. Other instances of the structuring principle of three in the novel include the three days of the narrative's capital event (Hadriana's wedding on Saturday, her funeral on Sunday, and her disappearance on Monday), the three-year age difference between Hadriana and Patrick, and Hadriana's role as "third" in her relationships with her closest girlfriends, the Kraft sisters (with whom she comprised "the three Creole graces") and with the twins Lolita and Klariklé Philisbourg.

23 Referring to the story of "real-life" zombie Felicia Felix, made famous by Zora Neale Hurston in *Tell My Horse: Voodoo and Life in Haiti and Jamaica* ([2009] 1938), Roger Luckhurst notes that after she had been freed from her zombification and returned to her family, nonetheless, "as was also standard, the village refused to accept her back into the community and she was cast out, eventually ending up in a mental hospital" (2015, 105).

24 Myriam J. A. Chancy (1997a) includes Depestre among those who are guilty of this tendency. See also Dayan's assertion that "the ideal of woman as property . . . is the residue of that time when women, like men, were property: 'movables' and 'things' for use by the master. Women's bodies, violated in colonial Saint-Domingue, would become the land mistreated and recalcitrant in independent Haiti" (1995, 130).

25 Ezili-Freda, often referred to as Erzulie, is one of the most significant aspects of the group of female spirits known as the Ezili. For a rich and thorough explanation of the complexity and significance of Ezili, see Karen McCarthy Brown's *Mama Lola: A Vodou Priestess in Brooklyn* (1991, esp. 220–57) and Omise'eke Natasha Tinsley's *Ezili's Mirrors: Imagining Black Queer Genders* (2018).

26 For a useful discussion of this novel as a fictional embodiment of the desired Caribbean community, see Celia Britton's *The Sense of Community in French Caribbean Fiction* (2011).

27 Paravisini-Gebert similarly reads this as the moment when "Depestre's text abandons the people of Jacmel to their sad fates" (1997b, 227).

28 In French as in English, the word-concept *source* refers at once to "a generative force," "a point of origin or procurement," and "the point of origin of a stream of

water" (*Merriam-Webster Unabridged Dictionary*). Accessed April 11, 2020. https://www.merriam-webster.com/dictionary/source.

29   "The Ezili are watery spirits whose name derives from Lac Aziri in Benin, and are associated with seas, rivers, waterfalls, springs, and other bodies of fresh and salt water in Haiti" (Tinsley 2018, 5).

30   "Mirrors, resembling pools of captured water, are associated with water: both have reflective surfaces that can be used to communicate with other worlds" (Houlberg 1996, 31).

31   *Hadriana* also features a second zombie, the young and beautiful Gisèle K., a woman of color and member of the Jacmelian elite who managed to escape from a similar zombification almost exactly thirty years before Hadriana's death at the altar. This other former zombie is long gone by the time Hadriana's adventure begins: we learn that after having been rescued from her zombified state, Gisèle K. spent some time as a Hollywood actress and then moved to Paris before ultimately settling in a French convent, where she became the mother superior. Since named Sister Lazara of the Christ Child, Gisèle K. appears in the novel's second movement as the author of letters written to Patrick's uncle, her former lover, in which she passionately denounces global geopolitical dramas ranging from Hitler's impending invasion of France to Mussolini's invasion of Ethiopia and Franco's atrocities in Spain to Trujillo's massacre of Haitians in the Dominican Republic. Hadriana is not, then, the only zombie who has her say in Depestre's novel. And this other, "original" zombie presumably is not white.

32   In Dayan's eloquent words, "Negritude condemned women in the Caribbean to a crushing loss of presence," to being "part of someone else's history, someone else's celebration," "appropriated and metaphorized out of existence" (Dayan 1999, 69). The woman "bears the tremendous responsibility," Dayan argues, "of being inspiration for the long-silenced Caliban's regaining of voice: yet she needs no voice of her own in order to effect such reclamation" (Dayan 1986, 581). Or, as Carole Pateman has asserted forcefully, "'The eternal Woman' is a figment of the patriarchal imagination" (2004, 17).

33   In this instance, Dayan is referring to protagonists Mayotte and Claire in Mayotte Capécia's *Je suis martiniquaise* (I Am a Martinican Woman) and Marie Vieux Chauvet's *Amour* (Love), respectively.

3. SELF-DEFENSE | Lotus

1   Depestre evokes this distinction explicitly, writing, "Marie Vieux cannot be harnessed to Haitian literary traditions in the same fashion as Roumain, Alexis or myself. . . . It's difficult to identify her intellectual origins. There is a singularity to Marie Vieux-Chauvet in Haitian literature" (2016, 69).

2   Nearly all of those associated with Haïti Littéraire were forced into exile during the 1960s. See Anthony Phelps's lecture, "Haïti littéraire: Rupture et nouvel espace poétique; Exemplaire fraternité" (2005). See also Zimra (1993, 80–81).

3   Her final completed novel, *Les rapaces* (Birds of Prey), was published posthumously in 1986, more than a decade after her untimely death from brain cancer in 1973.

4   I place these labels in quotes here to signal their contingent nature. Their use throughout the remainder of this chapter should be understood as idiosyncratic to the Haitian context. As M.-R. Trouillot has cautioned, "Terms such as mulâtre and noir do not simply mean—and sometimes do not mean at all—'mulatto' or 'black' in the U.S. sense. . . . Haitian color categories refer not only to skin color and other somatic features, but to a large range of sociocultural attributes that do not have a somatic referent" (1994, 149).

5   As Charles points out, "In Haiti, less than 10 percent of the population received more than 46 percent of the national income. Wealth and power have been concentrated in the hands of a small economic elite of Creole whites, mulattoes, and Blacks supported by a violent military institution. These groups rule through an alliance with a small urban middle class residing mostly in the capital. . . . To that extreme class and power inequality are added cleavages of color, language, religion, and culture, separating the rural poor, illiterate mass of peasants from the urban, educated, and affluent elites" (1995, 143). Lee-Keller also notes, "From the administration of Jean-Jacques Dessalines (1804–1806) forward, successive regimes rigidly maintained a system of social castes and hierarchies. With despotic leadership exacerbating and manipulating racial politics and social inequalities, the conflict between the elite mulâtres-aristocrates [Mulatto-aristocrats] and the poor became increasingly more entrenched" (2009, 1294).

6   "Throughout her writings," notes Colin Dayan, "Chauvet exposes how the revolution, proclaimed in the name of the people, did not change the broad outlines of the social system. Mulattoes and blacks merely took over the top ranks of society" (1995, 89).

7   Haitian writer Yanick Lahens posits that "in Haiti, politics defeated Indigenism, since Duvalier himself claimed to derive his own ideology from Indigenism" (1993, 80). This ideology, which translates literally as "Blackism," undergirded a politics of radical Black supremacy in Haiti.

8   As David Nicholls has rightly explained, "Duvalier himself claimed to be a product of the masses, whose policy was designed to eliminate economic and social inequalities. His was a revolutionary government, and 'revolutions' must be total, radical, inflexible" (1996, 236).

9   Literally translated as "people on the outside," this disparaging term refers to Haiti's rural majority population.

10   In 1959, having disbanded the army, Duvalier created the Milice de volontaires de la sécurité nationale (MVSN; Militia of National Security Volunteers), a private paramilitary organization commonly known as the *tonton-macoutes*. Loyal only and entirely to Duvalier, the macoutes were granted automatic pardon for any crime they committed and so had full legal carte blanche to extort, rape, torture, murder, and otherwise terrorize Haiti's citizens.

11 Charles affirms, "The gender of those in the opposition did not prevent repression or torture. As many women refugees and political exiles testify, women were held accountable not only for their own actions but also for those of their relatives" (1995, 140).

12 "During the François Duvalier era, the women's movement went undercover. Most of its outspoken leaders went into exile and the remaining members turned the movement into a kind of charitable organization in order to avoid persecution by the government" (N'Zengou-Tayo 1998, 131). Ironically, the very feminist organizing that had culminated in Duvalier's ascension to the presidency (women were first granted suffrage for the 1957 presidential elections) was suppressed in anything but its explicitly nationalist dimensions under his government.

13 Thomas C. Spear presents a compelling and thorough account of the trilogy's publishing history in his essay "Marie Chauvet: The Fortress Still Stands" (2015).

14 In "The Letters of Marie Chauvet and Simone de Beauvoir: A Critical Introduction," Régine Isabelle Joseph presents a rich and fascinating account of Chauvet's epistolary relationship with de Beauvoir and introduces the broader question of the "practice of global feminism" she names *compagnonnage* (mentoring) (2015, 26).

15 "Marie Chauvet was herself aware not only of the role of the writer, but of that of the mother, of the Haitian citizen. She was also at complete odds with her social class" (Frankétienne 2016, 83).

16 Marie Chauvet's April 16, 1967, letter to Simone de Beauvoir is from "Lettres reçues de lecteurs." The preceding and subsequent citations to letters from Chauvet are from this collection.

17 "You know well why I have to succeed and to what point I need to be a little *independent*" (March 23, 1968; emphasis mine). "Writing is the only thing I am capable of doing in life, and sooner or later this work (because that is what it is) must earn me enough to allow me to become *independent*" (April 9, 1969; emphasis mine). The matter of self-sufficiency is primary for Chauvet.

18 Chauvet revisits this precise historical context in *Amour*, the first novella in the celebrated trilogy and the last work she published before leaving Haiti for good. The heroine of this later work, Claire Clamont, is no less "equivocal," no more "clear-cut" or "coherent," than her predecessor, Lotus.

19 Though *Fille d'Haïti* has garnered little attention since its publication, it enjoyed significant success in its time, winning the Prix de l'Alliance Française (Alliance Française Prize) and L'Ordre Universel du Mérite Humain (Universal Order of Human Merit).

20 Anne Marty's discussion of these phenomena is among the most thorough and perceptive: "The feminine figures in these novels of the soil are very much idealized and their schematic nature recalls that of women from fairytales and other such stories, like the myth of the 'grandmother' and other characters whose psychological perspective is scarcely developed. Incarnation and symbol

of the country, they are attached to hero-narrators preoccupied with translating a collective consciousness, with transmitting or illuminating the destiny of their fellow citizens. This is why we speak of collective fantasies when it comes to these representations of women, emerging from a narrative consciousness wherein the 'I' is nearly indistinguishable from the 'we'" (2000, 99).

21 See M. J. Smith (2009); Deibert (2011); and Polyné (2011). Both Matthew J. Smith and Michael Deibert point out that Estimé was "not exactly a noirist himself" but followed Lescot's colorist mulatto government and "drew his political base from the country's disenfranchised black majority" (Deibert 2011, 160); his policies also "deepened black radicalism" (Polyné 2011, 170) for subsequent noiristes, including Duvalier. In his insightful account of the colorist rhetoric and politics of the 1946 moment, M.-R. Trouillot explains, "The fusion of noirisme, indigénisme, and négritude—facilitated by the general indignation over Lescot's practices and the reevaluation of the nation in the light of the occupation—created an ideological tidal wave unprecedented in Haitian history, which imposed the presidency of Dumarsais Estimé.... In 1946 this general resentment against the mulâtre faction of the elites gave Estimé a political mandate of rare dimensions in Haitian history—as it would also give Duvalier, in 1957, the benefit of the doubt" (1994, 167–68).

22 A popular rural doctor before his involvement in national politics, Duvalier was appointed director general of the National Public Health Service by Estimé and then went on to serve as minister of both health and labor in Estimé's government. "[Duvalier] inherited a vision of Haitian society that ... presupposed continuity in change, the desire to complete an unfinished 'revolution'" (M.-R. Trouillot 1994, 169). Duvalier had Estimé's remains reinterred in Port-au-Prince in 1968.

23 In her essay "Toward a Literary Psychoanalysis of Postcolonial Haiti: Desire, Violence, and the Mimetic Crisis in Marie Chauvet's *Amour*," Doris Garraway makes this claim regarding Claire Clamont, but her assessment might easily apply to Lotus Delgrave or to any other of Chauvet's anti/heroines, each of whom is a "fundamentally paradoxical subject whose emotional and fantasy life alternates between expressions of love and hatred, power and victimization, desire and repression, revolt and submission, justice and criminality" (2013, 206).

24 "You are, dear Haitian women, the educators of the human race. You must above all save the young, your children, in the midst of the turmoil of today, that is you must safeguard the future" (Lhérisson 1955, 298, quoted in Munro 2007, 218).

25 I am thinking here, for example, of Dora Soubiran's sexual mutilation by the Black-power government official Calédu in *Amour* and of Rose's brutalization by "the Gorilla" in *Colère*.

26 Scholars have made ample use of Bhabha's insights regarding the blurred boundaries between the public and the private, the political and the domestic space, in thinking through gendered psychosocial cartographies of the postcolonial. Martin Munro's compelling consideration of the unhomely with respect to

Danticat's *Breath, Eyes, Memory,* for example, addresses the particularly tragic twinned traumas of exile and sexual violence (2007), and Celia Britton makes use of the concept in analyzing the central woman character of Édouard Glissant's novels. Thinking with Bhabha, these and other scholars affirm the phenomenon by which, without a "secure 'home' in either time or place, the individual becomes acutely vulnerable to the outside world" (Britton 1999, 120). Britton further points out that "all of Bhabha's literary examples of unhomely individuals are women . . . since women have traditionally been assigned to the domestic space that is being penetrated by the public, political outside world" (120).

27 See chapter 2 of this monograph for a discussion of Depestre's intertextual dialogue with *Masters'* conclusion in his novel *Hadriana in All My Dreams*.

28 These are the names of the equally "complex, tortured, angry, libidinous, explosive, spectacular women characters" (Tinsley 2016, 131) of *Fonds des Nègres, La danse sur le volcan, Amour,* and *Colère,* respectively.

4. SELF-PRESERVATION | Xuela

1 In her introduction to *Jamaica Kincaid: Writing Memory, Writing Back to the Mother,* J. Brooks Bouson provides a thorough overview and assessment of Kincaid's autobiographical affirmations in interviews conducted between 1985 and 2002.

2 The *Autobiography* won the Cleveland Foundation's Anisfield-Wolf Award and *Boston Book Review*'s Fisk Fiction Award. It was also nominated for a National Book Critics Circle Award in fiction and was a finalist for the PEN/Faulkner Award.

3 It must be noted that Susheila Nasta, Leigh Gilmore, and Sandra Pouchet Paquet allude only minimally, if at all, to *The Autobiography of My Mother* in their reflections on Kincaid's investment in a practice of "serial autobiography" (Gilmore 2001, 98). See also Nasta (2009) and Paquet (2017). This is arguably due to the contrast between the novel's self-declaration as autobiography and its relative remove from the known signposts of Kincaid's life. Moreover, the anchoring of the narrative in the space of an island not Kincaid's own renders it relatively dissimilar to her other works.

4 "This account of my life has been an account of my mother's life as much as it has been an account of mine" (Kincaid 1996, 227).

5 Poet and essayist Dionne Brand describes a similar experience from her childhood in colonial Trinidad: "We were inhabited by an unknown self. The African. This duality was fought every day from the time one woke up to the time one fell asleep. As we went to be schooled in Englishness and as we returned home to say our Christian prayers in the evenings. One had the sense that some being had to be erased and some being had to be cultivated" (2002, 17).

6 Césaire, Lamming, and Retamar are the authors of the 1969 play *A Tempest,* the 1960 essay *The Pleasures of Exile* and its novelistic reversioning *Water with Berries* (1971), and the 1971 essay "Caliban: Notes toward a Discussion of Culture in Our America" (see Retamar 1989), respectively.

7 I refer here to Nuñez's novel *Prospero's Daughter* (2006) and Paule Marshall's short story "Brazil," from the collection *Soul Clap Hands and Sing* (1988). While these works push back forcefully against the silencing of the feminine in both Shakespeare's play and subsequent anticolonial rewritings of the play, they also remain anchored in the Prospero-Miranda-Caliban paradigm. An arguably more obliquely subversive feminist reworking of *The Tempest* and *A Tempest* emerges in Nuyorican playwright Migdalia Cruz's *Fur: A Play in Nineteen Scenes* (1995). Armando García does the compelling work of linking *Fur*'s central query—"how bodies are stripped of their humanity . . . and how far it is possible, in such conditions, to create and live in freedom" (2016, 344)—to demonic grounds situated in implicit relation to, yet explicitly beyond, Shakespeare's text and its countertexts.

8 Notably, Wynter has come to occupy a "curious place" in Caribbean (and) feminist scholarship: as "both the progenitor of a Caribbean feminist intellectual tradition, as well as its most fierce and recalcitrant opponent" (N. Barnes 2010, 38).

9 The phrase "water with berries" is spoken by Caliban in act 1, scene 2, of Shakespeare's *The Tempest*:

> When thou camest first,
> Thou strok'st me and made much of me, wouldst give me
> Water with berries in 't, and teach me how
> To name the bigger light, and how the less,
> That burn by day and night: and then I loved thee.

10 Singh also critiques male postcolonial rewriters of *The Tempest* for not having imagined "the possibility of a fruitful partnership with a native woman—a native mate for Caliban" (1996, 195).

11 Scholar Caroline Rody posits that "the most pointed literary revision performed by *The Autobiography of My Mother* is its rejection of cross-ethnic connections, of the more hopeful multiracial visions now common in Caribbean women's novels" (2001, 130). Rody points to Xuela's antipathy toward Philip's first wife as a particularly remarkable instance of this provocation in Kincaid's writing: "Xuela seems to mock the love of Condé's Tituba for a white woman, which is symbolized in a white flower. Not only does Kincaid's narrative associate white flowers with sickness, rot, and death (62), but her heroine actually brings about the death of the white woman with a white flower" (131). It bears noting, however, that Condé, too, as I have shown earlier, questions the possibility of true interracial gender solidarity, both via the failed alliance between Tituba and Elizabeth Parris and via the parody of feminism enacted by Hester Prynne. Moreover, Tituba similarly uses plants to sicken her mistress, Susanna Endicott, a white lady who reduces her to the degraded status of nonwhite woman.

12 Here I mean to evoke Fanon's celebrated 1961 work *Les damnés de la terre* (*The Wretched of the Earth*).

13 As the playwright, Césaire himself does not meet his character's demand: he does not change Caliban's name in the stage directions.

14 The novel is set in Dominica, one of only two eastern Caribbean islands (with Saint Vincent) with a population of pre-Columbian natives remaining.
15 Elsewhere Wynter very astutely traces a "genealogy of Afro-Caribbean 'indigenization'" (Newton 2013, 117), though she does not contest it or acknowledge its cost to Native American populations. Wynter writes, "The more total alienation of the New World Negro has occasioned a cultural response, which had transformed that New World Negro into the indigenous inhabitant of his new land. His cultural resistance to colonialism in this new land was an *indigenous* resistance. The history of the Caribbean islands is, in large part, the history of the *indigenization* of the black man" (1970, 35).
16 "It is worth noting," writes Belinda Edmondson, "that if one attempts to find direct and precise parallels in Caribbean history then Caliban would be best represented as the figure of the original inhabitant, the Amerindian, and not the African slave. However, in the debates for independence in Caribbean nations from the nineteenth century through the twentieth Europeans were not concerned with the fitness of Amerindian populations to rule—there was no possibility of such an event since they were all but extinct" (1999, 113).
17 Whereas scholars have increasingly paid attention to narratives by indigenous writers that move away from the notion of Native American extinction and concomitant reliance on notions of ethnobiological purity or authenticity, Kincaid makes no effort to counter the "myth of the disappearing Indian" in the *Autobiography*. In keeping with her emphasis on Xuela's nonbelonging, Kincaid emphasizes Black Caribbean hostility toward aboriginal peoples, as a means of contesting self-righteous nationalist community.
18 To be clear, the wrongness of "what they saw" pertains not only to their disregard for Xuela's multi-ethnicity but also to the idea of the Carib people's complete destruction (extermination).
19 From Césaire's *Discourse on Colonialism*: "What, fundamentally, is colonization? To agree on what it is not: neither evangelization, nor a philanthropic enterprise, nor a desire to push back the frontiers of ignorance, disease, and tyranny, nor a project undertaken for the greater glory of God, nor an attempt to extend the rule of law. To admit once for all, without flinching at the consequences, that the decisive actors here are the adventurer and the pirate, the wholesale grocer and the ship owner, the gold digger and the merchant, appetite and force . . . that neither Cortez discovering Mexico from the top of the great teocalli, nor Pizzaro before Cuzco (much less Marco Polo before Cambaluc), claims that he is the harbinger of a superior order; that they kill; that they plunder; that they have helmets, lances, cupidities; that the slavering apologists came later; that the chief culprit in this domain is Christian pedantry, which laid down the dishonest equations *Christianity = civilization, paganism = savagery*, from which there could not but ensue abominable colonialist and racist consequences, whose victims were to be the Indians, the yellow peoples, and the Negroes" ([1950] 2000, 33).
20 It is in fact Madame Labatte who makes the deal with Xuela's father; an indifferent Monsieur Labatte is presented with the fait accompli.

21 Here, too, there is an echo of Indian Warner's tragic circumstances.
22 I am thinking here of the way in which Xuela's strategies of self-preservation echo, through a queer practice of disidentification, misogynist characterizations of the "narcissistic female," that is, "Nietzsche's complaint about woman—that woman is always acting, that every woman is an artist" (Isaak 2005, 54).
23 See my discussion of Tituba's self-discovery through masturbation in chapter 1 of this study.
24 It ultimately becomes apparent that her stepmother's inability to love Xuela is also a function of gender, which Xuela comes to understand in observing her stepmother's relationship to her own daughter, Xuela's half-sister: "[My father's wife] valued her son more than her daughter. That she did not think very much of the person who was most like her, a daughter, a female, was so normal that it would have been noticed only if it had been otherwise" (52). "It was her own son my father's wife favored, not loved more, for she was incapable of it—love; she favored him because he was not like her: he was not female, he was male" (53).
25 Here again we might turn to *The Tempest* and its avatars for some insight given that "the structure of the exchange of women as gifts" is fundamental to Shakespeare's play, and anticolonial writers did little to undermine that foundation: "Césaire leaves intact the intractable system of gender categories that are the centerpiece of Prospero's ostensibly benevolent mastery" (Singh 1996, 196).
26 "That doubled articulation of motherhood as both colonial and biological explains why the mother-daughter relations in her fiction seem so harshly rendered, a fact that has constantly unsettled reviewers" (M. Ferguson 1994, 1).
27 *Truth-for* is a Wynterian formulation that describes the inevitably biased epistemic structures by which any given society organizes and understands itself.
28 In the quotation here, Forbes is referring to Kincaid's 2002 novel, *Mr. Potter*.
29 As Paravisini-Gebert aptly posits in her 1999 monograph, "Xuela's narrative seeks, if not to build the foundations for the 'new man' (or woman) that Fanon envisioned, at least to reject collusion in a process that can only result in self-hatred and self-destruction" (162). Paravisini-Gebert is also right to point out, however, that "Xuela's narrative departs from Fanon in its rejection of political action as a path to liberation" (163).
30 "The inferiority complex can be ascribed to a double process: First economic. Then, internalization or rather epidermalization of this inferiority" (Fanon [1952] 2008, xiv–xv).
31 The quotation embedded in Isaak's quote is from Freud's essay "Humour," in which he writes, "Humour is not resigned; it is rebellious. It signifies not only the triumph of the ego but also of the pleasure principle, which is able here to assert itself against the unkindness of the real circumstances" ([1927] 1957, 162). I would argue that the word-concept *humor* might be replaced with *narcissism* for the purposes of analyzing Xuela's strategies of self-preservation.

32 "If cannibalism is the ultimate image of consuming flesh then another delicacy of the flesh is sexual promiscuity. Both deviances connote excessive bodily appetite and an animalistic physicality. Because these two 'othering' discourses are 'of the body,' they become metonyms for the Carib people" (Morris 2002, 958).

33 In a passage that, given my earlier reading of the *Tempest* intertext in the *Autobiography*, indirectly sheds light on Xuela's views on marriage, Jonathan Goldberg brings Kant to bear on *The Tempest*, specifically with respect to the philosopher's musings on gender and race, as useful to understanding Miranda's relationship with and to Caliban: "Kant worries that the sexual relationship may constitute a form of slavery, and he solves this problem by imagining marriage to be the only possible egalitarian arrangement. Kant's view ... is that sexual desire is problematic precisely because it is natural; it is nothing but appetite. It seeks another person not as a person but as a sexual object.... Marriage is the social institution that solves the problem of overcoming human nature, the sexual drive as mere appetitiveness" (2004, 131–32). Xuela's position on marriage categorically refuses the Eurocentric-cum-postcolonial-respectability problem-solution model outlined here.

34 I must point out that whereas for Lorde, individual connection to the erotic is a means to the end of becoming a better feminine self in (feminine/feminist) community, Xuela's erotic drive has no such noble, communalist objective.

35 Žižek reflects on femme fatale in the context of the film noir or detective novel, wherein she plays a secondary role and serves as foil to a hero who eventually emerges—her breakdown serves as the catalyst for "the moment of triumph for the hard-boiled detective" once he rejects her (Žižek 1992, 65). Kincaid's configuration of this character, however, defies this trope. Her femme fatale is no "bric-a-brac of hysterical masks" (Žižek 1992, 65) because from the very beginning she has held herself accountable to herself and never imagined herself other than as she is. She has never sought to wear a mask.

36 The coincidence of Philip's first name with that of Philip Warner is noteworthy.

5. SELF-REGARD | Lilith

1 See Hartman's powerful deconstruction of abolitionist John Rankin's empathetic appropriation of slave suffering in chapter 1 of *Scenes of Subjection: Terror, Slavery, and Self-Making in Nineteenth-Century America*, titled "Innocent Amusements: The Stage of Sufferance" (1997, 17–48).

2 Both novels also feature the same cover art: Marie-Guillaume Benoist's 1800 salon painting *Portrait de Madeleine* (Portrait of Madeleine), formerly *Portrait d'une négresse* (Portrait of a Negress), a striking depiction of a free woman of color who gazes directly at the viewer.

3 Both Forbes and Sáez present insightful and compelling analyses of James's linguistic intervention in their respective essay and book chapter, "Bodies of Horror in Marlon James's *The Book of Night Women* and Clovis Brown's Cartoons" (Forbes 2017) and "Writing the Reader," in *Market Aesthetics: The Purchase of the Past in Caribbean Diasporic Fiction* (Sáez 2015, ch3).

4   See prominent Haitian sociologist Jean Casimir's (2018) analysis of "the captive's" self-understanding against the imposed identity of "the enslaved" in *Une lecture décoloniale de l'histoire des Haïtiens: Du Traité de Ryswick à l'occupation américaine, 1697-1915* (A Decolonial Reading of the History of Haitians: From the Treaty of Ryswick to the American Occupation, 1697-1915).

5   In the titular essay of her volume of collected writings, *The Source of Self-Regard*, Toni Morrison reflects on her configuration of *Beloved*'s protagonist, Sethe, a formerly enslaved woman haunted by the ghost of the daughter she was compelled to murder. "I was interested in what contributed most significantly to a slave woman's self-regard. What was her self-esteem? What value did she place on herself? And I became convinced, and research supported my hunch, my intuition, that it was her identity as a mother," writes Morrison. "But when Sethe asks, 'Me? Me?' at the end of *Beloved*, it's a real movement toward a recognition of self-regard" (317-18). Whereas, for Morrison, the question of the Black woman's self-for-self would not be answered under slavery or in its immediate aftermath—"a generation or two later" (Morrison 2019, 318)—James leapfrogs into an imagination of its possibility in the present of enslavement.

6   I am indebted in my reflections here to Sianne Ngai's insights regarding Morrison's *Sula* in "Competitiveness: From 'Sula to Tyra.'" I depart, however, from Ngai's cautiously optimistic reading of Sula's and Naomi Campbell's refusal of sisterly alliance "as a profoundly political desire for the ideal state of being the 'only one' to be paradoxically held by all" (2006, 119), that is, as ultimately communal—or selfless!—in intention.

7   Myal is an Afro-Jamaican spiritual practice that incorporates elements of ritualistic magic, healing techniques, possession, and dancing.

8   I am thinking here of Tinsley's *Thiefing Sugar: Eroticism between Women in Caribbean Literature* (2010) and Hartman's "Venus in Two Acts" (2008).

9   "Nothing equals the anger of a creole woman who punishes the slave that her husband has perhaps forced to dirty the nuptial bed. In her jealous fury she doesn't know what to invent in order to satisfy her vengeance" (Dayan 1994, 15).

10 The scene of the murder of Lilith's friend, the much-abused Dulcimena, borrows heavily in its details from Mary Prince's *The History of Mary Prince, a West Indian Slave, Related by Herself* ([1831] 2017), in which Prince writes of the fate of the enslaved woman Hetty, beaten to death for failing to properly tie up a cow.

11 James alludes here to Jean Rhys's *Wide Sargasso Sea* (1982), echoing both the name of the Coulibri plantation, Antoinette Cosway's infamous childhood home in Jamaica, and its fiery fate at the hands of its formerly enslaved workers.

12 We have seen this phenomenon play out in other texts in this corpus: specifically, in Tituba's battle with Susanna Endicott and Xuela's undoing of her husband Philip's first wife, Moira Bailey. In each instance, an unspoken and inappropriate rivalry develops between the two women—inappropriate in that the power differential between the Black and the white woman should preclude the very possibility of competition between them.

13 In addition to the echoes of her biblical avatar, Lilith is haunted by a second disorderly ancestor, the Haitian Iwa Ezili Je Wouj (Ezili Red Eyes), a violent and unforgiving iteration of the Haitian goddess Ezili. Ezili Je Wouj is a "raging, vengeance-red" spirit whose "revenge has no end." Overcome with "cosmic rage," she desires only red blood and white flesh (Tinsley 2018, 118, 116).

14 In a wink to the reader, James includes a scene of Lilith and Isobel riding into Kingston on their own to buy things for the latter's wedding trousseau. In response to Humphrey's worried protestations that "it not too safe for two womens to be riding all the way to Kingston with no man for protection," Isobel cheekily tells him to "have no fear, no pirates have been seen for ages. . . . She can use a musket and a cutlass better than most man and to get her they would have to catch her first" (310). For the space of an afternoon, then, Lilith and Isobel resume, albeit without the carefree innocence, the waywardness of their preadolescent girlhood.

15 Although James presents what looks to be a "heterosexual love plot" that will allow for Lilith's "liberation from oppressive circumstances and the resolution of difference with a move into domesticity" (Francis 2010, 5), he ultimately confirms the unlikelihood of such a happy ending. Quinn is not, in fact, the master. As a white man, he has the right to dispose of Lilith as he wishes sexually, but he is not her owner. As such, in the deviant context of the colonial plantation, he cannot protect her, really. And in the end, it is Lilith who is in the position to save his life.

16 Nash maps somewhat different critical terrain in her study, which is a focused analysis of Black female pleasure in the context of racialized pornography. Nonetheless, I have found her premises useful to understanding James's choices, specifically her formulation of "reading for" alternative possibilities of signification—reading for ecstasy rather than injury ("evidence of the wound"; 2014, 2).

17 And, of course, as Annette Gordon-Reed has argued in reference to Thomas Jefferson and Sally Hemings's relationship, "The romance is not saying that they may have loved one another. The romance is in thinking that it makes any difference if they did" (quoted in C. Sharpe 2010, 22).

18 Both *Night Women* and Condé's *I, Tituba* use "in-trust" narrators, defined by Renée Larrier as "observers or sister witnesses, who are themselves transformed into surrogate storytellers, translators, and/or scribes" (2000, 55). This is another close resemblance between the books.

WORKS CITED

Adorno, Theodor W. 2014. *Problems of Moral Philosophy*. New York: John Wiley & Sons.

Alexander, M. Jacqui. 2005. *Pedagogies of Crossing: Meditations on Feminism, Sexual Politics, Memory, and the Sacred*. Durham, NC: Duke University Press.

Alexis, Jacques-Stéphen. (1960) 1988. "Chronique d'un faux-amour." In *Romancero aux étoiles*, 103–49. Paris: Gallimard.

American Psychiatric Association. 2013. *Diagnostic and Statistical Manual of Mental Disorders*. 5th ed. Arlington, VA: American Psychiatric Association.

Araujo, Nara. 1994. "The Contribution of Women's Writing to the Literature and Intellectual Achievements of the Caribbean: *Moi, Tituba Sorcière* and *Amour, colère et folie*." *Journal of Black Studies* 25, no. 2 (December): 217–30.

Arnold, A. James. 1993. "The Novelist as Critic." *World Literature Today* 67, no. 4 (Autumn): 711–16.

Arnold, A. James. 1994. "The Erotics of Colonialism in Contemporary French West Indian Literary Culture." *New West Indian Guide/Nieuwe West-Indische Gids* 68, nos. 1–2 (January): 5–22.

Bailey, Carol. 2014. *A Poetics of Performance: The Oral-Scribal Aesthetic in Anglophone Caribbean Fiction*. Kingston, Jamaica: University of the West Indies Press.

Balutansky, Kathleen M. 1990. "Naming Caribbean Women Writers." *Callaloo* 13, no. 3 (Summer): 539–50.

Barnes, Paula C. 1999. "Meditations on Her/Story: Maryse Condé's *I, Tituba, Black Witch of Salem* and the Slave Narrative Tradition." In *Arms Akimbo: Africana Women in Contemporary Literature*, edited by Janice Lee Lidell and Yakini Belinda Kemp, 193–204. Tallahassee: University Press of Florida.

Barnes, Natasha. 2010. *Cultural Conundrums: Gender, Race, Nation, and the Making of Caribbean Cultural Politics*. Ann Arbor: University of Michigan Press.

Baskin, Judith. 2015. *Midrashic Women: Formations of the Feminine in Rabbinic Literature*. Hanover, NH: Brandeis University Press.

Beaulieu, Elizabeth Ann. 1999. *Black Women Writers and the American Neo-Slave Narrative: Femininity Unfettered*. Westport, CT: Greenwood.

Beckles, Hilary McDonald. 2008. "Kalinago (Carib) Resistance to European Colonisation of the Caribbean." *Caribbean Quarterly* 54, no. 4 (December): 77–94.

Bellegarde-Smith, Patrick. 2006. "Broken Mirrors: Mythos, Memories, and National History." In *Haitian Vodou: Spirit, Myth, and Reality*, edited by Patrick Bellegarde-Smith and Claudine Michel, 19–31. Bloomington: Indiana University Press.

Bellegarde-Smith, Patrick, and Claudine Michel, eds. 2006. *Haitian Vodou: Spirit, Myth, and Reality*. Bloomington: Indiana University Press.

Benedicty[-Kokken], Alessandra. 2013. "Questions We Are Asking: Hegel, Agamben, Dayan, Trouillot, Mbembe, and Haitian Studies." *Journal of Haitian Studies* 19, no. 1 (Spring): 6–64.

Benedicty-Kokken, Alessandra. 2015. *Spirit Possession in French, Haitian, and Vodou Thought: An Intellectual History*. New York: Lexington Books.

Benjamin, Jessica. 1980. "The Bonds of Love: Rational Violence and Erotic Domination." *Feminist Studies* 6, no. 1 (Spring): 144–74.

Benjamin, Jessica. 1988. *The Bonds of Love: Psychoanalysis, Feminism, and the Problem of Domination*. New York: Pantheon Books.

Bercovitch, Sacvan. 1975. *The Puritan Origins of the American Self*. New Haven, CT: Yale University Press.

Bernabé, Jean, Patrick Chamoiseau, and Raphaël Confiant. (1989) 2000. *Éloge de la créolité/In Praise of Creoleness* (Bilingual Edition). Paris: Gallimard.

Bernard, Louise. 2002. "Countermemory and Return: Reclamation of the (Postmodern) Self in Jamaica Kincaid's *The Autobiography of My Mother* and *My Brother*." *MFS: Modern Fiction Studies* 48, no. 1 (Spring): 113–38.

Best, Stephen. 2012. "On Failing to Make the Past Present." *Modern Language Quarterly* 73, no. 3 (September): 453–74.

Bey, Marquis. 2017. "The Trans*-Ness of Blackness, the Blackness of Trans*-Ness." *Transgender Studies Quarterly* 4, no. 2 (May 1): 275–95.

Bhabha, Homi K. 1994. *The Location of Culture*. New York: Routledge.

Boehmer, Elleke. 2005. *Stories of Women: Gender and Narrative in the Postcolonial Nation*. Manchester: Manchester University Press.

Bogues, Anthony. 2008. "Writing Caribbean Intellectual History." *Small Axe* 12, no. 2 (26) (June): 168–78.

Boisseron, Bénédicte. 2014. *Creole Renegades: Rhetoric of Betrayal and Guilt in the Caribbean Diaspora*. Gainesville: University Press of Florida.

Bongie, Chris. 1998. *Islands and Exiles: The Creole Identities of Post/Colonial Literature*. Stanford, CA: Stanford University Press.

Bongie, Chris. 2008. *Friends and Enemies: The Scribal Politics of Postcolonial Literature*. Liverpool, UK: Liverpool University Press.

Boucher, Philip P. 1992. *Cannibal Encounters: Europeans and Island Caribs, 1492–1763*. Baltimore: Johns Hopkins University Press.

Bouson, J. Brooks. 2006. *Jamaica Kincaid: Writing Memory, Writing Back to the Mother*. New York: SUNY Press.

Brand, Dionne. 2002. *A Map to the Door of No Return: Notes to Belonging*. Toronto: Vintage Canada.

Brathwaite, Kamau. 1974. *Contradictory Omens: Cultural Diversity and Integration in the Caribbean*. Mona, Jamaica: Savacou Publications.

Brathwaite, Kamau. (1977) 2001. *Ancestors: A Reinvention of Mother Poem, Sun Poem, and X/self*. New York: New Directions Books.

Brathwaite, Kamau. 1994. *Barabajan Poems*. New York: Savacou North.

Braziel, Jana E. 2009. *Caribbean Genesis: Jamaica Kincaid and the Writing of New Worlds*. Albany: SUNY Press.

Breton, André. (1928) 1964. *Nadja*. Paris: Gallimard.

Breton, André. (1937) 1976. *L'amour fou*. Paris: Gallimard.

Britton, Celia. 1999. *Edouard Glissant and Postcolonial Theory: Strategies of Language and Resistance*. Charlottesville: University of Virginia Press.

Britton, Celia. 2010. *The Sense of Community in French Caribbean Fiction*. Cambridge: Liverpool University Press.

Brown, Karen McCarthy. 1991. *Mama Lola: A Vodou Priestess in Brooklyn*. Los Angeles: University of California Press.

Bucknor, Michael A., and Kezia Page. 2018. "Authorial Self-Fashioning, Political Denials and Artistic Distinctiveness: The Queer Poetics of Marlon James." *Journal of West Indian Literature* 26, no. 2 (November): i–xiv.

Butler, Judith. 1999. *Gender Trouble: Feminism and the Subversion of Identity*. New York: Routledge.

Butler, Judith. 2001. "What Is Critique? An Essay on Foucault's Virtue." *Pensées critiques contemporaines*. Accessed April 11, 2020. https://pcc.hypotheses.org/files/2012/03/butler-2002.pdf.

Butler, Judith. 2005. *Giving an Account of Oneself*. New York: Fordham University Press.

Butler, Octavia E. (1979) 2003. *Kindred*. Boston: Beacon Press Books.

Campbell, Elaine. 2010. "Narcissism as Ethical Practice? Foucault, Askesis and an Ethics of Becoming." *Cultural Sociology* 4, no. 1 (March): 23–44.

Campt, Tina Marie. 2019a. "Black Visuality and the Practice of Refusal." *Women and Performance: A Journal of Feminist Theory* 29, no. 1: 79–87.

Campt, Tina Marie. 2019b. "The Visual Frequency of Black Life: Love, Labor, and the Practice of Refusal." *Social Text* 37, no. 3 (September): 25–46.

Capécia, Mayotte. 1948. *Je suis martiniquaise*. Paris: Éditions Corrêa.

Caserio, Robert L., Lee Edelman, Judith Halberstam, José Esteban Muñoz, and Tim Dean. 2006. "The Antisocial Thesis in Queer Theory." PMLA 121, no. 3 (May): 819–28.

Casimir, Jean. 2018. *Une lecture décoloniale de l'histoire des Haïtiens: Du Traité de Ryswick à l'occupation américaine (1697-1915)*. Port-au-Prince, Haiti: published by the author.

Cavarero, Adriana. 2000. *Relating Narratives: Storytelling and Selfhood*. Translated by Paul A. Kottman. London: Routledge.

Césaire, Aimé. (1939) 2013. *The Original 1939 Notebook of a Return to the Native Land* (Bilingual Edition). Edited and translated by A. James Arnold and Clayton Eshelman. Middletown, CT: Wesleyan University Press.

Césaire, Aimé. (1950) 2000. *Discourse on Colonialism*. Translated by Joan Pinkham. New York: Monthly Review.

Césaire, Aimé. 1955a. "Réponse à Depestre poète haïtien." *Présence Africaine* 1–2 (April–July): 113–15.

Césaire, Aimé. 1955b. "Sur la poésie nationale." *Présence Africaine* 4 (October–November): 39–41.

Césaire, Aimé. (1969) 1992. *A Tempest*. Translated by Richard Miller. New York: Theater Communications Group.

Chamoiseau, Patrick, Raphaël Confiant, Jean Bernabé, and Lucien Taylor. 1997. "Créolité Bites." *Transition*, no. 74: 124–61.

Chancy, Myriam J. A. 1997a. *Framing Silence: Revolutionary Novels by Haitian Women*. New Brunswick, NJ: Rutgers University Press.

Chancy, Myriam J. A. 1997b. *Searching for Safe Spaces: Afro-Caribbean Women Writers in Exile*. Philadelphia: Temple University Press.

Chang, Shu-li. 2004. "Daughterly Haunting and Historical Traumas: Toni Morrison's *Beloved* and Jamaica Kincaid's *The Autobiography of My Mother*." *Concentric: Literary and Cultural Studies* 30, no. 2 (July): 105–27.

Channer, Colin. 1998. *Waiting in Vain*. New York: One World/Ballantine.

Charles, Carolle. 1995. "Gender and Politics in Contemporary Haiti: The Duvalierist State, Transnationalism, and the Emergence of a New Feminism (1980–1990)." *Feminist Studies* 21, no. 2 (Spring): 135–64.

Charles, Carolle. 2014. "A Sociological Counter-Reading of Marie Chauvet as an 'Outsider-Within': Paradoxes in the Construction of Haitian Women in *Love, Anger, Madness*." *Journal of Haitian Studies* 20, no. 2 (Fall): 66–89.

Chauvet, Marie [Vieux-]. (1954) 2014. *Fille d'Haïti*. Léchelle, France: Zellige.

Chauvet, Marie [Vieux-]. (1957) 2014. *La danse sur le volcan*. Léchelle, France: Zellige.

Chauvet, Marie [Vieux-]. (1960) 2014. *Fonds des Nègres*. Léchelle, France: Zellige.

Chauvet, Marie [Vieux-]. (1968) 2015. *Amour, colère et folie*. Paris: Maisonneuve et Larose.

Cheng, Anne Anlin. 2009. "Psychoanalysis without Symptoms." *Differences: A Journal of Feminist Cultural Studies* 20, no. 1 (Spring): 87–101.

Clark, Vèvè A. (1991) 2009. "Developing Diaspora Literacy and *Marasa* Consciousness." *Theatre Survey* 50, no. 1 (May): 9–18.

Claude-Narcisse, Jasmine. (1997) 2002. *Mémoire de femmes*. UNICEF-Haiti. Accessed April 11, 2020. http://memoiredefemmes.com.

Clitandre, Pierre. (1980) 2013. *Cathédrale du mois d'août*. Brooklyn: Éditions Ruptures.

Cohen, Charles Lloyd. 1986. *God's Caress: The Psychology of Puritan Religious Experience*. New York: Oxford University Press.

Colin-Thébaudeau, Katell. 2005. "René Depestre: La terre faite chair." *Etudes françaises* 41, no. 2: 43–56.

"Conclusion: Points de vue sur la poésie nationale." 1956–57. *Présence Africaine* 11 (December–January): 100–102.

Condé, Maryse. (1979) 2000. *La parole des femmes: Essai sur des romancières des Antilles de la langue française*. Paris: Harmattan.

Condé, Maryse. (1986) 1994. *I, Tituba, Black Witch of Salem*. Translated by Richard Philcox. New York: Random House.

Condé, Maryse. 1988. *En attendant le bonheur (Hérémakhonon)*. Paris: Robert Seghers.

Condé, Maryse. 1992. *Les derniers rois mages*. Paris: Mercure de France.

Condé, Maryse. 1993. "Order, Disorder, Freedom, and the West Indian Writer." *Yale French Studies*, no. 83: 121–35.

Condé, Maryse. 1998. "*Créolité* without the Creole Language?" In *Caribbean Creolization: Reflections on the Cultural Dynamics of Language, Literature, and Identity*, edited by Kathleen M. Balutansky and Marie-Agnès Sourieau. Gainesville and Kingston, Jamaica: University Press of Florida/University of the West Indies Press: 101-9.

Condé, Maryse. 2001. "Fous-t-en, Depestre; Laisse dire Aragon." *Romanic Review* 92, nos. 1-2 (January-March): 177-84.

Condé, Maryse, and Madeleine Cottenet-Hage, eds. 1995. *Penser la créolité*. Paris: Karthala.

Cooper, J. California. 1991. *Family*. New York: Anchor Books.

Cottenet-Hage, Madeleine, and Lydie Moudileno. 2002. *Maryse Condé: Une nomade inconvenante: Mélanges offerts à Maryse Condé*. Petit-Bourg, Guadeloupe: Ibis Rouge.

Cotton, John. 1645. *The Way of the Churches of Christ in New-England, or, The Way of Churches Walking in Brotherly Equalitie, or Co-ordination, without Subjection of One Church to Another: Measured and Examined by the Golden Reed of the Sanctuary, Containing a Full Declaration of the Church-Way in All Particulars*. London: M. Simmons.

Couffon, Claude. 1986. *René Depestre*. Paris: Seghers.

Cruz, Migdalia. (1995) 2000. *Fur: A Play in Nineteen Scenes*. In *Out of the Fringe: Contemporary Latina/o Theatre and Performance*, edited by Caridad Svich and Teresa Marrero, 71-113. New York: Theatre Communications Group.

Dalleo, Raphael. 2011. *Caribbean Literature and the Public Sphere: From the Plantation to the Postcolonial*. Charlottesville: University of Virginia Press.

Dash, J. Michael. 1998. *The Other America: Caribbean Literature in a New World Context*. Charlottesville: University of Virginia Press.

Dash, J. Michael. 2003. "Vital Signs in the Body Politic: Eroticism and Exile in Maryse Condé and Dany Laferrière." *Romanic Review* 94, nos. 3-4 (May-November): 309-17.

Davies, Carole Boyce, and Elaine Savory Fido. 1990a. "Introduction: Women and Literature in the Caribbean: An Overview." In *Out of the Kumbla: Caribbean Women and Literature*, edited by Carole Boyce Davies and Elaine Savory Fido, 1-24. Trenton, NJ: Africa World Press.

Davies, Carole Boyce, and Elaine Savory Fido, eds. 1990b. *Out of the Kumbla: Caribbean Women and Literature*. Trenton, NJ: Africa World Press.

Davies, Carole Boyce, and Elaine Savory Fido. 1990c. "Preface—Talking It Over: Women, Writing and Feminism." In *Out of the Kumbla: Caribbean Women and Literature*, edited by Carole Boyce Davies and Elaine Savory Fido, ix-xx. Trenton, NJ: Africa World Press.

Davis, Angela Y. 1992. Foreword to *I, Tituba, Black Witch of Salem*, by Maryse Condé. xi-xiv. Translated by Richard Philcox. New York: Random House.

Davis, Charles, and Henry Louis Gates Jr. 1985. *The Slave's Narrative*. New York: Oxford University Press.

Dayan, Colin [Joan]. 1986. "'Hallelujah for a Garden-Woman': The Caribbean Adam and His Pretext." *French Review* 59, no. 4 (March): 581-95.

Dayan, Colin [Joan]. 1989. "Caribbean Cannibals and Whores." *Raritan* 9, no. 2 (Fall): 45-68.

Dayan, Colin [Joan]. 1992. "Playing Caliban: Césaire's *Tempest*." *Journal of American Literature, Culture, and Theory* 48, no. 4 (Winter): 125-45.

Dayan, Colin [Joan]. 1993. "France Reads Haiti: René Depestre's *Hadriana dans tous mes rêves*." *Yale French Studies*, no. 83: 154-75.

Dayan, Colin [Joan]. 1994. "Erzulie: A Women's History of Haiti?" *Research in African Literatures* 25, no. 2 (Summer): 5–31.

Dayan, Colin [Joan]. 1995. *Haiti, History, and the Gods*. Berkeley: University of California Press.

Dayan, Colin [Joan]. 1996. "Erzulie: A Women's History of Haiti?" In *Postcolonial Subjects: Francophone Women Writers*, edited by Mary Jean Matthews Green, 42–60. Minneapolis: University of Minnesota Press.

Dayan, Colin [Joan]. 1999. "Women, History and the Gods: Reflections on Mayotte Capécia and Marie Chauvet." In *An Introduction to Caribbean Francophone Writing: Guadeloupe and Martinique*, edited by Sam Haigh, 69–82. New York: Berg.

De Ferrari, Guillermina. 2012. *Vulnerable States: Bodies of Memory in Contemporary Caribbean Fiction*. Charlottesville: University of Virginia Press.

Deibert, Michael. 2011. "Notes on *Red and Black in Haiti*." *Small Axe* 15, no. 3 (36) (November): 155–63.

De Lauretis, Teresa. 2011. "Queer Texts, Bad Habits, and the Issue of a Future." *GLQ: A Journal of Lesbian and Gay Studies* 17, nos. 2–3 (June): 243–63.

Depestre, René. (1946) 2005. *Étincelles, suivi de Gerbes de sang*. Port-au-Prince: Presses Nationales d'Haïti.

Depestre, René. (1973) 1981. *Alléluia pour une femme-jardin*. Paris: Gallimard.

Depestre, René. 1974. *Pour la revolution, pour la poésie*. Ottawa, Canada: Leméac.

Depestre, René. 1975. *El palo ensebado*. Havana: Arte y Literatura.

Depestre, René. 1979a. *Le mât de cocagne*. Paris: Gallimard. Edited translation of *El palo ensebado*. Havana: Arte y Literatura, 1975.

Depestre, René. 1979b. "René Depestre Speaks of Negritude, Cuba, Socialist Writing, Communist Eros, and His Most Recent Works." Interview by Hal Wylie (1976). *GAR* 33 (February): 14–15, 18–21.

Depestre, René. (1988) 2017. *Hadriana in All My Dreams*. Translated by Kaiama L. Glover. New York: Akashic Books.

Depestre, René. 1998a. *Ainsi parle le fleuve noir*. Grigny, France: Paroles d'Aube.

Depestre, René. 1998b. *Le métier à métisser*. Paris: Stock.

Depestre, René. 2016. "Témoignage de René Depestre." In *En amour avec Marie*, edited by Emmelie Prophète, 64–69. Port-au-Prince, Haiti: Imprimeur, S.A.

Deren, Maya. 1953. *Divine Horsemen: The Living Gods of Haiti*. New York: McPherson.

Devadas, Vijay, and Jane Mummery. 2007. "Community without Community." *Borderlands* 6, no. 1 (May). Accessed April 11, 2020. http://www.borderlands.net.au/vol6no1_2007/devadasmummery_intro.htm.

Douaire-Banny, Anne. 2011. "'Sans rimes, loin des mares, toute une saison': Enjeux d'un débat sur la littérature nationale." *Études d'œuvres*. Accessed April 11, 2020. http://pierre.campion2.free.fr/douaire_depestre&cesaire.htm.

Douglass, Frederick. (1845) 1982. *Narrative of the Life of Frederick Douglass, an American Slave*. Edited and with an introduction by Houston A. Baker Jr. New York: Penguin.

Dubois, Laurent. 2011. *Haiti: The Aftershocks of History*. New York: Metropolitan Books.

Dukats, Mara. 1998. "The Hybrid Terrain of Literary Imagination: Maryse Condé's Black Witch of Salem, Nathaniel Hawthorne's Hester Prynne, and Aimé Césaire's Heroic Poetic Voice." In *Race-ing Representation: Voice, History, and Sexuality*, edited by Kostas Myrsiades and Lynda Myrsiades, 141–54. New York: Rowman and Littlefield.

Dumm, Thomas L. 1999. *A Politics of the Ordinary*. New York: New York University Press.

Edmondson, Belinda. 1999. *Making Men: Gender, Literary Authority, and Women's Writing in Caribbean Narrative*. Durham, NC: Duke University Press.

Edwards, Brent H. 2003. *The Practice of Diaspora: Literature, Translation, and the Rise of Black Internationalism*. Cambridge, MA: Harvard University Press.

Ellis, Nadia. 2015. *Territories of the Soul: Queered Belonging in the Black Diaspora*. Durham, NC: Duke University Press.

Evans, Lucy. 2014. *Communities in Anglophone Caribbean Short Stories*. Liverpool, UK: Liverpool University Press.

Fanon, Frantz. (1952) 2008. *Black Skin, White Masks*. Translated by Richard Philcox. New York: Grove.

Fanon, Frantz. (1961) 2006. *Les damnés de la terre*. Paris: La Découverte.

Ferguson, Kennan. 2012. *All in the Family: On Community and Incommensurability*. Durham, NC: Duke University Press.

Ferguson, Moira. 1994. *Jamaica Kincaid: Where the Land Meets the Body*. Charlottesville: University of Virginia Press.

Fessenden, Tracy, Nicholas F. Radel, and Magdalena J. Zaborowska. 2001. Introduction to *The Puritan Origins of American Sex: Religion, Sexuality, and National Identity in American Literature*, edited by Tracy Fessenden, Nicholas F. Radel, and Magdalena J. Zaborowska, 1–20. New York: Routledge.

Flaugh, Christian. 2013. "Crossings and Complexities of Gender in Guadeloupe and Martinique: Reflections on French Caribbean Expressions." *L'esprit créateur* 53, no. 1 (March): 45–59.

Forbes, Curdella. 2002. "The End of Nationalism? Performing the Question in Benítez-Rojo's 'The Repeating Island' and Glissant's 'Poetics of Relation.'" *Journal of West Indian Literature* 11, no. 1 (November): 4–23.

Forbes, Curdella. 2008. "Fracturing Subjectivities: International Space and the Discourse of Individualism in Colin Channer's *Waiting in Vain* and Jamaica Kincaid's *Mr. Potter*." *Small Axe* 12, no. 1 (25) (February): 16–37.

Forbes, Curdella. 2012. "Between Plot and Plantation, Trespass and Transgression: Caribbean Migratory Disobedience in Fiction and Internet Traffic." *Small Axe* 16, no. 2 (38) (July): 23–42.

Forbes, Curdella. 2017. "Bodies of Horror in Marlon James's *The Book of Night Women* and Clovis Brown's Cartoons." *Small Axe* 21, no. 3 (54) (November): 1–16.

Forsdick, Charles. 2010. "Late Glissant: History, 'World Literature,' and the Persistence of the Political." *Small Axe* 14, no. 3 (33) (November): 121–34.

Foucault, Michel. 1980. *An Introduction*. Vol. 1 of *The History of Sexuality*. Translated by Robert Hurley. New York: Random House.

Foucault, Michel. (1984) 1987. "The Ethic of Care for Self as a Practice of Freedom: An Interview with Michel Foucault on January 20, 1984." Interview by Raúl

Fornet-Betancourt, Helmut Becker, and Alfredo Gomez-Müller. Translated by J. D. Gautier, S.J. *Philosophy and Social Criticism* 12, nos. 2–3 (July): 112–31.

Foucault, Michel. 1988. *Technologies of the Self: A Seminar with Michel Foucault*. Edited by Luther H. Martin, Huck Gutman, and Patrick Hutton. Amherst: University of Massachusetts Press.

Foucault, Michel. 1997a. "The Ethics of the Concern for the Self as a Practice of Freedom." In *Ethics: Subjectivity and Truth*, vol. 1 of *Essential Works of Michel Foucault, 1954–1984*, edited by Paul Rabinow. Translated by Robert J. Hurley, 281–301. London: Penguin.

Foucault, Michel. 1997b. "What Is Critique?" In *The Politics of Truth*, edited by Sylvère Lotringer, 41–82. New York: Semiotext(e).

Fouron, Georges Eugene, and Nina Glick Schiller. 2001. *Georges Woke Up Laughing: Long-Distance Nationalism and the Search for Home*. Durham, NC: Duke University Press.

Fox-Genovese, Elizabeth. 1990. "Autobiographical Writings of Afro-American Women." In *Reading Black, Reading Feminist*, edited by Henry Louis Gates Jr., 176–203. New York: Meridian.

Francis, Donette. 2010. *Fictions of Feminine Citizenship: Sexuality and the Nation in Contemporary Caribbean Literature*. New York: Palgrave Macmillan.

Frankétienne. 2016. "Marie Chauvet affirmait sa vie par l'écriture." In *En amour avec Marie*, edited by Emmelie Prophète, 82–88. Port-au-Prince, Haiti: Imprimeur, S.A.

Freud, Sigmund. (1914) 1957. "On Narcissism: An Introduction." In *The Standard Edition of the Complete Works of Sigmund Freud*, vol. 14 *(1914–1916)*, edited and translated by James Strachey, 73–102. London: Hogarth.

Freud, Sigmund. (1927) 1957. "Humour." In *The Standard Edition of the Complete Works of Sigmund Freud*, vol. 21 *(1927–1931)*, edited and translated by James Strachey, 161–66. London: Hogarth.

Froula, Christine. 1983. "When Eve Reads Milton: Undoing the Canonical Economy." *Critical Inquiry* 10, no. 2 (December): 321–47.

Fuentes, Marisa J. 2016. *Dispossessed Lives: Enslaved Women, Violence, and the Archive*. Philadelphia: University of Pennsylvania Press.

Fulton, Dawn. 2008. *Signs of Dissent*. Charlottesville: University of Virginia Press.

García, Armando. 2016. "Freedom as Praxis: Migdalia Cruz's *Fur* and the Emancipation of Caliban's Woman." *Modern Drama* 59, no. 3 (Fall): 343–62.

Gardiner, Madeleine. 1981. *Visages de femmes, portraits d'écrivains*. Port-au-Prince, Haiti: Henri Deschamps.

Garraway, Doris. 2005. *The Libertine Colony: Creolization in the Early French Caribbean*. Durham, NC: Duke University Press.

Garraway, Doris. 2013. "Toward a Literary Psychoanalysis of Postcolonial Haiti: Desire, Violence, and the Mimetic Crisis in Marie Chauvet's *Amour*." *Romanic Review* 104, nos. 3–4 (May): 199–222.

Gerima, Haile (director/writer). 1993. *Sankofa*. Washington, DC: Mypheduh Films.

Gilmore, Leigh. 2001. *The Limits of Autobiography: Trauma and Testimony*. Ithaca, NY: Cornell University Press.

Glissant, Édouard. 1981. *Le discours antillais*. Paris: Gallimard.

Glover, Kaiama L. 2010. *Haiti Unbound: A Spiralist Challenge to the Postcolonial Canon*. Liverpool, UK: Liverpool University Press.

Glover, Kaiama L. 2019. "'Blackness' in French: On Translation, Haiti, and the Matter of Race." *L'esprit créateur* 59, no. 2 (Summer): 25-41.

Goldberg, Jonathan. 2004. *Tempest in the Caribbean*. Minneapolis: University of Minnesota Press.

Gouraige, Ghislain. 1982. *Histoire de la littérature haïtienne (de l'indépendance à nos jours)*. Port-au-Prince, Haiti: Editions de l'Action Sociale.

Gregg, Veronica Marie. 2002. "How Jamaica Kincaid Writes the Autobiography of Her Mother." *Callaloo* 25, no. 3 (Summer): 920-37.

Halberstam, Judith [Jack]. 2008. "The Anti-social Turn in Queer Studies." *Graduate Journal of Social Science* 5, no. 2 (January): 140-56.

Hall, Stuart. 1989. "Cultural Identity and Cinematic Representation." *Framework: The Journal of Cinema and Media*, no. 36: 68-81.

Hall, Stuart. 1994. "Cultural Identity and Diaspora." In *Colonial Discourse and Postcolonial Theory: A Reader*, edited by Patrick Williams and Laura Chrisman, 392-403. New York: Columbia University Press.

Harrison, Sheri-Marie. 2018. "Marlon James and the Metafiction of the New Black Gothic." *Journal of West Indian Literature* 26, no. 2 (November): 1-17.

Hartman, Saidiya. 1997. *Scenes of Subjection: Terror, Slavery, and Self-Making in Nineteenth-Century America*. New York: Oxford University Press.

Hartman, Saidiya. 2008. "Venus in Two Acts." *Small Axe* 12, no. 2 (26) (June): 1-14.

Henry, Paget. 2000. *Caliban's Reason: Introducing Afro-Caribbean Philosophy*. New York: Routledge.

Hewitt, Leah. 1995. "Condé's Critical Seesaw." *Callaloo* 18, no. 3 (Summer): 641-51.

Hine, Darlene Clark. 1989. "Rape and the Inner Lives of Black Women in the Middle West." *Signs* 14, no. 4 (Summer): 912-20.

hooks, bell. 1992. *Black Looks: Race and Representation*. Boston: South End.

hooks, bell. 2003. "The Oppositional Gaze: Black Female Spectators." In *The Feminism and Visual Culture Reader*, edited by Amelia Jones, 94-105. New York: Routledge.

hooks, bell. 2015. *Black Looks: Race and Representation*. New York: Routledge.

Horn, Maja. 2014. *Masculinity after Trujillo: The Politics of Gender in Dominican Literature*. Gainesville: University Press of Florida.

Houlberg, Marilyn. 1996. "Sirens and Snakes: Water Spirits in the Art of Haitian Vodou." *African Arts* 29, no. 2 (Spring): 30-35.

Hoving, Isabel. 2001. *In Praise of New Travelers: Reading Caribbean Migrant Women Writers*. Stanford, CA: Stanford Unversity Press.

Hulme, Peter. 1986. *Colonial Encounters: Europe and the Native Caribbean, 1492-1797*. New York: Methuen.

Hulme, Peter. 2000. *Remnants of Conquest: The Island Caribs and Their Visitors, 1877-1998*. Oxford: Oxford University Press.

Hurston, Zora Neale. (1938) 2009. *Tell My Horse: Voodoo and Life in Haiti and Jamaica*. New York: Harper.

Ingebretsen, Ed. 2001. "Wigglesworth, Mather, Starr: Witch-Hunts and General Wickedness in Public." In *The Puritan Origins of American Sex: Religion, Sexuality, and National Identity in American Literature*, edited by Tracy Fessenden, Nicholas F. Radel, and Magdalena J. Zaborowska, 21–40. New York: Routledge.

Ippolito, Emilia. 2000. *Caribbean Women Writers: Identity and Gender*. Rochester, NY: Camden House.

Isaak, Jo Anna. 2005. "In Praise of Primary Narcissism: The Last Laughs of Jo Spence and Hannah Wilke." In *Interfaces: Women, Autobiography, Image, Performance*, edited by Sidonie Smith and Julia Watson, 49–68. Ann Arbor: University of Michigan Press.

Jacobs, Harriet. (1861) 2001. *Incidents in the Life of a Slave Girl*. New York: Dover Thrift.

James, Marlon. 2009. *The Book of Night Women*. New York: Riverhead Books.

James, Marlon. 2014. *A Brief History of Seven Killings*. New York: Riverhead Books.

James, Marlon. 2015. "From Jamaica to Minnesota to Myself." *New York Times Magazine*, March 10, 2015. https://www.nytimes.com/2015/03/15/magazine/from-jamaica-to-minnesota-to-myself.html.

Jones, Bridget. 1981. "Comrade Eros: The Erotic Vein in the Writing of René Depestre." *Caribbean Quarterly* 27, no. 4 (December): 21–30.

Jones, Gayl. (1987) 2019. *Corregidora*. Boston: Beacon.

Joseph, Régine Isabelle. 2015. "The Letters of Marie Chauvet and Simone de Beauvoir: A Critical Introduction." In "Revisiting Marie Vieux Chauvet: Paradoxes of the Postcolonial Feminine," edited by Kaiama L. Glover and Alessandra Benedicty-Kokken. Special issue, *Yale French Studies*, no. 128: 25–42.

Josephs, Kelly Baker. 2013. *Disturbers of the Peace: Representations of Madness in Anglophone Caribbean Literature*. Charlottesville: University of Virginia Press.

Kaisary, Philip. 2014. *The Haitian Revolution in the Literary Imagination: Radical Horizons, Conservative Constraints*. Charlottesville: University of Virginia Press.

Kaussen, Valerie. 2008. *Migrant Revolutions: Haitian Literature, Globalization, and U.S. Imperialism*. New York: Lexington Books.

Kincaid, Jamaica. 1986. *Annie John*. New York: New American Library.

Kincaid, Jamaica. 1996. *The Autobiography of My Mother*. New York: Farrar, Straus and Giroux.

Kincaid, Jamaica. 2003. *Mr. Potter*. New York: Farrar, Straus and Giroux.

King, Jane. 2002. "A Small Place Writes Back." *Callaloo* 25, no. 3 (Summer): 885–909.

Kohut, Heinz. 1966. "Forms and Transformations of Narcissism." *Journal of the American Psychoanalytic Association* 14, no. 2 (April): 243–72.

Kottman, Paul A. 1997. "Translator's Introduction." In Adriana Cavarero, *Relating Narratives: Storytelling and Selfhood*, vii–xxxi. New York: Routledge.

Lahens, Yanick. 1993. "Haitian Literature after Duvalier: An Interview with Yanick Lahens." Interview by Clarisse Zimra. *Callaloo* 16, no. 1 (Winter): 77–93.

Lamming, George. (1960) 1992. *The Pleasures of Exile*. Ann Arbor: University of Michigan Press.

Lamming, George. (1970) 1991. *In the Castle of My Skin*. Ann Arbor: University of Michigan Press.

Lamming, George. (1971) 2015. *Water with Berries*. Leeds, UK: Peepal Tree.
Larrier, Renée. 2000. *Francophone Women Writers of Africa and the Caribbean*. Gainesville: University Press of Florida.
Lasch, Christopher. 1979. *The Culture of Narcissism: American Life in the Age of Diminishing Expectations*. New York: Norton.
Lee-Keller, Hellen. 2009. "Madness and the *Mulâtre-Aristocrate*: Haiti, Decolonization, and Women in Marie Chauvet's *Amour*." *Callaloo* 32, no. 4 (Fall): 1293–311.
"Lettres reçues de lecteurs" [Letters from readers]. Simone de Beauvoir papers. BNF NAF 28501. Bibliothèque Nationale de France, Paris.
Lhérisson, Louis Carius. 1955. "Appel aux femmes haïtiennes." In Lélia J. Lhérisson, *Manuel de littérature haïtienne*, 288. Port-au-Prince, Haiti: Département de l'Education Nationale.
Lindsey, Treva B., and Jessica Marie Johnson. 2014. "Searching for Climax: Black Erotic Lives in Slavery and Freedom." *Meridians: Feminism, Race, Transnationalism* 12, no. 2 (September): 169–95.
Linton, Jennifer. 2010. "The Art of Hannah Wilke: 'Feminist Narcissism' and the Reclamation of the Erotic Body." *Lady Lazarus*, December 31, 2010. https://jenniferlinton.com/2010/12/31/the-art-of-hannah-wilke-feminist-narcissism-and-the-reclamation-of-the-erotic-body/.
Lionnet, Françoise. 1989. *Autobiographical Voices: Race, Gender, Self-Portraiture*. Ithaca, NY: Cornell University Press.
Lionnet, Françoise. 1995. *Postcolonial Representations: Women, Literature, Identity*. Ithaca, NY: Cornell University Press.
Lorde, Audre. (1984) 2007. *Sister Outsider*. Berkeley, CA: Crossing.
Lovejoy, David S. 1967. "Samuel Hopkins: Religion, Slavery, and the Revolution." *New England Quarterly* 40, no. 2 (June): 227–43.
Luckhurst, Roger. 2015. *Zombies: A Cultural History*. London: Reaktion Books.
Lunbeck, Elizabeth. 2014. *The Americanization of Narcissism*. Cambridge, MA: Harvard University Press.
Manzor-Coats, Lillian. 1993. "Of Witches and Other Things: Maryse Condé's Challenges to Feminist Discourse." *World Literature Today* 67, no. 4 (Autumn): 737–44.
Mardorossian, Carine M. 2005. *Reclaiming Difference: Caribbean Women Rewrite Postcolonialism*. Charlottesville: University of Virginia Press.
"Marie Chauvet: Première lauréate de l'Alliance Française." 1953. *Le nouvelliste*, April 11, 1953, 1,6.
Marshall, Paule. (1961) 2016. *Soul Clap Hands and Sing*. Mansfield Centre, CT: Martino.
Marty, Anne. 2000. *Haïti en littérature*. Paris: Maisonneuve et Larose.
McClintock, Anne. 1995. *Imperial Leather: Race, Gender, and Sexuality in the Colonial Contest*. New York: Routledge.
McKinney, Kitzie. 1996. "Memory, Voice, and Metaphor in the Works of Simone Schwarz-Bart." In *Postcolonial Subjects: Francophone Women Writers*, edited by Mary Jean Matthews Green, 22–41. Minneapolis: University of Minnesota Press.
Meeks, Brian. 2002. "Reasoning with Caliban's Reason." *Small Axe* 6, no. 1 (11): 158–68.

Miller, Monica L. 2009. *Slaves to Fashion: Black Dandyism and the Styling of Black Diasporic Identity*. Durham, NC: Duke University Press.

Mitchell, Angelyn. 2002. *The Freedom to Remember: Narrative, Slavery, and Gender in Contemporary Black Women's Fiction*. New Brunswick, NJ: Rutgers University Press.

Moody, Joycelyn K. 1990. "Ripping Away the Veil of Slavery: Literacy, Communal Love, and Self-Esteem in Three Slave Women's Narratives." *Black American Literature Forum* 24, no. 4 (Winter): 633–48.

Morgan, Jennifer L. 2004. *Laboring Women: Gender and Reproduction in New World Slavery*. Philadelphia: University of Pennsylvania Press.

Morris, Kathryn E. 2002. "Jamaica Kincaid's Voracious Bodies: Engendering a Carib(bean) Woman." *Callaloo* 25, no. 3 (Summer): 954–68.

Morrison, Toni. (1970) 2007. *The Bluest Eye*. New York: Vintage.

Morrison, Toni. (1974) 2004. *Sula*. New York: Vintage.

Morrison, Toni. (1987) 2004. *Beloved*. New York: Vintage.

Morrison, Toni. 2019. "The Source of Self-Regard." In *The Source of Self-Regard: Selected Essays, Speeches, and Meditations*, 304–21. New York: Knopf.

Mortimer, Mildred. 2007. *Writing from the Hearth: Public, Domestic, and Imaginative Space in Francophone Women's Fiction of Africa and the Caribbean*. Lanham, MD: Lexington Books.

Moss, Jane. 1999. "Postmodernizing the Salem Witchcraze: Maryse Condé's *I, Tituba, Black Witch of Salem*." *Colby Quarterly* 35, no. 1 (March): 5–17.

Moudileno, Lydie. 1995. "Portrait of the Artist as Dreamer: Maryse Condé's *Traversée de la mangrove* and *Les derniers rois mages*." *Callaloo* 18, no. 3 (Summer): 626–40.

Moudileno, Lydie. (2005) 2007. "*Moi, Tituba, sorcière noire de Salem* . . . : Les déplacements d'un récit d'esclave inédit." In *Revisiting Slave Narratives/Les avatars contemporains des récits d'esclaves* (Bilingual Edition), edited by Judith Mizrahi-Barak, 471–85. Montpellier, France: Presses Universitaires de la Méditerranée.

Mudimbe-Boyi, Elisabeth. 1993. "Giving Voice to Tituba: The Death of the Author?" *World Literature Today* 67, no. 4 (Autumn): 751–56.

Muñoz, José Esteban. 2009. *Cruising Utopia: The Then and There of Queer Futurity*. New York: New York University Press.

Munro, Martin. 2000. *Shaping and Reshaping the Caribbean: The Work of Aimé Césaire and René Depestre*. London: Maney and Sons.

Munro, Martin. 2007. *Exile and Post-1946 Haitian Literature: Alexis, Depestre, Ollivier, Laferrière, and Danticat*. Liverpool, UK: Liverpool University Press.

Musser, Amber Jamilla. 2005. "Masochism: A Queer Subjectivity." Women, Gender and Sexuality Studies Research, Paper 17. Accessed April 11, 2020. http://openscholarship.wustl.edu/wgss/17.

Musser, Amber Jamilla. 2015. "BDSM and the Boundaries of Criticism: Feminism and Neoliberalism in *Fifty Shades of Grey* and *The Story of O*." *Feminist Theory* 16, no. 2 (August): 121–36.

Nancy, Jean-Luc. 1991. *The Inoperative Community*. Edited by Peter Connor. Minneapolis: University of Minnesota Press.

Nash, Jennifer C. 2014. *The Black Body in Ecstasy: Reading Race, Reading Pornography*. Durham, NC: Duke University Press.

Nasta, Susheila. 1993. "Motherlands, Mothercultures, Mothertongues: Women's Writing in the Caribbean." In *Shades of Empire in Colonial and Post-colonial Literatures*, edited by C. C. Barfoot and Theo D'Haen, 211–20. Amsterdam: Rodopi.

Nasta, Susheila. 2009. "'Beyond the Frame': Writing a Life and Jamaica Kincaid's Family Album." *Contemporary Women's Writing* 3, no. 1 (June): 64–85.

Nehl, Markus. 2016. *Transnational Black Dialogues: Re-imagining Slavery in the Twenty-First Century*. Bielefeld: Transcript.

Newson, Adèle S., and Linda Strong-Leek, eds. 1998. *Winds of Change: The Transforming Voices of Caribbean Women Writers and Scholars*. New York: Peter Lang.

Newton, Melanie J. 2013. "Returns to a Native Land: Indigeneity and Decolonization in the Anglophone Caribbean." *Small Axe* 17, no. 2 (41) (July): 108–22.

Ngai, Sianne. 2006. "Competitiveness: From 'Sula to Tyra.'" *Women's Studies Quarterly* 34, nos. 3-4 (Fall-Winter): 107–39.

Ngate, Jonathan. 1986. "Maryse Condé and Africa: The Making of a Recalcitrant Daughter?" *A Current Bibliography on African Affairs* 19, no. 1 (September): 5–20.

Nicholls, David. 1974. "Ideology and Political Protest in Haiti, 1930–46." *Journal of Contemporary History* 9, no. 4 (October): 3–26.

Nicholls, David. 1996. *From Dessalines to Duvalier: Race, Color, and National Independence in Haiti*. New Brunswick, NJ: Rutgers University Press.

Nixon, Rob. 1987. "Caribbean and African Appropriations of *The Tempest*." *Critical Inquiry* 13, no. 3 (Spring): 557–78.

Nuñez, Elizabeth. 2006. *Prospero's Daughter*. New York: Ballantine Books.

N'Zengou-Tayo, Marie-José. 1998. "'Famn se poto mitan': Haitian Woman, the Pillar of Society." *Feminist Review*, no. 59 (Summer): 118–42.

Orlando, Valérie K. 2001. "Writing New H(er)stories for Francophone Women of Africa and the Caribbean." *World Literature Today* 75, no. 1 (Winter): 40–50.

Orlando, Valérie K. 2003. *Of Suffocated Hearts and Tortured Souls: Seeking Subjecthood through Madness in Francophone Women's Writing of Africa and the Caribbean*. New York: Lexington Books.

Paquet, Sandra Pouchet. 2002. *Caribbean Autobiography: Cultural Identity and Self-Representation*. Madison: University of Wisconsin Press.

Paquet, Sandra Pouchet. 2004. "Foreword." In George Lamming, *The Pleasures of Exile*. Ann Arbor: University of Michigan Press.

Paquet, Sandra Pouchet. 2017. "The Mediated Self in the Contested Domain of Caribbean Autobiography." In *Auto/Biography across the Americas: Transnational Themes in Life Writing*, edited by Ricia Anne Chansky, 112–26. New York: Routledge.

Paravisini-Gebert, Lizabeth. 1997a. "Women Possessed: Eroticism and Exoticism in the Representation of Woman as Zombie." In *Sacred Possessions: Vodou, Santería, Obeah and the Caribbean*, edited by Margarite Fernández Olmos and Lizabeth Paravisini-Gébert, 37–58. New Brunswick, NJ: Rutgers University Press.

Paravisini-Gebert, Lizabeth. 1997b. "Writers Playin' Mas': Carnival and the Grotesque in the Contemporary Caribbean Novel." In *A History of Literature in the Caribbean*, vol. 3, edited by A. James Arnold, J. Michael Dash, and Julio Rodríguez-Luis, 215–36. Amsterdam: J. Benjamins.

Paravisini-Gebert, Lizabeth. 1999. *Jamaica Kincaid: A Critical Companion*. Westport, CT: Greenwood.

Parkman, Patricia. 1990. *Insurrectionary Civic Strikes in Latin America, 1931–1961*. Cambridge, MA: Albert Einstein Institution.

Pateman, Carole. 2004. *The Sexual Contract*. Stanford, CA: Stanford University Press.

Penier, Izabella. 2010. "Globalization, Creolisation and 'Manichaeism Delirium': Jamaica Kincaid's Dialogue with Postcolonial 'Radically Non-racial Humanism' in *The Autobiography of My Mother*." *Orbis Linguarum* 36: 241–54. http://dspace.uni.lodz.pl/xmlui/bitstream/handle/11089/1068/ORBIS.pdf?sequence=1&isAllowed=y.

Phelps, Anthony. 2005. "Haïti littéraire: Rupture et nouvel espace poétique; Exemplaire fraternité." Video. *Île-en-île*. (October 20). Accessed April 11, 2020. http://ile-en-ile.org/anthony-phelps-haiti-litteraire/.

Pineau, Gisèle. (1993) 2007. *La grande drive des esprits*. Paris: Éditions Philippe Rey.

Polyné, Millery. 2011. "To the 'Sons' of Dessalines and Pétion: Radicalism and the Idea of a 'New' Haiti." *Small Axe* 15, no. 3 (36) (November): 164–72.

Pratt, Mary Louise. 1992. *Imperial Eyes: Travel Writing and Transculturation*. New York: Routledge.

Pressley-Sanon, Toni. 2013. "One Plus One Equals Three: *Marasa* Consciousness, the *Lwa*, and Three Stories." *Research in African Literatures* 44, no. 3 (Fall): 118–37.

Prince, Mary. (1831) 2017. *The History of Mary Prince, a West Indian Slave, Related by Herself*. In *Six Women's Slave Narratives*, edited by William L. Andrews, 12–40. Chapel Hill: University of North Carolina Press.

Ramsey, Kate. 2011. *The Spirits and the Law: Vodou and Power in Haiti*. Chicago: University of Chicago Press.

Réage, Pauline. 1954. *The Story of O* [*L'histoire d'O*]. Internet Archive. Accessed April 11, 2020. https://archive.org/stream/TheHistoryOfO/the%20history%20of%20O_djvu.txt.

Retamar, Roberto Fernández. 1989. "Caliban: Notes toward a Discussion of Culture in Our America." In *Caliban and Other Essays*, 3–45. Minneapolis: University of Minnesota Press.

Rhys, Jean. 1982. *Wide Sargasso Sea*. New York: Norton.

Rodriguéz, Juana María. 2011. "Queer Sociality and Other Sexual Fantasies." *GLQ: A Journal of Lesbian and Gay Studies* 17, nos. 2–3 (June): 331–48.

Rody, Caroline. 2001. *The Daughter's Return: African-American and Caribbean Women's Fictions of History*. New York: Oxford University Press.

Roumain, Jacques. (1944) 1988. *Masters of the Dew*. Translated by Langston Hughes and Mercer Cook. Oxford: Heinemann Educational.

Sáez, Elena Machado. 2015. *Market Aesthetics: The Purchase of the Past in Caribbean Diasporic Fiction*. Charlottesville: University of Virginia Press.

Saint-Grégoire, Erma. 1992. "Interview with Erma Saint-Grégoire." Interview by Charles H. Rowell. Translated by Mohamed B. Taleb-Khyar. *Callaloo* 15, no. 2 (Spring): 462–67.

Salien, Jean-Marie. 2000. "Croyances populaires haïtiennes dans *Hadriana dans tous mes rêves* de René Depestre." *French Review* 74, no. 1 (October): 82–93.

Sartre, Jean-Paul. 1964–65. "Black Orpheus." Translated by John MacCombie. *Massachusetts Review* 6, no. 1 (Autumn–Winter): 13–52.

Scarboro, Ann. 1992. Afterword to *I, Tituba, Black Witch of Salem*, by Maryse Condé, 187–225. Translated by Richard Philcox. New York: Random House.

Scharfman, Ronnie. 1996. "Theorizing Terror: The Discourse of Violence in Marie Chauvet's *Amour, Colere et Folie*." In *Postcolonial Subjects: Francophone Women Writers*, edited by Mary Jean Green, Karen Gould, Micheline Rice-Maximin, Keith L. Walker, and Jack A. Yeager, 229–45. Minneapolis: University of Minnesota Press.

Schine, Cathleen. 1996. "A World as Cruel as Job's." *New York Times*, February 4, 1996. https://www.nytimes.com/1996/02/04/books/a-world-as-cruel-as-job-s.html.

Schipke, Timothy. 2017. "Narcissism, Ego, and Self: Kohut—A Key Figure in Transpersonal Psychology." *Journal of Transpersonal Psychology* 49, no. 1: 3–21.

Schultheis, Alexandra. 2001. "Family Matters in Jamaica Kincaid's *The Autobiography of My Mother*." *Jouvert: A Journal of Postcolonial Studies* 5, no. 2 (Winter). https://legacy.chass.ncsu.edu/jouvert/v5i2/Kincai.htm.

Schwartz-Bart, Simone. 1995. *Pluie et vent sur Télumée-Miracle*. Paris: Seuil.

Scott, Darieck B. Forthcoming. *Keeping It Unreal: Comics and Black Queer Fantasy*. New York: New York University Press.

Scott, David. 1999. *Refashioning Futures: Criticism after Postcoloniality*. Princeton, NJ: Princeton University Press.

Serynada. 2015. "The Real Being." *New Inquiry*, March 12, 2015. https://thenewinquiry.com/real-human-being/.

Shakespeare, William. 1611. *The Tempest*. In *The Complete Works of William Shakespeare*. Accessed April 11, 2020. shakespeare.mit.edu/tempest/full.html.

Sharpe, Christina. 2010. *Monstrous Intimacies: Making Post-slavery Subjects*. Durham, NC: Duke University Press.

Sharpe, Jenny. 1996. "'Something Akin to Freedom': The Case of Mary Prince." *Differences: A Journal of Feminist Cultural Studies* 8, no. 1 (Spring): 31–56.

Sharpley-Whiting, Tracy D. 1999. *Black Venus: Sexualized Savages, Primal Fears, and Primitive Narratives in French*. Durham, NC: Duke University Press.

Sheller, Mimi. 2012. *Citizenship from Below: Erotic Agency and Caribbean Freedom*. Durham, NC: Duke University Press.

Shelton, Marie-Denise. 1990. "Women Writers of the French-Speaking Caribbean." In *Caribbean Women Writers: Essays from the First International Conference*, edited by Selwyn R. Cudjoe, 346–56. Wellesley, MA: Calaloux.

Shelton, Marie-Denise. 1993. "Condé: The Politics of Gender and Identity." *World Literature Today* 67, no. 4 (Autumn): 717–22.

Silverman, Kaja. 2009. *Flesh of My Flesh*. Stanford, CA: Stanford University Press.

Simmons, J. Aaron. 2006. "A Review of Judith Butler, *Giving an Account of Oneself*." *Journal for Cultural and Religious Theory* 7, no. 2 (Spring): 85–90.

Simmons, K. Merinda. 2009. "Beyond 'Authenticity': Migration and the Epistemology of 'Voice' in Mary Prince's *History of Mary Prince* and Maryse Condé's *I, Tituba*." *College Literature* 36, no. 4 (Fall): 75–99.

Singh, Jyotsna G. 1996. "Caliban versus Miranda: Race and Gender Conflicts in Postcolonial Rewritings of *The Tempest*." In *Feminist Readings of Early Modern Culture: Emerging Subjects*, edited by Valerie Traub, M. Lindsay Kaplan, and Dympna Callaghan, 191–209. Cambridge: Cambridge University Press.

Smith, Matthew J. 2009. *Red and Black in Haiti: Radicalism, Conflict, and Political Change, 1934–1957*. Chapel Hill: University of North Carolina Press.

Smith, Michelle. 1995. "Reading in Circles: Sexuality and/as History in *I, Tituba, Black Witch of Salem*." *Callaloo* 18, no. 3 (Summer): 602–7.

Spear, Thomas C. 2015. "Marie Chauvet: The Fortress Still Stands." In "Revisiting Marie Vieux Chauvet: Paradoxes of the Postcolonial Feminine," edited by Kaiama L. Glover and Alessandra Benedicty-Kokken. Special issue, *Yale French Studies*, no. 128: 9–24.

Spillers, Hortense J. 1987. "Mama's Baby, Papa's Maybe: An American Grammar Book." *Diacritics* 17, no. 2 (Summer): 64–81.

Spillers, Hortense J. 2003. *Black, White, and in Color: Essays on American Literature and Culture*. Chicago: University of Chicago Press.

Stout, Harry S. 1986. *The New England Soul: Preaching and Religious Culture in Colonial New England*. New York: Oxford University Press.

Strongman, Roberto. 2008. "Transcorporeality in Vodou." *Journal of Haitian Studies* 14, no. 2 (Fall): 4–29.

Szeles, Ursula. 2011. "Sea Secret Rising: The Lwa Lasirenn in Haitian Vodou." *Journal of Haitian Studies* 17, no. 1 (Spring): 193–210.

Thomas, Bonnie. 2006. *Breadfruit or Chestnut? Gender Construction in the French Caribbean Novel*. Lanham, MD: Lexington Books.

Thomas, Deborah A. 2011. *Exceptional Violence: Embodied Citizenship in Transnational Jamaica*. Durham, NC: Duke University Press.

Thomas, Deborah A. 2016. "Time and the Otherwise: Plantations, Garrisons, and Being Human in the Caribbean." *Anthropological Theory* 16, nos. 2–3 (June–September): 177–200.

Thomas, Greg. 2001. "Sex/Sexuality and Sylvia Wynter's 'Beyond . . .': Anti-colonial Ideas in 'Black Radical Tradition.'" *Journal of West Indian Literature* 10, nos. 1–2 (November): 92–118.

Thomas, Greg. 2008. "Review of Linda Lang-Peralta, ed. *Jamaica Kincaid and Caribbean Double Crossings*. Newark, NJ: University of Delaware Press, 2006." MFS: *Modern Fiction Studies* 54, no. 4 (Winter): 919–21.

Tidd, Ursula. 2002. "Gendering Depersonalization: Simone de Beauvoir's 'Monologue' and R. D. Laing." *French Studies* 56, no. 3 (July): 359–69.

Tinsley, Omise'eke Natasha. 2010. *Thiefing Sugar: Eroticism between Women in Caribbean Literature*. Durham, NC: Duke University Press.

Tinsley, Omise'eke Natasha. 2011. "Songs for Ezili: Vodou Epistemologies of (Trans)gender." *Feminist Studies* 37, no. 2 (Summer): 417–36.

Tinsley, Omise'eke Natasha. 2015. "Femmes of Color, 'Femmes de couleur': Theorizing Black Queer Femininity through Chauvet's *La danse sur le volcan*." In "Revisiting Marie Vieux Chauvet: Paradoxes of the Postcolonial Feminine," edited by Kaiama L. Glover and Alessandra Benedicty-Kokken. Special issue, *Yale French Studies*, no. 128: 131–45.

Tinsley, Omise'eke Natasha. 2018. *Ezili's Mirrors: Imagining Black Queer Genders*. Durham, NC: Duke University Press.

Torres-Saillant, Silvio. 2013. *Caribbean Poetics: Towards an Aesthetic of West Indian Literature*. Leeds, UK: Peepal Tree.

Trouillot, Evelyne. 2003. *Rosalie l'infâme*. Paris: Éditions Dapper.

Trouillot, Michel-Rolph. 1994. "Culture, Color, and Politics in Haiti." In *Race*, edited by Steven Gregory and Roger Sanjek, 146–98. New Brunswick, NJ: Rutgers University Press.

Udé, Iké. 1995. "The Regarded Self." *Nka: Journal of Contemporary African Art*, no. 3 (Fall/Winter): 17.

Varga, Somogy, and Charles Guignon. 2014. "Authenticity." In *The Stanford Encyclopedia of Philosophy* (Fall 2017 Edition), edited by Edward N. Zalta. Article first published September 11, 2014. Accessed April 11, 2020. https://plato.stanford.edu/archives/fall2017/entries/authenticity.

Vasquez, Sam. 2012. "Violent Liaisons: Historical Crossings and the Negotiation of Sex, Sexuality, and Race in *The Book of Night Women* and *The True History of Paradise*." *Small Axe* 16, no. 2 (38) (July): 43–59.

Vejdovsky, Boris. 2001. "'Remember Me': The Wonders of an Invisible World—Sex, Patriarchy, and Paranoia in Early America." In *The Puritan Origins of American Sex: Religion, Sexuality, and National Identity in American Literature*, edited by Tracy Fessenden, Nicholas F. Radel, and Magdalena J. Zaborowska, 56–71. New York: Routledge.

Verduin, Kathleen. 1983. "'Our Cursed Natures': Sexuality and the Puritan Conscience." *New England Quarterly* 56, no. 2 (June): 220–37.

Vergès, Françoise. 1999. *Monsters and Revolutionaries: Colonial Family Romance and Métissage*. Durham, NC: Duke University Press.

Vergès, Françoise. 2017. *Le ventre des femmes: Capitalisme, racialisation, féminisme*. Paris: Albin Michel.

Vintges, Karen. 2001. "'Must We Burn Foucault?' Ethics as Art of Living: Simone de Beauvoir and Michel Foucault." *Continental Philosophy Review* 34, no. 2 (June): 165–81.

Vintges, Karen. 2004. "Endorsing Practices of Freedom: Feminism in a Global Perspective." In *Feminism and the Final Foucault*, edited by Diana Taylor and Karen Vintges, 275–99. Chicago: University of Illinois Press.

Walcott, Derek. 1990. *Omeros*. New York: Farrar, Strauss and Giroux.

Walcott-Hackshaw, Elizabeth. 2005. "My Love Is like a Rose: Terror, *Territoire*, and the Poetics of Marie Chauvet." *Small Axe* 9, no. 2 (18) (September): 40–51.

Walker, Margaret. (1966) 2016. *Jubilee*. New York: Mariner Books, Houghton Mifflin Harcourt.

Warren, Wendy. 2016. *New England Bound: Slavery and Colonization in Early America*. New York: Norton.

Weheliye, Alexander G. 2014. *Habeas Viscus: Racializing Assemblages, Biopolitics, and Black Feminist Theories of the Human*. Durham, NC: Duke University Press.

West, Elizabeth J. 2003. "In the Beginning There Was Death: Spiritual Desolation and the Search for Self in Jamaica Kincaid's *The Autobiography of My Mother*." *South Central Review* 20, nos. 2–4 (Summer–Winter): 2–23.

Williams, Sherley Anne. 1986. *Dessa Rose*. New York: Harper Collins.

Winthrop, John. 1630. "A Model of Christian Charity." Accessed April 11, 2020. http://www.john-uebersax.com/pdf/John%20Winthrop%20-%20Model%20of%20Christian%20Charity%20v1.01.pdf.

Wolin, Richard. 1986. "Foucault's Aesthetic Decisionism." *Telos*, no. 67 (March): 71–86.

Wylie, Hal. 1981. "Creative Exile: Dennis Brutus and René Depestre." In *When the Drumbeat Changes*, edited by Carolyn A. Parker and Stephen H. Arnold, 279–93. Washington, DC: Three Continents.

Wylie, Hal. 1999. "Review of *Ainsi parle le fleuve noir*." *World Literature Today* 73, no. 2 (March): 378.

Wynter, Sylvia. 1968. "We Must Learn to Sit Down Together and Discuss a Little Culture—Reflections on West Indian Writing and Criticism." *Jamaica Journal* 2, no. 4 (December): 23–32.

Wynter, Sylvia. 1970. "Jonkonnu in Jamaica." *Jamaica Journal* 4, no. 2 (June): 34–48.

Wynter, Sylvia. 1989. "Beyond the World of Man: Glissant and the New Discourse of the Antilles." *World Literature Today* 63, no. 4 (Autumn): 637–48.

Wynter, Sylvia. 1990. "Beyond Miranda's Meanings: Un/Silencing the 'Demonic Ground' of Caliban's 'Woman.'" In *Out of the Kumbla: Caribbean Women and Literature*, edited by Carole Boyce Davies and Elaine Savory Fido, 355–72. Trenton, NJ: Africa World Press.

Wynter, Sylvia. 2000. "The Re-enchantment of Humanism: An Interview with Sylvia Wynter." Interview by David Scott. *Small Axe* 4, no. 2 (8) (September): 119–207.

Wynter, Sylvia. 2001. "Towards the Sociogenic Principle: Fanon, Identity, the Puzzle of Conscious Experience, and What It Is Like to Be 'Black.'" In *National Identities and Sociopolitical Changes in Latin America*, edited by Mercedes F. Duran-Cogan and Antonio Gomez-Moriana, 30–66. New York: Routledge.

Zimra, Clarisse. 1990. "Righting the Calabash: Writing History in the Female Francophone Narrative." In *Out of the Kumbla: Caribbean Women and Literature*, edited by Carole Boyce Davies and Elaine Savory Fido, 143–59. Trenton, NJ: Africa World Press.

Žižek, Slavoj. 1992. *Looking Awry: An Introduction to Jacques Lacan through Popular Culture*. Cambridge, MA: MIT Press.

INDEX

Academia: identity politics in 1–2; ordering practices of 1–5, 12, 33, 37, 220–21
"Adieu à la revolution" (Depestre), 71
Adorno, Theodor, 228n21
Agard-Jones, Vanessa, 21
Ainsi parle le fleuve noir (Depestre), 71, 233n10
Alexander, M. Jacqui, 11, 16, 21, 29, 138, 169
Alexis, Jacques Stephen, 35, 69, 82, 113, 126–27, 235n16, 235n20, 237n1
Alléluia pour une femme-jardin (Depestre), 69, 75, 77, 81
American Psychiatric Association, 8
Amour, colère et folie (Chauvet), 112, 115, 126, 144–45, 239n13, 241n28; publication woes of, 120–24. *See also Love, Anger, Madness*
Anderson, Benedict, 226n11
Annie John (Kincaid), 152
Anisfield-Wolf Award, 241n2
Antigua, 146
Antillanité, 15, 53, 227n13
antisocial, the (Halberstam), 32, 36, 161, 169, 183
anti-superstition campaign, 235n20
Aragon, Louis, 78–79, 234n12
Araujo, Nara, 230n11
Archive, 188, 191, 202, 215–16
Arnold, A. James, 43, 53, 227n13
articulation (Hall), 31, 228n27
authenticity, 18, 41, 69, 79, 171, 243n17
autobiography, 25, 49, 75; Jamaica Kincaid and, 147, 149–50, 241n1; narcissism and, 8, 227n19
Autobiography of My Mother, The [AOMM] (Kincaid), 4, 36, 148–87; critical discomfort with, 146–49, 171; critique of community in, 150; maternity in; as work of philosophy, 36, 150, 151; and *The Tempest*, 152–55

Bailey, Carol, 193, 201–2, 205, 217
Baker, Theodore, 69
Balutansky, Kathleen M., 112, 157
Barnes, Natasha, 242n8
Barnes, Paula C., 62, 231n20
BDSM (bondage, discipline, and sadomasochism), 29; AOMM and, 182; *Fille d'Haïti* and, 35–36, 112, 127, 130, 133–40. *See also* Deviance; Sadomasochism
Beaulieu, Elizabeth Ann, 62
Beauvoir, Simone de, 90, 138; Marie Chauvet and, 35, 112, 119–24, 128, 239n14
Beckles, Hilary McDonald, 160
Bellegarde-Smith, Patrick, 96, 109
Beloved (Morrison), 191, 232n24, 246n5
Benedicty-Kokken, Alessandra, 11, 78, 101
Benítez-Rojo, Antonio, 14, 15
Benjamin, Jessica, 112, 125, 134, 138, 139–40
Bercovitch, Sacvan, 44–46, 48–49, 229n4
Bernabé, Jean, 41–43
Bernard, Louise, 147–49
Best, Stephen, 37, 191–94, 201, 216
Bey, Marquis, 168
"Beyond Miranda's Meanings: Un/Silencing the 'Demonic Ground' of Caliban's 'Woman'" (Wynter), 154–55
Bhabha, Homi K., 36, on the unhomely, 141, 240n26
"Black Orpheus" (Sartre), 7
Black radicalism, 6, 14, 16, 157; in Haiti, 35, 113–14
Bluest Eye, The (Morrison), 104
Black Skin, White Masks (Fanon), 9
Bloncourt, Gérald, 69
Boehmer, Elleke, 140
Bogues, Anthony, 153
Boisseron, Bénédicte, 39, 42, 226n9

Bongie, Chris, 72, 77
Book of Night Women, The (James), 4–5, 36–37, 190, 192–217
Boston Book Review, 241n2
Boucher, Philip P., 161
Bourse Goncourt de la Nouvelle, 233n2
Bouson, J. Brooks, 241n1
Brand, Dionne, 241n5
Brathwaite, Kamau, 14, 98, 157–58, 176, 226n12
Braziel, Jana Evans, 178
"Brazil" (Marshall), 242n7
Breath, Eyes, Memory (Danticat), 240n26
Breton, André, 69–70, 78, 83
Brief History of Seven Killings, A (James), 188
Britton, Celia, 14–15, 97, 108, 226n10, 236n26, 241n26
Brown, Clovis, 190, 245n3
Brown, Karen McCarthy, 96–97, 236n25
Bucknor, Michael A., 188, 190
Business of Mixing, The (Depestre), 233n7. See also *Le métier à métisser*
Butler, Judith, 23–29, 32, 172, 228n21; on recognition, 26, 134, 143
Butler, Octavia E., 191, 232n24

Caliban (character), 6, 153–58, 174, 176–84, 237n32, 242nn7–13, 243n16, 245n33
"Caliban: Notes toward a Discussion of Culture in Our America" (Retamar), 241n6
Campbell, Elaine, 23, 25, 227n19
Campt, Tina Marie, 183, 195, 225n2
cannibal, 157, 167, 245n32
Capécia, Mayotte, 237n33
Carib, 36, 158–61, 175, 182, 243n18; cannibalism and, 245n32. See also Kalinagos
Caribbean Artists Movement, 15, 226n12
Caribbean women's writing, 18–23
Carnival: in *HIAMD*, 87–89, 98–99, 107
Caserio, Robert L., 168
Casimir, Jean, 246n4
Castro, Fidel, 70–71, 76, 234n11
Cathédrale du mois d'août, La (Clitandre), 99
Cavarero, Adriana, 1, 35, 49, 230n12; on empathy as trap, 2, 228n20; Orpheus myth and, 104–6
Césaire, Aimé 17, 36, 40, 43, 53, 153–58, 161, 179–84, 234n14, 241n6, 242n13, 243n19, 244n25; "Debate on National Poetry," 78–80, 234n12
Césaire, Ina, 98
Chamoiseau, Patrick, 14, 18, 39, 43; dispute with Maryse Condé 41–42
Chancy, Myriam J. A., 19, 20, 95–96, 112, 114, 236n24
Chang, Shu-li, 150, 172, 185
Channer, Colin, 228n23
Char, René, 78
Charles, Carolle, 36, 114, 119, 144–45, 238n5, 239n11
Charlier, Aymon, 115
Chauvet, Marie (Vieux), 4, 6, 35–36, 111, 237n33; biography of, 115–17, 119–20; correspondence with Simone de Beauvoir, 112, 119–24; silencing of, 112; Duvalier and, 121; feminism of, 116, 125; non-involvement in Haitian politics, 113–14, 116–17, 145
Chauvet, Pierre, 115, 119
Cheng, Anne Anlin, 5, 216, 219; on identity politics among academics, 2, 15; on empathetic identification, 3, 107
chiasmus, 206, 208–09
"Chronique d'un faux amour" (Alexis), 82
Cixous, Hélène, 57
Clark, Vèvè A., 17, 32, 99, 236n22
Claude-Narcisse, Jasmine, 16
Clément, Catherine, 57
Cleveland Foundation, 241n2
Clitandre, Pierre, 99–100
Cohen, Charles Lloyd, 46
Colimon, Marie-Thérèse, 115
Colin-Thébaudeau, Katell, 68, 72, 233n3
Colonial Encounters: Europe and the Native Caribbean, 1492–1797 (Hulme), 155
communism, 34, 78–80, 113. See also French Communist Party
community, 1–6, 8, 10–11, 19–20, 23, 25–33, 35, 225n1; academia and, 1–3, 5, 13, 69; Audre Lorde on, 3; Caribbean anti-colonial nationalism and, 13–16, 114; in Caribbean culture, 1, 2–3, 13–14, 29, 204; in Caribbean literature, 2–4, 13–15, 97, 236n26; genealogy and, 20–22; as political premise, 2–3, 13–14; regulating impulse of, 10–12, 15, 29, 108, 204, 222; women and, 16, 20–22, 29, 204, 221–23

Condé, Maryse, 4, 6, 33–34, 79, 152, 161, 167, 185, 193, 212, 226n9-10, 227n13, 234n12, 235n18; biography of, 39–40; conflict with Creolists, 41–42; theoretical contributions of, 17–19
Confiant, Raphaël, 18, 39, 43; dispute with Maryse Condé, 41–42
Cooper, Carolyn, 19
Cooper, J. California, 232n24
"Corinne, muchacha amable" (Montero), 98
Cottenet-Hage, Madeleine, 39, 41
Cotton, John, 229n5
Creole, 4, 34, 44, 77, 93, 205, 226n9, 234n8, 236n22, 238n5; Hadriana, 92–93, 98, 103, 109; language, 41–42, 207; as political identity, 16; white women, 6, 82, 87, 101, 176, 199, 246n9
Créolité, 15, 227n13
Cruz, Migdalia, 242n7
Cuba: René Depestre and 70–73, 76–77, 80, 82, 98, 112–13

Dalleo, Raphael, 112
Danforth, Samuel, 45
Danse sur le volcan, La (Chauvet), 112, 115, 241n28
Dash, J. Michael, 13, 22, 39, 66, 142; critique of René Depestre, 81, 98–99; on Marie Chauvet, 112
Danticat, Edwidge, 240n26
Davies, Carole Boyce, 19, 20, 22, 227n14
Davis, Angela Y., 43, 57–58
Davis, Charles, 231n20
Dayan, Colin, 33, 89, 105–6, 143, 159, 204, 207, 236n24, 237n32, 246n9; critique of René Depestre, 71, 73, 81, 83–84, 86, 90–91, 94, 99, 232n1; on Ezili, 29, 82, 101–2, 109, 205; on Fille d'Haïti, 126; on Marie Chauvet, 112, 126, 238n6
dechoukaj, 233n5
De Ferrari, Guillermina, 166, 169, 182
Deibert, Michael, 240n21
De Lauretis, Teresa, 228n25
Depestre, René, 4, 6, 34–35, 68–110, 112–13, 241n27, 237n1; 1946 student strike and, 70, 78, 113; biography of, 69–71, 76–77; critical discomfort with, 68–69, 71–75, 87, 90–91, 97–100, 103–4, 236n24; Cuban experience, 70–73, 76–77, 80, 82, 98, 112, 113; narcis-

sism of, 98, 107–8; "Debate on National Poetry," 78–80, 234n12; solar eroticism of, 72, 75–76, 109
Deren, Maya, 101
Derniers rois mages (Condé), Le, 230n16
Desroy, Annie, 17, 115
Dessalines, Jean-Jacques, 79, 117, 238n5
Devadas, Vijay, 225n1
deviance, 182, 206; cannibalism and, 245n32; motherhood and, 166; sexual, 11, 28–29, 32.
Dewisme, C.-H., 235n16
Discourse on Colonialism (Césaire), 234n14, 243n19
Dominica, 159–60, 178, 243n14
Douaire-Banny, Anne, 80
Douglass, Frederick, 62
Dubois, Laurent, 235n20
Dukats, Mara, 230n13
Dumm, Thomas L., 182
Duvalier, François "Papa Doc," 36, 70, 72, 101, 112–14, 233n11, 238n7; Marie Chauvet and, 111–12, 119–23, 129, 140; feminism under, 118–19, 239n12; noirisme, 117–18
Duvalier, Jean-Claude "Baby Doc," 70, 233n5

Éditions Gallimard (publishing house), 72, 233n2; Marie Chauvet and, 119, 121–23
Edmondson, Belinda, 11, 16, 18–19, 21, 31, 64, 227n16, 243n16
Edwards, Brent Hayes, on articulation, 228n27
Ellis, Nadia, 183
Éloge de la créolité (Bernabé), 41. See also In Praise of Creoleness
empathy, 24–25; Adriana Cavarero on trap of, 2; Anne Anlin Cheng on, 2–3, 228n20
erotic, the, 12, 29–30, 33–35, 42, 222; Audre Lorde on, 29, 95, 109; René Depestre and, 34, 72–74, 81, 86, 95, 98, 109; as practice of refusal, 29, 109
érotisme solaire, 72, 81, 109, 233n7
Erzulie, 98, 101, 236n25. See also Ezili
Estimé, Dumarsais, 117, 129, 240n21, 240n22
ethics, 1, 3–5, 7, 12, 14, 23, 33, 37, 106–7; critique as practice of, 24–27; Foucault and, 24–27, 32, 227n19; history and, 191; narcissism and, 7–8, 177, 222; self-regard as, 1, 10, 28, 33
Étincelles (Depestre), 69

INDEX 269

Eurydice, 87, 104–8
Evans, Lucy, 14, 15
Ezili, 29, 82, 97, 99–102, 104, 109, 205, 236n25, 237n29; Ezili Dantò, 82; Ezili Freda, 82, 97, 101, 236n25; Ezili je wouj, 82, 247n13; Marinèt, 82. *See also* Erzulie; Lasirenn

Fanon, Frantz, 7, 90, 157, 159, 167, 174–75, 242n12, 244n29, 244n30; narcissism and, 9, 109, 226n5
Federn, Paul, 225n4
feminism, feminist, 10, 12, 18–19, 21–23, 28, 33–36, 43, 49, 55, 57, 68, 105, 108, 120, 225n2, 227n16, 228n20, 228n24, 242n7; French, 57, 124, 226n8; in Haiti, 35, 114–19, 239n12; Lilith's incompatibility with, 202, 216; Marie Chauvet and, 116–17; Tituba's refusal of, 42, 55–58, 242n11; Xuela's incompatibility with, 149, 176, 181, 185, 245n34
femme fatale, 177, 245n35
femme-jardin, 75
Ferguson, Kennan, 182
Ferguson, Moira, 244n26
Fessenden, Tracy, 45, 229n4
Fido, Elaine Savory, 18–22, 227n14
Fille d'Haïti (Chauvet), 4, 35–36, 112, 115, 124–45; academic critique of, 112, 124–28, 144–45; class and color in, 125–26, 128–31, 144; rape in, 131, 139–41; sadomasochism in, 131–40
Fisk Fiction Award, 241n2
Flaugh, Christian, 21
Folch-Ribas, Jacques, 232n1
Fonds des Nègres (Chauvet), 115, 241n28
Forbes, Curdella, 14, 16, 36, 185, 229n2; on *The Book of Night Women*, 190–91, 194, 203, 216, 245n3; individualist texts, 28–29, 36, 149; on Jamaica Kincaid, 148, 167, 170, 228n23, 244n28
Forsdick, Charles, 72–73
Fort Dimanche, 118
Foucault, Michel, 23–29, 32, 45, 65, 228n22; *askesis*, 227n19; critiques of, 24, 26; on freedom, 24; narcissism and 24, 227n19; technologies of the self, 32, 133
Fouron, Georges Eugene, 118–19
Fox-Genovese, Elizabeth, 232n22
Francis, Donette, 11, 95, 137, 168, 176, 247n15; antiromance genre 228n24

francophonie, 72–73, 234n12
Frankétienne, 128, 239n15
French Communist Party, 79
Freud, Sigmund, 7, 9, 22, 134, 141, 144, 172–73, 177, 180–81, 226n4, 228n26, 244n31
Froula, Christine, 109
Fuentes, Marisa, 191
Fulton, Dawn, 55
Fur: A Play in Nineteen Scenes (Cruz), 242n7

Gallimard, Claude, 122
Garcia, Armando, 184, 186, 242n7
Gardiner, Madeleine, 111
Garraway, Doris, 48, 130, 139–40, 210, 220, 240n23
Gates Jr., Henry Louis, 43, 231n29, 231n20
gaze, the, 7, 10–11, 26, 133, 222; in *AOMM*, 151, 178, 186, 245n2; bell hooks on, 151, 194; in *The Book of Night Women*, 194–96, 200, 203, 206–07, 210; in *Fille d'Haïti*, 134; Frantz Fanon and 7; Edouard Glissant and, 7; in *I, Tituba, Black Witch of Salem*, 43–44, 50; Jean-Paul Sartre and, 7; as form of violence, 50
Gerima, Haile, 191
Gilmore, Leigh, 147, 241n3
Glissant, Édouard, 14, 17–18, 72–73, 148, 241n26; *antillanité*, 15, 43, 227n13; on the gaze, 7; maroon figure, 53, 230n15; opacity, 7; relation, 15
Goldberg, Jonathan, 157, 174–76, 184–85, 245n33
Gordon-Reed, Annette, 247n17
Gouraige, Ghislain, 124, 126–27, 130, 144–45
Grande drive des esprits, La (Pineau), 231n17
Gratiant, Gilbert, 79
Gregg, Veronica Marie, 148, 151, 185
Guignon, Charles, 171–72
Guillén, Nicolás, 70

Hadriana in All My Dreams/Hadriana dans tous mes rêves [*HIAMD*] (Depestre), 4, 34–35, 68–69, 77–110, 241n27; academic critique of, 69, 71–75, 77, 81, 83–84, 90–91, 98–99, 108, 233n3; "I"-narrator in, 77–78; reception in France of, 68, 110; surrealism in, 78–79, 83–84; structure of, 73, 83, 236n22; vodou in, 81, 88–89.
Hadriana Siloé (character), 6, 34–35, 73, 82–110; escape from zombification of,

102–6, 110; queerness of, 92, 100; race and, 75, 94, 99–101, 104, 109; sacrifice of, 87–88, 91–96, 108; sexuality of, 91–96, 106, 109; as Simbi-la-Source, 100; whiteness of, 99–104, 109; zombification of, 89–96, 108
Haiti, 17, 34–36, 68–71, 73, 80, 68–110, 111–45; 1946 national strike in, 78, 113, 129, 131; American occupation of, 69, 113, 116–17; carnival in, 87–89, 98; class and color politics in, 100, 112–18, 128, 240n21; women in, 114–19, 137, 239n12, 240n24; literary tradition in, 111–12, 128, 239–40n20; radicalism in, 113–14, 117, 240n21; state violence in, 118. See also Jacmel, Haiti
Haitian Communist Party, 113
Haïti Littéraire, 115, 237n2
Halberstam, Jack, 32, 178, 180; on the antisocial, 36, 161, 169. See also Queer studies
Hall, Stuart, 13, 15, 226n11; on articulation 228n27
Harris, Lyle Ashton, 226n6
Harris, Wilson, 14, 98
Harrison, Sheri-Marie, 213
Hartman, Saidiya, 37, 190–91, 193, 195, 201–2, 212–13, 216, 225n2, 245n1, 246n8
Hegel, Georg Wilhelm Friedrich, 134
Heidegger, Martin, 171
Henry, Paget, 162, 171, 175, 186
Hérémakhonon (Condé), 40–41, 229n2. See also Veronica Mercier
Hester Prynne (character), 52, 54–59, 242n11
Hewitt, Leah, 39
Hine, Darlene Clark, 63
Histoire d'O, L' (Réage), 133–34, 137–39
historiographic metafiction, 42, 229n3
Hooker, Thomas, 45
hooks, bell, 1, 149, 151, 186; on the gaze, 194
Horn, Maja, 11
Hoving, Isabel, 19
Hulme, Peter, 155, 160, 179
Humor, 184, 228n26, 244n31
Hurston, Zora Neale, 232n22, 235n16, 236n23
Hutcheon, Linda, 229n3
Hutchinson, Anne, 230n9

indigeneity, 36, 154, 242n15; in *AOMM*, 154, 158–61
Indigenism, 17, 43, 126, 238n7, 240n21
individualist texts, 28–29, 36

Ingebretsen, Ed, 46–48, 230n9
intramural, the (Spillers), 36
In Praise of Creoleness, 41. See also *Éloge de la créolité*
Ippolito, Emilia, 231n17
Isaak, Jo Anna, 6, 8, 175, 244n22, 244n31
I, Tituba, Black Witch of Salem (Condé), 4, 33–35, 42–67, 192. See also *Moi, Tituba, sorcière . . . noire de Salem*

Jacmel, Haiti, 73, 78, 82, 84–89, 91–96, 99, 102, 104, 108–9
Jacobs, Harriet, 34, 59–63, 231n21, 232nn22–23, 232n25
Jamaica, 90, 94–95, 100, 192; homophobia in 188–90; representations of Jamaica, 190
James, C. L. R., 98
James, Marlon, 4, 6, 34, 36–37, 188–217; biography of, 188–92
Je suis Martiniquaise, 237n33
John Indian (character), 44, 48–49, 51, 54, 56, 63, 167–68, 231n18, 232n25
Johnson, Jessica Marie, 188, 212–13, 234n7
Jones, Bridget, 81, 88, 108
Jones, Gayl, 62, 232n24
Joseph, Régine Isabelle, 112, 239n14
Josephs, Kelly Baker, 227n18

Kaisary, Philip, 72
Kalinagos, 160. See also Carib
Kant, Emmanuel, 245n33
Kaussen, Valerie, 112, 120; on *Fille d'Haïti*, 126–27, 131, 142
Kernberg, Otto, 226n4
Kincaid, Jamaica, 4, 6, 34, 36, 146–87, 228n23; biography of, 147–48; critical discomfort with, 147–48; relationship with mother, 146
King, Jane, 148
Kohut, Heinz, 8–9, 225–26n4; cosmic narcissism, 184
Kottman, Paul A., 49

Lacascade, Suzanne, 17
Lahens, Yanick, 112, 238n7
Lamming, George, 15, 153, 157–58, 241n6
La Rose, John, 226n12
Larrier, Renée, 19, 247n18; on "dual authorship," 20

Lasch, Christopher, 8
Lasirenn, 103
Lee-Keller, Hellen, 15, 114, 238n5
Légende des fleurs, La (Chauvet), 117
Lescot, Elie, 70, 113, 129, 235n20, 240n21
Lettres françaises, Les (journal), 78–79
Ligue Feminine d'Action Sociale, 114–16; *La voix des femmes*, 114
Lilith (character), 6, 36–37, 192–217; homophobia of, 201–2; mirrors and, 195–96, 200, 203–4, 206–7, 209–10, 212; narcissism of, 195, 200, 216–17; pleasure and, 211–12; racial ambivalence and, 210; rape and, 192–94, 203–4, 211; refusal of sisterhood and, 194–96, 201–2, 213–17
Lindsey, Treva B., 188, 212–13, 234n7
Linton, Jennifer, 177
Lionnet, Françoise, 19, 30–31
Lorde, Audre, 75, 96, 202, 215; on community, 3; on the erotic, 29, 82, 95, 109, 177, 245n34
Lotus Delgrave (character), 6, 35–36, 125–45; class ambivalence of, 125–26, 129, 144; narcissism of, 142; psychoanalytic reading of, 128–29, 143; racial ambivalence of, 125–26, 129, 144; rape and, 131, 139–41
Love, Anger, Madness (Chauvet), 112. See also *Amour, colère et folie*
Lovejoy, David S., 45
Lovelace, Earl, 98
Luckhurst, Roger, 236n23
Lunbeck, Elizabeth, 169, 225n4

Mabille, Pierre, 78
Madness, 23, 65, 227n18
Man Booker Prize, 188
Manzor-Coats, Lillian, 66
Marasa consciousness, 17, 32, 91, 99, 236n22. See also Vèvè Clark
Mardorossian, Carine, 31, 227n17
Maroon, the, 79, 172, 214, 234n13; Édouard Glissant and, 230n15; in *I, Tituba, Black Witch of Salem*, 44–45, 52–54, 58–59
marronage, 198
Marshall, Paule, 153, 242n7
Marty, Anne, 128, 143, 239n20
Marxism, 40, 72, 74, 97, 113, 129, 142, 144, 234–35n14, 235n15; Aimé Césaire and, 79; René Depestre and, 69, 72, 78, 81, 88, 108

Masters of the Dew (Roumain), 97–100, 142, 241n27
Masturbation, 49, 56, 63, 85, 163, 174, 175
Mât de Cocagne, Le (Depestre), 72, 77, 81, 108, 233n6. See also *El palo ensebado*
Mather, Cotton, 45
Mather, Increase, 45
Mather, Richard, 45
McClintock, Anne, 140–41
McKinney, Kitzie, 19
Meeks, Brian, 4
Memmi, Alfred, 90
Metamorphoses, The (Ovid), 106
Métier à métisser, Le (Depestre), 233n7. See also *The Business of Mixing*
métissage, 15, 30–31, 73, 104. See also Race, racialization
Métraux, Alfred, 235n16
Michel, Claudine, 96
Middle Passage, 44, 63
Miller, Monica, 9–10, 226n6
mirrors, 169; in *AOMM*, 172; in *The Book of Night Women*, 195, 200, 203–7, 209–10, 212; in *HIAMD*, 103, 109; in Vodou, 103, 237n30
Mitchell, Angelyn, 60, 62
Montero, Mayra, 98
Moody, Joycelyn K., 62
Mordecai, Pamela Claire, 19
Morgan, Jennifer, 191
Morris, Kathryn E., 175–76, 245n32
Morrison, Toni, 2–3, 62, 104, 191, 198, 212, 215–16, 219, 222, 246n5, 232n24; on community, 2–3; on motherhood, 246n5; on self-regard, 246n5
Mortimer, Mildred, 43, 47, 57, 231n17
Moss, Jane, 43, 229n3
motherhood, 21–23, 62, 246n5; in *AOMM*, 163–67, 169, 173, 244n24, 244n26; and temporality, 23, 167–68
Moudileno, Lydie, 39, 66, 231n19
Mudimbe-Boyi, Elisabeth, 57, 58
Mummery, Jane, 225n1
Muñoz, José E., 109, 183
Munro, Martin, 77–78, 99, 240n24; on *HIAMD*, 81, 87, 107, 110, 235n15; on the unhomely, 240n26
Musser, Amber Jamilla, 35, 112, 127, 133, 137, 145
Myal, 200, 246n7

Nancy, Jean-Luc, 10, 82, 203
narcissism, 7–11, 30, 107, 109, 169, 181, 221–22; Adriana Cavarero on, 49; American Psychiatric Association, 8; autobiography and 7; Christopher Lasch on, 8; as continuum, 8, 31, 173; Frantz Fanon on, 9, 109, 226n5; healthy, 9–10, 225n4; and humor, 228n26, 244n31; Maryse Condé on, 161; Monica Miller on, 9–10; as pathology, 7–9, 226n4; Otto Kernberg on, 226n4; Michel Foucault and, 24; Paul Federn on, 225n4; primary, 7; as self-defense, 7, 32, 104, 172–75, 222; Sigmund Freud on, 7, 226n4, 228n26; as threat to community, 8, 31–32; Timothy Schipke on, 9; women and, 8, 29, 32, 161; Jo Anna Isaak on, 6, 8; Heinz Kohut on, 8–9, 225n4; 30–32
Nash, Jennifer C., 212, 216, 247n16
Nasta, Susheila, 16, 19, 156, 182, 241n3
National Book Critics Circle, 241n2
nationalism, 16, 89; Duvalierism and, 118; masculinist foundations of, 3, 12, 169
"Debate on National Poetry," 79–80, 234n12
negritude, 15, 17, 40, 43, 52, 227n13, 237n32, 240n21
Nehl, Markus, 190
neo-slave narrative genre, 34, 43, 62–63, 193, 212, 232n25
New England Way, the, 45, 229n5
Newson, Adele S., 19, 58
Newton, Melanie J., 158–59, 243n15
Ngai, Sianne, 198, 212, 246n6
Ngate, Jonathan, 39
Nicholls, David, 70, 238n8
Nkrumah, Kwame, 40
noirisme, 117–18, 129, 238n7, 240n21
Notebook of a Return to the Native Land (Césaire), 53, 230n13
Nouvelliste, Le (newspaper), 116
Nuñez, Elisabeth, 153, 242n7
Nyong'o, Tavia, 178, 180
N'zengou-Tayo, Marie-José, 239n12

opacity, 7. *See also* Édouard Glissant
"Order, Disorder, Freedom, and the West Indian Writer" (Condé), 17, 52
L'Ordre Universel du Mérite Humain, 239n19
Orlando, Valerie K., 20, 227n15

Orpheus myth, 35, 104–6, 161
Ovid, 106

Page, Kezia, 188, 190
Palo ensebado, El (Depestre), 233n6. *See also The Festival of the Greasy Pole, Le mât de cocagne*
Pan-Africanism, 15, 40–41, 52, 79–80
Paquet, Sandra Pouquet, 60, 147, 148, 153, 241n3
Paravisini-Gebert, Lizabeth, 81, 235n16; critique of Jamaica Kincaid, 147, 149, 156, 244n29; critique of René Depestre, 84, 86, 94–95, 98–100, 103–4, 236n26
Parkman, Patricia, 70
Parole des femmes, La (Condé), 17, 19, 161
Pateman, Carol, 36, 111–12, 140–41, 144, 237n32
PEN/Faulkner Award, 241n2
Penier, Izabella, 148
Penser la créolité (Cottenet-Hage and Condé), 41
Phelps, Anthony, 237n2
Pineau, Gisèle, 231n17
pleasure, 64, 72, 85, 139, 173, 176–77, 247n16; in context of enslavement, 63, 66, 209, 211–12, 216; Depestre and, 91; Ezili and, 101; Hadriana, 85, 109; Lilith and, 211–12; Lotus and, 127; Tituba and, 49, 54–56, 63–64, 66; Xuela and, 163, 165, 167, 174–77
Pleasures of Exile, The (Lamming), 153, 241n6
Pluie et vent sur Télumée Miracle (Schwartz-Bart), 231n17
Polyné, Millery, 240n21
Pompilus, Pradel, 120
pornotroping, 37, 191, 212–13, 217
Portrait de Madeleine/Portrait d'une négresse (Benoist), 245n2
Practicing Refusal Collective, 225n2
In Praise of Creoleness (Bernabé, Chamoiseau, and Confiant), 41. *See also Éloge de la créolité*
Pratt, Mary Louise, 186
Présence Africaine (journal), 79, 234–35n14; "Debate on National Poetry," 79–80, 234n12
Pressley-Sanon, 236n22
Prince, Mary, 34, 59–63, 231n20, 246
Pringle, Mary, 193
Prix de l'Académie Royale de Langue et de Littérature Françaises de Belgique, 232n1
Prix de l'Alliance Française, 116, 239n19

Prix Renaudot, 68
Prix du Roman de la Société des Gens de Lettres, 231n1
Prospero (character), 153, 155–57, 177–83, 244n25
Prospero's Daughter (Nuñez), 242n7
Proudfoot, Ted, 120
puritans, puritanism, 34, 42, 44–49, 51, 66, 229n4; communal consciousness of, 45; constraints on female sexuality and, 46–48; fear of witches, 47, 49; Sacvan Bercovitch on, 44, 229n4; selfhood and, 46–48; sexuality and, 45, 47; slavery and, 60–61, 230n7

queerness, 29, 37, 109, 155, 222–23; and Hadriana, 92, 102–3; and Tituba, 55–56; and Xuela, 26, 92, 168, 228n22; Vodou and, 102
queer studies, 27–28, 35, 161, 167–69, 183, 228n25

race, racialization, 9, 30–32, 35, 90, 184–85, 219; Black inferiority complex and, 9; Carine Mardorossian on, 31; Françoise Vergès on, 29–30; Hadriana and, 104, 109; in Haiti, 115–18; Lilith and, 210; racial capitalism, 9; translation and, 233n4. *See also* métissage
Radel, Nicholas F., 45
Ramsey, Kate, 235n20
Rapaces, Les (Chauvet), 120
rape, 30, 86; Duvalierism and, 118, 238n10; in *Fille d'Haïti*, 131, 139–41; in *The Book of Night Women*, 192–95, 200, 203–4, 207, 211, 214; in *I, Tituba, Black Witch of Salem*, 44, 63–66;
Rastafarianism, 15
Réage, Pauline, 133–34, 137–39
réalisme merveilleux, 235n15
recognition (psychoanalysis), 26, 44, 127, 133–34, 137, 143. *See also* Judith Butler
"regarded self," 6–7, 169, 222
Relating Narratives: Storytelling and Selfhood (Cavarero), 9, 49, 104–5
Remnants of Conquest: The Island Caribs and Their Visitors, 1877–1998 (Hulme), 160
Retamar, Roberto Fernández, 153, 241n6
Rhys, Jean, 160
Rodriguéz, Juana María, 28, 183
Rody, Caroline, 16, 53, 62, 169, 242n11

Roumain, Jacques, 14, 17, 35, 43, 97–99, 108, 113, 126–27, 142, 235n20, 237n11; *See also Masters of the Dew*
Rousseau, Jean-Jacques, 144
La Ruche, 69–70
Rushdie, Salman, 189

sacrifice, 10, 16, 107–8, 114; Hadriana and, 87–88, 93–95, 106, 110; in "Corinne, muchacha amable," 98; in *Fille d'Haïti*, 141, 143; in *Masters of the Dew* 97–98, 142
sadomasochism, 130, 133–40. *See also* BDSM
Sáez, Elena Machado, 193–94, 245n3
Said, Edward, 226n11
Saint-Amand, Edris, 127, 235n20
Saint-Grégoire, Erma, 111, 120
Salien, Jean-Marie, 71, 77, 81–82, 236n21
Salkey, Andrew, 226n12
Sartre, Jean-Paul, 7, 90, 106
Scarboro, Ann, 43, 58
Scharfman, Ronnie, 112
Schiller, Nina Glick, 118–19
Schine, Cathleen, 149
Schipke, Timothy, 8
Schultheis, Alexandra, 172
Schwartz-Bart, Simone, 231n17
Scott, Darieck, 68, 221, 223
Scott, David, 12
Senghor, Léopold Sédar, 79
Serynada, 158
Sexual Contract, The (Pateman), 36, 111–12, 140–41
Shakespeare, William, 36, 152–58, 177–78, 182, 242n7, 242nn9–10, 244n25
Sharpe, Christina, 37, 151, 201, 207, 211, 247n17
Sharpe, Jenny, 58, 60, 231n20
Sharpley-Whiting, Tracy D., 157
Sheller, Mimi, 11–12, 16, 29, 34, 48, 66, 142, 144, 167–68
Shelton, Marie-Denise, 57, 112, 128–29, 131
Silverman, Kaja, 106, 109, 198
Simbi-la Source, 100
Simmons, J. Aaron, 25, 29
Simmons, K., 55
Singh, Jyotsna G., 153, 242n10, 244n25
slave narrative genre, 193; female slave narrative, 34, 42–43, 59–64, 213, 216, 231n19; sexuality and, 59, 63, 212; rape and, 63

Smith, Matthew J., 70, 113–14, 129, 240n21
Smith, Michelle, 54, 64–65
solar eroticism, 72, 233n7. *See also érotisme solaire*
Soul Clap Hands and Sing (Marshall), 242n7
Source of Self-Regard, The (Morrison), 246n5
Spear, Thomas C., 239n13
Spillers, Hortense J., 177, 184, 209, 212; "American grammar" and, 206; and the intramural, 36; on pornotroping, 37, 191, 212; on ungendering, 206
Stout, Harry S., 47, 229n5
Strong-Leek, Linda, 19, 58
Strongman, Roberto, 102, 107
Sula (Morrison), 219, 246n6
surrealism, 69, 78, 80–81, 83, 109, 235n15
Szeles, Ursula, 103

Taylor, Lucien, 42
Tempest, A (Césaire), 36, 241n6, 242n7; *AOMM* and, 153–58, 179–83, 244n25
Tempest, The (Shakespeare), 36, 177–78, 182–83, 242n7, 242nn9–10; *AOMM* and, 152–58, 244n25, 245n33
Thomas, Bonnie, 17, 22, 57, 231n17
Thomas, Deborah, 11–12, 167
Thomas, Greg, 148, 151
Tidd, Ursula K., 128
Tinsley, Omise'eke Natasha, 11, 16, 21, 191, 201, 236n25, 237n29, 241n28, 246n8; on Ezili, 99, 101, 103, 247n13
Tituba Indian (character), 6, 33–34, 42, 46–67, 185, 193, 242n11; Afro-diasporic spirituality of, 43–44, 47, 230n9; erotic freedom and, 61–66, 212, 217, 244n23; erotic self-regard of, 42, 48–49, 54–56, 58–66, 168, 213, 217; excluded from Black communities as witch, 51–52, 58; and Hester Prynne, 54–56, 58; queerness of, 55–56; refusal of motherhood and, 167
tonton-macoutes, 118–19, 238n10
Torres-Saillant, Silvio, 15, 72
Touré, Sékou, 40
Trouillot, Evelyne, 231n17
Trouillot, Michel-Rolph, 117–18, 238n4, 240n21, 240n22
truth-for (Wynter), 170, 172, 180, 221, 244n27

Udé, Iké, 6–7, 9–10, 104, 169–71, 222, 226n6
ungendering (Spillers), 206
unhomely, the (Bhabka), 141–42, 145, 240–41n26
University of the West Indies, 90, 189

Valcin, Cléante Desgraves, 115
Varga, Somogy, 171–72
Vejdovsky, Boris, 48, 49
Verduin, Kathleen, 44–45
Vergès, Françoise, 30–31, 226n8
Veronica Mercier (character), 41. *See also Hérémakhonon*
Vintges, Karen, 24–27, 31, 227n19
Visages de femmes, portraits d'écrivains (Gardiner), 111
vodou, 72, 79, 91, 103, 236nn21–23; anti-superstition campaign, 235n20; Depestre and, 79; in *HIAMD*, 81, 88–89, 94, 99–102, 236n21; and the erotic, 107, 109; women and, 96–97
voice, voicelessness, 4, 23, 34, 181–82; critical conflation of authorial and narrative "I," 41, 75, 77–78; first-person narration and, 20, 23, 25–26, 77, 91, 109–10, 127–28, 228n23; Tituba and, 53, 57, 62; women and, 19–23, 43, 155, 227n14, 237n32; Xuela and, 181–82
Voix des femmes, La (journal), 114. *See also* Ligue Feminine d'Action Sociale

Wade, Amadou Moustapha, 79
Walcott, Derek, 14, 78
Walcott-Hackshaw, Elizabeth, 112, 118
Walker, Margaret, 62, 231n34
Warner, Thomas "Indian," 159–60, 244n21
Warren, Wendy, 46, 230n7
Water with Berries (Lamming), 241n6, 242n9
Weheliye, Alexander, 157, 169
West, Elizabeth J., 149–50
Wide Sargasso Sea (Rhys), 160–61
Williams, John, 45
Williams, Sherley Anne, 232n24
Winthrop, John, 46; "City on a Hill" speech, 46, 230n6
Wolin, Richard, 24–25
Wylie, Hal, 76–77, 234n10
Wynter, Sylvia, 9, 36, 146, 150–52, 154–58, 161–62, 174–75, 177, 179–81, 184–86, 242n8, 243n15; "truth-fors," 170, 172, 180, 221, 244n27

"X/Self xth letter from the thirteen provinces" (Brathwaite), 157
Xuela Claudette Richardson (character), 6, 36, 149–87; Afro-Carib identity of, 156–61; BDSM and, 182; erotic autonomy of, 169, 176–77; narcissism of, 149–50, 163, 169, 170, 172, 176, 178, 180–83; pleasure and, 173, 175–77, 178; queerness of, 36, 168; refusal of community and, 151–52, 245n34; refusal of motherhood and, 157, 164–67, 173; sadism of, 167–69, 181–82; self-love and, 173–74, 177, 182; self-preservation and, 150, 162–65, 168, 170–72, 182, 244n31; self-regard and, 149, 151, 169–72; silence and, 181–82

Zaborowska, Magdalena J., 45
Zimra, Clarisse, 112, 120, 126, 142, 237n2
Žižek, Slavoj, 177, 245n35
zombie, zombification, 34–35, 68, 71, 81–84, 87–96, 101–4, 108–10, 232n1, 235n16, 236n23, 237n31